DISABILITY AND THE
TEACHING OF WRITING

DISABILITY AND THE TEACHING OF WRITING

A Critical Sourcebook

EDITED BY

Cynthia Lewiecki-Wilson
Miami University

Brenda Jo Brueggemann
The Ohio State University

with Jay Dolmage
West Virginia University

BEDFORD / ST. MARTIN'S   Boston   •   New York

For Bedford / St. Martin's

Executive Editor: Leasa Burton
Associate Editor: Joanna Lee
Production Associate: Maureen O'Neill
Production Supervisor: Jennifer Peterson
Senior Marketing Manager: Karita dos Santos
Text Design: Anna Palchik
Project Management: DeMasi Design and Publishing Service
Cover Design: Donna L. Dennison
Composition: LinMark Design
Printing and Binding: RR Donnelley & Sons, Inc.

President: Joan E. Feinberg
Editorial Director: Denise B. Wydra
Editor in Chief: Karen S. Henry
Director of Marketing: Karen Melton Soeltz
Director of Editing, Design, and Production: Marcia Cohen
Manager, Publishing Services: Emily Berleth

Library of Congress Control Number: 2006939562

Manufactured in the United States of America.

2 1 0
f e d c b

For information, write: Bedford / St. Martin's, 75 Arlington Street, Boston, MA 02116   (617-399-4000)

ISBN-10: 0-312-44725-6
ISBN-13: 978-0-312-44725-0

ACKNOWLEDGMENTS

Acknowledgments and copyrights are continued at the back of the book on page 282, which constitutes an extension of the copyright page.

PREFACE

*D*isability and the Teaching of Writing: A Critical Sourcebook introduces writing instructors to the many ways that disability—as topic, theory, identity, and a presence in our classrooms—calls for new practices in the teaching of writing. The essays collected here, both new and previously published, map the intersections of writing and disability studies. The introduction to this book, the headnotes that precede readings, and the "Reflecting on Your Teaching" and "Suggestions for Student Activities" sections accompanying readings demonstrate how an understanding of disability issues and perspectives can change and improve writing instruction in practical and creative ways. This book is meant to serve as a resource for teacher-training classes, graduate seminars, and faculty-development workshops. Experienced first-year and upper-level composition teachers, as well as those teaching first-year or honors seminars, will find clear explanations, activities, and assignments that can be used to inform teaching practices or be incorporated explicitly into course syllabi.

The philosophy behind this book is to encourage self-reflective teaching practices, foster critical thinking, and provide pedagogical suggestions that make use of multiple literacies and embodied learning. The phrase *embodied learning* points to the fact that all learning occurs with and through the body, and that ways of learning are constrained by the body. Our experiences as first-year writing teachers, as instructors of first-year writing teachers, and as authors of composition textbooks have shown us that writing instructors want both practical information and suggestions and the freedom to design or adapt ideas and develop their own approaches. Thus, while this book is pragmatically focused, it is not prescriptive. We believe informed reflection and critical thinking are the best methods for negotiating the many and different encounters with disability that a teacher may experience. We offer guidelines for using these materials, but most of all we encourage teachers to develop self-reflective habits.

LAYOUT OF THE BOOK

Part One, "Disability Awareness in Teacher Training," presents new research on disability and the teaching of writing with an overview of the pieces and their relation to each other. We hope that readers will begin with these five essays, because they highlight issues of disability that are already present in everyday language and assumptions, university structures, and writing classes and tutorials. These essays suggest that the places to begin implementing change are right in front of us, for example, in the way we ask students to compose texts or position themselves through pronoun choice, or the way we shape a writing assignment. The authors focus closely on the practices of tutoring and teaching writing and provide readers with an understanding of how small details of practice, such as being directive or nondirective, have different effects on different learners.

Part Two, "Embodied Writing: Perspectives from Teachers with Disabilities," features five essays by teachers of writing who have disabilities. These pieces explore the role of the body in learning and chart new possibilities for embodied learning. Based on the insights the authors provide, these selections allow teachers to develop strategies that foreground embodied difference, rather than demand bodily and creative conformity. Each selection is followed by specific and practical suggestions for implementing each essay's concepts in a writing class. Readers might want to look at the teaching ideas first, and then read the selections.

Part Three, "Resources for Teaching Disability Concepts in the Writing Classroom," provides disability studies resources for writing teachers who may be seeking information about working with disabled students and for those who may wish to include disability as a topic in their courses. The readings collected explore four themes: "Redesigning the Writing Classroom"; "Analyzing Language, Representation, and Narrative from a Disability Perspective"; "Using Disability Concepts: The Norm, Gaze, and Embodied Knowledge"; and "Entering Cultural Debates: A Politics and Poetics of Disability." Each reading explains a concept in disability studies that can be used to teach writing: Universal Design for Learning; views from a student with a learning disability; analyses of language, metaphor, and popular cultural representations; rhetorical and narrative schemes; critical looks at how "the gaze" and "the norm" function; and debates about access and aesthetics, to name just a few. Instructors may be interested in tracking down the original complete essays to use in their classrooms; however, the ideas for activities and writing prompts following the readings can be used independently of the texts. This section can serve both as a primer in disability studies and as a launchpad for further study.

We have collected the works cited in individual essays to create a single bibliography of resources in composition and rhetoric and disability studies. This single bibliography is an accessible reference tool for classroom teachers and students and can be consulted for research projects or further reading. It also includes resources that are referenced in many of the student activities.

Integrated throughout the book are many suggestions for informal in-class writing, small-group and whole-class discussion topics and activities, research projects, formal and informal paper assignments, and self-reflective activities and writing prompts for teachers. We hope the readings, activities, and assignments gathered here will help instructors teach with, to, and about all bodies. Most of all, we hope they lead to more questions. The most important move might just be to linger in the space between the question and the answer. We direct your attention to those spaces where teaching and learning occur—in the tensions between doubt and surprise, struggle and joy, individual and collaborative reflection, and discussion and writing.

ACKNOWLEDGMENTS

We would like to extend our grateful acknowledgment to the reviewers of this book. Their thoughtful responses and suggestions improved it immensely. To Laura Gray-Rosendale, Northern Arizona University; Kristen Harmon, Gallaudet University; Stephanie Kerschbaum, Texas A&M University; Sue Kroeger, University of Arizona; Paul Marchbanks, University of North Carolina at Chapel Hill; Celeste Martin, University of Rhode Island; Lucy Schultz, University of Cincinnati; Jill Swiencicki, California State University, Chico; and Abby Wilkerson, George Washington University—we give our thanks and appreciation for their contributions to making this volume successful. We especially want to acknowledge the care given to this project by editors Leasa Burton and Joanna Lee, and Katherine Bouwkamp, editorial assistant.

We are also grateful to the disability studies scholars who have given us permission to reprint excerpts from their work and the scholars whose essays are published here for the first time. By making their work accessible to a wide audience of instructors and students, these scholars and teachers are contributing to a broader understanding of disability and helping to change attitudes, actions, and institutions.

CONTENTS

Using Disability Concepts: The Norm, Gaze, and Embodied Knowledge

Entering Cultural Debates: A Politics and Poetics of Disability

DISABILITY AND THE
TEACHING OF WRITING

Rethinking Practices and Pedagogy: Disability and the Teaching of Writing

This book introduces teachers to key concepts of disability studies scholarship—such as claiming and naming, embodied learning and writing, and social stigma and the social construction and representation of disability—that are especially pertinent to writing instruction. The questions posed by disability studies ask us to think carefully about language and its effects, to understand the role of the body in learning and writing, to view bodies and minds as inherently and wonderfully divergent, to consider issues of access and exclusion in policies and in the environment, and to reengage with theories of difference and diversity. Included here are selections that explore the intersections of disability, race, and queer theories and push readers to navigate the complex terrain of identity and oppression. We suggest that if teachers do not learn about disability from the perspective of the disabled, they will not recognize a need to change their pedagogy. Learning about the new interdisciplinary academic field of disability studies is thus a key component in changing attitudes and practices.

Disability studies is an academic discipline that has emerged over the last twenty-five to thirty years. Rather than viewing disability solely as an individual-based deficiency or pathology, or through the lens of medical or therapeutic discourses, disability studies approaches the topic from the perspective of disabled people. It draws on critical, social, and constructivist theories in order to understand disability in the contexts of history, culture, and society and to provide an enriched and coherent view of disability as part of universal human experience, by understanding and analyzing disability as a phenomenon that simultaneously manifests itself at the bodily, personal, and societal levels.

Among the issues disability studies looks at are the way disability has been interpreted historically and within varying cultural contexts; disability as a social identity and locus for culture; political and material circumstances resulting from the assignment of value to certain kinds of bodies; how, historically, disability has influenced and is influenced by the distribution of resources, power, and status; how disability is expressed artistically; how disabled people have been and might be educated; how disabled people are excluded or included by physical and institutional environments; the ways disability is popularly imagined and represented; how professionals who work with disabled people can understand and respect disability culture; how language and rhetoric shape attitudes toward disabled people; and how other identities (such as race, class, or gender) intersect with and affect the lives and experiences of people with disabilities. The list could go on. In short, disability studies uses disability as a critical lens to interrogate history, art, literature, rhetoric, religion, philosophy, popular culture, political science, communications, speech therapy, nursing, education, architecture—indeed, all the disciplines of a university. As writing teachers learn about this rich field of study, they will start to see its applicability to composition and rhetoric and possibilities for future growth.

ACKNOWLEDGING DISABILITY, AND ITS MYTHS AND TENSIONS

The first—and most obvious—reason for thinking about disability issues and perspectives is the increasing number of students with disabilities in college classrooms. In the last twenty years, their numbers have tripled. Recent surveys have found that 7 to 9 percent of students enrolled in four-year colleges report having a disability, and the percentage of students with disabilities enrolled in two-year and community colleges is substantially higher. But because many students choose not to self-identify for fear of stigma, disability resource officers estimate that there are more students with disabilities in colleges than these numbers indicate. But even these numbers mean that students (and faculty and staff) with disabilities form a substantial group that contributes to diversity on college campuses. People with disabilities may, in fact, represent a larger minority group percentage at some campuses than do racial or ethnic minority groups. These designations often overlap, since disability cuts across cultural and social distinctions, and yet, because the *disabled* do not form a single, visible category with a set of common, identifiable features, people with disabilities typically are not construed as a unified group. As educators, we can and should all acknowledge and affirm the presence and the importance of embodied difference.

Whether acknowledged or not, disability does have an impact on the college classroom, and it often raises powerful, unexpected questions:

- What attitudes about disability and disabled people shape perceptions and actions by students and teachers?
- What social, physical, and learning barriers complicate access to learning for disabled students and to teaching for disabled teachers?
- What information and history (about disability and people with disabilities) do we not know that might change (our) attitudes and dismantle such barriers?
- What literacy skills are developed when embodied differences and disability are included as topics in the curriculum?
- In what ways does attention to disability forge connections across campus?

- How can we better understand learning and writing as embodied practices, foregrounding bodily difference instead of demanding bodily perfection?
- How can inclusion of disability improve the teaching of writing?

This book addresses these questions as well as common, unstated assumptions about and tensions related to disability in our society; for example, the tensions imbedded in stories of overcoming disability, passing as not disabled, and coming out as disabled. Disability is not necessarily a curse or a horrible affliction, it is not a static state, and it is not always something to be cured. But disability identity issues are fraught with tension. When we asked contributor Margaret Price for a teaching story about disability, she recalled when a student with a learning disability self-disclosed in her composition class. This student's coming out transformed the way others interacted with her and how she saw herself. Price recognized a complex web of desires in this exchange. The student, articulating how she felt about other students' responses to her, began to recognize the ways her own identity could change, and she also began to take control over her own position in the classroom and in relation to multiple and flexible identity positions.

Another common assumption we hope to dispel is that when disabled students do show up in college classrooms they "just want to be treated the same" and that ignoring their disabilities is, therefore, the best and fairest policy for instructors. Related to this assumption is another powerful myth: that the successes or failures of students with disabilities are entirely the result of individual effort and motivation, and institutional and material barriers—the ways we teach, what we teach, and the attitudes of the nondisabled—play no role in their success or failure.

A common response of educators is, "There are no students with disabilities in *my* class." That there are few persons with disabilities on campus would have been (mostly) true several decades ago for reasons of outright exclusion, but disabled students and faculty are on campus now because of thirty years of important legislation. Legislation such as Section 504 of the Rehabilitation Act of 1973 and Public Law 94–142 (The Education for All Handicapped Children Act of 1975), the Individuals with Disabilities Education Acts (IDEA) of 1975 and 1990, and the Americans with Disabilities Act (ADA) of 1990 has ensured children the right to free and appropriate public education at the K–12 level. This discourse on rights and responsibilities aimed at assuring "equal access with dignity" for the education of students with disabilities, under way for two decades, has led to achievement and built hopes and expectations for continuing education beyond high school. We have now seen an entire generation of school-age children go through their education with the ADA behind them, and as a result, they are—more and more—coming to college with a history of support and success in school.

Too often, though, when students with disabilities come to college, they face an environment that ignores them or is even hostile. One of the first realities they encounter is that they no longer have the legal protections afforded to public-school K–12 students. They are not guaranteed a right to education at the college level, they must themselves pay for any testing needed to document a disability, and they may ask for but not necessarily receive specific accommodations. When such requests are met with suspicion, and when the responsibility for disclosing a disability and then negotiating accommodations is primarily the student's, the difficulties and frustrations of obtaining appropriate academic services, support, and programs often have dire academic consequences.

It is not surprising, then, that even when people with disabilities negotiate around barriers to enrollment in postsecondary education, many experience difficulties completing their programs of study, or they achieve grade-point averages well below those of their nondisabled peers. Although the number of students with disabilities entering postsecondary programs has increased dramatically, higher education still struggles with how to support students with disabilities effectively. Providing support and services to postsecondary students with disabilities is a relatively new concept, and many faculty members outside the fields related to disabilities, education, and rehabilitation may not be aware of the many services available to assist students. When professors lack access to disability history, theories, and perspectives, and when they don't critically examine common assumptions about teaching and learning, it becomes all too easy to believe that students with disabilities cannot do the work or that they do not belong in college.

Just as the addition of other minority groups brought changes to higher education, so, too, should the inclusion of people with disabilities lead us to rethink our expectations and practices and to revise our canons. Making writing classrooms and curricula inclusive and accessible to those with disabilities means employing flexible and diverse approaches to the teaching of reading and writing to ensure pedagogical as well as physical access; using multiple teaching and learning formats; welcoming students who are disabled within the required disability statement on course syllabi; and including disability issues or perspectives in course content and faculty development workshops.

RETHINKING EXPECTATIONS AND PRACTICES

Including disability issues in the topics of a writing course makes sense, not just because students with disabilities are already present in our classes, but also because close attention to disability discourses sharpens critical thinking and improves literacy for everyone. Whether or not we are aware of it, discourses of disability are at work through the everyday language and images of popular culture. Indeed, critically analyzing a broad range of literature — from Homer to Shakespeare, Dickens to Dickinson, Toni Morrison to Marvel Comics — reveals the centrality of disability issues in cultural consciousness across eras. The critical concepts of disability studies help us and our students examine language and images with these issues in mind, thereby improving literacy skills and leading writers to give greater consideration to their rhetorical choices and the effects their choices may have on people and practices.

Throughout this book we ask teachers and students to reflect on their language choices—Who is named? Who gets to name? Who is excluded? What are the real-world consequences of particular language choices? We do not prescribe rules for talking about disability, however. One reason is that the label by which a group names itself changes over time as political goals change. Currently, disability activists prefer the term *disabled,* but we recognize that this term may also be contested and, further, that not everyone who has a disability identifies him- or herself as being disabled. This preferred label indicates that disability is an important part of one's identity, not something to be erased or overlooked or gotten beyond. Although disabilities differ greatly, claiming the identity *disabled* affords a diverse group of people a way to form alliances and more effectively promote social change for better treatment of all people with disabilities. In the past, other terms, such as *handicapped,* were preferred. There is nothing special about a term that makes it correct outside of the context of its use. What writers should consider is *who* is using a term, for *what purposes,* and in *what contexts* as they decide what language to employ.

As you will see from this collection, the field of disability studies makes important contributions to the teaching of writing and rhetoric, to literacy studies, and to writing center work. Those now engaged and those future teachers and scholars who will be engaged in these sites of practice have much to gain from disability studies insights. A shared knowledge of disability theory helps to articulate the links and connections and encourage cross-talk among university spaces—from teacher-training classes and writing programs to writing and tutorial centers and disability resource offices. And the insights and analysis gained from an attention to disability can be extended to other areas of the writing curriculum. For example, we can draw connections between the tutoring of deaf students in the writing center and working with students labeled "basic writers" or multilingual students in writing classrooms. We can be more aware of how writing programs call out and label streams of "difference" and "deficiency." Students with the label English as a Second Language (ESL), students with the label Learning Disability (LD), and students with the Basic Writing (BW) label, are often defined and pitted against each other and against the "normal" stream. Such sorting reaffirms the idea of disqualification and deficiency while also allowing the so-called mainstream to continue in its rutted path with few changes made to its practices. In short, attention to disability issues and theory makes us better writing teachers and more fully and thoughtfully engaged participants in the university.

Negotiating Pedagogy and Research in the Classroom

Disability studies reminds us that making accommodations for students (and teachers) can lead to more creative and productive university communities for all members—particularly when we move beyond accommodation and into challenging the culture of the writing classroom to evolve. But incorporating disability studies material into a classroom is not by itself enough to

change the landscape of the university, to make it accessible and fully responsive to its new and increasing population of people with disabilities. That is
why this book includes both research and pedagogy—new and previously
published studies on disability-related issues, and suggestions for ways to
implement these new ideas in classroom activities and writing assignments.
Research and pedagogy go hand in hand, helping us to reimagine teaching
and learning through the lens of disability.

The editors and many contributors to this volume work at the intersection of writing and disability studies and have been incorporating disability
issues into their writing classes for some time. When we talk about our experiences teaching writing informed by disability studies, the first question we
are often asked goes something like this: "I have a student with _____ disability in my composition course. What should I do?" This question suggests
the desire for an expert solution, a quick fix, a simple set of practices, each tai-
lored to a different kind of disability, that "solve" the challenge which the particular student presents. The philosophy of this book is quite different from
that implied in such a question. Rather than approaching a student with a disability as a "problem" needing a particular cure that brings the student back
to conformity with the "normal way of doing things," the inclusion of students with disabilities and the topic of disability offer an opportunity to
change teaching methods and content so that they provide more flexibility
and choice for various kinds of students. Universal Design for Learning
(UDL), developed out of the accessibility movement of the ADA, emphasizes
a range of flexible, multimodal practices and a philosophy for teaching that
stresses the importance of addressing different learning needs and styles by
offering many pathways to achieve class goals.

Readings on UDL and pedagogy influenced by it are integrated throughout this book. The *universal* in UDL means that one should design a class in
anticipation of a variety of student learners, not for a single type of universal,
idealized, abstract student. That all of us are uniquely embodied learners is
another and related core philosophy of this book. Too often teachers, particularly in postsecondary education, ignore embodied aspects of learning and
treat students as detached minds. We offer suggestions for learning activities
that put students' bodies in motion and that ask them to consciously reflect on
how their embodied senses function in their learning and writing.

We include in this book readings and teaching activities related to various
kinds of disabilities: learning disabilities, more severe cognitive disabilities
like Down syndrome, autism, mental illness, physical disabilities, and major
disease. We provide examples of an inclusive pedagogy, but our goal is to
nurture the habits of self-reflective practice in writing teachers, not to prescribe methods. It would be impossible, in any case, to cover the ways to work
with all disabled students within even one of these disability categories. The
label *learning disability*, for example, is applied to a variety of learning differences, from mild organizational problems to more severe impairments. No
two people with a similarly labeled cognitive disability have precisely the
same learning strengths and weaknesses. However, after more than thirty

years of laws guaranteeing the right of an appropriate education to children with disabilities, we do know that many people with disabilities outperform the often limited and morose expectations that accompany labels.

We provide not therapies for specific kinds of disabilities but critical research and writing projects, prompts for student and teacher self-reflection, and discussion and activity ideas. If an instructor needs specific advice or information about a particular disability—for example, ways to work with a student who has ADHD—we recommend first conferencing with the student. By the time students with disabilities get to college, they know how they learn best. Ask and listen; then, together teacher and student can develop and negotiate approaches to completing assignments. We also recommend making use of campus resources such as an Office of Disability Resources, or a learning disability center. On many campuses, resource offices have computer programs (such as those that turn speech into text, or text into speech) that can help students with particular learning needs; such offices may also provide extra tutoring, study skills classes, or just a quiet place to study. Their staffs are trained to provide assistance. The Internet is also an invaluable resource for finding factual information and support groups. However, a flexible and inclusive pedagogy remains the best foundation for addressing the needs of all students, with and without disabilities.

A self-reflective teacher is always learning from her students. Contributor Amy Vidali shares an important lesson she learned when she taught her first disability-themed composition class: Vidali incorporated disability as a theme but taught the writing class without changing her pedagogy. "In hindsight," she told us, "I can see that I left no wiggle room at all: no place for creative idea generation; no alternative ways to produce or revise writing; and few ways to improve writing beyond 'practicing' writing. . . . In short, while I was clearly teaching disability studies 'content,' I was not engaging a disability studies pedagogy that attended to the different strategies various students could use to produce and revise their writing. As an instructor, I understood disability, but I did not understand how to use the concept of disability to challenge the traditional writing process." She told us that she is "still haunted" by the memory that she failed one student: her one student with a disability. "Sure, he missed a conference, refused some extra help, etc., but looking back, I think that perhaps my pedagogy disabled him in significant ways." Vidali came to the realization that disability studies curriculum must translate into disability studies pedagogy.

While there is a dearth of information about successful practices, policies, and processes for teaching students with disabilities in writing courses, many of the best practices of composition—including scaffolding writing in stages and encouraging revising, small group work, one-on-one conferencing, and attention to developing meaning first and revising for correctness last—are also quite helpful for students with disabilities. Many writing instructors already incorporate alternate modes into their teaching practices, such as using audio recordings to respond to student writing. Sound recordings, whether using old-fashioned audiotapes or newer MP3 files, are helpful not only for blind or visually impaired students, but also for students with dyslexia or other difficulties in the processing of written language. Blackboard, WebCT, and class and teacher Web sites also offer multiple forms of access, although teachers should be careful to make Web sites simple and clearly organized to ensure accessibility for people with disabilities. Web pages that have descriptions for all images, or have text only versions, are more easily navigated using screen-reading programs. High contrast color helps those with visual impairments. Sound captions help deaf users.

Almost any disability probably does affect—not necessarily just "interfering" with, but intersecting with, altering somehow—the way a person carries out the complicated and critical literacy skills that are often required in college and that are being introduced in a college writing classroom. Writing is hard work; writing well is even harder. Add a disability to that and the work can easily become unmanageable, especially if students must do it all on their own.

But we have witnessed and can affirm the successes of people with disabilities in academic spaces, while also acknowledging the complexity and struggle of such "success." While we believe writing teachers should be knowledgeable about disability theory and pedagogy so as to provide support for their students, teachers also should understand that students with disabilities *can* do college work. In fact, they can accomplish amazing feats through hard work, for example, using a Johnston head switch to compose a paper, laboriously, letter by letter; listening to audio-recorded books and memorizing long passages for exams and papers; faithfully attending tutorial sessions and writing four extra drafts in order to achieve the clear and correct prose that initially emerges entangled because of a learning disability.

Even with such extraordinary effort and motivation, there will be students sitting in our writing and first-year classrooms who need our understanding and support. They may need to approach the writing process or offer their written products in ways that are not entirely familiar to us (yet). We will likely learn a lot from and with them. We will all, teachers and students, benefit from the presence of people with disabilities, and their increased presence on college campuses is changing the overall academic landscape.

Teachers with disabilities form an important part of that landscape and have valuable insights to offer. In talking to us about this book project, one of our contributors, Georgina Kleege, recalled an instance in which student and teacher accommodations productively met: Kleege is a college writing teacher and author who is blind. She works to accommodate the learning needs of her students, just as they accommodate her needs. When a student with dyslexia sought help for her writing, she accommodated Kleege by submitting her work electronically. A digital file of a student paper can be enlarged for low-vision readers, or it can be "read" using screen-reading software for the blind. Kleege then used "show markup" options in a word processing program to accommodate the student's preference as a visual learner. In recognizing each other's best abilities—the student's ability to process information visually and the teacher's ability to pinpoint key moments in the student's writing and explicate them using electronic technology—the two found more than just a way around a problem; they also created a mutually productive learning relationship.

Kristin Lindgren, another contributor to this volume, told us about a moment in class when she followed an impulse and told her class of her brother's schizophrenia. This unplanned move unexpectedly deepened a teaching moment as her students came to understand that the essays and stories they were reading connected with real lives. Later on that year, when students in her class remarked that there are no people with disabilities on their campus, Lindgren was stunned and decided to reveal her own illness. Both of these revelatory moves challenged her former beliefs about keeping a critical stance and not self-disclosing in the classroom: "There is no practical reason that I need to disclose my disability to my students. Yet I've come to believe that there are other important reasons to do so," she said.

Contributors told us these stories when we asked them how they came to incorporate disability into their teaching and writing. Even asking such a question, of course, implies that our academic lives (ironically, even when we have a disability or live in the world of disability) exist somewhere and somehow apart from disability, in spite of it, overcoming it, without acknowledging it. Each vignette evinces the dominance of an "able" world. This world, however, is constructed; it's a tenuous, troubled, and troubling fiction. When students and teachers recognize that disability is always a part of our culture, our society, our relationships, and our lives, then the fictional perspective of an "able" world shifts. In this shift, a new space emerges. This new space is one we may not previously have recognized as our own, but it is, nevertheless, a place we have actually inhabited all of our lives, one where disability is everywhere a part of our life.

Making disability a part of a writing class or a first-year seminar can enable teachers and students to think differently as they gain new insight into the subject of disability and the disabled subject/person. This enabling and insightful pedagogical result combined with the fact that disability really is everywhere in our global, national, and local cultures and histories creates powerful reasons why a disability-themed writing class can be so effective. Whether examining the political and social issues around disability, rethinking disability as an identity, or questioning historical and cultural representations of disability, a disability-themed writing class can move teachers and students to think, discuss, and write about difference and diversity and engage in critical thinking.

We hope you will use the materials gathered here as you begin (or continue) your own exploration of disability, bring disability into a writing or first-year classroom, make "visible" what is already everywhere around us, and engage the tensions surrounding access, stigma, equality, and "passing" when disability and people with disabilities enter the academy. We invite you into the exciting triangulated space of disability, teaching, and writing, and we wish you and your students an enabling journey of change as you encounter and negotiate disability together and continue to reshape this space.

PART ONE

Disability Awareness in Teacher Training

Introduction to Part One

Disability issues, disability studies theories, and disability perspectives may at first seem just another add-on to composition curricula. But the five new essays collected in this section suggest otherwise. Disability, unseen, unacknowledged, and unexamined, is already always present in the spaces and practices of writing instruction. It is present as students in our classes, in the language we use, the ways that we teach and tutor, even in physical spaces and institutional structures. Assumptions about disability pervade the academic landscape and also script attitudes about its counterpart, ability. Gaining a greater awareness of disability's presence should thus be part of teacher training, not as an add-on, but as a conscious surfacing of habitual practices and discourses for critical examination. The essays and teacher-training activities included here can help writing instructors become more self-reflective practitioners by encouraging them to develop an awareness of how disability impacts the teaching of every writing class, not just one with disabled students or a disability theme.

1 Mapping Composition: Inviting Disability in the Front Door

JAY DOLMAGE

Working with the notion of space—both the physical space of the institution and the pedagogical space of the classroom—Jay Dolmage explores how students with disabilities have been excluded, how institutes of higher education have attempted to accommodate them, and how learning can be improved with advances made in disability studies. Working with the metaphors of steep steps and retrofitting, and with the concept of Universal Design, Dolmage explores how instructors can increase access to both the literal and ideological maps of composition. Dolmage notes that "how disability 'fits' into our structures and practices reveals much about their potential for inclusion and exclusion." The steep steps characterize the academy's hierarchical and exclusive culture: difficult to climb, and representing a barrier more than an invitation to enter; this traditional image of the intellectual gateway to higher education proclaims that not all can succeed and many will be excluded. The retrofit—the ramp in the back or around a corner—symbolizes a slightly improved but still grudgingly accommodating culture more than a decade after the passage of the Americans with Disabilities Act (ADA). As an identity or as a social, political, medical, legal, and economic issue, disability, and people with disabilities, can come in a back or side entrance, while the mainstream remains the same. The concept of Universal Design for Learning offers hope and another tone of voice, Dolmage argues, for truly enabling attitudes, spaces, and practices. For more information on UDL, please see "Universal Design for Learning: A Brief Annotated Bibliography of Online Resources" on pg. 171.

Composition is not always an accessible space. The work of scholars like Tom Fox has shown us that writing teachers must consider access and that there is much work to do in order to open the doors of the university, to understand and combat economic, social, and political forces of exclusion. We must also provide access to students with disabilities, who are often excluded from the physical spaces of the university in which we teach and learn. Composition has much to learn from issues of disability access. How disability "fits" into our structures and practices reveals much about their potential for inclusion and exclusion. Attention to disability shows that physical structures equate with ideological structures. For all students to have access to those things composition has to offer—literate "skills," a voice, the words to write the world—we must ensure that disability is recognized and respected. Concurrently, as we redistribute access, the possibility for composition to change will increase, but with a difference. We will have to stop believing that access is distributed from the top down. Access can only be fully realized as a circuit of interchange borne of interdependency. As we include more students with diverse goals and different backgrounds, teachers learn from their perspectives. In the following pages, I sketch a new map of composition, one that recognizes how students with disabilities have been excluded, how the academy has accommodated them, and how disability, as an identity and an epistemology, has and will continue to push us to see teaching and learning in new, broader, and more empowering ways.[1]

My three spatial metaphors come from the field of disability studies and articulate the ways space excludes, or can be redesigned, to be more inclusively conceived. My criteria for selecting these metaphors are simple: I want them to be readily recognizable. You might "see" these spaces every day as you come to work—in the approach to or layout of your classroom or studio, in course texts, in your response to student writing, in your paper prompts, or in your workshop design. The metaphors are also spaces that are produced, ideologically, in the world in which you move. First of all, the university erects *steep steps* to keep certain bodies and minds out. Second, to *retrofit* our structures for access, we add ramps at the sides of buildings and make accommodations to the standard curriculum. Still, disability can never come in the front. But finally, in theory and practice, we can recognize the ways that teaching composition through *Universal Design* creates an enabling space for writing and a way to think broadly about ability.

The academic discipline of composition developed, struggled for acceptance and for space, during a period of literacy "crisis" and during the advent of open admissions. A more diverse and "universal" student body came into the university, at a time when the diagnosis of literate "ability" was a key institutional agenda. So, the discipline of composition grew as diversity grew, as the space for writing and writers expanded. But, composition grew at a time when issues of ability were framed according to a deficit model. As notions of literacy developed from the idea of illiteracy, so, too, has ability been developed only as disability has been (often arbitrarily) defined.[2] Composition has been, from the very beginning, concerned with approaching an expanding institutional space in an egalitarian manner while responding critically to the demand for ever more narrow interpretations of the bodies within it. Tom Fox critiques these narrow interpretations, which he identifies as standards: "When access threatens change, standards are always the tools used to resist that change" (Fox, *Defending Access*, 8). Despite such critiques of standards and the discipline's respect for student diversity and difference, teachers of writing are still asked to erect steep steps in front of some students. Because the work of composition has always been to confront the tension between our work in service to standards and to expanding diversity, I see the discipline of composition as a place from which to consider space and disability. Disability studies can help us reimagine the spaces of composition because it best conceptualizes the tension between diverse bodies and narrow diagnoses (see Linton, Mello, and O'Neill).

As Brendan Gleeson has written, "disabled people in Western societies have been oppressed by the production of space . . . due in part to their exclusion from the discourses and practices that shape the physical layout of societies" (2). Disability is a reality—in the lives of those affected, and in the lives of those who believe themselves immune. Disability is also *produced,* sometimes most powerfully by our uses of space. If the composition teacher wants to treat students ethically and respectfully, she must consider the spaces where she teaches in terms of disciplinary attitudes, but also in terms of bricks and mortar, walls and steps that exclude bodies. The disciplinary and the institutional, the discursive and the physical, must be considered always in interaction. For this reason, we must map composition in terms of the exclusionary potential of spaces and see the potential for constructing alternative modes of access.

STEEP STEPS

The *steep steps* metaphor puts forward the idea that access to the university is a movement upwards—only the truly fit survive this climb. The steep steps, figuratively, lead to the ivory tower. Not only have these steps been impossible for many to climb, but because they seem to get more steep as we grow more tired climbing them, and because the final step itself comes to look like the side of a canyon, it is clear that the steps are steep for a reason. It is impossible not to think of the English professor as one of the architects of this numinous impediment. From the window of his office on the top floor, the professor can watch students struggle up and come to understand that one of his jobs is to preside over the failure of the many and the success of the few. The tower is built upon standards. In many ways, this is an identity that the university has embraced.

I suggest that we have mapped the university in this way—as a climb up the stairs of the ivory tower—for particular reasons. Often, maps are created not to reveal exclusion but to *create* it. Mapping is traditionally a mode of closing off, of containment—of, as Kathleen Kirby writes, structuring a dominant subjectivity "through the delimitation of the external environment" (46). David Sibley, the cultural geographer who has perhaps most extensively theorized the exclusionary potential of spatialization, extends this idea of "structuring subjectivity": "space and society are implicated in the construction of the boundaries of the self but . . . the self is also *projected* onto society and onto space" (86). As a discipline, the way we see ourselves is *projected* onto our classroom space. The steep steps metaphor sums up the ways the university constructs spaces that exclude. The self or selves that have been projected upon the space of the university are not just able-bodied and what is considered normal, but exceptional, *elite*. The university is the place for the very *able*.

Making disability seem inimical to the university has been a strategy used to shore up the identity of those invested in higher education. If those who do not "qualify" can be vilified, set apart, and kept away, then those who make it up the stairs must deserve to. The creation of steep steps has always also been a means of creating "pure" cultural, ethnic, and class divisions — delimiting space delimits culture.

In composition, such steep steps come in the form of a restrictive grammar and usage rules that allow writing to be added up. As Mike Rose suggests, one of the most damaging assumptions about writing is that ability can be quantified via counting errors (347). Tom Fox concurs that historically there has been pressure to "reduce writing to a set of discrete skills to be learned, especially the countable ones" (*Defending Access*, 52). As Patricia Dunn points out, it is now the case that many "students who make the most surface errors end up on the lowest track" ("Talking," 103). Ira Shor ties this to the discipline's history as a "curricular cop and sorting machine" at Harvard; this is the dominant view of "composition for containment, control and capital growth" (92). He adds that, following the advent of open admissions and the remediation of students, "basic writing has added an extra sorting-out gate in front of the composition gate" ("Our Apartheid," 92), to "slow the output of college graduates" and "manage some disturbing economic and political conditions on campus and off" (93). This sorting is, of course, more than just a managing of space; it is a discursive marking that reaches into minds and bodies. As Mike Rose notes, "to be remedial is to be substandard, inadequate and, because of the origins of the term, the inadequacy is metaphorically connected to disease and mental defect" (349). Lennard Davis points out that "language usage, which is as much a physical function as any other somatic activity, has become subject to an enforcement of normalcy" (*Bending*, 104). This focus on standardization, Fox argues, also "mak[es] writing much more suited to the business of class and cultural discrimination" (*Defending Access*, 26). Crowley and Hawhee point out that "usage rules are the conventions of written language that allow Americans to discriminate against one another. Questions of usage are tied to social attitudes about who is intelligent and well-educated, and who is not" (23). The result might be that we now teach "courses in coercive socialization" (Fox, *Defending Access*, 28). When the standards cannot be used to keep certain bodies out, they might be used to shape those bodies and minds that get up the stairs.

Of course, the reality is that disability is always present. There is no perfect body or mind. And there is no normal body or mind. The United States is a country within which one-fifth of the population is affected by disability. "Even" in the Western world, we live in an age when, despite physical/medical efforts to avoid it and psychological/medical efforts to disavow and pathologize it, we all may experience disability at some point in our lives. According to the National Center for Education Statistics, in 1996, 6–9 percent of undergraduate students reported having a disability (iii). Of these, 35 percent were learning disabilities (iii). We might also assume that many students with less visible disabilities "pass" by hiding their disability or attempting to overcome it (see Brueggemann "On Almost Passing"). As teachers of composition, we recognize the diversity of the students we teach. But we must also recognize our roles within institutions and disciplines, and perhaps even our personal pedagogical agendas, in which we may seek to avoid and disavow the very idea of disability—to give it no place. This avoidance and disavowal brings with it its own spatial metaphor, and I use the steep steps to express this negative force. That these steps are real in the lives of people with disabilities adds to the power of the metaphor. The steps have a strong connotation in the disability community, and not just for people who use wheelchairs and crutches. In March 1990, ADAPT (American Disabled for Accessible Public Transit) staged a protest, which was nicknamed the Capitol Crawl, calling for passage of the ADA (subsequently passed). Hundreds of people with disabilities crawled and climbed up the Capitol steps to show how the seat of power in the United States was physically inaccessible to them, and also to make a metaphorical statement about their struggle for power.

When I say that the academy *erects* steep steps, I am suggesting that the steep steps are constructed for a reason. It could be said that the academy is a primary enforcer of cultural norms. As James Trent and others have shown, the history of eugenic research, testing, and programmatic implication in institutions such as Stanford and Harvard reveals that universities have been the arbiter of ability in the United States. American academics have delineated and disciplined the border between able and disabled, "us" and "them." These line drawers were able to solidify their own positions as they closed the doors on others. The disabled, in this history, were more than left out: disabled people have been sterilized, imprisoned, and killed. As Trent and others have pointed out, American academics systematically developed the means to segregate society based on arbitrary ideas of ability. The university was the place for the most able, the mental institution the space for those thought to be the least able. One way to map the spaces of academia and disability would be to look at the ways land was parceled out in the United States in the 1800s. While land-grant universities were popping up in rural places, asylums were popping up in other rural settings—on old farms and abandoned land. From within one privileged space, academics were deciding the fate of others in similar, yet now pathologized, other and impure spaces.

Interrogating the steep steps metaphor works to highlight not just how space and spatialization are exclusionary, but also the ways that the distance between the hypothetical us and the them, the able and the disabled, has a particular structure. In the writing classroom, when teachers try to ascertain what this structure of exclusion looks like, they search students' writing. Mina Shaughnessy's work perhaps best expresses this search, a search for error. In her diagnosis of basic writing, Shaughnessy suggests that "for the basic writing student, academic writing is a trap, not a way of saying something" (7). She says that basic writers are "paralyzed" as they move across the "territory of language" as though "being forced to make their way across a mine field" (11). Each of their errors, in this space, becomes a further "barrier" to progress (11). The risers on the stairs could represent these barriers or mines. Of course, Shaughnessy goes on to say that the errors are also, perhaps only, the fault of the teacher. Despite this statement, decades later our institutions continue to diagnose the problem by analyzing the student. Kathleen Yancey writes that "as English teachers, we may not be sufficiently and or technically educated or trained to help the LD [learning disabled] student" (341). Despite this, she seems quite comfortable saying that students with learning disabilities "do structure the world differently than the rest of *us* do" (342; italics mine). Her suggestion is that "they can mimic structures provided to them" and then "practice, practice and practice again" to hold on to "typical ways of patterning information" (342). I picture students being put through a training regimen, being run up and down a set of steep stairs. David Bartholomae suggests we need to do a "large, longitudinal study" to identify a "'natural' learning sequence" for basic writers and second-language learners ("Study of Error," 267). The writers could then be pushed through this sequence, through another training regimen. Ironically, though Bartholomae indicates that his intention is to map how students learn, he charts only their ("they" are the re-named students that he diagnoses) errors and miscues. Essentially he is mapping how students fall down the stairs. Writing about students with learning disabilities, as I will later show, follows the same pattern. Clearly, disability in the college classroom is not respected. It is something to fix. The method of fixing disability focuses on patterns of the "typical," and the "natural," implying that disability is neither. As Tom Fox reminds us, "We fall into the trap of imagining that language standards and social boundaries are one and the same" (*Defending Access,* 6). Mastering writing does not ensure academic access for students. As Fox also points out, mastering writing does not ensure class mobility or socioeconomic success. In this way, normalizing students with disabilities not only perpetuates the myth of typical or natural learning, it also reinforces standards that, even when mastered, do not offer greater access. Instead, the process of *normalizing* (making typical or natural) the process of writing is used in service of exclusion, delineating the "abnormal." *They* are not *us.*

   Bruce Horner and Min-Zhan Lu suggest that errors are often seen as "linguistic confusion" or as "cultural difference" (147–51). In these two models, the writer's errors are identified so that the writer (not just the error) might be placed outside of the rational order of language, or outside of the dominant mode of discourse. Kimber Barber-Fendley and Chris Hamel, creating an inventory of our disciplinary attitudes toward learning disabled students, suggest that learning disabilities have always been identified with "bizarre errors" (512). These errors are characterized as having no rhyme or reason. In the case of the basic writer or the learning disabled (LD) writer, the disability is the writer's, and the university thus marks the writer as foreign and irrational. Not surprisingly, foreignness and irrationality are two of the most commonly applied metaphors for people with (all types of) disabilities in the history of the Western world. Of course, the similarity between treatment of basic writers and treatment of students with disabilities does not adhere across contexts. But the similarities suggest a common architecture. Both basic writers and LD writers are stigmatized *socially* by their labels. Bruce Horner suggests that the "distinction between error and its social implications is false" (140). Error, in his opinion (as in Fox's), is a social achievement (141). Certainly, by labeling LD errors as bizarre, teachers absolve themselves of responsibility for understanding the error or the student. They stop teaching. But, more remarkably, this allows the teacher to label anything bizarre, or beyond their comprehension or imagination, as disabled. The move is to disavow the error and dismiss the student and his or her writing, as bizarre, far from normal. This version of foreign and irrational, bizarre disability serves to reinforce the fiction of the writing teacher's natural, typical, rational ability.

Conceptualizing the existence of steep steps, steps built by us as teachers, between us, the eminently able, and them, the irrevocably disabled, might help us to understand that spatial metaphors and social attitudes are (at least) as persistent as physical structures. These persistent practices, and persistently exclusive spaces, are part of the map of composition. As compositionists, we often like to believe that our classes are the most accessible, the most broadly applicable. All students take our classes, across the campus and across the curriculum. We are keenly aware of issues of class, race, and gender, and when this is not the subject matter of our classes, it is at least a key consideration of our pedagogy. Yet we need to ask ourselves some important questions. Are our classes physically accessible? When we conceptualize the openness of our classes, our awareness of important issues of identity, are there identities that we leave out? How do these two questions necessarily entail one another? How can we have an open intellectual space if we have a closed physical space? How might we chart the steps of our own "ascendance" up the steps? What forces move up and down, what snakes and ladders exist, affecting students' progress? What are the attitudes, requirements, and practices that might represent boundaries, risers on the steps?

THE RETROFIT

To *retrofit* is to add a component or accessory to something that has already been manufactured or built. This retrofit does not necessarily *make* the product function, does not necessarily fix a faulty product, but it acts as a sort of correction. It adds a modernized part in place of, or in addition to, an older part. Often, the retrofit allows a product to measure up to new regulations. The retrofit is often applied to automobiles and concerns the need to get them "up to spec." Cars are consistently retrofitted with new parts so that they can pass new emissions guidelines. A home might be retrofitted with a new furnace for similar reasons. Retrofits may be seen as mechanical, or as a matter of maintenance and thus are not creative. Retrofitting is also often forced or mandated. Another entailment of the retrofit is that it is a stopgap measure. This leads to the attitude that a retrofit can, in fact should, be given low priority. Thus, as a building is retrofitted to accommodate disability, as per the "specs" of the ADA, ramps are added to the side of a building, or around back, instead of at the main entrance. The ADA calls for *reasonable accommodation*. Common reason then seems to dictate that disability is supplemental to society, that it is an afterthought.[3]

The construction of elevators or ramps instead of steep steps are well-intentioned ideas; they speak to our desire for equality. Yet, as Patricia Sullivan has written, this democratic ideal, when faced with "a broad and diverse cross-section of American culture . . . in college classrooms" led the university to respond with "a humane disregard for difference under an egalitarian ethic" (39). This egalitarian ethic might be labeled "fairness." As Barber-Fendley and Hamel point out, however, fairness is an underdefined term. They see fairness spatialized, metaphorized, as the level playing field. This is a field that makes LD writers invisible, the authors argue (512). In these ways, disability in writing programs is made invisible most of the time, and called bizarre when necessary—when the paradigm needs to assert its boundaries; when teachers need to impose the visibility of standards; when they need or want to define themselves and their classrooms as *not* bizarre; when they want to identify their work as typical or natural; when they stop learning and teaching. The retrofit is the level-playing-field response to disability. It is a sort of cure, but halfhearted, and so it *begins* by negating disability and *ends up* only partially succeeding, thus leaving many people with disabilities in difficult positions.

The retrofit is also a part of composition pedagogy, particularly in relation to issues of difference. Too often, we *react* to diversity instead of planning for it. We acknowledge that our students come from different places, and that they are headed in different directions, yet this does little to alter the vectors of our own pedagogy. Instead, we add one week of readings on issues of gender, one week on issues of race, and we often place these weeks near the end of a course, where they might be preempted if other concerns spill over. Most often, the only time disability is spoken or written about in class is in the final line of the syllabus, when students are referred to Disability Services should they desire assistance. The message to students is that disability is a supplementary concern. The sentence about Disability Services gets the syllabus up to spec. Teachers "deal with" disability via the ideological equivalent of a ramp. Disability as an identity category can come in the side or the back entrance if it is to be included at all.

Of course, the intellectual implications of the retrofit are many. When we look at the buildings of our universities and cities, we see how thought about disability has almost always been an *after*thought. Count the appended ramps, the painted-in parking spots, the adapted freight elevators. In our own theoretical history, similar oversight and after-sight is evident: in Tom Fox's groundbreaking article "Standards and Access," disability is not mentioned. Or, rather, it is a part of the ubiquitous "other marginalized groups" (37). Yet, disability might have provided a crucial category for the consideration of access. Indeed, as Fox concentrates on the myth of standards and the problem of believing that access to skills equates with access to power, disability could provide perfect examples.

Linda Feldmeier White exposes the possibility that, in fact, what I would call the retrofit can also be used to further exclude students with disabilities in writing classes. The accommodations model, much like the retrofit, seeks to level the playing field and, quite literally, get the classroom up to spec.[4] Responses to this makeover of space come in three main forms:

1. **Rank.** On one hand, students with "disabilities" get ranked, sorted. As Linda Feldmeier White writes, "Learning-Disabled students will remain vulnerable as long as schools are organized less to educate than to sort, a function that requires the convenient fictions of standardized testing in order to make some children Others" (Brueggemann et al., "Becoming Visible," 375). Incorporating discussion of accommodations into a discursive field relying on the language of testing, diagnosis, and sorting perpetuates the vulnerability and also leads some students to choose to "pass," to avoid being identified as disabled at all costs.

2. **Greater Demands.** The other response comes from teachers who, as Patricia Dunn writes, "[find] or, if necessary [invent] an extreme example of LD students' 'demands.'" The validity or veracity of a student's claim to disability is debated by the teacher, rather than defined by the student or even by the legal and medical paradigm. Students with learning disabilities come to be seen as "jumping the queue, cutting the line, pushing patient, suffering 'average' kids out of the way and into the shadows while they, waving their LD label, rush to the front to grab an oversized piece of the shrinking pie" (*Learning Re-Abled*, 378).

3. **Charity.** On the other extreme, accommodation and retrofitting are often seen as acts of charity. Really *good* teachers and administrators, who really *care* about "them," *help* them to overcome themselves.

Finally, whether the student is "processed" via testing and then seen as flouting disability, or the academy makes accommodation its moral mission, re-creating students with disabilities as objects of pity, or the student evades this process and remains "invisible"—LD students face a difficult terrain. I want to suggest that, in some cases, a retrofitting can be useful, can aid students in their navigation of this space just as an elevator or a bridge might enable mobility. It is important, however, to recognize that the retrofit is often only an after-the-fact move because the facts refuse to recognize disability as a reality, or the factors cast disability as a strategy, or the benefactors claim accessibility not as everyone's right but as their opportunity to provide charity.

I want to suggest that we need a more sophisticated form of negotiation in order to retrofit structures and practices in the best possible way. With the above-mentioned attitudes toward disability, negotiation is rarely evident. Instead, people with and without disabilities are forced to work around an inaccessible environment, never cooperating because too often their concerns are perceived as divergent. I want to say that the violence of literacy, in our classes, will continue until negotiation becomes common practice. The first step is to recognize disability as an embodied fact, an identity. To ignore this fact is to do violence. We know, perhaps too well, that we neither compose "normal" nor ever fully recognize what normal is. That said, we need to allow for an environment in which students can claim difference without fear of discrimination. This environment *must* include disability, although currently, it rarely does. Further, disability cannot be seen as something one person diagnoses in another. Disability must be seen as socially negotiated; people with disabilities must be seen as the moderators, the agents of this negotiation.

Deborah Metzel and Pamela Walker emphasize the importance of *negotiative* roles for people with disabilities. The authors write that "individualized approaches are designed to enhance community presence and participation" (127). This individualized negotiation would expand "social-spatial lives of people with developmental disabilities and [promote] increased control and spatial choice" (127). In the field of composition studies, Horner and Lu write the most extensively about the importance of negotiation, of working *with* students rather than on, at, or around them. What we have learned, following theorists like Fox, Horner, and Lu, is that the inclusion of each individual in the discussion forever changes that discussion. Further, each party to the conversation has a stake. It is in this way that writers with disabilities can be allowed to "evolve"—not toward cure, but toward an identity through negotiation, a negotiation in which all abilities and disabilities have a means of communication. As Horner writes, error, in this conversation, would be "a failure on both the part of the writer and reader to negotiate an agreement" (141). The teacher, in this scenario, has no need, and no right, to define her students' disabilities. Nor is the responsibility for retrofitting the classroom solely hers. Instead, all students and teachers, coming to the conversation with varying abilities, must redefine what they are able to do together. This would be what Paolo Freire called "co-intentional education," emphasizing the right of every student to be the re-creator of the world (*Pedagogy of the Oppressed*, 69). Patricia Dunn, one of the only scholars in composition and rhetoric to have done extensive qualitative research into student perspectives on learning disabilities, finds that LD students have a sophisticated metacognitive awareness of themselves as learners (*Learning Re-Abled*, 152). She concludes that these students themselves are experts on learning and have much to offer to the "mainstream." Yet she warns that "total immersion in the mainstream, without altering the mainstream, will not work" (132). Therefore, changing the spaces in which we teach is necessary if we want to teach and learn from all students. Students with disabilities have a right and an insight that should allow them to re-map, re-create and re-write the world in which they learn.

UNIVERSAL DESIGN

In looking at the steep steps and the retrofit, one thing becomes clear—we can recognize these metaphors as physical structures. Yet we also need to recognize these as temporal metaphors. The steps are steep, and they are also steeped in tradition, in traditional university life. My point is that students with disabilities are excluded not just from campus space, but from the entirety of collegiate history and lore. The retrofit is an after-the-fact construction. It is always *supplemental*—always nonoriginary. But as a supplement, to retrofit is to *fix* in some way. Unfortunately, this fixing provides little opportunity for continued refitting, for process. In developing my third concept, I want to emphasize the importance of the *priority* of Universal Design (UD). The word *universal* is problematic for many. I hope to show the ways we can respond to this trouble productively. However, I choose to write about Universal Design mainly because of the verb, *design*. This suggests that UD is a way to plan, to foresee, to imagine the future. The *universal* of UD also suggests that disability is something that is *always* a part of our worldview. Thus, when UD is successful, it is hopeful *and* realistic, allowing teachers to structure space in the broadest possible manner.

UD is defined as "the design of products and environments to be usable by all people, to the greatest extent possible, without the need for adaptation or specialized design" (Center for Universal Design). Principles for Universal Design, developed by a team of researchers at North Carolina State University, and now widely accepted as definitive of the concept, include these design considerations:

Equitable Use. Useful and marketable to people with diverse abilities.

Flexibility in Use. Accommodates a wide range of individual preferences and abilities.

Simple and Intuitive Use. Easy to understand, regardless of the user's experience, knowledge, language skills, or current concentration level.

Perceptible Information. Communicates necessary information effectively to the user, regardless of ambient conditions or the user's sensory abilities.

Tolerance for Error. Minimizes hazards and the adverse consequences of accidental or unintended actions.

Low Physical Effort. Can be used efficiently and comfortably and with a minimum of fatigue.

Size and Space for Approach and Use. Appropriate size and space is provided for approach, reach, manipulation, and use regardless of user's body size, posture, or mobility. (Center for Universal Design)

I want to point out that Universal Design, as a list, and as applied solely to the physical environment, as in this example, looks a lot like a set of specifications. Indeed, UD is often interpreted in this way. But institutions like Ohio State University and the University of Washington have used these criteria to design pedagogy. They, too, provide lists, suggesting that teachers encourage collaboration and cooperative learning; that they fluctuate teaching methods and diversify media; that they allow students to show their knowledge in a variety of ways. Most important, however, in documents like Ohio State's "Fast Facts for Faculty" on UD, teachers are encouraged to "permit," "listen," "update," "guide," "clarify," "review," and "allow" (3). These are the verbs of Universal Design, and they function as much more than specifications. UD, registered as action, is a way to move. In some ways, it is also a worldview. UD is not a tailoring of the environment to marginal groups; it is a form of hope, a manner of trying. The listed verbs all could be read as reacting to terms of standards: *limit, write, repeat, direct, test, produce, ration.* I would suggest (and hope) that composition methodically and philosophically challenges these standard verbs.

One of the central tenets of UD is that it helps all students, regardless of their ability.[5] Steve Jacobs, in his article the "Electronic Curb-Cut Effect," suggests that many of the things we now take for granted, technologies that improve everyone's quality of life, were originally designed for people with disabilities. If disability had not broadened our conception of access to technology, made it more universal, we would not have the typewriter, the stereo recorder, the transistor radio, the flatbed scanner, the personal digital assistant, the pager, watch alarms, or e-mail. Universal Design has already changed our world.

Universal Design offers composition a way to locate itself not in response to changing hostile geographies but as a proactive architect of future possibilities. Universal Design is a means of seeing the whole world at the same time while seeing that space as in process and new spaces as being constantly renegotiated. The emphasis on design allows us to recognize that we are involved in the continued production of space. Universal Design is *kairotic*—in this sense, seeking the opportune, but also acknowledging that context forever shifts.

Universal Design as epistemology also seems to entail new theories of subjectivity and agency. Universal Design responds to the idea, here expressed by Lennard Davis in *Bending Over Backwards,* that "what is universal in life, if there are universals, is the experience of the limitations of the body" (32). Difference, Davis asserts, "is what we all have in common" (26). This is not to say that we are all disabled, but to show that "we are all non-standard" (32). In response to this, we can either disavow our difference and project it upon others, or we can join in an "ethic of liberation" (29). Davis suggests that disability epistemology, or "dismodernism," to borrow his phrase, shows us that identity is not fixed but malleable, that technology is not separate but part of the body, that dependence, not individual independence, is the rule (26). Negotiation gains importance. In an academy, a classroom, or a conversation that is truly accessible, that strives to acknowledge (and create) a place for our different bodies and minds, that has the power to lay bare the workings of societal discourse, and to affirm identity, UD is disability praxis. We are not set free into an undifferentiated universe, but we begin to look for the broadest spaces in which we all share experience. Making space for others does not deny their difference but affirms a shared connection based on this difference.

UD as praxis is still a matter of social justice. If composition is asked to take part in its own design, if we see this as a possibility, then we can also recognize the priority of negotiation, the importance of including everyone in the discussions that create space. For UD to be a transformative agenda, we are reminded that our work must be change enhancing, interactive, contextualized, *social;* must allow individuals to rewrite institutions through rhetorical action (see Porter, Sullivan); and must push us all to think broadly and generously. UD as a concept and as a rubric does seem to include and embrace such possibilities in ways others cannot.

On the other hand, of course, there is the possibility that this embrace is too large, too broad. Unfortunately, the idea of the universality of this concept also leads to its nearly universal dismissal. We see ourselves as teaching in highly localized contexts. For this reason, our skepticism about the universe of UD is well founded. Whose universe will this be? Yet, UD does offer ways to move, theoretically, that have everything to do with the universal—not as a means of homogenization but as a way to complicate divisive notions of difference with new models of cooperation. The Ohio State document insists that "Universal Design does not remove academic challenges; it removes barriers to access. Simply stated, Universal Design is just good teaching." However, it is telling that this defense is necessary. Many object that "just good teaching" could lead to the same old neglect of and the same old invisibility for disabled students. For this reason it is not enough to focus only on UD. At the same time, we need to recognize the persistence of the steep steps and the consequences of the retrofit. Doing so, we can be reflective teachers *as* we become progressive teachers, committed to respecting the rights of all students to design the spaces of composition.

NOTES

1. I am indebted to Nedra Reynold's mappings of composition's "imagined geographies, " and to Ellen Cushman's metaphorical interpretation of the steps at the Rensselaer Polytechnic Institute, as starting points for my thinking in this paper.

2. I allude here to the fact that *literacy* in its contemporary sense only came into use in the late nineteenth century. Previously, to be literate meant to be familiar with literature. Also, as disability geographer Brendan Gleeson reminds us, the factory "produced physical disability on an industrial scale" (109). Preindustrialization, though there were ideas of ability and disability, society did not comprehensively "sort" its citizens using disability as criteria. Illiteracy has been a way to sort society, determining the strata of the labor force in similar ways. And so the ideas of *dis*ability and *ill*iteracy might be seen to have developed in similar ways, at similar times, in the Western world, the prefixes being used with particular and similar (perhaps connected) ends in mind.

3. Since the passage of the Americans with Disabilities Act in 1990, the public has begun to see disability as an issue of space. This issue is constructed as a matter of compliance, as the dominant terminology of the act is the idea of "reasonable accommodation." Disability comes to be seen in physical artifacts such as the elevator, the automated door, the ramp, the wheelchair parking space. These spaces, seen first, are then connected to people with disabilities only when they traverse this "other space," when they park their car, for instance. These spaces are in fact somewhat prosthetic: they are correctives, substitutions. These spaces are noticeably exclusive—they are explicitly not for the able-bodied. Yet I don't want to be too critical of such additions. Since the ADA, at the very least, people with disabilities have been given space. This access to space has been a crucial part of the lives of people with disabilities as they have moved through the world (historically, moving outside of institutions like the sanitorium and into institutions like the bank or dance club). What should be unsurprising about this history is that space has always been an issue of social justice. Think of buses in the South before 1956, with their front and back, and buses now, some with chair lifts. Even post-ADA, and certainly outside of the United States, people with disabilities are still fighting to have their rights recognized, still fighting for equal access and for reasonable accommodation. The ADA, then, has brought the connection between disability and space into the public consciousness.

4. The accommodations have always been initiated or carried out, or otherwise anchored, by the actions of university offices, which, first and foremost, are concerned with enforcing the "reasonable accommodations" mandated by the ADA.

5. There is some danger here of falling into what Critical Race Theorists would call *interest convergence*—the idea that conditions for the minority group improve only once the effort can be justified as helping the majority as well. In arguing for Universal Design instead of accommodations, many have suggested that UD is of greater benefit to more students—UD can take adaptations and use them to help everyone. Yet such an argument can lead to a situation in which the needs of the majority once again trump the needs of those who traditionally have been excluded—people with disabilities. The argument "better for all students" must be continually interrogated.

REFLECTING ON YOUR TEACHING

Practices of Accommodation

Consider the ways that your daily teaching practices may function as steep steps (a barrier to learning) or a retrofit (an accommodation that does not change and challenge the mainstream) or may be reimagined to be fully inclusive. Make four columns on a sheet of paper. List three or four teaching practices vertically in the left column—one example might be having students read their drafts aloud in small peer-response groups. Label the next column "steep steps," and list in this column students who may be excluded by this practice—for example, a deaf student. Label the next column "retrofit" and list here an accommodation for those excluded. Finally, label the fourth column Universal Design for Learning (UDL), and imagine redesigning your practices to be more inclusive of all kinds of student learners. If you do this exercise in a faculty development workshop or training class, the next step is to gather in small groups and discuss your charts: Do certain kinds of accommodations stigmatize some students? Do we as teachers resent making accommodations? Why? Do you agree or disagree with Dolmage when he writes that the inclusion of disability as an issue and of people with disabilities will "push us to see teaching and learning in new, broader, and more empowering ways"? Why or why not? Complete this exercise by spending five to ten minutes writing a reflection, and if time permits, share these with your small group or class.

2   *Tutoring Deaf College Students in the Writing Center*

REBECCA DAY BABCOCK

Rebecca Day Babcock turns our attention to the writing center. Babcock notes "the relative absence of discussions of deafness and other sensory and physical disabilities in tutor training texts"—a lack that led her to analyze the interactions of tutor, deaf tutee, and interpreter in writing center sessions. She found that a single set of practices will not work for all students. She suggests that insights from disabled students may be extended to other groups of students such as English as a Second Language (ESL) and Learning Disabled (LD) students. "Common tutoring practices are based on aural/oral processing of language or Hearing cultural values such as nondirectiveness," Babcock writes. These practices may be ineffective not only for d/Deaf students but also for ESL and LD students. Babcock concludes that effective tutoring practices should be "negotiated between the tutor, tutee, and interpreter."

Writing center workers and scholars have not yet fully examined the implications of deafness on their tutoring theories and practices. Many, if not most, common tutoring practices are based on aural/oral processing of language or Hearing cultural values such as nondirectiveness. Common peer tutoring practices such as reading papers aloud are effective for auditory learners, but as Margaret Weaver writes, they may exclude the deaf student and others who process language differently. The writing center commonplace of nondirectiveness can be seen as problematic not only for deaf students but for ESL and LD students as well. A focus on the learning needs of deaf students can not only help writing center people to tutor them better, but can force them to rethink their practices in light of others who learn differently.

Tutor training rarely focuses on helping students who have a sensory or physical disability. A quick look at tutor guides reveals little emphasis on physical difference. I thought no tutoring books talked about deafness at all, until my colleague Crystal Bickford referred me to *The Tutor Book* by Arkin and Sholler. According to my research, in the last twenty years only this one general tutor training book had addressed more than a sentence or two to tutoring deaf students in writing, until Murphy and Sherwood included Margaret Weaver's 1996 article about tutoring a deaf student in the writing center in the second edition of *The St. Martin's Sourcebook for Writing Tutors.* The relative absence of discussions of deafness and other sensory and physical disabilities in tutor training texts is evident. Considering the numbers of deaf and hard-of-hearing students in mainstream institutions, and those with other disabilities as well, this is a glaring oversight. There is clearly a need for more investigation and description of these tutorials. To this end, I conducted a study, the first to describe in detail the dynamics among hearing tutor, deaf tutee, and interpreter.[1] While tutorials conducted through the communication modes based on English—such as lipreading and speaking, as well as writing, both on paper and computer screens—have been documented, before my study there had been no previous documentation of writing tutorials conducted through an interpreter. The few articles in the writing center literature are all first person narrative accounts of tutoring a single deaf student. My study is the first to study tutoring sessions in writing with deaf students in mainstream institutions through naturalistic observation. The previous articles also show only one person's view of the process: the tutor's. My study shows the perspectives of all involved: researcher, tutee, tutor, interpreter, and administrator.

I conducted a naturalistic study of tutors working with d/Deaf[2] tutees in writing center or learning center contexts. I observed tutoring sessions with deaf tutees and hearing tutors, and as a point of comparison, I also observed tutoring sessions with these same tutors and their hearing tutees. I followed up the tutoring sessions with interviews with all the stakeholders in the tutoring session: tutor, tutee, interpreter, and administrator. I also made general observations of the context and collected relevant documents such as tutor-training materials, writing center documents, and the students' texts that they worked on in the tutorial. After transcribing the video- and audiotaped tutoring sessions and interviews, I coded and analyzed them using the grounded theory approach. I also submitted transcripts and drafts to participants for member checking. The resulting "storyline" (Strauss and Corbin's term) tells what happens in a tutoring session between a deaf tutee and a hearing tutor (and an interpreter).

First I give a brief overview of the findings of this study and relate the relevant points of the study to specific experiences of the participants. I then present recommendations for practice and tutor training.

SAMPLE CASE STUDY: BLUE

Blue is an acting major and a tutee at Davis College. She is a nineteen-year-old deaf Black woman. She is slender with a pretty face. She has one deaf brother. When I first saw Blue, she was wearing a blue-and-orange jacket. I asked her if she was a Chicago Bears fan. She replied that she just liked the colors. Her hair was pulled back in twists. She was also wearing Air Jordan sneakers and jeans. Blue dressed like a typical college student, but with a bit of style.

She is interested in dancing. I confirmed this with her after reading a paper she wrote about a dance she created with her family for her grandmother's birthday party, the presentation she did about Janet Jackson, and her interest in Janet Jackson as a dancer. Blue is a motivated learner and enjoys the time she has with her tutor. In an interview she informed me,

> Well, honestly, I feel pretty motivated to learn how to write. I feel like I'm ready to do it. You know, I feel more like I want to learn about verbs and adjectives. I feel pretty inspired to get that information and to learn about it.[3]

She also said she would like to improve her reading and English vocabulary. During the course of the study, she won a cash award for being the most-improved tutee. She was nominated by her tutor, Newby, who also won a cash award.

Blue attended the State School for the Deaf (SSD). She graduated from City Vocational Career Academy (CVCA; I have withheld the name of the state and city for confidentiality reasons). At SSD she was exposed to American Sign Language (ASL), but she reported that at CVCA they signed differently. She reported that at SSD, "There was more expressiveness, more joking capability, more social humor. But it seems there wasn't really much of that going on in the language [at CVCA]." She prefers when people use ASL, but she is not really sure if she prefers English or ASL in an academic context. Her interpreter, Jay, tends to transliterate word-for-word in English with Blue in the tutoring session.

The first semester I met Blue, she was taking Intro to College Writing, and the second semester she was taking English Composition I. She also discussed work for her science class in the tutorial. She felt that her writing had improved greatly as a result of coming to the tutorials. The main issue she wanted to work on in the tutoring sessions was grammar, and through the tutoring sessions she was able to learn how to correct her own errors. She said the idea that grammar was important came from her teachers. She also wanted to work on understanding her homework assignments. She appreciated the presence of the interpreter in the tutoring session but also did not have a problem with conducting the tutoring sessions without an interpreter, in writing.

I asked Blue why she chose a general university rather than a school for the d/Deaf, and she replied that she preferred to live at home rather than in dorms. Also, at SSD she did not like the food, and I think she generalized that all residence halls have bad food. She currently lives with her mother, her mother's boyfriend, and her siblings. Her mother works for United Parcel Service. She said she would like to move into her own apartment. She was looking for a job the summer I met her, but she had not found one by the following fall when our observations were complete.

Findings

The session content and tutoring practices between a hearing tutor and a hearing student and a hearing tutor and a deaf student are very similar. As I had anticipated, the common tutoring practices of reading aloud and nondirectiveness can be problematic for deaf students as well as other students who learn differently, such as LD students. I also discovered that in tutorials on writing, reading is a major factor. Students' reading behavior and background appear to directly affect their writing performance and attitude and their school performance in general. I learned that deaf students, like other students, are all different, and we cannot expect them all to learn in the same way. In general, all students are unique, and our work with deaf students both reinforces that fact and displays in a very real and practical way how we must adapt and adopt different tutoring practices for different students and populations.

Below I use some exchanges from Blue's tutoring sessions to illustrate some of the important points that emerged from this study. The following exchange happened during the first tutoring session I observed between Blue and Newby (her tutor); Linda was the interpreter.

> NEWBY: Let's look at this. I'm gonna read [aloud]. You tell me how it sounds. OK?
>
> LINDA: What do you mean?
>
> NEWBY: I mean [I want her to be able to see the mistakes she's made]. She should be able—
>
> LINDA: Do you want me to interpret?
>
> NEWBY: Don't fix it. I want her—
>
> LINDA: Do you want her to just read along while you're reading?
>
> NEWBY: She could do that.

This short exchange illustrates that tutors have a penchant for reading aloud. It's so automatic that they seldom think about the appropriateness of reading aloud with deaf students. The interpreter in this exchange recommends that the student read along with the tutor, stressing different learning styles and learning channels. The tutor also implies an assumption that written English can be reproduced faithfully on the hands. The tutor says, "Don't fix it," implying that she knows if the text is translated into ASL the English errors will disappear. The interpreter gently guides the tutor into more appropriate behaviors. This highlights the advocacy role of the interpreter, even though Linda said in the interview that she really did not know what the tutor meant when she asked the deaf student to "tell [her] how it sounds." At another point in one of Blue and Newby's tutorials, when Newby read quietly to herself, interpreter Jay signed, "She's reading," rather than interpret or transliterate the words on the page, which Blue could easily see from her position next to the tutor.

In an interview in which we reflected on the first exchange above, Linda said that she really did not know what the tutor meant:

LINDA: I think what happens is that tutors forget that deaf people have never heard English, and they don't know what it sounds like. And I don't think that they mean, "Does that—Is that a—Is that sentence grammatically correct?" I think they mean, "Does that sound correct?" I don't think that they're meaning metaphorically. I think they literally mean "What does that sound like?" And so—

REBECCA: That's the way they perceive English.

LINDA: That's the way they perceive English—

REBECCA: —through the ear.

LINDA: Any hearing person who's never spent, or had a real . . . even just a moment to really look, to go into themselves and think about this, they're not gonna get that. And it's just because, it's just, you know, not in a critical way, it's just ignorance. It's just that they don't know.

REBECCA: That's the way we talk, so we don't reflect, you know.

LINDA: On what our words really mean.

Traditionally, the goal of reading aloud is for the student to hear his or her own errors. In reference to ESL students, Judith Powers writes, "These techniques, which largely involve reading aloud and using the ear to edit, presume that the writer hears the language correctly and is more familiar and comfortable with the oral than the written word" (371). This may be true for deaf tutees as well. Deaf people can perceive English on paper, on the hands, and on the lips. The choice of whether to read aloud and have it transliterated or to read together on the paper is one that must be negotiated between tutor, tutee, and interpreter.

The following exchange illustrates the cultural and physical factors relating to deafness that can affect tutoring. Blue had used a word from a source, the meaning of which she did not know, and Newby attempted to have her put the phrase in question into her own words. The problem was that the content of the passage is outside the cultural and physical knowledge of a d/Deaf young lady:

NEWBY: [turns the page, reads] Do you know this word?

BLUE: No. I just got it on the Internet. [laughs]

NEWBY: You shouldn't use words if you don't know the meaning of them.

BLUE: But I got a B!

NEWBY: What do you think it means from what the sentence says?

BLUE: Maybe like she's a hard worker?

NEWBY: [takes pen, points to paper] What does she do here, just tell me. This sentence, when you say she culled from one album seven top-five singles. What does it mean that she "culled"? In your own words, how would you say that?

BLUE: That Janet Jackson was dancing, she was doing a lot of hard work.

NEWBY: OK, look. She made an album. She had five singles that, that went to number one. OK. So, you're saying here she was the first artist in history. So, if you were telling me that she did that, how would you tell me in your own words? [takes off glasses, rubs eyes]

BLUE: I would just say the same story. I mean, that's just all I know. That she was a dancer and that she worked really hard.

NEWBY: No, no. Tell me about this album where she had five singles that were top five, or five singles that were number one.

BLUE: OK. [smiles, covers face with hands] I have to copy what you just said, right?

NEWBY: I want you to tell me in your own words. Just tell me, tell me, sign it for me.

BLUE: I'm sorry. I don't understand.

NEWBY: I want you to tell me in your own words that Janet Jackson made an album that she got five number-one singles from the album and that she was the first artist to ever do that.

BLUE: OK. She's the best dancer in history, so far?

NEWBY: We're not talking about dancing. We're talking about singing. Tell your girlfriend, tell your girlfriend that you write to about Janet Jackson's album. What was the name of it? [puts on glasses, looks at paper] *Rhythm Nation*, I guess. Tell your girlfriend about *Rhythm Nation* and how many singles Janet Jackson had. Just tell your girlfriend about it.

BLUE: Guess what! In all of history there are five songs! I don't know. It's hard.

NEWBY: [puts on glasses, shows Blue paper]

BLUE: I don't understand.

Deaf young people do not listen to popular music like hearing young people do. As a person who cannot hear music, it is extremely hard for Blue to understand the concept of a "top-five single." She primarily relates to Janet Jackson as a dancer, an actress, and a hard worker. It is obvious here that Blue cannot understand the task that Newby has set up for her, and also cannot understand the concepts being discussed, because songs, top-five singles, and albums are not a part of her d/Deaf reality.

Cultural and physical factors should also be kept in mind when tutoring deaf students. If we take for example this exchange with Newby and Blue about Janet Jackson, we see that it is extremely difficult for a d/Deaf student to relate to a hearing experience, namely listening to music, and related topics, such as top-five singles. Perhaps in this case the tutor or interpreter could have intervened and explained what a top-five single was. Also, when Blue insisted on describing Janet Jackson as a dancer and a hard worker, the tutor could have discussed how hearing people see Janet Jackson as primarily a singer. Newby got close to this when she said, "We're not talking about dancing. We're talking about singing." But then we have to take a step back and remember that deaf people do not listen to and enjoy music the same way hearing people do. Tonya Stremlau Johnson writes, "Lack of knowledge about popular music is a communication barrier for a deaf person in the hearing world, especially for a deaf student among hearing classmates in a culture where popular music is especially important to teenagers and young adults" (33).

This is just one example of a cultural factor, but I invite the reader to imagine other, like situations in the classroom or the writing center where we assume people can hear, and the results of those assumptions on deaf people. My study led me to reflect on an assignment I give in freshman composition in which I ask students to analyze a song. This kind of assignment is unfair to deaf students. Johnson also discusses several common writing assignments that are biased against deaf students, such as an activity that asks students to imagine they cannot hear and then reflect on the experience. How is a deaf person to relate to this activity? For one, it implies that deaf students are not considered as a possible audience for the assignment.

I had expected to find more situations of ASL interference in the tutoring session than I actually did. The clearest example of possible ASL interference in English was in an exchange with Blue, Newby, and Jay, the interpreter during this session. Blue was working on a paper about her observations on the train, and Newby was reading through it with her, making corrections in response to teacher comments, when she came upon a problematic sentence:

NEWBY: Could you sign this sentence for me and have Jay tell me what it says?

BLUE: Woman who had the red—Woman who have red hair with ponytail holder, with ponytail holder and green eyes.

NEWBY: Oh, OK. So, this is—I was a little confused right here. OK. OK. Now, "the woman who has."

BLUE: [signs, with a closed fist at the back of her head]

JAY: Holds. Ponytail holder

NEWBY: With, with, if it's a—we'll get to that. So, hold, ponytail holder. You need to tell me what kind of holder it is. OK. This is like, [holds book to chest] she holds the book. This is, right, and that's OK. But you need to—

JAY: I kind of messed it up. She didn't say ponytail holder.

NEWBY: Right. It's not on there.

JAY: But she did "hold." I probably should have said "hold." That was my interpretation of what she said. I probably should have—

NEWBY: And this is where, this is where she has problems with writing. Because in signing, you can say so much more with fewer words. I guess when you have ideas and concepts and all that, you can sign it. But on a paper you've gotta write it out. OK. So, I mean this is much more complex and probably harder. Although sign language is pretty hard for me. So, yeah, signing, it's perfect the way you're doing it. It's just that when you put it on paper, I need to—I need more to understand.

BLUE: I got it. All right.

NEWBY: So you need to tell me and this would be "holder" instead of "holds" with an *s*. A ponytail holder. You need to tell me what kind. That's—yeah. It's got to have much more stuff than you're used to. Most of us when we start to write we probably have to put in more stuff on the paper than when we speak. Just probably if you remember that you need to add more to make me see. When you sign, when you sign, she [the interpreter] can see it, OK? But in order for me to see it, you've gotta put the words on your paper. OK. Just like learning a foreign language. OK? So, you're doing great. You're doing great. So you know what to do with that one.

What is interesting about this exchange is that they explicitly discuss the miscommunication, how it happened, and how to correct it. Then Newby discusses the situation and result, using the problem as a learning opportunity. What Blue had actually written was, "Now, the woman who has a red hair with bow holds and green eyes." Newby assumed that if Blue signed it, then the missing words or unclear meaning would become clear. The problem here is that in writing, Blue had used the noun "bow" as an adjective, rather than "ponytail," as Jay interpreted and as Newby expected. Also, "holds" was written as a verb, rather than the expected noun form, "holder," which Jay also supplied. The way Blue signed it, with a closed fist on the back of the head, she was signing "holds" in a different position. The sign HOLDS is usually articulated with a closed fist, palm up, in the signing space in front of the signer, but Blue signed it with a closed fist at the back of the head, representing the position of the ponytail. That this construction was clear to Jay is obvious: She interpreted the word correctly as "ponytail holder." This event could be seen as an instance of ASL interference, or of the interpreter inserting words that were not the word choice of the deaf tutee. In either case, ASL interference was sporadic and not highly significant in the data corpus.

Recommendations for Tutoring

Some specific techniques worked well in the tutoring sessions I observed, and some were not as effective. I frame this section as advice to the practitioner.

Most of all, try to find out what the deaf person needs and wants out of the session, and gear your tutoring toward that. This will be uncomfortable, for instance, if the tutee asks for help with editing and proofreading and the tutor's training forbids that kind of help. Remember that for deaf people, and for hearing students who speak nonstandard dialects or English as a second language, reading aloud as a technique to catch errors may not work. These students need to learn to see the errors on the page, and in order to do this they must be familiar with the conventions of print in English, and that is best done by reading.

Many deaf college students are not as familiar with print as we would expect a college freshman to be. Be patient and understanding as you find ways to help students find and correct their own errors. In addition, you need to pay special attention to reading comprehension and paraphrase/summary in a tutorial with a deaf tutee, much more so than you would in a tutoring session with a hearing person. To this end, the tutor has to be a cheerleader for reading. Find out if your deaf tutee reads a lot. If the answer is yes, you should notice a more standard product. If the answer is no, then encourage your tutee to read. You could do as Newby did and recommend books, go to the library together, or even give your tutee a book that you think she might enjoy. I gave the deaf participants in the study gift certificates to Barnes & Noble. I was encouraged during the member-checking phase of this study when Blue said she could not respond to the chapters I gave her to review, since she was reading a book and did not want to divide her attention between the book and the chapters. Composition scholars Tonya Stremlau Johnson and Brenda Brueggemann both attribute their success with English to early, voracious reading. Newby, deaf study participant Kali, and I feel the same way. Marlon Kuntze says reading and a strong foundation in ASL are the keys to d/Deaf students' literacy success (pers. comm.).

Make sure you give the deaf person opportunity for more than one-word answers. To check understanding, you could ask the student to rephrase what you have been talking about. And although it is sometimes uncomfortable for hearing people to leave silences, rather than talk on and on, wait and give the deaf person a chance to enter the conversation. What hearing people think of as open-ended questions deaf people may find vague. Try asking direct, pointed questions, but not ones that require only a yes or no answer. As JoAnn Johnston recommends, you could use imperatives, which lead to more talk than do questions.

Although nondirective techniques are valued in many writing centers (and by hearing culture), these techniques may not work as well with deaf writers. I have also learned from observation and research that these techniques may not work with LD and ESL writers either. However, all writers still need to be pushed to find their own answers when possible. I recommend that with deaf and LD students tutors try nondirective techniques but abandon them if they prove unproductive. Deaf culture values directness, and nondirective coaching may frustrate d/Deaf students.

Blue valued Newby's practice of sitting next to her and putting the paper in view of both of them. An important technique when working with a deaf student is sharing text as written. Other uses of written text are those that study participants Rae, a student, and John, her tutor, used: Rae typed her answers directly into the computer so John could read them on screen and comment as she typed. Also, John took notes for Rae as she signed her answers. Both of these techniques are promising ways to share language, text, and ideas. Be careful when discussing text not to split the tutee's attention between the text and the interpreter. A deaf person cannot attend to the text *and* the interpreter at the same time, although a hearing person can sometimes read and listen at the same time. If you want to tell a deaf person something while she is looking down at the text, you will have to stop her and wait until her attention is focused on the interpreter, then give your message. Likewise, if you are talking and want the deaf person to attend to something on the paper, finish talking, let the interpreter finish interpreting, then focus the deaf student's attention on the paper. It is hard for hearing people to take in an aural and a visual message at the same time, but a deaf person can only take in one visual message at a time, either the interpreter's signs or the words on the paper.

When working with deaf students on grammar and mechanical conventions, it is important for tutors to be sensitive to tutees' needs. A tutee might want a verbal explanation, a handout, a trip to the grammar book, or just an error to be corrected. I recommend the tutor ask the tutee what kind of help is needed, and if a detailed explanation is welcomed, give it, in the format the tutee prefers. Deaf participant Rae values her tutor's giving advice and explanations, but not ones that are too technical in reference to grammatical rules. The explanations can be given in technical or nontechnical terms, depending on the student's interest in grammar as a topic of study. Also, modeling a correction can also be effective for a visual learner, with or without an explanation. This is especially true for difficult rules of grammar that the tutor might not even know, such as the rules of article use in English. In a tutorial when Kali asked her tutor, Gustav, about article use, he modeled the correction and told her the rule was too complicated and he did not know it himself. This kind of honesty is superior to giving a half-learned or half-correct version of a rule.

When working with an interpreter, make sure you address the deaf person and not the interpreter. Also, consult the deaf person about the ideal seating arrangements. Consult with the deaf person and interpreter, too, about the best way to communicate written information. Sometimes the best idea is to refer the deaf person's attention to the written text, sometimes the tutor can read it aloud and the interpreter interpret, and sometimes the deaf person can sign what is written on the page. Linda, one of the interpreters in the study said that "when you're interpreting something that's related to English, it makes sense to actually have people read in English." These techniques can be used for the student's own writing as well as other texts. Which one is appropriate should be negotiated between the tutor, tutee, and interpreter. When the student is producing text, she can write for the tutor directly on paper or the computer screen, or she can sign while the interpreter interprets and the tutor takes notes. Again, the format and technique should be negotiated among the participants. Sometimes the tutor will have a genuine educational reason for preferring one or the other, or the interpreter or student will have a communication or linguistic preference for one or the other. For instance, interpreter Linda reflected that it is easier for a deaf person to brainstorm in ASL because the ideas can come freely without the need to translate them into English. In another example, John, the tutor, asked the interpreter, "OK, should I read this out loud and then you just relay it to her, or—" and then Rae responded, "I'll read it myself." This is a good model of how to negotiate how the communication and information transfer take place.

In an interview, Rae told me about a faculty tutor she had who took up her precious tutoring time with his own questions about her deafness and her language. Remember, the tutoring time belongs to the tutee, not to you. Do not waste the tutee's time with questions that are meant to satisfy your curiosity. You as a tutor are being paid to help the student, not for the student to educate you about deafness. If you are interested in the topic, and you should be if you are tutoring a deaf student, you can read a book on the subject, such as *Deaf in America* by Carol Padden and Tom Humphries, *A Journey into the Deaf-World* by Harlan Lane, Robert Hoffmeister, and Ben Bahan, *Reading between the Signs* by Anna Mindess et al., or *American Deaf Culture* edited by Sherman Wilcox, or talk to your school's disabilities services coordinator. Some schools offer courses in Deaf Culture and ASL. If you are particularly interested in talking to the tutee personally about these issues, ask to meet outside the tutoring session at a mutually convenient time and place, so as not to monopolize the tutee's tutoring time. Perhaps you could tell the tutee of your interest, and the tutee could answer your questions on a day when she does not have an assignment to work on in the tutoring session. If you are interested in Deaf culture and deaf people, another idea is to volunteer to be an in-class note taker for a deaf student.

IDEAS FOR FURTHER RESEARCH

This study is only the first step in learning about tutoring deaf college students in writing. Further research needs to be done on the use of writing for communication in the tutorial between deaf tutees and hearing tutors. Both Gail Wood and Tonya Stremlau Johnson recommend this practice so that deaf people can get complete access to English through writing. Unfortunately, I was unable to observe enough tutorials conducted in writing to include them as a category in my analysis. Research also needs to be done on tutorials conducted entirely in sign language. A researcher would need fluent sign language skills to conduct such research. An ambitious study could compare tutorials conducted in writing, through an interpreter, with those conducted in sign language (both ASL and contact sign) to see if, as Gail Wood claims, there is any difference in achievement based on the communication model used in the tutorial. One question that remains to be answered is, What are or should be the roles of ASL and English, respectively, in the tutoring session? Since Gail Wood reported that students tutored in ASL did not progress, but much of the sign language used in educational contexts is English based, the dimension of language needs to be added to that of modality as a dimension for study. Research also needs to be done on various technological options that could be used to facilitate communication with deaf people. Some colleges are using live captioning systems such as CART or C-PRINT in the classroom. The possibility for their use in the tutoring session could be investigated. Also, the possibility of tutoring deaf students using online technologies could also be investigated. These technologies offer the advantage of allowing tutorials to be conducted entirely in English, in writing, and thus eliminating the need for an interpreter. A drawback of these techniques is that a tutorial conducted entirely in English would not be effective for a student who is struggling with English.

NOTES

1. The International Writing Centers Association Graduate Research Grant and the Rock Valley College Foundation Grant provided funding for this research.

2. Throughout this article, I use *Deaf* or *Hearing* with capital letters to indicate cultural status, *deaf* and *hearing* with lowercase letters to indicate auditory status and as neutral terms, and both separated by a slash (d/Deaf) to consciously include both cultural and auditory groups.

3. All deaf people's words are transcribed as voiced by an interpreter.

REFLECTING ON YOUR TEACHING

Conferencing

Babcock's study demonstrates how "normal" habits and practices favor certain kinds of embodied ways of learning that may not suit every learner and every body. An important move in disability studies is to critically examine the construction of "normal"—its history, power, and rules—so as to understand how the norm operates to maintain an invisible hierarchical structuring effect.

Many writing teachers use one-on-one conferences with students, in addition to classroom time, for instruction. What are the rules of normalcy in conferencing with students? Working with a small group, brainstorm a short list of steps in conducting an individual writing conference with a student. Then, discuss the norms that underlie the practices; can you discern an invisible hierarchical structuring effect? How might you change the way you conference with students? Could you adapt Babcock's advice for tutoring and develop a protocol for negotiating with a student about how to conduct a conference? What would such a protocol look like?

3

Discourses of Disability and Basic Writing

AMY VIDALI

Amy Vidali reengages with the debates over the benefits and drawbacks of separate or inclusive classrooms, not only for students with disabilities but also for students labeled "basic writers." Vidali asks why these two marginalized groups — "basic writers" and "students with disabilities" — have so often been defined and pitted against each other to compete for limited resources within the university. Revisiting the history of basic writing by using insights gained from disability studies, Vidali "explore[s] [how] the concept of deficit functions in both basic writing's theories of cognitivism and disability studies' claims about how disability is perceived." She notes the social construction and "elasticity" of both basic writing and disability identities. For both groups, she argues, the "overcoming" myth functions to deflect attention away from the social forces that oppress and disenable and tend to make people focus only on the individual's ability to conquer obstacles. While both groups now "more often struggle against each other than against common sources of oppression" what might happen, she asks in her conclusion, if we were to connect basic writing and disability in writing programs?

In general, my study of basic writers — their strategies, processes, and products — leads me to believe that they have not attained the level of cognitive development which would allow them to form abstractions or conceptions.

> —ANDREA LUNSFORD, "COGNITIVE DEVELOPMENT AND THE BASIC WRITER"
> (1979, REPRINTED IN VILLANUEVA)

Briefly, the medicalization of disability casts human variation as deviance from the norm, as pathological condition, as deficit, and, significantly, as an individual burden and personal tragedy. ... The disability studies' and disability rights movement's position is critical of the domination of the medical definition and views it as a major stumbling block to the reinterpretation of disability as a political category and to the social changes that could follow such a shift.

> —SIMI LINTON, *CLAIMING DISABILITY* (1998)

Though the two quotes above were published nearly two decades apart and purport to discuss different populations, Simi Linton's critique of the medicalization of disability can be applied to Andrea Lunsford's description of the "deficits" of basic writers. For instance, the lack of "cognitive development" described by Lunsford in 1979 could be critiqued—in Linton's words—for treating basic writers as if they have some sort of pathological condition, deficit, or deviance from supposedly normal writers. And as Linton claims, such false perceptions of people with disabilities (and basic writers) obscure the social and political issues that are really at play regarding people with disabilities (and basic writers). The connections between basic writing and disability studies go well beyond such wordplay, as I explain in the following pages. First, I explore the concept of *deficit* as it functions in both basic writing's theories of cognitivism and disability studies' claims about how disability is perceived. This initial analysis sets the stage for a more detailed exploration of the relationship between the seemingly disparate disciplines of basic writing and disability studies.

The sort of cognitivist theory famously expressed by Andrea Lunsford decades ago was part of a movement in composition known as cognitivism, developmentalism, and later, deficit theory. As discussed by Lester Faigley in "Competing Theories of Process," cognitivism attempted to bring a "science consciousness" to composition research and drew on cognitive science and psychology. For example, scholars like Barry Kroll and Andrea Lunsford adapted Jean Piaget's concept of "Egocentrism" in order to talk about the various developmental stages that children, and arguably basic writers, move through. While Kroll argued that children's ability to imagine another perspective, or to "decenter," develops more slowly in writing than in speaking, Lunsford extended this idea and argued that the tendency of basic writers to produce personal narrative in writing situations that ask for "abstract" discourse indicates they are arrested in an "egocentric stage" (Faigley, 43–44).

Such approaches focus on the "cognitive ability" or "cognitive development" of the writer, and basic writers were often relegated to prewriter or even preadult status. As David Bartholomae notes in "Tidy House: Basic Writing in the American Curriculum," thinking of basic writing in terms of such development allows the reproduction of "existing hierarchies but as evidence of natural patterns—basic writers are just like other writers, but not quite so mature" (14). Bartholomae intimates that the "problems" of basic writers are imagined to be "naturally" located within such students, rather than resulting from previous schooling experiences, home language issues, discrimination, and so forth. In the classroom, a "developmental" approach to writing meant that basic writers were repeatedly drilled on the "building blocks" of writing, rather than being treated as students capable of (or interested in) producing complex pieces of writing (Reynolds and Bruch, 12). Within cognitivism/developmentalism, the slip from identifying deficits in basic *writing* (which may or may not actually exist) to detecting deficits in basic *writers* is an easy one. Furthermore, as Bruce Horner argues, such developmental models situate basic writers not only in a cognitive and "natural" sense, but also in a civic sense, "locating them at a particular stage in a natural sequence of learning and attributing to them the aspiration to join with rather than disrupt mainstream American society" (14).

The heyday of cognitivism and developmentalism was the 1970s and early 1980s, though even during this period scholars such as Mike Rose and David Bartholomae challenged these concepts: Bartholomae argued in 1980 that basic writing "is not evidence of arrested cognitive development, arrested language development, or unruly or unpredictable language use" (though Bartholomae's early critique still relies on "diagnosing" the errors of basic writers) ("Study of Error," 176). Since then, casting basic writers in terms of their developmental/cognitive deficits has been largely repudiated by basic writing scholars. For instance, in "Basic Writing and the Issue of Correctness," Patricia Bizzell divides the history of basic writing into three phases, clearly locating cognitivist approaches in the bygone first phase that "dat[es] to about twenty years ago," or 1980 (4). Bizzell argues that most current basic writing scholarship is either in the second phase, which seeks to initiate students into academic discourse while respecting their home language and cognitive abilities, or the third phase, where "the unitary nature of traditional academic discourse as a target for composition teaching is called into question" (5). Mary Soliday also places theories that emphasize cognitivist deficits in the past: "Deficit imagery has of course been challenged as a result of research in composition, cultural studies, sociolinguistics, and the anthropology of education" (132).

While basic writing scholars situate such deficit theories as debunked approaches of the past, disability studies scholars emphasize that deficit theories dominate the perception of disability in the present. Similar to the way cognitivist approaches treat basic writers as incomplete or developing writers/adults/citizens, people with disabilities are often perceived as being partial or flawed because of their so-called deficits. While cognitivism recommends a developmental approach to teaching writing to address the "deficits" of basic writers, people with disabilities are directed to doctors and rehabilitation specialists to fix theirs. From this dominant clinical perspective, disability is treated as a nonpolitical, nonsocial aspect of identity that has exclusively personal and medical features. Simi Linton refers to this as the "medicalization of disability," which—as noted in her quote above—views disability as "deviance," "pathological condition," "deficit," and "individual burden and personal tragedy," thereby denying the complex relationship of disability, culture, and identity. Paul Longmore explains that this "deficit" or "medical model" problematically defines disability as "physiological pathologies located within individuals" that must be cured or corrected so people with disabilities can achieve social acceptance ("The Second Phase," 217), thereby relegating disability to hospital hallways, physical therapy tables, and remedial classrooms (Davis, *Disability Studies*, 1–2).[1] And, though Tom Fox claims that deficit theories will persist as long as "racism and sexism and classism affect education" (*Defending Access*, 51–52), I would argue that deficit models also endure (in basic writing and elsewhere) because they are the dominant discourses of disability and ability—discourses which often underlie and intermingle with discussions of capacity based on race, class, and gender.

While the medical model of disability does not imagine that various sorts of bodies should exist and can lead enjoyable lives, disability studies theorizes disability identity and culture in conjunction with the goals of disability activism in order to recognize that disability is social, political, and historical. This minority or social model of disability argues that while material bodies exist, disability is also socially constructed, and disability studies scholars have emphasized that discrimination, not physical or mental limitation, may be the biggest burden facing those with disabilities. In this sense, disability is not simply a medical or physical characteristic of bodies but, as Rosemarie Garland-Thomson writes, "a product of cultural rules of what bodies should be or do" (6). Garland-Thomson does not locate disability as a "deficit" in a "problem body," but instead notes that disability is "located in the interaction between bodies and the environment in which they are situated" ("Integrating Disability Studies," 296). Similarly, Linda Ware notes that disability studies problematizes the medical model "such that questions of civil rights and social justice are privileged over those cast as personal problems," making disability "a way of thinking about bodies rather than something that is wrong with bodies" (110).

Disability studies' challenge of the medical model can help basic writing scholars understand why deficit models persist in basic writing, even after most basic writing scholars have shunned them, and the social and political model of disability identity can be used to conceptualize a similarly informed model of the basic writer. I will explore these ideas by examining the "discourses of disability" in basic writing, and "reading" basic writing scholarship using the insight of disability. This allows a better understanding of basic writing and basic writers and importantly engages discussion about student writers with disabilities in the composition classroom.

Ellen Barton's discussion of the "discourses of disability" helps define what I mean by this term and how I will examine such discourses in basic writing scholarship. In her investigation of how expertise is negotiated among parents, disabled children, and doctors, Barton notes:

> This social nature of disability is created and reflected by various discourses of disability—stretches of language as short as a conversational exchange or as long as the literature of an academic discipline—and an analysis of some of these discourses, their underlying assumptions and unstated attitudes, their themes and conventions, points to a critical view of the social nature of disability in American society. (300)

While Barton employs the methods of discourse analysis to study the conversations of her subjects, I will focus on the discourses of disability in "the literature of an academic discipline"—in this case, basic writing scholarship. Like Barton, I examine discourses of disability in order to emphasize "the social nature of disability." Furthermore, to use Brenda Brueggemann's terms, I am interested in using disability as insight ("Enabling," 795), so as to "enable" basic writing theory in such a way that benefits both basic writers and writers with disabilities.

SLIPPERY IDENTITIES: BASIC AND DISABLED SUBJECTIVITIES

Before moving to a discussion of how basic writing scholarship and disability studies can inform each other, it is important to recognize that the identities of writers with disabilities and basic writers are not always distinct—there are certainly basic writers with disabilities. Further, the identities of basic writers and writers with disabilities have not only been overlapping but interchangeable; that is, a particular set of students might be labeled "basic" at one historical or institutional moment and "disabled" the next. For example, in "Bureaucratic Order and Special Children: Urban Schools, 1890s–1940s," Joseph Tropea explores how students were variously labeled as disciplinary cases, "backward," "vocational" or "mentally handicapped," depending on the usefulness of the label for maintaining order in the schools at particular historical moments.[2] In a more recent study of the principles that undergird placement decisions, Jean Crockett and James Kauffman note that "many urban districts short on resources and long on low-achieving students use special education as a means of dealing with general education's nondisabled fallout" (29–30).[3] Mary Soliday traces how this plays out in terms of writing policies and programs, clarifying that the "special programs" in which basic writers are enrolled are not necessarily employed because they are particularly beneficial to the students; rather, "specific institutional histories suggest that these programs may also help institutions to manage their growth during periods of crisis and change" (60).

Such analyses clarify that "basic" and "disabled" labels may be used interchangeably by institutions seeking particular ends; however, my goal is not to show that these two groups of students are pretty much interchangeable in educational environments. Indeed, these two groups receive rather different treatment in colleges and universities, and discussion of these two categories of students occurs in disparate disciplines. The sort of shared identity referred to (but not endorsed) by Tropea, Crockett and Kauffman, and Soliday results from attempts to (re)marginalize these students by casting them all into a "wastebasket" category conveniently labeled "other." The alliances I hope to establish between these two groups look toward a shared future of social justice that recognizes their differences.

CONSTRUCTING BASIC WRITERS AND STUDENTS WITH DISABILITIES

Both basic writing theory and disability studies have attended to how identity is socially and discursively constructed, lending insight into the relationship and differing elasticity of such identities. Disability studies emphasizes that disabled identities are socially and discursively constructed, like other identities, while retaining more attention on the material body than do other identity-related discussions.[4] The constructed nature of disability identity is emphasized by Linton, who posits that disability is what society makes of an impairment (138–41). Foucauldian disability scholars have pushed the socially constructed nature of disability even further, arguing that conceiving of impairment as "prediscursive" and "natural" inadvertently legitimizes and extends discriminatory attitudes toward those with disabilities (Tremain, "Foucault, Governmentality," 10–11).[5] Disability studies also seeks to reveal the constructedness of "normal" identity, or what Rosemarie Garland-Thomson calls "normate" identities, a term that "names the veiled subject position of cultural self, the figure outlined by the array of deviant others whose marked bodies shore up the normate's boundaries" (*Extraordinary*, 8).

Similarly, basic writing theory has embraced the constructedness of identity. Marshall Alcorn argues for a Lacanian theory of subjectivity in composition, noting that the construction of student subjectivities is currently informed by an "insufficiently complex understanding of subjectivity" that has not changed as the "subject matter" of composition courses has (2). Taking a different stance, Gail Stygall analyzes the possible subject positions basic writers can inhabit, interpreting Foucault's author function via basic writers. She clarifies that the author function has four characteristics and notes that the author function allows for a multiplicity of selves in the same author. But, Stygall concludes, when these concepts of the author function are applied to basic writers, they are disallowed from being authors in Foucault's sense because their transgressions are treated as trivial; because they are allowed limited change; and because they are constructed as being nonliterate, preconceptual thinkers with unitary identities (324–25). Disability studies suggests that disability identity is also imagined as static, singular, and nontransgressive.

Disability identity, however, generally differs from other identities (such as gender, race, and class) in that it is highly permeable—anyone can become disabled at any time, and most people will likely have a disability if they live long enough (hence the term "temporarily able bodied," or TAB).[6] The identities of basic writers should also be permeable, assuming that writers can indeed improve their writing and will be recognized by those around them for having done so (and these are large assumptions). However, the factors that make the basic writer "basic"—lack of resources, poor schooling, race and class discrimination—are not necessarily "remedied" when the basic writer learns to write well, making the identity of the basic writer less permeable than it seems. Indeed, such sociocultural and economic factors are typically ignored, and instead, the basic writer becomes pathologized as the "problem" of the basic writer's "basic-ness" is decontextualized and located in the basic writer's writing, and by extension, in the basic writer herself. According to these assumptions, the identity of the basic writer is only permeable, or changeable, by some supreme expression of personal will or stamina (which stand in for social justice).

THE OVERCOMING MYTH IN BASIC WRITING SCHOLARSHIP

As highlighted in the earlier discussion of cognitivism, basic writing theorists have employed the language of ability and disability (and particularly deficit) in order to describe basic writers. Such descriptions are typically accompanied by assertions of how the "problems" of basic writing, and basic writers, will be "fixed." For example, in his discussion of collaborative learning,

Kenneth Bruffee explains that students need to revise their apparently insufficient identities and communities, a process he calls "reacculturation": "To be acculturated to those perfectly valid and coherent but entirely local communities alone has severely limited their freedom. It had prepared them for social, political, and economic relations of only the narrowest sort" (6). Bruffee's notion of reacculturation expects students to overcome what is considered to be inadequate ways of thinking and knowing in order to embrace academically sanctioned versions of social, political, and economic relations. Linda Adler-Kassner and Susanmarie Harrington also note that conversations regarding "deficits" in basic writers are often followed by "a discussion of curricular strategies meant to alleviate the problems identified in the research" — a move which tends to elide discussion of the political nature of such "deficits" (20). Whether certain identities are blatantly identified as narrow, or whether such identities are assumed to be in need of fixing as implied by curricular "solutions," the idea that a person must overcome an undesirable identity in order to be successful is problematic, and the expectation "to overcome" has been criticized by disability studies scholars. Understanding their developed critique of "overcoming" lends further insight into its use in basic writing.

Disability studies explains that society expects those with disabilities to work extra hard in order to "overcome" or "compensate for" their disabilities, predominantly through superhuman acts of talent, kindness, and inspiration. While there is nothing wrong with a talented or hardworking person with a disability, it is the expectation or demand that a person with a disability "overcome" their "tragic" state that disability studies scholars find problematic. Rosemarie Garland-Thomson explains, noting that the expectation of overcoming "suggests that one's body is the recalcitrant object that must be surmounted," meaning that because the body of a person with a disability is "flawed," it must be conquered or defeated by the disabled person ("Integrating Disability Studies," 304). The expectation of overcoming is so persistent, Mitchell and Snyder argue, that narratives of disability "must inevitably show how we conquer our disabilities or how they eventually conquer us." This expectation of overcoming "refuses us the pursuit of anonymity in ordinary involvements" (xii). Disability studies instead emphasizes that people with disabilities accomplish their goals *with* their disabilities, rather than by overcoming or conquering them.

Expectations of overcoming also play out in basic writing, similarly negating marginalized ways of being and knowing. Careful examination of Marilyn Sternglass's discussion of two of the nine subjects in her longitudinal study reveals expectations of overcoming at work. In one part of her analysis, Sternglass describes Donald, an African American student who she notes is "willing to do the required work, but . . . interested in finding the most efficient ways to carry out his response" (xx). In the conclusion of her chapter on the effects of complex social histories, Sternglass notes that Donald "could use his awareness that minorities had been discouraged from applying to respected colleges; he could try to urge others in his community to overcome such obstacles" (112). Here, Sternglass recommends that Donald embrace college and urge his friends and family to apply, despite the fact that minorities are discouraged from applying in the first place. In a strange sleight of hand, compensating for the lack of outreach to minorities, a lack which the college is certainly responsible for, becomes Donald's responsibility. A more appropriate move would be to pursue the issue with the college rather than placing the obligation to overcome obstacles on the minority student. Sternglass makes no such assertion of institutional responsibility, and indeed, we may make the same mistake in some of our basic writing courses by praising the few students who "make it" rather than questioning the system that denied so many like them.

Disability studies scholar Simi Linton neatly sums up what occurs when an individual is expected to overcome barriers erected by society, rather than society removing those barriers. Though Linton is addressing people with disabilities, her statement clearly applies to Donald's situation as well: "If we, as a society, place the onus on individuals with disabilities to work harder to 'compensate' for their disabilities or to 'overcome' their condition or the barriers in the environment, we have no need for civil rights legislation or affirmative action" (19).

Similarly, expecting basic writers to "overcome" or "normalize" themselves excuses institutional responsibility and negates the identities of basic writers. Tom Fox levies a critique similar to Linton's when he notes that the "issues" of basic writers are cast as "individual maturity problems, lack of organization, intellectual deficits, psychological problems, lack of preparation, and other individual faults of the students," thereby ignoring the social and political context that defines basic writing and writers (*Defending Access*, 11).

The expectation to overcome is also prominent in Sternglass's discussion of Delores, who Sternglass describes as a Latina student who "displayed initiative and fortitude in taking on complex original projects, even when her financial situation made excruciating demands on her" (xix). Sternglass explains that Delores received a C— on her paper with the following teacher remark: "What could have been quite a good paper is hampered by poor writing." Sternglass responds: "Delores took these kinds of admonitions to heart and she worked on overcoming these problems" (118). While I would not argue that the (largely grammatical second-language) writing issues in Delores's work will have no effect on how she is perceived, the "moral" of this particular anecdote is that Delores can and will overcome her writing errors, which sidesteps the effect her heavy workload outside of school might have had on her schoolwork. Again, the "burden" is placed on the student to overcome, rather than on an institution that cannot or will not provide the sort of support Delores deserves in order to be able to succeed in school (grants, loans, and so forth).

Implicit in these discussions is that individuals are able to, and should, overcome such obstacles. While the discussions are more overt in disability studies, disabled and basic writers share a need to recast the "problem" or "burden" of their othered identities, not as inherently existing traits but as fallout of environments that create such others. However, it may be difficult for basic writing scholars to reject the myth of overcoming, since many such scholars pride themselves on overcoming difficult obstacles.[7]

DEFINING WRITERS WITH DISABILITIES AND BASIC WRITERS AGAINST EACH OTHER

Basic writing and disability studies thus share much in common, including a belief in the constructedness of identity, a history of and resistance to deficit theory, and shared terminology for and expectations of overcoming marginalization. While interaction between disability studies and composition has not generally focused on these issues, disability studies scholars have argued for increased inclusion of writers with disabilities. For instance, Kimber Barber-Fendley and Chris Hamel explore the treatment of learning disability in composition theory, concluding that "the medical model of LD has precluded the more in-depth and holistic study of LD that the field of disability studies calls for." Looking to the future, they note that disability studies motivates compositionists to ask "what truly constitutes writing: what form or forms must expression take for it to be considered 'writing,' and what alternative formats are acceptable" (512).

Similarly, Patricia Dunn emphasizes how composition teachers may "disable" skilled thinkers by "overusing one pathway—writing—in the many intellectual tasks leading up to a finished piece: written journals, written peer responses, freewriting, written proposals or outlines, written e-mail discussions, and so on" (Brueggemann et al., 379). In *Learning Re-Abled,* Dunn critiques Shaughnessy, Bartholomae, and Bizzell for disregarding learning disabilities. Dunn claims that Shaughnessy's assumption that basic writers' troubles result from an unfamiliarity with terms discounts that students may have seen the terms and are perhaps struggling to internalize standard spelling because of a learning disability (64), and she also notes that Bartholomae's marking of certain errors as "accidental" dismisses the possibility of learning differences (67). Finally, she claims that Bizzell's research presupposes that a "clash" between home and school cultures causes students' problems, when a learning disability may (also) be involved (69).

While the fields of basic writing and disability have ignored each other's needs at times, as Dunn suggests, basic writers and writers with disabilities have also been cast as competing entities, rather than minority groups that might have some shared goals. Dunn herself problematically pits learning disabled writers against basic writers:

> If teachers assume a student is using simplistic words because he or she *does not know* more sophisticated ones, they might also make inaccurate assumptions concerning the student's intelligence, which might in turn impact how they treat that student and what expectations they overtly or subtly convey. If, however, teachers are acquainted with the LD theory that poor vocabulary might be due to poor recall and not to ignorance of words, they might be more inclined to treat the student with more respect and to have appropriately higher expectations. (*Learning Re-Abled,* 63; italics in original)

Dunn regards writing issues resulting from learning disabilities as justified and deserving of appropriately higher expectations, while basic writing issues are relegated to a state of ignorance that warrants low expectations. Rather than arguing that the "normal" classroom is unsuitable for both types of students, she labels basic writers as the problematic "other" from which students with disabilities can, and should, be distinguished.

Dunn makes a similar move in *Talking, Sketching, Moving: Multiple Literacies in the Teaching of Writing*, a text which importantly invites composition teachers to challenge their reliance on linguistic pathways and engage exciting pedagogical approaches such as e-mail journals, "rhetorical proof cards," and discussion-oriented peer review. However, Dunn is again careful to distinguish writers with disabilities from basic writers:

> What if some students who have the most difficulty with one level of writing—with surface correctness for example—have complex, sophisticated ideas, but their "grammar" problems peg them as "basic writers," slot them in a lower academic track, and wring out of them any confidence they might have had about themselves or any enthusiasm they might have had for learning? (24)

While it is certainly possible that students with disabilities might be labeled as basic writers and placed in a basic writing class (note I'm resisting the implications of the terms *pegged* and *slotted*), Dunn's description of basic writing as a "lower academic track" where students have all of the "enthusiasm they might have had for learning" and "confidence they might have had about themselves" wrung out of them is unjustifiably bleak. Instead, I would argue that basic writing students produce some of the richest writing and are often more in tune with critical pedagogy than "standard track" students, and further, that the basic writing classroom often provides a place for community among a group of students who may not easily fit in with their upper-middle-class white peers. Lastly, Dunn's statement denies the possibility that the "grammar problems" of learning disabled writers and basic writers may be tolerated, and even addressed, in a shared environment.

Disability historian Douglas Baynton is critical of how able-bodied, marginalized populations have wrongfully used disability to contest their own mistreatment, and his work is helpful in understanding Dunn's unintentional castigation of basic writers. Baynton notes that "not only has it been considered justifiable to treat disabled people unequally, but the concept of disability has been used to justify discrimination against other groups by attributing disability to them" (33). He uses the tactics of suffragists as an example, noting how disability was problematically deployed using three approaches:

> [O]ne, women were not disabled and therefore deserved the vote; two, women were being erroneously and slanderously classed with disabled people, with those legitimately denied suffrage; and three, women were not naturally or inherently disabled but were made disabled by inequality—suffrage would ameliorate or cure these disabilities. (43)

While Baynton claims that the argument typically is put forward by an able-bodied marginalized group noting that "they were not disabled . . . and therefore were not proper subjects of discrimination" (34), the opposite occurs in Dunn's text: Disability is justified at the expense of basic writers, casting the "problems" of basic writers as assumedly deserved and unproblematic.[8]

In the face of scant institutional resources, perhaps such competition among marginalized groups is expected, but in another sense it is surprising, given that the low-income and/or students of color who traditionally fill basic writing classes have a longer and more productive history of gaining access to colleges and universities than do students with disabilities. Because of this, it is surprising to see students with disabilities justified at their expense. In "Learning Disability, Pedagogies, and Public Discourse," Linda Feldmeier White provides a possible reason why this occurs:

> The attack on LD has been less successful than the attack on basic writing because conservatives and LD researchers share key beliefs in the certainty and objectivity of empirically produced knowledge and in the inevitability of hierarchical structures. (725)

White acknowledges that medical and scientific discourses are often required to "justify" LD, and that LD's association with dominant scientific discourse provides LD students with the "justification" basic writing students lack. However, attempting to provide basic writers with the "justification" LD students already have would not only endorse scientific criteria and erase social causes, it would also lead back toward cognitivist approaches in which basic writers are defined by intrinsic "deficits." Instead, both basic writing and disability studies scholars must recognize the risk of remarginalizing each other when fighting for recognition and change.

THE DIFFERING PLACEMENT OF BASIC WRITERS AND WRITERS WITH DISABILITIES

Though basic writing and disability studies often roam the same theoretical terrain, the writers themselves typically inhabit different classroom spaces (except when such students bear both identities, in which case they will likely be in basic writing classrooms). In postsecondary education, for the most part, basic writing students have had their own classrooms and programs, while writers with disabilities have often been placed into "standard" classes (where they may or may not have been accommodated). This disparate placement is informed by differing disciplinary discourses, with discussions of students with disabilities centering around inclusion and Universal Design (UD), and basic writing scholarship focusing on "mainstreaming," as illustrated by the 2001 collection entitled *Mainstreaming Basic Writers: Politics and Pedagogies of Access,* edited by Gerry McNenny. Examining these disparate discourses allows a rethinking of how these groups might function as allies in the practical (and complicated) space of the classroom, program, and department.

In "The Tidy House," Bartholomae demonstrates basic writing's tendency to argue for mainstreaming, an approach which adds "other" students to "standard" classrooms. Bartholomae argues that the "tidy distinction between basic and mainstream . . . enforce[s] a commonness among our students by making the differences superficial, surface-level, and by designing a curriculum to both insure them and erase them in 14 weeks" (12). Bartholomae imagines some other rhetorical/institutional place where basic writers could be: "We could imagine not tracking students at all. We could offer classes with a variety of supports for those who need them" (14). Such a classroom or program accords with the new application of UD to learning. UD is a familiar concept to disability advocates because it promotes full accessibility as a prerequisite for buildings. The Council for Exceptional Children describes its application to learning:

> Universal design for learning is achieved by means of flexible curricular materials and activities that provide alternatives for students with differing abilities. These alternatives are built into the instructional design and operating systems of educational materials—they are not added on after-the-fact. (qtd. in Bowe, 45)

Though Bartholomae's call for a "variety of supports" vaguely points toward UD principles, he does not ultimately call for such a reconfiguration of the classroom, and he backs away from abolishing basic writing programs because he "fear[s] what would happen to the students who are protected" by basic writing. His approach exemplifies basic writing's tendency to explore only two options: basic writers are "added" to "standard" classrooms, or they stay in their own classrooms.

In contrast, disability scholars have largely repudiated segregation and mainstreaming and instead argue for inclusive education. Harry Daniels and Philip Garner explain the difference between mainstreaming (also known as integration) and full inclusion as "a focus on changing individuals to fit existing systems, and changing systems in order that the endemic and often subliminal practices of exclusion and marginalization are avoided" (1). In theory, the inclusion model based on principles of UD would likely benefit both basic writers and writers with disabilities. In practice, figuring this all out is a bit harder.

THOUGHTS TOWARD A PROGRAM FOR BASIC WRITERS AND WRITERS WITH DISABILITIES

Can writers with disabilities and basic writers be served through unified writing programs and classrooms? This "practical" task is difficult in part because a theoretical "base" that connects these two groups does not much exist (yet), and also because of the myriad practical realities involved in imagining such a program or project (How is it funded? What happens to existing programs? Who are the experts? And so forth). I do not have the space here to flesh out a complete program or even a well-developed theory of a program; however, by further engaging placement debates in basic writing, as well as a recent argument for writing programs that focus on LD students, I will begin the discussion of the benefits and challenges of such a unified program.

The inclusion of students with disabilities in basic writing classrooms does not demand that basic writing programs disappear altogether, though the change required to create a program that truly serves both groups would likely reengage the ongoing debate regarding whether basic writers should have separate programs and classes. The debate has emphasized that basic writing programs segregate basic writers for the wrong reasons, or that the removal of basic writing programs would result in the disappearance of basic writers from the university. Soliday also points out that making "practical" changes that affect how basic writers are dealt with requires very different sorts of conversations and commitments, and she criticizes Min-Zhan Lu for making the assumption that a change in "ideas" will lead to a change in "politics." Given that the "bureaucratic machinery of institutions" is slow to change (Soliday, 83), it's understandable that basic writing scholars may hesitate to disassemble basic writing programs, even when inclusive classrooms are the goal.

Conceiving a program that serves both basic writers and writers with disabilities is made more challenging by the fact that even within current basic writing classrooms, some students are underserved. In "Basic Writing and Second Language Writers: Toward an Inclusive Definition," Paul Kei Matsuda argues that "all basic writing teachers—or better yet, all writing teachers— need to be prepared to work with ESL writers" (83), who will continue to be enrolled in basic writing courses, despite ongoing debate as to whether this is appropriate placement. In making this argument for increased understanding and inclusion of English as a Second Language (ESL) students, Matsuda importantly clarifies that it would be unfair to place the responsibility of learning to teach such a diverse student body solely on basic writing teachers, because "the lack of attention to ESL writers in basic writing is more systemic in nature" (83). He explains that the marginalization of ESL issues in basic writing is influenced by "the persistence of the disciplinary division of labor," which imagines composition and second-language studies as separate. Forming a program that brings together composition studies and/or basic writing with the perspectives of disability studies means bridging an even larger disciplinary gap.

Kimber Barber-Fendley and Chris Hamel propose a writing program focused on serving LD students while also reiterating important calls for heightened disability awareness in composition. They preface their proposal with an examination of how much attention the field of composition has paid to learning disability, concluding that "[a]s a field, we do not truly know what a LD writer is" nor do we "truly know how accommodations affect writing processes" (512). They argue for programs that specifically attend to writers with learning disabilities; claiming that such programs should be "inclusive, process-based, customized, department-initiated programs . . . infused into established writing programs and . . . designed to assist with the distinct writing needs of local students with LD at particular campuses" (530).

Barber-Fendley and Hamel boldly describe a program that goes a long way toward theorizing what programs can do to serve LD writers. However, I would caution that any such program must more fully include basic writers; indeed, as with previous discussions of LD writers, Barber-Fendley and Hamel's recent proposal remarginalizes basic writers in order to argue for the rights of students with disabilities.[9] Conversely, basic writing programs must pay more attention to writers with disabilities, and it is worth thinking through the issues that might arise by combining the sort of alternative assistance programs that Barber-Fendley and Hamel discuss with existing basic writing programs. Such a combination may prove successful because such alternative assistance programs could build on basic writing's institutional standing in universities and its historical commitment to underprivileged groups.

To date, most of the conversation about basic writers and students with disabilities has consisted of side comments in work focused on other issues, and such "asides" consistently highlight the differences between basic writers and students with disabilities. And yet, similarities abound: theoretically, both groups have been discussed in terms of their deficits and have been problematically expected to overcome such deficits; historically, students with disabilities and basic writing students have often shared identities and classrooms; and presently, basic writers and writers with disabilities are both defined according to a dominant (white, male, abled) other. Despite these similarities, they more often struggle against each other than against common sources of oppression. We should consider how we can recognize their differences in productive ways, casting writing classrooms and programs as models of how marginalized groups can form a diverse but united progressive left.

NOTES

1. Some disability studies scholars have differentiated between a "functional limitations/ rehabilitation" model of disability, which is produced by such programs as vocational rehabilitation and Social Security Insurance (Hahn, 43), and a "medical" model, which is not likely to result in any sort of civil legislation or aid. However, Lennard Davis notes that both approaches are problematic because while the medical model treats disability as in need of cure, the rehabilitation model treats disability as in need of repair, concealment, remediation, and supervision ("Crips," 506).

2. For more recent statistics and analysis of the relationship of race and disability in education, see Losen and Orfield's *Racial Inequity in Special Education*.

3. Historically, such recategorizations were appealing because schools were often not held accountable for their students with disabilities, particularly in standardized testing reports. More recently, Jay Heubert notes that federal legislation (IDEA 1997 and Improving America's Schools Act 1994) requires that students with disabilities be included in large-scale testing programs with appropriate accommodation, and that schools report performance data for students with disabilities (publicly and in disaggregated form) (138). However, Heubert clarifies that the legislation does not require that high-stakes consequences be imposed on students with disabilities who fail such tests (140), and some schools continue to exclude scores from students with disabilities (146).

4. For disability studies' critiques of the consideration of the material body in social construction theories, see David Mitchell and Sharon Snyder's *Narrative Prosthesis: Disability and the Dependencies of Discourse* and Jim Swan's "Disabilities, Bodies, Voices."

5. Similar to Tremain, Barry Allen complicates the notion of impairment, arguing that while impairment is indeed real (as much as a credit rating or an income tax bracket), it is not "something missing, not a lack or absence; it is something added, an unasked-for supplement contributed by disciplinary knowledge and power" (94).

6. To be fair, racial identity is also porous (one can adopt racial identities one is not born into, or be erroneously assigned to a racial group, and so forth); gender identity is elastic and changeable (again, through claiming and/or revising various identities, or more radically through sex change operations or forced gender reassignment); and one can supposedly move from one class to another (though this may be a harder argument to make). However, there is little chance that a white lower-middle-class woman will awaken tomorrow to find herself an upper-class Korean man. Conversely, waking up tomorrow with a disability, or gaining one in the remaining hours of today, is entirely possible.

7. For Horner notes the contradiction Shaughnessy faces in discussing how she "overcame" material obstacles: her explanation serves "not only as a call to improve conditions" but also as seeming acceptance that teachers must be "powerless altruists who work to achieve under grotesque conditions" (26).

8. Basic writing sometimes justifies its writers at the expense of those with disabilities, which more closely exemplifies Baynton's theory. For instance, in arguing against erroneous perceptions of basic writers, Deborah Mutnick notes: "Only a fraction of individuals are admitted, despite evidence like unreadable placement exams, who seem doomed to fail due to disabilities of various, often unrelated kinds" (xiv). In this quote, it isn't clear if she is actually talking about students with disabilities or using disability metaphorically, but either way, Mutnick does not contest the connection between disability and failure in justifying basic writers.

9. Barber-Fendley and Hamel note that part of their goal "is to assist student writers with LD with their specific and unique writing needs within the policy of inclusion that keeps students with LD in mainstream writing programs and with mainstream populations" (505). Though the authors refer to "the policy of inclusion," the use of the term "mainstream" implies that there are some students who rightfully remain outside the stream, and this unnamed population seems to be basic writers. Indeed, like some of the other texts I've examined, the authors are also careful to distinguish writers with LD from basic writers, as in the authors' critique of Amy Richards's 1985 article in the *Journal of Basic Writing:* "According to Richards, LD writing is indicated through 'unusual' (72), 'strange constructions' (74), consisting of 'distorted' and 'random' spellings' (71). Punctuation errors have the 'odd look of a wild scatter' (74), which occur 'erratically,' 'with no comprehensible rationale for error' (73). Capitalization is 'irrational' and 'random' (73), tossed into the paper 'indiscriminately' (74). Sentences are 'garbles' (75), appearing 'erratic[ally]' and 'seemingly hopeless' (75). These words as descriptions of LD writing offer little, if any, technical distinction from basic writing (507)."

While Barber-Fendley and Hamel appropriately critique Richards for assuming that there is no rhyme or reason for the patterns in the writing of those with LD, they seem comfortable with the idea that the traits Richards describes are appropriate descriptions of basic writing. Here, basic writing seems "hopeless," "distorted," and has "no comprehensible rationale for error."

REFLECTING ON YOUR TEACHING

Inclusive Teaching and the Writing Curriculum

Vidali helps us to see how including disability in debates about basic writing might lead to new kinds of integrated writing courses. Imagine you will be teaching a writing class composed of diverse students—perhaps LD students, those labeled basic writers; mainstream first-year writers; and multilingual students. What expectations do you have for each of these types of students? How would you construct a course that would create a sense of inclusiveness among so diverse a population of students? Spend a few minutes listing the practices you might opt to use and some notes explaining why. Then share your list and ideas with a partner. Discuss the strengths and drawbacks of the ideas on your list. Finally, write a reflection on how an integrated writing course might change how you teach. How might practices change? How would the curriculum change?

4

Writing from Normal: Critical Thinking and Disability in the Composition Classroom

MARGARET PRICE

Just as habits of practice do, language use carries with it a culture's discourse and assumptions about "normal," with its power to center, marginalize, or "other" people, their ways of thinking, and their choices of actions in the world. Putting questions about "normalcy" at the very center of a disability-themed composition course she taught, entitled "Exploring Normalcy," Margaret Price studied the discourses students used as they read and wrote about disability issues—in particular, the way they positioned themselves in relation to disability in their pronouns (using "I" and "they," "us" and "them" as binaries, for example). Even when one student consciously wished to adopt a disability studies perspective, Price found that the student wrote from the central, unmarked position of "normal" because other discourses about disability from our culture seep into students' texts to complicate conscious positions. Price learns through her interview with the student that although he does not consciously hold ableist stereotypes, his discourse bears their traces. From another student who identified both as disabled and nondisabled, Price learned that her shifting pronouns could signal more than mere grammar error, but indeed could have been a survival strategy of shifting identification.

Price's close analysis of students' positioning in language offers teachers a useful model for responding to student writing when the topic may be personally and politically charged. Although Price points out students' pronoun shifts and asks her students questions related to their language and the way they position themselves as narrators, she does not directly challenge the ideology of their discourses, because she understands how dominant cultural norms make their way into texts and because she respects her students. "I didn't want to tell her, in effect, 'The way you think about your disability is flawed,'" Price writes. "This is an old problem for teachers, especially teachers who hope to offer their students new and perhaps transformative ways to view the world. . . . It seemed more respectful simply to try to understand where [the student] was coming from."

I never really thought about it before," said Tara[1] when I asked her how she identifies in relation to disability. Tara identifies as nondisabled, but not explicitly. She tends to leave her nondisabled status implicit, both in speech and in writing. In doing so, she exercises the privilege that most nondisabled people exercise—that of having an unmarked body and the attendant power to gaze "from nowhere" (Nagel). By contrast, another student, Kathleen, speaks from her experience of having a disability: "I think that, just because I've had a disability . . . I could relate to her [a disabled author] and write, like, understand how she felt and stuff." In fact, Kathleen seems to find it difficult, if not impossible, to write about disability without referring to her own experiences and identity: "I had to, like, put mine out first, like explain my whole disability and stuff like that even, in order to relate myself to her. So I realized, like, that was the only way that it would work out."

Both Tara and Kathleen were students in an Introduction to College Writing class I taught at the University of Massachusetts, Amherst (UMass). The class, themed "Exploring Normalcy," incorporated disability studies (DS) discourse and attempted to use it as a means to foster students' critical thinking. While teaching that semester, and for six months afterward, I conducted a case study of the class and its students in order to learn more about the processes through which students incorporate discourses of DS into their writing. When DS is presented as one possible lens through which to read and write, in what ways do students take it up—or not take it up? How does DS interact with other discourses that students bring to their writing? How might DS foster critical thinking (and how is "critical thinking" defined as part of such an endeavor)? When does resistance arise, and why?

These questions rest on my assumption that the writing classroom is not simply a place to improve writing "skills," but a place to think critically. When we write, we align ourselves with particular worldviews; we step into and out of subject positions; we signal our alliances and our enmities. This play of ideologies, language, and subject positions is far from abstract. It's actualized every moment in a material world, a world where bodies are prevented from moving off curbs, entering public buildings, caring for themselves, remaining safe. Learning to write with more self-awareness— becoming more able to identify, consider, and change the ideologies that are enacted in our writing—is a key goal of the critical writing classroom. In these classrooms, DS is becoming an important topic because it brings forward the interplay of writing, ideology, and material life in fundamental and vivid ways.

"EXPLORING NORMALCY": THE COURSE OF THE COURSE

I taught the "Exploring Normalcy" class as a graduate student instructor. Having taught composition, basic writing, and other writing classes for seven years, I felt confident in my ability to lead a writing class (if not in my ability to conduct a qualitative study of one). I identify as nondisabled and as queer, identities which I specified to the class in the course of our discussions.[2] I was accustomed to coming out as queer, but not to coming out as nondisabled, and I struggled to talk coherently about ways that my nondisabled identity impacts my life and my writing. Talking about my queer identity was comparatively easy. This paradox—trying to speak from a specific location and finding myself almost imprisoned by my own tendency to use the "view from nowhere"—came up in my students' work as well.

Although, for the purposes of this study, I was most interested in the ways that students engaged with DS discourse, I organized the course so that we theorized normalcy from a variety of identifications, including race, class, gender, and sexuality, as well as disability. Readings included Lennard Davis's "Constructing Normalcy" from his book *Enforcing Normalcy,* Malcolm Gladwell's "The Sports Taboo: Why Blacks Are Like Boys and Whites Are Like Girls," and Eli Clare's essay "The Mountain," from hir book *Exile and Pride: Disability, Queerness, and Liberation.*[3] We also viewed films including *Vital Signs: Crip Culture Talks Back* and *Tough Guise: Violence, Media, and the Crisis in Masculinity.* Students wrote six essays, including two "text-wrestling" (literary analysis) essays, a documented essay, and a reflective review at the end of the semester.

The critical pedagogy that I strive for in my writing classroom shares some features with Henry Giroux's "pedagogy of difference," which emphasizes attention to the operation of power as it intersects with knowledge in the classroom. Experience is an important part of such a pedagogy, but not experience as a romanticized or static entity. Rather, experience in a pedagogy of difference is understood to be constructed through discourses of power as well as through subjugated discourses. I wanted my students to examine their own positions, to think about the relations of power that gave rise to those positions, and to take action in their writing to challenge, and perhaps change, relations of power that they perceived as unequal. However, I was also acutely aware of the resistance that they would probably bring to our introductory composition class. Even if students are not feeling resistant to a required writing class in the first place, they often—in my experience—respond to critical pedagogies with resistance, since their notion of a writing class as a place to pick up quantifiable skills may seem to conflict with a class that asks them to examine social relations of power and their own roles in those relations.

I defined "critical thinking" in my syllabus as "the ability to extend your own thinking by getting a sense of other perspectives—what other people think, how you respond, and why. Critical thinking involves questioning your own views (although you may or may not change your mind on any given issue) and considering multiple perspectives." This wording, with its qualifiers and careful choice of terms such as "questioning" and "considering," was based on my assumption that students would exhibit at least some resistance to our course's theme and approach. However, to my surprise, students in the "Exploring Normalcy" class were markedly less resistant to a pedagogy of difference, and in particular to DS, than any class I had taught before. Just after responding to their essays on Eli Clare, I wrote in my teaching journal, "There was a stunning—compared to other semesters—sense of acceptance about Clare's ideas. . . . Some students disagreed with Clare . . . [but] the really offensive stuff that I usually brace myself for when reading a batch of essays on 'The Mountain' was dramatically not in evidence." I can't say for sure why this was. One possible reason was my newly revised syllabus, especially its emphasis on the deconstruction of "normalcy" before approaching the topic of disability. Resistance still emerged, as I will discuss later, but was less of a factor than I had anticipated. As a result, my dual focus on resistance and critical thinking shifted more exclusively toward critical thinking.

Another change occurred as the semester went on—a change in my own way of understanding critical thinking. I realized that "critical thinking" was not something I had to define in my syllabus and then try to make students enact throughout the semester. Rather, it was an activity that we would, inevitably, define together over time. I began to see that I could not effectively study critical thinking about disability—at least not in this classroom—without focusing on students' identities and subject positions as they related to disability. Again and again, students made comments that tied their own identities to the ways they read. For example, Tara wrote in an exercise, "I think my interpretation of the world is different from the way someone who is impaired interprets it because of the fact that I don't have an impairment." In my study of the class after the semester ended, I turned my attention to such questions of subject position and identity, feeling that these might be important keys to understanding how my students worked with discourses of DS in their writing.

METHODOLOGY

Few studies of writing classrooms that involve DS exist, and of those, most tend to be framed as descriptive narratives rather than as qualitative studies. The shape of my study, therefore, was exploratory; I experimented with methods, initially using a variety and then zeroing in on the ones that seemed most useful. The overall design was of a case study in three parts, which can be visualized as three concentric circles. The outer circle represents the "Exploring Normalcy" class overall; the middle circle represents the seven students who volunteered their writing for analysis and were invited to participate in two group interviews; and the inner circle represents the three students—Kathleen, Joe, and Tara—with whom I conducted individual interviews and the most intensive analysis.

Teacher research offers the teacher-researcher the benefit of being an "insider" to the study environment, but also the danger of "coercion or undue influence" (Kirsch, 41). I wanted my students to feel, as much as possible, that their participation in the study would be voluntary and would in no way impact our relationship as students and teacher. At the same time, I wanted students to be aware that I did plan to conduct a study, so they did not feel surprised or tricked at semester's end. With this in mind, I handed out a letter at the beginning of the semester explaining the study and its purposes. Aside from my teaching journal, the only data collected during the semester were students' "quickwrites," which I did not read until after semester's end.[4]

My overall plan for the study involved collecting data in five major categories. Two of these were collected during the semester: my teaching journal, which I wrote in after each class period and generally a few other times during the week; and students' quickwrites, which were completed at four points, more or less evenly spaced, throughout the semester. The other three data sources (group interviews, individual interviews, and student texts) were collected during the spring semester, after our "Exploring Normalcy" class had come to a close. Using Sharan Merriam's description of category construction (179–81), I read my teaching journal and students' quickwrites and developed a list of themes, drawing both from students' accounts of their critical thinking and from my own observations. One way of enacting critical thinking, for example, which was described by four students in their quickwrites, was to "think about what isn't there" or find a "deeper meaning"; another, described by eight students, was to position oneself in relation to an Other. With this list of themes in hand, I asked the volunteers to participate in an initial group interview. My aim in conducting the group interview was to learn more about students' perceptions of thinking critically about disability in a writing class, and to learn more about directions they felt it was important to go in on this topic. After the group interview, it was evident to me that subject position and identity in relation to disability remained crucial areas for exploration.

To carry out text analysis and individual interviews, I narrowed my focus still further. I selected three students — Kathleen, Joe, and Tara — out of the original seven and called them "focal students." My selection was guided by a desire to find a range in students' own identities and ways of approaching the discourse of DS, as described by the students themselves. Kathleen is white, from a working-class background, describes herself as "a small-town girl," and has a learning disability. Joe is black, from a working-class background, describes himself as "very focused," will be the first in his family to graduate from college, and is nondisabled. Tara is white, from a middle-class background, describes herself as "creative and motivated," and is nondisabled.

As I identified categories of critical thinking in my data and sorted all the data according to these categories, I found that two primary concepts emerged again and again: students' use of pronouns and students' use of what I came to call "key terms." Students' use of pronouns was an early indication that something interesting was going on in terms of subject position and disability. I first noticed it in an exercise that Kathleen wrote. In response to a question about the phenomenon of "supercrip,"[5] Kathleen expanded on the phenomenon in terms of her own experience, which includes having a learning disability, but also includes participation in ableist society. As she does so, she shifts between the subject positions disabled/supercrip and nondisabled/ableist. She writes, "We really truly have no control over the whole thing. We just react that way and it hurts them but we don't even realize it. It has happened to me and my disability was different but I still feel bad for them and give them sympathy when I know it hurts."[6] Reading this, I was struck by the way that the first-person pronouns shift from positioning Kathleen as the nondisabled viewer of a person with a disability ("We just react that way and it hurts them") to positioning her as a person with a disability who is being constructed as a supercrip ("It has happened to me"). The pronouns — "We" as nondisabled viewers, then "I" as disabled putative supercrip — indicate the shifting subject positions that Kathleen moves through on a daily basis.

Key terms, too, were something that emerged repeatedly as I analyzed different sources of data. I noticed that students' uses of certain terms, such as "overcome" or "suffer," seemed to indicate moments in their writing or speech that were heavily loaded with significance. These were moments in which students' adherence to one or more discourses on disability, such as a DS discourse or an individual/medical discourse, seemed to occur most clearly; they were also moments that tended to be highly charged in terms of students' own identities in relation to disability. For example, in his essay on Clare's "The Mountain," Joe seems to struggle to fit the terms "normal" and "same" into his writing about disability: "So what I am asking is that you treat a disabled person with the same respect and same normality, that you would treat someone who is not disabled, but keep in mind the differences that do exist, and take them into account, and react accordingly." In this passage, Joe seems to be trying to choose between two subject positions: one that believes in treating people with disabilities with the "same normality" as anyone else, and one that believes in treating them in ways that account for differences.

In order to develop a list of key terms to be identified in students' writing, I drew on the second chapter of Simi Linton's *Claiming Disability*, "Reassigning Meaning" (an excerpt of which is reprinted on p. 174 of this volume), which discusses the construction and operation of social/cultural beliefs about disability. Linton's goal is to identify "the linguistic conventions that structure the meanings assigned to disability and the patterns of response to disability that emanate from, or are attendant upon, those meanings" (8). I also drew on Clare's "The Mountain," a text about DS concepts as well as a personal narrative about living with cerebral palsy. This was the text on disability that our "Exploring Normalcy" class studied most closely. My rationale for using these texts was that their DS terms, such as "impairment" and "supercrip," were likely to be picked up by students as they worked to incorporate DS discourses into their own thinking and writing, or to challenge such discourses. The list of terms I selected follows: *afflict(ed), challenge(d), crip, disability or disabled, freak, gimp, handicap(ped), impaired or impairment, nondisabled, normal or norm, overcome, pity, special, suffer, supercrip, victim.* When I analyzed the transcripts of my individual interviews with Joe, Tara, and Kathleen, and their writing from our class, I coded those data sources using the list of key terms.

TARA: "I AM AN OUTSIDER LOOKING IN"

Tara positions herself consistently, from my first notes about her in my teaching journal to our final group interview, as a person who is nondisabled and who therefore came to our class with little knowledge of disability. In other words, she perceives a link between her own identification as nondisabled and her lack of knowledge about disability as a concept. In her individual interview, she said, "I never really thought about [disability] before [our class], because it's not like a part of my life at all." She also tends to assume that people with disabilities will understand DS automatically and will always adhere to a DS point of view. In her essay on Clare, for example, she writes that Clare has "inside knowledge" on the subject of disability because Clare has cerebral palsy. In her individual interview, she elaborated on this view when describing her process of writing an essay on Clare's "The Mountain": "If I had been disabled, then the whole piece would be totally different, because . . . [I was] thinking, like, 'Wow, I never thought of these things before.' . . . [But] if someone who had been disabled was writing it, they wouldn't have had a realization like that, because they would have already been familiar with what Clare was saying." According to Tara, having a disability gives one special knowledge about the discourse of DS, while being nondisabled means that encountering this discourse must entail a change in perspective, a "realization."

Because Tara worked from the assumption that she had no knowledge of disability, she at first felt at a loss about how to approach her analysis of Clare's "The Mountain." Eventually, acting in part on a suggestion from me, she decided to focus her essay on access. The idea that environments construct disability is a cornerstone of DS discourse and was the main idea that Tara "realized" while working on her text-wrestling essay. As she phrased it during her interview: "Society places these disabilities on people, and I think that was the main point of my essay." In the essay, she analyzed several environments she was familiar with (her classes, her dorm, and a T. J. Maxx store in Hadley, Massachusetts) as a means to showing how environments construct disability. Her intended audience, she said, was "an ableist society, an able person."[7] She used concrete examples, she explained, because she wanted to give her readers access to the new ideas about disability that she had discovered, and which she assumed they—as nondisabled readers—would also not know, and would want to realize. Tara's essay took access as both its *topic* and as its *main goal:* she wanted her nondisabled audience to gain access to the discourse of DS, as she had. Moreover, she found a way to make use of her nondisabled identification as a means to analyzing disability: she spoke in her essay (albeit implicitly) as a nondisabled person, one who had not directly experienced disability but who could nevertheless examine an environment from a DS point of view.

Tara's use of pronouns reflects her sense that disability involves a concrete divide between insiders and outsiders, "us" and "them." In her speech and her writing, "I" and "we" signal nondisabled people; "they" and "them" signal people with disabilities. Significantly, however, "I" in her writing is not an *explicitly* nondisabled person; it refers to Tara, who as narrator of the essay is not marked as disabled, nondisabled, or anything else. When I asked her why she left her own identification in relation to disability implicit, she seemed somewhat at a loss, saying, "I don't know. I, it just didn't, didn't really come up. . . . I think it was maybe . . . unintentional. You know, it just didn't come to my mind as something important to write in." This, of course, is the privilege of occupying an unmarked position such as nondisabled, white, straight, or male; one's position is assumed to be the case until stated otherwise. Tara's explanation of her writing process bears this out: "I wasn't thinking about myself when I was writing it. I was more thinking about my opinions and my perspectives." When writing her essay she used, although not consciously, the "view from nowhere." The body of the narrator in her essay is the body of the "normate," a putatively normal body "outlined by the array of deviant others whose marked bodies shore up [its] boundaries" (Garland-Thomson, *Extraordinary Bodies,* 8). With her nondisabled body thus shored up, Tara was able to leave it out of her essay and focus only on "my opinions."

Although Tara used a number of key terms in her speech and writing, I focus here on her use of the term "normal," which occupied most of our attention when we talked about her essay during our interview. In her process letter about the essay and later in the interview, Tara emphasized her desire to write from a DS point of view. However, analysis of her use of the term "normal" demonstrates that other discourses also infuse her writing. At one point in the essay, she writes, "Sie [Clare] couldn't act like a normal person in a grocery store because her shaky writing led the cashier to believe she wasn't capable of caring for herself."[8] Here, the term "normal" seems to assume that normalcy is both stable (i.e., not constructed by context) and nondisabled. In her individual interview, however, when shown this sentence along with two other variations, Tara rejected it and indicated a preference for a different phrasing. She explained her choice as follows: "Just because someone's shaking it doesn't mean they're not normal . . . where really the point was that even though she can function in an environment like a grocery store, it's the way others look at hir." In other words, Tara identified her original use of "normal" in this sentence (although she did not remember which one she had actually written in the essay) as an interdiscursive signal of ableist discourse.

Further elaborating her DS reading of this sentence, Tara added, "There's no one meaning for 'normal.' It's just how you think of it, what you're used to, what the situation is, what the context is." However, as she reflected aloud on the use of "normal" in that sentence, it became clear that Tara's use of "normal" tended to shift even as she spoke:

> So in my essay, I think "normal" would be a person who can function in society, who is nondis—actually, not even nondisabled, because "Clare couldn't be perceived as normal," like, she's in a grocery store, it's normal, whatever she was doing in the grocery store was normal, picking out food and going up to the cashier and checking out. Like, there's nothing not normal about that. So, in every example, "normal" could be treated as different. Like, in a grocery store, it's normal to go in and pick out the groceries. Like, it's not normal to steal the groceries [laughs].

As this comment makes clear, Tara's view of "normalcy" seems to align most closely with a DS discourse as articulated by Lennard Davis, Eli Clare, and others we read and viewed. But other ways of using "normal" sometimes pop up in her speech or writing, interdiscursive echoes that show how powerfully assumptions about normalcy enclose us and our thinking.

Tara seems to be aware that her ideas about what "normal" means—and hence, what discourse(s) she is adhering to when using it—are in flux. Her quick reversal ("nondis—actually, not even nondisabled") indicates this. "Normal" is a term that she began discussing early in class, and one that she continues to think about, and revise her perspective on, even after the class has ended.

JOE: "IT KIND OF HIT HOME"

Like Tara, Joe's self-identification in relation to disability is fairly stable. He identifies himself as nondisabled and tends to refer to people with disabilities as "them." However, Joe's approach differs from Tara's in that he had extensive experience with people with disabilities before starting our "Exploring Normalcy" class, and he tends to filter information about disability through this experience. In fact, it's somewhat misleading to say simply that he identifies himself as nondisabled, because the first time I asked him this question, during our interview, he didn't refer to himself at all:

> MARGARET: How do you identify in relation to disability?
>
> JOE: I have a cousin that's, has cerebral, cerebral palsy. So I kind of, it kind of, it kind of hit home. . . . Also I went to a school where there was a lot of disabled kids. Like, first and third grade. You know, so I had a classmate, I think, fourth and fifth grade, I had a classmate that was in a wheelchair, and another one that also had cerebral palsy. So I've been around it a lot.

In my overly focused researcher's quest to discover what I thought of as "the" answer to my question, I asked Joe again about his own identification, and he replied that he identifies as nondisabled. However, as our conversation went on, I began to realize that for Joe, it does not make sense to discuss disability without referring to his experiences with his cousin, his classmates, and his mother (who has sickle-cell anemia). His failure to include himself in his response to my question could be seen as a way of using the "view from nowhere." But seen another way, Joe is citing his experience precisely *in order to* identify himself. His identification is channeled through others' identities; the two seem too intertwined to separate meaningfully.

Although he would not have labeled it as such, Joe entered the "Exploring Normalcy" course with a perspective already strongly allied with DS discourse. His essay on Eli Clare, entitled "Same Respect Please, but Realize That There Are Some Differences," is framed as a combination argumentative and how-to essay. It argues that people with disabilities should be accommodated, rather than ostracized, and offers practical suggestions for how to provide accommodations. The essay's main point is to explain the rationale behind accommodation: treating people with disabilities "exactly the same" as nondisabled people, it argues, amounts to discrimination, because "circumstances" may be constructed in such a way that people with disabilities face unfair disadvantages. Instead, the essay maintains, people with disabilities should receive different treatment but "the same respect."

In his speech and writing, Joe consistently views people with disabilities as individuals. Unlike Tara, who describes people with disabilities as a fairly undifferentiated mass, Joe usually refers to them as specific people whom he knows. Perhaps as a result of this, his use of pronouns tends more toward the singular than the plural. Like Tara, he positions himself in the essay as "I," and uses third-person pronouns to position people with disabilities. In Joe's case, however, the third-person pronouns are mostly singular; that is, they refer to one particular person. Often this person is Clare, although there are also passages that refer to his cousin or other students in his school: "I've helped my cousin carry things, he has needed extra time to finish some tasks."

One paragraph in Joe's essay does make use of an abstract "they" to refer to people with disabilities. Here, Joe seems to be trying to explain to the reader how to treat people with disabilities, that is, to develop the idea that's expressed in his title:

> I can't say that if I hadn't had these life experiences, that I would not view disabled people differently than I do right now. I have somewhat of an understanding of their world and what they go through, from being around people with disabilities when I was young. Someone that does not have the experiences that I have had in my life, may not know what to expect, or how to treat disabled people. It's probably hard on them and they might not know where to start, but from my point of view you have got to look past the disability and treat them as you would treat anybody else, but keep in mind that disabled people, at times, do have different needs. There are times and circumstances that will require you to cater to their needs, even though you should treat them equally, you should still recognize that they are different than you are.

In this passage, the subject (that is, the person acting in some way toward people with disabilities) is first "I," and refers to Joe, with his specific experiences. Then, as the passage moves into more generalized advice about how to treat people with disabilities, the subject becomes "they," the person who "might not know where to start." Lastly, it's "you": "you have got to look past the disability." Briefly, "they" acts ambiguously, because it has two antecedents: it refers both to people in general ("they might not know where to start"), and to people with disabilities ("treat them as you would treat anybody else"). People with disabilities in this passage are consistently "they." Again, Joe's self-identification seems to be intertwined with his knowledge of specific people with disabilities. In this paragraph, when he leaves behind his specific focus on Clare, his cousin, and his classmates, his self-identification seems to destabilize.

Like Tara, Joe used a number of key terms in his speech and writing. I focus here on "pity," because his essay discusses Clare's critique of this term and uses that critique as a springboard into its central argument for accommodation:

> Sie also, when sie is complaining about how people don't allow hir the leeway to get certain things done, dismisses the notion that sie is asking for pity, by saying that sie is telling us about impairment and disability. I think this shows us one reason why hir sentiments say anything but, disabled people should be treated exactly the same as nondisabled people.

In this passage, Joe enlists Clare's argument against pity so that it supports his own argument about accommodation, although he does not explain exactly how this connection works. However, another term jumped out at me in this passage—not one that I'd identified as a key term, but one which is charged in DS discourse: "complaining." References to Clare in "Same Respect Please" include several such charged terms: in addition to "complaining," there's "obsesses" (used twice), "cry," and "cries out." I was struck by these word choices because, although Joe's essay makes use of DS discourse, that discourse seems to be braided with others—in this case, an ableist discourse, which assumes that a person with a disability who asks for accommodation must be either unreasonable ("complaining," "obsesses") or pitiful ("cries out").

In our interview, I asked Joe about his use of some of these charged terms. I was interested particularly in "cry," both because it appeared twice and because it seemed to contradict his essay's main point that accommodation does not have to do with pity, but rather with fairness of treatment. He responded, "'Cries out' to me says she's real, real passionate. Like, really crying out, like you can feel her, like if you're reading it you can hear her crying." I took from this response that his reading of "cry" was less negative than mine; for him, it could indicate passion rather than helplessness. Still, we are not always cognizant of the discourses that circulate in our writing. I believe that several discourses were at work simultaneously in Joe's writing: a DS discourse in his argument for accommodation, and a more mainstream discourse on disability as well, one which assumes that people with disabilities are more likely to "complain" about their circumstances, to "obsess" over them, or to "cry" when faced with unequal treatment.

The movement between discourses in Joe's and Tara's writing reminds me that critical thinking occurs dynamically and remains in process all the time, for teacher as well as students. As Amy Lee points out, "There is not an *end* at which one is successfully and finally anti-racist or liberated from misogyny or classism. Rather, new texts, new interactions, new contexts provide us with new challenges to our existing concepts" (151). As teachers making use of DS discourses, our job is not so much to ask whether students are "getting it," but instead to ask how they are, when they are, and why.

KATHLEEN: "YOU WANT SOMEONE TO HELP YOU, BUT YOU DON'T."

Kathleen was one of two students in the class of twenty-three who identified herself to me as having a disability. (The other student, Rebecca, initially volunteered to take part in interviews but later withdrew because of other time commitments.) She "came out" about halfway through the semester, after a class session during which we had had a long discussion of Clare's "The Mountain." She explained to me that day that she had a learning disability and added, "I've pretty much overcome it." I was surprised at her choice of words, since we had only minutes before been discussing the DS critique of the term "overcome." Kathleen's complex stance on overcoming would continue to be a theme in her writing and speech throughout the semester, and during the following semester as well.

Kathleen used her own experience of disability as a touchstone when analyzing Clare's essay. In fact, she indicated during our individual interview that it was only through her own experience that she could approach discussion of Clare: "I had to, like, put mine out first, like explain my whole disability and stuff like that even, in order to relate myself to her. So I realized, like, that was the only way that it would work out." However, Kathleen's identification as a person with a disability is dynamic (unlike Tara's and Joe's identifications, which remained stable). At times she said that she "had" a learning disability "when I was little"; at other times, she said that she "has" a learning disability. I asked her about these shifts during our interview. She explained that she was diagnosed with a disability in kindergarten, but the way her schools handled accommodations left her unsure about whether she still had the disability as she got older. She was told during high school that she could choose to stop being "pulled out" of classes for special education; however, she remained officially diagnosed throughout high school, and at UMass, registered for tutoring with the disability services office. Of her own sense of her disability, and how it affects her learning, she said in her interview, "I know it's still there."

Perhaps in part because of this dynamic identification, Kathleen's writing and speech take up a variety of subject positions around disability. Sometimes she identifies as a person with a disability, sometimes as a person who used to have one; sometimes she aligns herself with DS discourse, and sometimes distances herself from it. Although her writing and interviews are filled with rich examples of these phenomena, I focus here on two: first, her use of pronouns, and second, her use of the term "overcome."

It was Kathleen's use of pronouns that first alerted me to the multiple subject positions she occupies around disabilities. During the first group interview, conducted just after the class ended, Kathleen's use of pronouns in reference to herself and to others shifts:

> I kind of think from my point of view it's different, because I've grown up with a disability. I had a learning disability when I was little. . . . If you haven't had a disability you don't understand where you're coming from. Like, I kind of agree with her [Clare]. Like, you want people to feel bad for you, but you don't at the same time.

This was the first time during the group interview that Kathleen's speech exhibited this kind of pronoun shift (in this case, from "I" to "you"). It was also the same statement in which she "came out" to the group as having a disability, something that she had never mentioned during class. This was a high-stakes moment for her (while she spoke, she flushed red, and the room became very quiet), and it is worth noticing that the dynamism of her pronoun use emerged during it.[9] The key sentence in this passage seems to be the one that uses "you" for two different antecedents ("If you haven't had a disability . . ."), one of whom has a disability, and one of whom does not. A more logical way to arrange the pronouns here might have been to say, "You don't understand where *I'm* coming from." However, this would have required Kathleen to locate the person with a disability as "I" while simultaneously making the confrontational statement that a nondisabled person cannot understand where that other person "is coming from." Perhaps in an effort to bring her perspective closer to that of her listeners — that is, to use it as a persuasive strategy — she temporarily located the person with a disability as "you," then returned to "I" in the next sentence.

The midprocess draft of Kathleen's essay exhibits "I/you" shifts similar to the ones that appear in her speech during the group interview. If anything, in writing, the shifts are even more sudden, sometimes occurring within the same sentence:

> In my own experience in life when I see somebody with a disability, you feel bad for them. Even if you're not trying to your first reaction is to feel bad about the whole situation. Well in my life especially. I watched and had people do that for me. When you are sitting in your kindergarten class at age 5 and everyone around you can sing and spell out the alphabet. And you're the only one having a problem. You began to realize that life is going to be a lot harder. (2)

Here, Kathleen first positions herself as someone who is viewing a person with a disability. Although it is not stated, my assumption is that this viewer is nondisabled. Initially this viewer is "I" ("when I see somebody with a disability") and then "you" ("you feel bad for them"). She then shifts to identifying herself as someone with a disability — "I watched and had people do that for me." Again, this subject is first "I" ("I watched") and then "you" ("you are sitting in your kindergarten class"). These shifts seem to signal a sort of toggling between subject positions as nondisabled and disabled.

During the individual interview, I asked Kathleen to comment on these shifts. When we focused on the first part of the passage (from "when I see" to "the whole situation"), she said that she would prefer to use "you," because she was trying to make a more general point here, and wanted to position herself as a "normal" (i.e., nondisabled) speaker: "That [part] was just like normal . . . that was, like, normal, everyone feels that way." But for the second part (from "When I was sitting" to "a lot harder"), she said that she would prefer to use "I." She explained why she would make this choice:

> I definitely, now, for this one, I would choose "I." Because . . . I'm sitting in the class, and I remember just looking around, and all the kids, and everyone was doing so good, and I just remember the teacher calling my mom, and my mom kind of being, like, she'd be, "[Kathleen], yeah, she tries really hard." . . . I remember the teacher bought me a poster and it was, like, the alphabet. And it was hanging in my room for so long. It had, like, different animals on it. I'll never forget it. And it was just like, it was sitting there on my wall, and it just like—that was me. . . . I knew I was going to be different.

In this part of the passage, as Kathleen explains, the point is that she has had an experience that is unusual and "different." She draws upon the particulars of this experience in her essay to make a point about what it is like to approach the topic of disability from the perspective of a person with a disability.

My aim here is not to uncover Kathleen's "real" intention as a writer, but rather to emphasize that she is forced to shift between subject positions in order to get her ideas across. She is drawing on different kinds of authority when writing this essay. On the one hand, she is drawing on the authority of her experience as a person with a disability: "that was me." But on the other hand, she also draws on the authority that she sees accruing to a nondisabled speaker. Because she (like all of us) has assimilated ableist discourse (for example, to "feel bad" when encountering someone with a disability), she accurately identifies this subject position as the dominant point of view. Hence, this subject position also carries with it needed authority. Kathleen desires more than one subject position in order to give her writing as much "effect," as she put it, as possible.

Kathleen's essay incorporates DS discourse in various ways. However, it also incorporates a discourse that calls on an individualized model of disability. The way the term "overcoming" manifests in her writing demonstrates that her use of DS discourse can be neither simple nor easy.

Disability studies rejects the notion of "overcoming" in relation to disability, arguing that this locates disabilities in individuals who are then charged with "overcoming" their disabilities in order to avoid being treated as tragic less-than-humans. But for Kathleen, overcoming has a positive charge. Having assured me that she had "pretty much overcome" her disability when she first told me about it, Kathleen's use of a discourse that values individual achievement remained strong throughout the semester and the study. For example, her final portfolio was titled "I Made It!" And in her individual interview, when asked what "ideas or images" stuck with her from the materials we had read in class, Kathleen said that what stuck with her about "The Mountain" was that "I kind of like understood what she meant by, like, you had to keep getting up and trying again. . . . Like, she said that she didn't accomplish climbing the mountain, but she was going to." This description of Clare's essay surprised me, because not only did Clare not advocate an individualistic "keep trying again" approach to having a disability, sie argued that the mountain itself (a metaphor for overcoming) should be "collapsed in volcanic splendor" (Clare, *Exile*, 12).

Kathleen's (mis)reading of Clare's desire to overcome appears in her essays as well. In the midprocess draft, she summarizes Clare's stance toward Mount Adams as follows: "The fact that she was disabled and tried to do things on her own and didn't want help from anyone. That she was going to try really hard to make it up that mountain. Even if it was the hardest mountain to climb." This reading continues throughout the essay; in its closing lines, Kathleen reasserts the importance of individual achievement for herself, and again uses this assertion to ally herself with Clare: "The point is that we [Clare and I] want it and we have taught ourself that we won't stop until we get it."

As her teacher, I focused on the issue of "overcoming" in my comments to Kathleen. For example, I wrote in the margin of her midprocess draft, "But does this idea—of overcoming—make you and Clare 'supercrips'?" In part in response to my challenges (I assume), Kathleen focused more closely on the issue of pity and supercripdom in her final draft. However, in the last paragraph of that draft, she again returns to the concept of "overcoming," and again expresses its positive value for her:

> With me, I have a learning disability that I believe I have somewhat overcome on my own. I have fought a battle all my life to feel the normal. It kind of like Eli Clare says here I the story The Mountain "They focus on disabled people 'overcoming' our disabilities" (P. 72, Eli Clare). The feeling that we both get when we succeed is that we have overcome somewhat of our disability. When Eli Clare makes it up that mountain just a little more every time and completes the whole path of the entire mountain she has overcome her disability. When I got into my reach colleges, that everyone had warned me I could never get into, I had somewhat overcome my learning disability.

Kathleen seems to have recognized my negative valuation of overcoming, and hence she qualifies her own overcoming as having "somewhat overcome." However, she sticks firmly to this value as one that is important to her. Moreover, she reads Clare in such a way that overcoming becomes positive for hir as well.

As Kathleen's teacher, I felt reluctant to challenge her too closely on the question of overcoming. This feeling persisted during the next semester, as we became closer through interviews, e-mails, and occasional chats at Learning Disabilities Support Services (where Kathleen received tutoring, and where I worked as a tutor, although not hers). Teaching students with disabilities has shown me that there are many different ways to conceptualize disabilities, and—perhaps more to the point—there are many different ways to survive in an ableist world. I read Kathleen's valuation of her own ability to "overcome" as a survival strategy, a way to think about herself and her disability positively. While my knowledge of DS also pointed out the problems with this strategy, I did not want to tell her, in effect, "The way you think about your disability is flawed." This is an old problem for teachers, especially teachers who hope to offer their students new and perhaps transformative ways to view the world. As Anne Herrington and Marcia Curtis argue, in some cases it may be a more respectful choice to "validate" a student's thinking by "listen[ing] *with* him" rather than challenging him (129). Challenging a student's thinking can also be a gesture of respect, but as my work with Kathleen reminded me, sometimes it seemed more respectful simply to try to understand where she was coming from.

Moving from mainstream discourses of disability to DS discourse requires a radical shift of mind, and it is unsurprising that Kathleen finds it difficult to adopt this discourse fully into her writing. The stakes for her are higher than they are for Tara, who adopted DS discourse fairly seamlessly. For Tara, who writes from the privileged position of a nondisabled person, taking up DS discourse impacts her thinking and writing only insofar as she wishes to let it. As she said during her individual interview, "[Disability is] not like a part of my life at all." For Kathleen, on the other hand, taking up a new discourse around disability may also mean recognizing the material effects that it will have in her life. What would it mean for Kathleen to assume that her disability is not her own individual problem, her own issue to "overcome," but instead something that is unjustly created on a daily basis by people she likes and trusts—such as me, her writing teacher? This is a tremendous mental shift, and one with serious consequences in Kathleen's immediate life. "I have fought a battle all my life to feel the normal," she writes in her essay. DS discourse challenges, or at least complicates, the value of that statement. No wonder, then, that her writing exhibits inconsistent use of DS discourse. The stakes are extremely high.

THE STAKES OF A NEW DISCOURSE

It is important to note that the stakes for Tara, Joe, or any other nondisabled student *should* be as high as they are for Kathleen. DS discourse is not a "special" (to borrow a key term) discourse that impacts only people with disabilities. Indeed, one of its main points is that everyone "works the hyphen" (Fine) between disability and nondisability. Which side of that binary we fall on is constructed by many factors, including medical, academic, and legal discourses. All of us *in theory* face the same dilemmas that Kathleen faces. However, if we are identified as "nondisabled," then we can draw on the privilege of being "normal" and can choose to ignore the dilemmas that Kathleen cannot avoid. This is the key difference I had in mind when I titled this article "Writing from Normal." In some cases, as in Tara's, a student must approach the topic of disability from normalcy, that is, write from a subject position that has always been viewed as normal. In other cases, however, like Kathleen's, a student must write her way away from normalcy, using her own nonnormative subject position as a springboard into analysis of disability. Different subject positions, different identities, do not determine how students approach the topic of disability or their facility with DS discourse. However, the major finding I made during the course of my study is that *students' own subject positions and identities cannot be avoided when teaching DS in the writing classroom—nor can my own.* The only way to take up DS in a writing classroom and *not* focus on identities and subject positions would be to ask every student to employ a "view from nowhere"—and hence to assume that we are all, in the most static and damaging sense of the term, normal. Those of us who are nondisabled must begin to see that our stakes in DS discourse are as high as the stakes held by people with disabilities. Although some of us write "from normal" in the sense that our sociopolitical positions mark us as "normal," we must also write "from normal" in the sense of "away from normal"—challenging ableist discourses, and insisting on access to the topic of disability.

NOTES

1. Some names used here are pseudonyms and some are not; I followed students' preferences as expressed on their consent forms.

2. Deborah Marks argues that teaching DS from a nondisabled position raises "the spectre of colonization of the 'Other' . . . [and] the course risks slipping into an examination of 'Others'" (70). Moreover, in terms of research, studying students, students with disabilities, and the topic of disability in general all carry the risk that a nondisabled researcher will contribute to unequal distributions of power by "studying down" (Fine). On the other hand, I believe that nondisabled people can make valuable contributions to disability studies, just as I believe that straight people can make valuable contributions to queer studies. In my work as a teacher and researcher, I try, in Owen Wrigley's phrase, "to recognize both the biases of my position and the privileges of my gaze" (vii). Ironically, in the years following the semester during which I taught the "Exploring Normalcy" class, my identity shifted from nondisabled to disabled, as the result of both physical and psychological disabilities. Although I was surprised, I should not have been: numerous DS scholars have pointed out the tendency of disability to de- and rematerialize in our bodies and lives. Brenda Brueggemann et al. put it this way: "We are sitting next to you. No, we *are* you" (371).

3. Eli Clare identifies as genderqueer. "Sie" and "hir" (rather than "he/she" or "his/her") are gender-neutral pronouns. Other such pronouns sometimes used are "ze" and "zir."

4. In designing my study I relied on both the CCC's "Guidelines for the Ethical Treatment of Students and Student Writing in Composition Studies" and Gesa Kirsch's *Ethical Dilemmas in Feminist Research.* I applied for and received permission to conduct the study from UMass's Institutional Review Board, the Human Subjects Review Committee. I gave the first consent form to students near the end of the semester. Seven students indicated an interest in participating in the interviews that would take place during the spring semester, and after the winter break all elected to sign the more formal consent form.

5. A supercrip is a person with a disability who is believed to have "overcome" that disability by performing ordinary tasks (for example, a girl with Down syndrome who has a boyfriend) or extraordinary tasks (for example, a man with one arm who becomes a major-league pitcher). See Clare, *Exile* (1–13) and Shapiro (16) for fuller discussion of "supercrip."

6. In all students' quoted writings, spelling errors have been corrected; but grammar, syntax, and punctuation remain as written.

7. In this statement, Tara continues to conflate being "able" with being ableist, even though her essay in fact showed that a nondisabled person can also write from an antiableist point of view.

8. The pronouns here, which begin with the gender-neutral "sie" but then switch to "she"/"her," indicate the interaction of two other discourses in Tara's writing: one that I call a queer discourse, which makes use of gender-neutral pronouns, and a mainstream discourse, which insists upon pronouns that uphold a binary concept of sex and gender. This kind of switching is common among those who have just begun to use gender-neutral pronouns.

9. Reflecting on this moment during her individual interview, Kathleen used it as an example of the reason that she, as a person with a disability, has a different perspective on disability

than the other students participating in the interview: "Like, that whole roomful of people didn't know until I said that, when we were in the meeting that night, that I had a disability. And that's why I felt different ways [from them]. Like, I mean, I probably had a different opinion on probably everything that was said that night than anyone else." In this remark, Kathleen also acknowledges that, because her disability is not visible, her public manifestation as a person with a disability is usually something that she must effect by announcing it verbally.

REFLECTING ON YOUR TEACHING

Responding to Student Writing

Price's study suggests that constructions of and responses to disability are implicitly present in student discourses as well as in our pedagogies, even when disability is not specifically being taught. Including disability topics explicitly in writing courses can give students opportunities to think critically about such constructs. We need, though, to give some thought to how we ask students to write about disability issues. Price's advice is that writing teachers ask students to attend closely to attitudes about disability embedded in language and to the real-life effects of their own and others' language use. Price reminds us to attend to language use and pronoun positioning, ask questions, and listen; in short, to respect students rather than debating ideology with them or "correcting" what seems to us an "unenlightened" point of view.

The following is a teacher-training exercise in responding to student writing, one that requires student papers written on controversial topics. Gather some examples of student writing and make copies for each person in the teacher-training workshop. Ask instructors in the workshop to read and respond to one of the papers by attending to the way the writer positions him- or herself (and others) in relation to the topic through pronoun use, specific or peculiar language choices, and embedded and explicit figurative language. Next, in small groups, exchange ideas about patterns of language use seen in the paper and discuss how the writer's language use affects the paper's argument, not just its surface features. Also share ideas about how you might cast suggestions for revision so as to engage the student in rethinking the substance of the draft through an attention to language. Next, have everyone practice writing formative end comments on this paper, toward the goal of getting the student to make substantive revisions. To complete this exercise in ways of responding to student writing, volunteers read their end comments aloud to initiate whole-class discussion of the following issues: Is focusing on the student's pronouns and language use helpful in constructing a teacher response? Do you feel this narrow focus skirts the serious issues a teacher should address in end comments? Did this focus help you to address the substantive problems in the draft?

5 Add Disability and Stir: The New Ingredient in Composition Textbooks

DEB MARTIN

Deb Martin asks what role writing textbooks play in maintaining or challenging a culture's views and discourses about disability. In the process, she examines seven composition textbooks, analyzing their treatment of disability, their structure (where and how disability is included) and "the relationship between the language, the text producers, and consumers"—all of which contribute to the social construction of disability. Most textbooks, Martin found, exclude disability or do not advertise its presence. When disability is included, it is often simply an "add-on," presented in a "simplified, essentialized, and/or dichotomized" way "as a pro/con debate" or "just another unexamined kind of difference in a long line of difference." Martin argues that the way most textbooks include disability limits critical thinking. She noticed "an overall tendency to promote an 'us/them' divide," and a "talk-show approach" that asks students to take sides in a simple binary debate that "distorts the reality of cultural dynamics by ignoring the role of power in conflict." These textbooks also teach detachment: They do not invite students to write about personal passions or experiences in relation to disability. They treat students as democratic citizen-managers of social problems "out there" (e.g., What should "we" do about a policy?) but do not ask students to consider their own roles in constructing disability nor as possible recipients of such policies. Textbooks typically narrate from an ableist voice and present disability as a problem that can be solved through writing.

In this chapter I explore dis-ability[1] at the intersection of language and writing. The site of investigation, the college composition textbook, is one place where the topic of dis-ability is increasingly being introduced. I focus here on how dis-ability is being integrated and to what effect. As teachers and scholars in composition and rhetoric continue to redefine our discipline, we cannot afford to neglect the dynamic role textbooks play in maintaining, challenging, and transforming culture, the discipline, and the tradition of teaching writing (Olson, Foreword, 4). Textbooks are key sites of influence for teachers as they select and organize course content and design writing assignments. For students, textbooks represent authority. Students come to depend on textbooks to help them navigate the meaning of new and difficult concepts. By looking at the kinds of discourse generated about dis-ability and the relationship between the language, the text producers, and consumers, I explore the ways in which language signifies the construction of dis-ability.

I believe that language both allows and constrains expression. All writers code invisible assumptions in their use of language. The very mechanisms in place designed to elicit good writing—for example, genre rules, grammar, and other prescribed writing conventions—can, ironically, work to subvert it. By raising the collective understanding of such devices at work in our language and in the dominant pedagogy, we are better able to understand how such structures inscribe attitudes and influence behavior. I want to invite others in the profession to consider with me both the possibilities and pitfalls of adding dis-ability into the mix of strategies for teaching writing and how doing so inevitably influences the way students create understanding of what it means to be dis-abled.

First, I address the conspicuous absence of dis-ability in composition texts generally, and I attempt to explain why that might be. Following that discussion I consider the implications of including dis-ability when it is packaged, as it often is, as an add-on to the existing structures and approaches of writing texts—be they the standard argument or the burgeoning cultural studies forms. I investigate how these approaches often disguise the structures framing the prevailing view of dis-ability and writing. And I include suggestions for how, as writing instructors and textbook authors, we can blend dis-ability content into our writing courses in a manner that fosters a more sophisticated understanding of language as social action and help student writers realize their responsibility as creators of discourse. From my initial investigation of over twenty-five textbooks,[2] I use seven representative texts to present the key points just listed, and to illustrate my findings.

EXCLUDING DIS-ABILITY

There is a profound absence of dis-ability as a subject through which to teach writing. That is to say, far more textbooks exclude than include dis-ability. While the meanings of silence are complicated and often misinterpreted, Brenda Jo Brueggemann offers one reading regarding silence and dis-ability; "Just as sex was the ubiquitous unspoken subject in the Victorian world, disability—the harbinger of morality—is the ubiquitous unspoken topic in contemporary culture" (Brueggemann et al., 2). It is there. We know it but do not talk about it. Simi Linton makes similar claims in her study of the academy: "The perspective of disabled people and the field of disability studies are conspicuously absent across a broad range of endeavors, but most notably from those in the higher education curriculum" (89).

Considering the pervasive nature of dis-ability in our daily lives and in our literature, how can entire books whose stated purposes are to investigate cultural boundaries avoid a discussion of dis-ability as difference? This absence of dis-ability is conspicuous when it would seem consistent or well within the parameters of the topic to include it.

The answers to the question lie, at least in part, in the explanation of logonomic systems. As in Kenneth Burke's theory of dramatism and paralleled in social semiotics, logonomic systems act to constrain social behavior through rules prescribing semiotic production, that is, who is able/forbidden to produce or receive what meaning under what circumstances and in what codes. Logonomic systems at any specific time are social facts or what passes as reality. In order to function they must rely on known categories and enforced rules. Dis-ability as a major topic of discussion seems to be generally off limits (not considered polite conversation) in some textbooks, yet, as an ever-present part of what it means to be human, it stands as a contradictory version of reality. While some books have chapters on ethnicity, religion, and other fields of multicultural study, thus making them a major topic of discussion, dis-ability has yet to be recognized as a field of study and a point of view in most composition textbooks. Despite the increasing number of students with disabilities in our classrooms, dis-ability, for the most part, remains invisible, albeit present.

This dichotomy can be illustrated in the marketing of Andrea Lunsford's *St. Martin's Handbook* (5th edition). For the first time in any writing handbook, this text includes almost twenty notes and sidebars addressing dis-ability concerns in composition. Specifically, sidebars and boxes "point writers with disabilities to resources and strategies" and "help make work accessible to readers with disabilities" (v). On a larger scale, these considerations represent an important shift in awareness of inclusion, access, and privilege in producing and consuming texts, yet no mention is made of this innovation in its advertising.

To appreciate how truly innovative this feature is, a more comprehensive description is necessary. While a good number of the nineteen sidebars devote attention to accessibility issues on the Web, most address the entire student audience, not exclusively students with dis-abilities. Certain boxes give alternative strategies for writing, such as speaking into a voice recorder rather than drafting by hand. One box suggests that comparing different perspectives on note taking within a cooperative learning group is beneficial for all students. "Know Your Readers" is similarly aimed at all writers; it states that "living with a disability is more the norm than many previously thought" (519) and that considering all members of your audience is an important rhetorical move. Concerns with handwriting, spelling, and color contrasts in Web designs are approached more as a matter of learning differences and communication issues rather than disabilities to overcome. The effect of these kinds of concerns trains attention on the material choices students make and their rhetorical implications. This move is in concert with chapter 25, "Considering Others: Building Common Ground," where paying attention to difference in general is addressed.

I examined promotional material by Bedford/St. Martin's on their Web site, as well as a two-page print advertisement the publisher placed in the

February 2003 issue of *College Composition and Communication* (between pages 412 and 413). Interestingly, there is no mention anywhere of this innovation concerning writing pedagogy. In a link off the Bedford/St. Martin's main page titled "New to This Edition," the publishers inform potential buyers of the changes and updates to the fifth edition, yet omit any reference to the inclusion of dis-ability related materials. While Bedford/St. Martin's demonstrates the need to include such material within the text, addressing specific writing concerns of students with disabilities in marginal notations does not seem to merit advertising; that is, it is not a selling point. The publishers made choices. Including the noticeable brown boxes throughout the text speaks of one reality: the multitude of reasons for addressing dis-ability concerns in writing. The absence of this feature in advertising speaks of another reality: dis-ability's tacit invisibility for those who use textbooks. In logonomic terms, there is no proper mechanism in place in public discourse for dis-ability to be discussed. Shared values and assumptions about the importance of these differences and their implications to writing do not yet exist for the majority of those who would buy or use a textbook, although publishers—and their authors—are making some attempts to address these differences. Indeed, the fact that you are reading this very essay, which looks at how textbooks need to change in order to address and make use of dis-ability in composition, means that things are changing.

THE PACKAGING OF DIS-ABILITY

The few but growing number of textbooks that are addressing dis-ability — such as *Between Worlds: A Reader, Rhetoric, and Handbook* (3rd edition) by Susan Bachmann and Melinda Barth; *Rhetorical Context* by Suzanne Strobeck Webb and Lou Ann Thompson; *Cultural Conversations: The Presence of the Past* by Stephen Dilks, Regina Hansen, and Matthew Parfitt; *In Context: Participating in Cultural Conversations*, by Ann Merle Feldman, Nancy Downs, and Ellen McManus; and *Uncommon Threads*, written by Robert D. Newman, Jean Bohner, and Melissa Carol Johnson—are breaking the taboo that mandated silence on the subject. Dis-ability is gaining acceptance as an included category of difference and as a topic of discussion. If *The St. Martin's Handbook* is any indication, featuring dis-ability for various purposes will continue as a trend in composition texts, one that parallels the growing interest in dis-ability worldwide. In the mid-1990s, the field was hard-pressed to offer seven composition textbooks where authors or editors directly and openly discussed dis-ability issues in first-year texts. Today that number has grown exponentially. But simply adding dis-ability and stirring it into the predominating mix creates unintended consequences.

I believe that authors who do incorporate dis-ability topics do so with the best intentions. Although its presence seems to be increasing, more often than not, dis-ability, as portrayed in composition texts, is simplified, essentialized, and/or dichotomized. Several reasons explored here combine to ensure critical thinking about dis-ability is kept at a minimum. Factors include the following: (1) the manner in which dis-ability is presented—often as a pro/con debate or as just another unexamined kind of difference in a long line of difference, that is, the pluralist approach; (2) the constricting formats used in presenting dis-ability concepts; and (3) an overall tendency to promote an "us/them" divide.

Packaging Dis-Ability as Debate

Gary Colombo, Robert Cullen, and Bonnie Lisle identify two major approaches that multicultural readers (books focused on diversity and difference issues) employ: either they adopt a pluralist approach and conceive of American society as a kind of salad bowl of culture, or they take what might be called the talk-show approach and present American culture as a series of pro-and-con debates (vii). The talk-show approach, in general, creates problems for student writers. It distorts the reality of cultural dynamics by ignoring the role of power in conflict. Real-world arguments are rarely a matter of rational and reasonable disputes. Differences, in real life, are rarely negotiated on equal terms. Debate, in the traditional sense of the word, does not work when addressing cultural issues, because it implies two equal and reasoned sides. Dis-ability, like many other cultural issues presented in composition texts, pertains to the struggles between the dominant culture and those seeking legitimacy. The limitations of such an approach will be illustrated with examples from *In Context,* but I would like to emphasize that the "dis-ability as debate" approach is by no means limited to this particular text.

As well as being a popular composition text, *In Context* has a large unit (forty-eight pages) devoted to dis-ability issues. "Deliberating about Disability" is a section within a larger unit called "Participating in Civic Conversations." Included in the dis-ability subsection are essays, mostly in the academic genre, written by dis-ability scholars Paul Longmore, Simi Linton, Michael Berube, and Rosemarie Garland-Thomson, as well as a letter to the editor written by former press secretary James Brady, who was disabled by a stray bullet during an assassination attempt on then-president Ronald Reagan. The readings include excerpts from the Senate debate on the Americans with Dis-abilities Act (ADA) and excerpts from the actual document. The section ends with an essay by Rosemarie Garland-Thomson on the FDR Memorial that segues into the case study for the chapter, "Negotiating Art for Public Space" (440).

"Deliberating about Disability" opens with an image of the front cover of *The Disability Rag & Resource* (now *The Ragged Edge*), an activist publication. The September/October 1995 issue of that publication featured a reproduction of a work of art by Robert Styles, an abstract oil painting on canvas titled "Quickie" (391). Within the rhetorical rubric—or as it is often called, the editorial apparatus—duplicated in every chapter, the textbook authors inquire about the image in terms of "Context," "Genre," "Language," and "Consequences," changing the order of the discussion to best address the material. In addition to being the brand name of a kind of wheelchair, the word "quickie" has a sexual connotation, a reference to a lively, brief sexual interlude. Curiously, no mention of sexuality is made here in the discussion of the painting. Under "Language" the authors instead focus on the technique of painting with a wheelchair and miss the opportunity to explore how the words and images play with multiple meanings.

On the following page begins an introductory discussion about disability framed as a two-sided debate: "special interest groups" versus the public (393). Here students learn about the dispute between Christopher Reeve, most familiar to them as the actor who played Superman, and the disability movement (probably not very familiar at all). The authors supply background information about "people with disabilities" (392)[3] and how "they claimed the right to become full members of society" (392), how "their efforts sparked discussion in the media," and how "they continue trying to realize the full economic and political power promised by the ADA" (393).

The framework for considering the readings similarly enforces the presentation of dis-ability as a two-sided debate. The authors of the first four essays are primarily people with disabilities writing about people with disabilities for an audience of people who care about dis-ability issues. The title of the unit, "Deliberating about Disability" (391), first signals the "us" versus "them" approach to the issues presented. "Deliberation" connotes courtroom images of judges and juries deciding between guilt and innocence, right and wrong, truth and lies. Framing dis-ability as a one-dimensional issue within the confines of a two-sided debate, as these authors/editors do, works to perpetuate stereotypes and encourages one-dimensional thinking.

Such an approach is rendered more problematic because no mention is made of the political pressures surrounding the outcome of the ADA debate. First, we have to consider that elected officials are servants of their constituents and do not always vote solely on the merits of an argument. Political debates (even the ADA) are decided against a backdrop of deals and concessions. To pretend that the ADA passed into law strictly on its own merits is to ignore the most vital context of all: influence in politics. For example, in the current political climate businesses are coercing rollbacks of some of the ADA provisions they find too costly. Textbooks (and often teachers) imply that the best-constructed arguments "win," but the reality is far more complicated. Texts distort the reality of conversational dynamics by presenting conflict as a winnable debate.

As the remainder of the chapter consistently positions dis-ablity as a debate, it becomes apparent that the discussion of Christopher Reeve is intended to complicate the otherwise two-sided argument. Because Reeve was widely known as a former superman paralyzed from a steeplechase accident, he is a sympathetic anomaly, a doppelganger or troubling double, our worst nightmare. His wealth and status as a Hollywood movie star gave him direct access to the "public" conversation on dis-ability. Students learn from the introduction that dis-ability rights activists did not like him, however, because he often framed dis-ability as a medical or technological issue. His ambiguous status is explained in part as perpetuating the damaging cultural myth of the "crippled hero." This book's willingness to complicate public debate about dis-ability is encouraging in that it provides fertile ground for critical thinking.

Packaging Dis-Ability as One More Way to Be Different

The problem with the salad bowl's celebration of diversity, as Colombo, Cullen, and Lisle suggest, is that it ignores the issue of cultural dynamics, the push and pull resulting from forces of power operating in an environment of limited resources. It also ignores the tensions that result from the expectations established by our dominant cultural myths and the diverse realities that these myths often contradict (viii). How, for example, can we reconcile the myth of equality and fairness within a capitalist system, in which the "best" decision is often one based on immediate gain and financial expediency? If, as Brenda Jo Brueggemann, Linda Ward, and others have suggested, teaching dis-ability potentially means calling attention to inconsistencies, rather than glossing over them, then textbook authors have to start addressing these contradictions wherever they are and making social context and the complexity that constitutes social realities a larger concern in writing about social issues. Instead of asking, for example, "What self-image issues might physically challenged and able-bodied persons have in common?" (Ackley, 154), we should be challenging students to consider specifically the ways dis-ability might complicate the already complicated subject of self-perception.

In Bonnie Smith-Yackel's *My Mother Never Worked*, an essay featured in Laurie Kirszner and Stephen Mandell's *Patterns for College Writing*, disability is not just one more way to be different; for Smith-Yackel, dis-ability is part and parcel of the already existing fabric of the protagonist's life as a woman working at home on the family farm. Her mother's position as a disabled person who works hard (a cultural contradiction) is used by the textbook authors in the table of contents to entice the reader: "From her wheelchair she canned pickles, baked bread, ironed clothes . . ." (xvi). But her status as a person with a dis-ability is never interrogated in the discussion questions. While the protagonist shatters the cultural myth of the sick or dependent person in a wheelchair, the textbook authors, focusing only on the death benefits denied Smith-Yackel's mother as a woman who worked in the home, missed the opportunity to connect that aspect to larger work issues. Why is it, they might have queried, that 79 percent of people with disabilities are unemployed in America? (U.S. Department of Labor). The answer is complicated, to be sure, and involves exploration into prevalent attitudes, cultural myths, environmental access, and discrimination. By isolating and defining problems on a small scale, we miss the bigger picture.

In this example and elsewhere, the salad bowl approach toward difference and diversity proves overly simplistic and misleadingly optimistic. The overriding "solution" implied in such an argument model is this: If we can only learn how to get along and live side by side, we would be so much better off. Applied to issues in dis-ability, however, the message appears to be a call for assimilation: If you, the disabled, act normally, people will think you are normal and we will all be better off. Students writing on such issues under the weight of this theoretical approach have two alternatives. They can argue for segregationist policies or argue for a better appreciation of and tolerance toward difference. However, authors who frame arguments in terms of what *we* can do with *the disabled* force a third conclusion—urging assimilation. The expectation of assimilation, either through the wonders of medical miracles or by tacitly suggesting people with disabilities "pass," works contrary to the intent of including diversity issues in textbooks in the first place.

When applied to dis-ability issues, the salad bowl view of diversity poses a further complication. *In Context*'s editorial comments lead readers to believe it is taking the salad bowl approach to diversity. For example, in the opening editorial for the unit, the authors state, "The issue of disability, even more than the issue of race, pushes us to consider what it means to live in an inclusively diverse society" (393). Yet the final writing prompt asks students to write a one-sided opinion piece like the kind we see in newspapers, one where writers "take a stand" (433). Dis-ability—and, I suspect, most other complex issues—does not fit into the "two sides to every argument" template and cannot easily be "solved" simply by writing about it.

In either approach, those students who represent the transparent culture of the dominant ideology find it impossible to situate themselves honestly within the conversation. Often, students are either asked to mediate debates between two disparate groups or directed to find a solution through writing. This places culturally privileged writers in the position of rewarding those seeking authenticity. Marginalized students are placed in the position of either requesting resources or ignoring their subjectivity and writing from an alien or inauthentic position.

Form Follows Function

Writing assignments are similarly designed to support the institutional version of truth in various ways. First, authors limit student writing to very specific and traditional genres. Students in *In Context* are asked to write in the following vein: an essay comparing two expert views (401), a research paper chronicling the changes in the way Down syndrome has been portrayed (424), a report on the disability studies program on campus (401). Finding truth about dis-ability for these writing acts requires students to revisit institutionally sanctioned versions of dis-ability, in the form of encyclopedias, medical texts, program administrators, and legislative-debate transcripts. Class members' opinions are omitted so that the "argument" can be claimed to have the structure and substance constructed independently of an individual's interest and experience in it. By controlling the ways students will research and write about dis-ability issues, the end result is a seemingly objective and sanitized view of dis-ability that also works to severely stifle students' opportunity to ask questions and form opinions of their own.

Hodge and Kress further explain how genre limits expression. As socially ascribed classifications of semiotic form, "genre-rules are exemplary instances of logonomic systems, and are a major vehicle for their operation and transmission (7). Excessive concentration on any normative system, whether it be a genre, an ideology, or a logonomic system, contains an inbuilt distortion and serves to reinforce the ideas of their dominance. These systems constrain thought and behavior insofar as they have been effectively imposed and not challenged (7). Those of us with public-school backgrounds or those who have had experience teaching first-year composition may know how the five-paragraph essay has dominated and constrained high school students' writing. Developing more flexible thinkers and writers means incorporating a variety of genres into the reading materials and teaching students to write and think in a variety of genres. Just as writing-across-the-curriculum efforts are enriched by reflection logs and the use of poetry in science and math courses as a way to approach difficult concepts from another angle, an interesting application of this principle to composition would be to investigate the ways genres alter the representation of dis-ability issues.

A second way assignments support the institutional version of reality is largely an issue of power. Students are often asked to engage, from a position of power, in conversations about dis-ability with educators and politicians. For example, in one writing prompt, students are asked to "imagine that you are a program director" (Feldman, Downs, and McManus, 401), an overt indication that students are writing from positions of advantage. Although these prompts are meant to give students a voice and a more powerful stake in the issue—rather than responding as bystanders—the danger is that these textbooks can relate to the dominant ideology and speak to mainstream culture while suppressing marginalized voices.

Asking students to write from fictional (nonauthentic) positions and limiting their truth seeking to institutional sources ignores the value of authenticity in the composing process. Kenneth Burke notes the importance of the writer's terministic screen in communicating. Terministic screens shape the direction and set limits on the observations a writer can make through the terms the writer uses (49). Oil producers and environmentalists view the Alaskan National Wildlife Area, for example, through significantly different lenses and use distinctly different terms to communicate about the same space. It is in this way that terms used in language fundamentally affect the nature of our communication (46–50). Terms, then, affect our actions and motives and, in a very concrete way, how we view the world. Bringing the concept of terministic screens back to dis-ability, students who are disabled or who have had close associations with dis-ability will perceive and write differently about it and, in my experience, are quicker to challenge textbook representations.

In these ways, textbooks teach detachment by asking students to consider language and writing about issues as if they had no personal interest in how they engage them. These textbooks, for the most part, do not ask students to relate their own knowledge, experience, hopes, and interests to the problem of writing about issues. They do not take into consideration or allow for the writer's own terministic screen. By excluding the writer's subjective self, the authors of these texts tacitly assume that students come to college as blank slates or always already rooted in the powerful, dominant center. From a disability perspective, this approach to writing teaches students that dis-ability is something that is happening "out there" to people not like themselves. Further, as seen in the examples in *In Context*, the authors imply that it is the students' responsibility as maturing adults living in a democratic system to decide what is to be done with "them." Conversely, students are seldom asked to examine their own role in the social construction of dis-ability. This kind of missed opportunity for critical self-reflection can also be extended to a consideration of the way other marginalized groups are addressed in composition pedagogy.

A more subtle way textbooks reinforce the institutional version of dis-ability through prescribed form is via the textbook narrator. Considering that difference is always marked, especially in multicultural texts, the authoritarian editorial voice rarely is. Considering that it is the textbook author/editor who is selecting the material, posing the questions about the material, and determining how students will write about the issues, perhaps the subjective editorial stance should be made known to the readers. No matter what that status is, readers, following cultural linguistic codes, interpret that the authors are situated in the dominant, that is, able-bodied, position.

There are occasions, however, when the authors unintentionally make their assumptions apparent. After Nancy Mairs's essay "On Being a Cripple," the authors of *Uncommon Threads* make explicit their position in "Writing Assignments," which asks readers to "create an image text showing how *we* might revise *our* attitudes toward the *physically challenged*" (207; emphasis mine). Intending the pronouns "we" and "our" to refer to abled-bodied people who need attitude adjustments, the authors make apparent not only that they are situated in the dominant category but that they expect that all of their readers are too. By setting up an us/them scenario "the physically challenged" become an essentialized group whose core essence is how they are treated.

Perpetuating the Binary

Because the very words used to speak and write about physical, sensory, and mental difference participate in the conception of it, words have been a particularly revealing point of contention. Through the unexamined use of the term *disabled*, for example, composition textbooks serve to perpetuate the ability/dis-ability binary that research and lived experience reveal as so harmful and limiting. A clear-cut category in the political or medical model does not necessarily reflect human experience. Whether it is race, sexuality, or religion, we are so much more than a category. People are more often abled or disabled depending on environment and circumstance. When also considering that claiming a dis-ability identity carries negative social consequences, words used in dis-ability discourse should be chosen with self-conscious awareness of their implications. Henri-Jacques Stiker, writing in *A History of*

Disability, posits that this history of linguistic confusion in labeling *(handicapped, disabled, people with disabilities, differently abled, physically challenged)* marks our insecurity and outright disagreement (153). Ultimately, the shift in thinking about dis-ability will come by the way it is defined, written about, and practiced, which makes the discussion of the terms pertinent in composition texts.

The debate model discussed previously further perpetuates the dichotomy. By arranging the debate between those in the dis-ability community and legislators, *In Context* formalizes an us/them dichotomy and further ingrains the divide by situating students as mediators. What the authors are asking students to do is something society as a whole is still grappling with—that is, how to ensure social justice for all. Again, as the presumed possessors of limited resources, students are placed in the position of benevolent guardian or hard-line defender of hard knocks. Although brief references are made to the multifaceted issues and changing definitions of dis-ability, in the end the student is placed in the role of deliberator, expected—privileged—to decide the outcome, as if such a decision could be made by any one individual about any aspect of dis-ability.

Another kind of binary is created by the standard practice of organizing chapters in textbooks so that they represent discrete issues. Isolating issues chapter by chapter is the typical approach of texts that pair composition with a more general subject or theme. In fact, the isolation of one issue from another is a customary form of postsecondary teaching and is analogous to the disconnections between departments and disciplines in universities. Approaching issues as if they were not interconnected hinders critical thinking, since related knowledge is increasingly divorced and connections harder to make. When dis-ability is contained in a single chapter, it can be thus dealt with as a separate and distinct issue instead of as an integral part of life affecting all other parts of the whole. The semiotic effect of arranging issues by chapter serves to portray dis-ability as an isolated issue removed from other related issues, such as work and sexuality, and suggests that they are, in fact, not related.

Although *Between Worlds,* like many of the texts I have used as examples, clusters its readings on dis-ability in a single chapter, "Between Perceptions," it takes a more integrated approach to the topic of dis-ability. It employs an expanded use of genres, including poetry, several personal essays, an article, and a book chapter. This is significant because more and diverse genres allow for a greater range of expression. The premise that dis-ability is called to illustrate is the uncomfortable and sometimes dangerous position of challenging and sometimes resisting how others see us as compared with how we see ourselves; it results in a smart pairing of dis-ability readings with discussions of identity formation.

The authors of the various readings argue for different points. Matthew Soyster, writing in "Living under Circe's Spell," tries to reconcile his changing identity within the context of a culture that has labeled him by his multiple sclerosis (MS). It is a powerful, emotional, and graphic essay that ends as it begins, with the protagonist "sprawled in the gutter behind [his] minivan, bits of glass and scrap metal chewing at [his] knees and elbows, a cut on [his] hand beginning to well crimson" (224). He has fallen in an attempt to free his wheelchair from its compartment, and as a result, he cannot get up. He lies there, contemplating and waiting. In "A Good Investment," Jerome Lee argues for employment rights. Like Soyster's piece, this article was originally published in *Newsweek*. Yet, unlike Soyster's unflinching focus on identity construction, the overriding message Lee puts forth is assimilation. Like every other American, he argues, he has defined himself through his work. He asks the government and employers to train and employ people in his situation. In the next piece, Ted Kooser writes from the point of view of a seeing person who articulates his anxiety about blindness and people who are blind. The poem, entitled "The Blind Always Come as Such a Surprise," has a decidedly sarcastic edge to it, one intended to call attention to the way people with sight relate to and feel about people with blindness. From these examples the reader takes away three very different aspects of dis-ability.

The textbook's template is ultimately a drawback, however, because it limits the kinds and order of questions asked. Through a series of questions and writing tasks, the textbook authors try to lead students to imagine "more constructive responses to living with disabilities" (233). First, the term "constructive" is problematic. As we have seen in so many of the textbooks here, students are called to be helpful, beneficial, and positive in response to readings (a covert issue of power but also an implication that dis-ability is somebody else's problem). But the issue of form I wish to explicate here pertains to the constraints of the text's chapter-by-chapter format. It works against coming to any fresh insights as to how, as individuals, students are to respond differently or what less conventional responses might be. For example, the standard devices of the text require that the readings in every chapter—regardless of the issues being presented—be addressed in the following order: "Thinking about the Text," "Writing from the Text," and "Connecting with Other Texts." This cookie-cutter approach to analysis does not allow for flexibility in addressing critical issues or invite innovative analysis or reflection.

"Thinking about the Text" guides students to identify and analyze rhetorical features and their effect without much focus on the content of the reading. Occasionally a content question is asked that will check comprehension of a particularly difficult passage. The first issue students are asked to consider after reading Soyster's intensely personal narrative is not about the emotional or cultural implication of dis-ability but rather a matter of technique:

> 1. This essay opens with the writer "sprawled in the gutter" and ends with him still "waiting" for a passing car or pedestrian to help. Analyze the effect of creating such a scene and of using the present tense (even though this event happened in the past). (226–27)

At best, ignoring the subject in an effort to focus on the rhetorical strategies represents a cognitive disjunction between the readings and how the authors of the texts ask students to engage them. At worst, it presents students with a hierarchy of values that places *techne* above readers' personal responses to texts as representations of the world.

The middle section, "Writing from the Text," usually involves addressing a given thesis that may or may not be related to the issue presented. Occasionally included in "Writing from the Text" is a chance to engage the text with a quasi-personal response; for example, "How do you feel when you meet a disabled person?" (232). From reviewing the kinds of questions and writing tasks that the authors ask of students, it becomes apparent that the issues function as backdrops for discussing writing techniques. A similar writing task is prefaced by the remark that "writing about personal trauma can be challenging because of the 'poor me' temptation. . . . Write an essay illustrating how one can write about personal trauma without succumbing to self-pity" (230). Following the Soyster essay, the textbook authors generalize and trivialize the author's experience of living with MS in a culture that privileges strength and normalcy by asking students to "write about a time when [they] felt different" (227).

In the "Connecting with Other Texts" feature, students compare and contrast two works by choosing from a range of given foci. For example, "Compare and contrast Lee's purpose, strategies, and tone with Soyster's" (231). In the next sample, students are asked to synthesize several readings and "write an essay about how and why people feel uneasy around *the disabled*—and what can be done about it" (227). Although a common constraint and guide found in most textbooks, one template applied to every chapter can hinder the critical thinking that the authors are supposedly encouraging.

The chapter is rounded out with readings about obesity, bulimia, and several essays interrogating skin color that work to expand the readers' notion of difference. The best that this chapter has to offer is in the final entry. A white female writer, Joan Steinau Lester, investigates the topic of multiple subjectivities and the phenomenon of passing. Students are then encouraged to use their own experiences to explore a range of issues presented throughout Lester's text as well as throughout the chapter. It is this complicating and interconnecting of issues that inspires students to think and write. *Between Worlds* moves closer to this interconnectivity in the section titled "Handbook," in which a student's research paper written on the social and cultural acceptance of dis-ability is used to demonstrate the research process and is also referenced in the "Connecting with Other Texts" sections.

The expressed goals of *Between Worlds* are more modest and, I believe, less troubling overall than most texts featuring dis-ability topics. Instead of placing students in refereeing positions debating the pros and cons of dis-ability, the book intends to have students examine their self-perceptions against those of the dominant culture. It uses dis-ability topics as a common ground for discussions on identity and perception. The authors include a variety of voices (authorities) and ask students to consider their own experiences with dis-ability in their investigations of identity.

Although the topic of dis-ability is engaged differently than in most texts, the effects are not as successful as I had hoped. *Between Worlds* resembles many other texts in its situating of dis-ability as a problem that students, through writing, can solve as they internalize the values of the textbook's authors and the pedagogy of writing to learn. An underlying assumption present in each of the three dis-ability entries in *Between Worlds* is that aid is the solution. Soyster is left in a gutter, in need of help; Lee needs a job; people who are blind need understanding and resources. Help, then, becomes the conclusion of the three readings, the "more constructive responses" the authors are after. A helpful attitude, supplied by the desires of readers, students sitting in a classroom completing the meaning of the texts with their own interpretations, is not necessarily what people with disabilities need or want, however. Ultimately, by asking students to solve the "dis-ability problem," the book presents dis-ability as someone else's need. Students are no closer to examining society's lack of accommodations or their own role in creating negative experiences for people with disabilities; nor are they interrogating language's role in perpetuating negative consequences.

DIRECTIONS FOR THE FUTURE

Most of the readings that editors select regarding dis-ability are compelling and can be used effectively when considering some of the critical points made in this chapter. Used in concert with a theoretical understanding of dis-ability studies—the cultural, political, economic, social, legal, and linguistic context in which all people live—and coupled with compatible composition methods, much of the reading material that posits a dis-ability perspective can be useful. Students, situated squarely inside their own cultural framework, can start taking notice of the cultures outside them that until now seemed remote or unrelated. Dis-ability interrogated as difference can start students pondering the complicated ways they themselves are related to the seemingly unfamiliar. This responsibility cannot be left to instructors and students alone. Textbook authors, editors, and publishers need to provide the framework to make this happen. The following is an example of how this synergy could be achieved, from chapter 7, "Writing an Autobiographical Narrative," of *The Allyn and Bacon Guide to Writing*.

The student essay "Phantom Limb Pain" is the narrative of a college student's suffering and guilt long after a childhood rival's arm amputation. The story ends with the protagonist freeing Miller, his former foe, from a fence where he became trapped when attempting to climb over it. In an unexpected move, Miller thanks the protagonist for "filling in" for him as quarterback on their high school football team, a position he lost when a motorcycle accident caused him to lose his right arm. The epiphany the student writer states directly is that "even without an arm he [his nemesis] was more of a leader. Damaged but not diminished" (Rammage, Bean, and Johnson, 161).

In the editorial apparatus entitled "Thinking Critically about 'Phantom Limb Pain,'" the editors ask students questions about the content in addition to having them notice rhetorical techniques, focusing on the essay's ending and its words. Had the authors taken on a direct discussion of how dis-ability functions and is represented in the story, as they had with race in the previous essay, they could have led readers to a more complex critique. In a discussion of theme and autobiographical writing presented earlier in the text, the authors ask questions about race and personal identity and the psychic damage of cultural dislocation. Dis-ability, as portrayed here, serves as a primary impetus of the storyteller's efforts. It serves to differentiate the characters—one "normal," one "damaged." A class discussion could center on David Mitchell and Sharon Snyder's concept of "narrative prosthesis," which situates the experiences and representations of dis-ability rhetorically within literature (6) (see excerpt from Mitchell, "Narrative Prosthesis and the Materiality of Metaphor, p. 183 in this volume). How, the authors might ask, do Miller's dis-ability and the overall lack of concrete details in the description of him together create a mysterious yet admirable persona? How does (or will) Miller's dis-ability complicate the already complicated relationship?

TOWARD INTEGRATION (TWO MODELS)

Cultural Conversations: The Presence of the Past has found a way to integrate (not simply add on) dis-ability material. Chapter 3, "Disabled Persons," begins by asking, "How Do Individuals Form a Culture?" and features a multi-genre investigation of Helen Keller. What is unique to this text is that issues are studied at the point of contention and from many different points of view. We read, for example, from Keller's own words, the words of her contemporaries (Alexander Graham Bell and Mark Twain), advertisements for her published works, and then finally how she is being read and interpreted today by dis-ability scholar Georgina Kleege. Photographs similarly juxtapose the Hollywood version of Keller against posed portraits and candid shots. Students are then asked to comment on the differences between the image and the person. Oliver Sacks, Harlan Lane, Simi Linton, and Slackjaw (Jim Knipfel) round out the contemporary voices.

Following most readings is the section labeled "Ideas for Rereading," which directs students in a variety of reading tasks: identifying particular rhetorical aspects, explaining certain passages, or extending the discussion by making inferences about the author or the cultural climate. Students are often asked to identify passages or concepts that surprised them in their first reading. This helps students identify dissonance between old and new ideas.

Immediately following, "Ideas for Writing" reinforces the main points made throughout the section. For example, after the Helen Keller series, students are asked to expand their view of Keller by viewing the film version of *The Miracle Worker*, focusing on the water pump scene. Then they, "write an essay examining the creation of Keller's public image and potential myth in the context of the depictions of this 'miraculous' moment in her life" (235). To additionally emphasize the chapter's focus, students are reminded that Keller herself was well acquainted with the film and play versions of her life. Students are also encouraged to examine their own sense of how the meaning of a life-defining event changes according to when and where and to whom the narrative is told (235). This text serves as a lucid example of how combining written text with readings of visual texts offers a powerful context for discovering incongruities.

Cultural Conversations concludes each chapter with a research section entitled "Extending Your Work." The authors offer ideas for research projects that concentrate on different aspects of the readings. In the third chapter, students can choose between writing about the cochlear implant controversy, the poster child as a fund-raising tool, and the empowering rhetoric of the American Federation for the Blind. "Ideas for Working across Chapters" invites students to make connections to other issues presented in the text, such as dis-ability and gender, dis-ability and race, and culture and difference.

By integrating dis-ability content throughout their rhetoric/reader, *Rhetorical Contexts,* Strobeck Webb and Thompson manage to avoid most of the pitfalls we've identified, while examining dis-ability in a social context. The text approaches writing via the rhetorical situation, focusing on implications of context, persuasion, *kairos,* audience, purpose, and Burke's idea of identification, a writer's attempt to reach the audience through the use of shared values and beliefs. The intended effect is that students become critics of language as it is used in the world. The readings introduce students to complex situations; the authors supply analytical tools to help students make sense of the text. As the introduction to John M. Williams's essay on dis-ability and advertising, "Images: Use of the Disabled in Advertising," illustrates, students are specifically reminded to "look for evidence that the author has certain presumptions about the interests and attitudes of his readers" (207).

Each of four essays on dis-ability is taken from magazines that target specialized audiences and focus on issues concerning people with disabilities, *WE Magazine* and its companion Web site, *WE Media,* and *New Mobility.* While the essays appear in different chapters categorized by aims—for example, "Exploring and Reflecting," "Making Judgments," and "Explaining and Interpreting"—the authors additionally cluster the essays under the dis-ability category in "Thematic Contents," a suggested alternative use of the text.

"An American in Albania," included in chapter 6, "Reporting and Recording," is written by war correspondent John Hockenberry. In this essay he weaves a reflection of himself as an American, a paraplegic, and a reporter and how these sometimes contrasting influences affect his view of Albanian refugees. Students, after reading, are prompted to explore this unique perspective and the challenges it may present to them as readers. The authors ask students to think of challenges Hockenberry might face in trying to communicate a multilayered message. Later, students are asked to judge the effectiveness or appropriateness of humor within the context of the essay. In this way, questions following the readings encourage students to analyze the context and language of each selection.

Responses to the writings are similarly focused on rhetorical elements situated in a social context. For example, after analyzing Williams's essay on dis-ability and advertising, students are asked to "examine a number of advertisements that are directed to a particular audience (children, young woman, sports fans), and write an essay in which you infer from those ads what assumptions the advertisers are making about that audience" (212). The writing prompt appearing after several print ads directs students to "look for any use of persons with disabilities in advertisements (on television, in magazines, or in newspapers). Write a paper in which you discuss the effects of increased use of people with disabilities in advertising, both for the advertisers and their consumers" (215). The essays, together with the ads, make a good launching-off point for such further explorations.

Rhetorical Context is not considered a multicultural reader, although it features a diverse range of writers and cultural issues. Its aim is not the critique of social issues, the unraveling of identity, or the use of writing to solve problems; rather, through its unrelenting focus on language in a social context, the textbook initiates students in thinking about the invisible constructions in language. It is, of course, not the only composition text using a rhetorical approach to the teaching of writing, but it is uniquely successful in integrating dis-ability into writing and suggests a useful direction for other authors.

CONCLUSION

Writing influences and is influenced by various perspectives—our own and others'. This influence and its consequences occur whether we are aware of it or not. We make a powerful statement through neglecting dis-ability as a part of our course content. Yet, simply "adding" dis-ability as one more diversity issue is not adequate and, in fact, often has negative consequences. Our goal as college composition professionals is to make these various, often competing, perspectives part of the classroom consciousness. Only then will constructions, such as dis-ability, be interrogated and writers come closer to understanding our own role in developing and perpetuating these constructs.

There is no precise recipe for including dis-ability in writing pedagogy—nor am I suggesting there should be. But we can, more often, do better. By being more willing to recognize contradictions, power imbalances, and cultural myths associated with the construction of dis-ability, and the constraints of textbooks in their prescribed forms, we not only have the potential for more open and honest discussions, but we honor writing's function in creating and understanding knowledge.

NOTES

1. To draw continual attention to the constructed nature of the dis-ability/ability dichotomy, I sever the word *dis-ability* textually with a hyphen here and throughout this text, except in cases where I have included direct quotes from others. Through its ubiquitous use by the dominant group, the concept of dis-ability has undergone exnominalization. That term, coined by French deconstructionist critic Roland Barthes, describes the process by which a group or an idea becomes accepted as "normal." The ideology supporting the status quo is in turn rendered invisible. Applied to dis-ability, readers become desensitized or perhaps are not even initially aware of dis-ability's formation through cultural traditions, so continual attention must be drawn to it.

2. In terms of a methodology, this study brings together three different but complementary perspectives on language as social practice: (1) critical discourse analysis as presented by Norman Fairclough, (2) the rhetorical analysis of Kenneth Burke, and (3) social semiotic analysis as defined by Robert Hodge and Gunther Kress.

3. "Person with a disability" is the preferred terminology within the formal structural systems that work with people with disabilities and within some advocacy and political organizations, at least in the United States, although this is changing. The thinking behind what is called people-first language is that the person with a dis-ability is a person first, and the dis-ability is incidental to that. It is a way of fighting against the stigma of the dis-ability and reemphasizing the humanity of the person. Geographically, this terminology varies widely. Within Canada, for example, there is a much different history of these descriptors, and it is much more common to use "disabled person" even in political, social, and academic discourses.

REFLECTING ON YOUR TEACHING

Designing Assignments

Martin's study speaks to the importance of how writing assignments are constructed, whether by teachers or textbooks. She did find some positive examples—for instance, textbooks that provide multiple points of view on disability; an assignment asking students to reflect on how an event (e.g., a disabling accident) changes its meaning as it is narrated at different times in one's life to different audiences; assignments asking students to research disability issues and draw connections to other, nondisability issues and readings; and an assignment asking students to critically examine the way language used in social contexts affects ideas and attitudes about disability and the disabled.

Creating good, scaffolded writing assignments is one of the most important (and difficult) elements of teaching writing. Working in small groups in a teacher-training workshop, collaboratively develop a writing assignment that in some way includes disability (it does not have to be the main feature of the assignment). With your team, scaffold two or three short preliminary writing or research assignments to lead to the major paper. Then return to the major assignment and flesh it out further. Make sure to consider the critical questions Martin raises: Does your assignment ask students to position themselves as experts when they are not? Does your assignment too easily split into an "us/them" binary? Complete this activity by sharing and discussing each group's series of assignments.

Embodied Writing: Perspectives from Teachers with Disabilities

Introduction to Part Two

Part Two explores how embodied knowledge emerging from disability experiences and perspectives shapes the teaching of writing. The essays included here are written by writing teachers with disabilities. Teaching writing from a disabled subject position creates opportunities for enacting imaginative and critical listening, for considering risks to teacher and student authority, for "bearing witness" to others' vulnerabilities and strengths, and for attending to "access" and "identity" in all their multiple forms. The authors' particular embodied experiences, as well as the activities following each essay, can help all writing instructors—whether disabled or not—to address the role of bodies in learning and in writing.

6   Body Language: Disability Narratives and the Act of Writing

KRISTIN LINDGREN

Using disability narratives as reading material in a composition classroom can help students think about the material contexts of composition. Kristin Lindgren uses her own teaching of disability narratives to illustrate how reading these texts can encourage students in composition classrooms to understand "themselves as embodied writers who also make use of specific writing technologies" and to explore how writing is a "physical and mechanical activity that cannot be separated from the body that produces it." Lindgren takes as her examples four narratives by authors who write about their (disabled) bodies and their own embodied practices of reading and writing. Excerpts from two of these authors, Georgina Kleege and Nancy Mairs, are included on pages 117 and 234 in this volume, respectively. Lindgren's argument follows upon but also disrupts both Walter Ong and Plato, who, as she notes, are famous for citing written text as "dead" — "a removal from the living human life-world," according to Ong. Lindgren shows how the use of disability narratives in a composition classroom can, in fact, revive "dead" writing by reinvigorating awareness of the embodied, physical nature of writing. In a provocative counter to Ong and Plato, Lindgren suggests, using Nancy Mairs's own words and work, that disability narratives "ask us to embrace literacy as a 'carnal act.'"

Forced by the exigencies of physical disease to embrace myself in the flesh, I couldn't write bodiless prose. The voice is the creature of the body that produces it. I speak as a crippled woman. . . . No body, no voice; no voice, no body. That's what I know in my bones.

—NANCY MAIRS

In *Carnal Acts*, poet and essayist Nancy Mairs explores how living in a body crippled by multiple sclerosis has shaped her voice as a writer. Concluding that body and voice are inextricably linked, Mairs claims that her writing voice is located "in the body-warmed breath escaping my lungs and throat" (281). When a writer talks about voice, we generally assume that she is referring to an abstract concept related to tone and style rather than to the sounds produced by the vocal organs. We seldom think of voice in a written text as emerging from the lungs and throat. Mairs's literalization of the concept of voice resonates more deeply if we know that she uses voice-recognition software to write. By linking body and voice, disability and writing, Mairs asks us to rethink what it means to write and to consider more fully how our bodies—disabled or not—shape the writing we do.

As teachers of writing, we want our students to understand the rhetorical situatedness of their own acts of writing. We ask them to consider voice, audience, context, and purpose. However, we rarely ask them to think about the material context of composition. How would their understanding of writing change if we integrated into our teaching discussions of writing as an embodied practice? And how might narratives about disability help students to think of themselves as embodied writers who make use of specific writing technologies? Nonfictional disability narratives—a category in which I include autobiography, memoir, the personal essay, and critical studies that incorporate first-person narrative—frequently employ rhetorical gestures that call attention both to technologies of writing, or "what I'm writing with," and to the politics of location, or "where I'm writing from." By highlighting the scene of writing, these narratives challenge the notion of writing as a purely conceptual act and present it as a physical and mechanical activity that cannot be separated from the body that produces it. Building on Mairs's notion of writing as a "carnal act," I will discuss embodied practices of writing and reading in four disability narratives: Robert Murphy's *The Body Silent*, Jean-Dominique Bauby's *The Diving Bell and the Butterfly*, Nancy Mairs's *Waist-High in the World: A Life among the Nondisabled*, and Georgina Kleege's *Sight Unseen*. Each of these narratives explores the intersections between body and technology, disability and composition. Situating these intersections in a practical context, I argue that teaching disability narratives in a writing classroom can complicate and enrich our understanding of what it means to compose, to write, and to read.

———

In his study of the transition from oral to literate cultures, Walter Ong argues that writing has a distancing and decontextualizing effect. Unlike the oral transmission of ideas, he suggests, writing "separates the knower from the known" (Ong, *Orality*, 46). In other words, the text as a material object exists apart from the time and place in which the knowledge was produced, and apart from the person—the embodied, knowing subject—who put his or her ideas into words. In the *Phaedrus*, Plato famously has Socrates argue that writing is a mere shadow, a calcified image of living speech. Ong suggests that Plato undermines his own argument by representing it in a written dialogue, but he follows Plato in asserting the "deadness" of the written text, its "removal from the living human lifeworld," a deadness that paradoxically enables its temporal endurance and its potential, over time, for entering other living contexts (Ong, 81).

Although writing, like speech, is produced by the body—usually by the hand—the printed text renders the author's body invisible. Even when a book is *about* its author's body, this body is absent. The textual effacement of material bodies has particular implications for disability narratives, which often depict the disabled body as hypervisible or invisible. As G. Thomas Couser points out, print media at once represents disability and conceals it from view ("Signifying," 114). While invisibility can sometimes serve the author of a disability narrative—for example, by enabling the author to reach readers who might be discomfited by the physical presence of a visibly disabled person—many disabled authors resist this bodily effacement. By writing not only about their bodies but also about their embodied practices of writing and reading, these authors rhetorically reconnect the written text to the body that produces or reads its signs. In doing so, they challenge the association of writing with disembodied and decontextualized knowledges.

Ong asserts that we have so fully interiorized the practice of writing that we are no longer able to understand it as a technology or to recognize how it shapes thought (*Orality,* 81). Theorists and historians of writing technologies point out that as new ways of writing are introduced—the pencil, the typewriter, the word processor—we gradually become accustomed to each mode of producing written text and become unaware of it as a technology. Dennis Baron, for example, in his essay "From Pencils to Pixels," suggests that when we are habituated to our writing tools, "we come to think of them as natural rather than technological" (51). In the introduction to their composition reader *Writing Material: Readings from Plato to the Digital Age,* Evelyn Tribble and Anne Trubek trace the history of writing in an effort to make visible the interaction between material and conceptual aspects of writing. They frame their anthology with the claim that "the materials we use to write, whether spoken voice, ballpoint pen or computer keyboard, influence what we write, what we read, and ultimately, how we think" (xi). Their selections emphasize moments of technological change, such as the invention of the printing press or the transition from a print-based culture to a digital one, and they argue that at these moments writing is denaturalized, made transparent *as* a technology.

While there is a substantial body of scholarship on technologies of writing, few scholars call attention to the relationship between writing technologies and the bodies that employ these technologies. A notable exception is Christina Haas, who points out that when technologies change, "aspects of writing are foregrounded that may not have been noticed before, including the writer's physical relationship to texts and the tools of text production" (24). Haas explores how technological change reshapes embodied writing practices, and she argues that various writing technologies produce "radically different spatial, tactile, visual, and even temporal relations" between body and text (226).[1] However, Haas focuses solely on how differences in technology affect the bodies of writers rather than on how bodily differences affect writing technologies. Addressing the relation between the writer's body and text from a different angle, I will discuss how disability and physical variation shape our practices of writing and reading, and I will suggest that the materiality of literacy can be brought to conscious awareness not only by changes in technology, but also by changes in our bodies.

As Drew Leder has pointed out, our bodies most often call attention to themselves at times of illness or disability, during a period of rapid bodily change, such as adolescence or pregnancy, or when we are learning a new physical skill. At other times, our bodies can disappear from consciousness (89–90).[2] When we become so habituated to the physical actions inherent in writing that we no longer notice them, writing can easily be conceptualized as a purely mental activity. However, when disability alters the writer's physical relationship to the text—especially when it requires the use of body parts that are not normative for writing and reading or when it requires collaborative writing or reading—it challenges our assumptions about literacy and calls attention to the physicality of literate acts.[3] As Jim Swan asserts, "writing is not only *about* the body but *of* and *from* the body too" (284; emphasis his). Disability narratives, by foregrounding the materiality of both body and text, can reembody reading and writing. These narratives emphasize that whether written text is created by a voice dictating to another person or to a computer; by a hand writing, typing, or signing American Sign Language; or by an eye blinking to indicate letters of the alphabet, its production is always grounded in the body.

In *The Body Silent*, a book that is both an ethnographic study and an autobiographical account of disability, the anthropologist Robert Murphy explains that his "long illness with a disease of the spinal cord has been a kind of extended anthropological field trip" (xi). Gradually paralyzed by a spinal tumor, Murphy is no longer able to travel to the Amazon to conduct fieldwork, and he turns his attention to studying the social and cultural effects of disability. Near the end of his book, Murphy chronicles the necessary changes he has made in writing technologies as his paralysis has become more severe. Incorporating into the narrative a detailed description of the writing tools he used to produce *The Body Silent*, Murphy foregrounds the physical act of writing and demonstrates that a progressively disabled body can trace a history of writing technologies.

As his fingers weaken and it becomes more difficult to press a writing implement onto a page, Murphy progresses from pencils to ballpoint pens to felt-tipped pens, and, finally, to a felt-tipped pen wrapped with latex foam, making it thick enough for his hand to grasp. To use a typewriter, he employs the foam-wrapped pen as a stylus, hitting the keys one by one with the eraser end; when it becomes too difficult for him to grasp the pen, he uses a device called a "universal cuff," a strip of plastic wrapped around the hand into which a pencil or eating utensil can be inserted, which enables him to use an implement without gripping it. Eventually, unable to roll the paper into the typewriter, he reluctantly buys a computer. Murphy comments a bit crankily on how the computer affects his writing:

> It makes for prolix and discursive writing, ill-planned sentences, and spongy syntax. The ease of revision and editing encourages messy composition. Sometimes I tell people that I no longer write—I process words. These are, however, avoidable drawbacks, and a small price to pay for great rewards. The computer has been a liberation, an extension of my useful professional life. (189)

Murphy was writing in the days before voice-recognition computer software was widely used, but had he lived into the twenty-first century he would very likely be using Dragon Naturally Speaking or another voice-activated system.[4] While the transition from pen to typewriter to word processor is typical for writers of Murphy's generation, these changes in writing materials are usually invisible to the reader. Murphy's description of his specific and adaptive use of each of these technologies not only renders his own acts of writing visible, it also makes clear that writing involves physical labor and continually evolving technologies.

By calling attention to the medium of his message, Murphy suggests that the materials we use to write, and the material conditions under which we write, influence the writing we produce. When I teach disability narratives, I use a passage such as Murphy's description of technologies of writing to highlight the material conditions under which each of us, disabled or not, is writing. I ask students to write a brief description of their preferred writing materials and to reflect on how these materials enhance or constrain the writing they do. When students are able to think of themselves as embodied writers who employ a specific writing technology, they are more likely to understand writing as a practice that is shaped by individual choices and by historical and cultural conditions. I would argue that this understanding makes them more self-reflective and finally more flexible writers—writers who understand that each act of writing is situated in a specific material and rhetorical context. Moreover, they come to understand that this context is an unstable one; as our bodies change, and as technology changes, so does our writing and thinking.

————

In his memoir *The Diving Bell and the Butterfly*, Jean-Dominique Bauby recounts a sudden and dramatic change in his physical abilities. Bauby, formerly the editor-in-chief of *Elle* magazine, explains that he is undergoing treatment and rehabilitation for "locked-in syndrome," a result of the stroke he suffered at age forty-three. He describes the syndrome in this way: "Paralyzed from head to toe, the patient, his mind intact, is imprisoned inside his own body, unable to speak or move. In my case, blinking my left eyelid is my only means of communication" (4). The central metaphors of Bauby's book— the diving bell and the butterfly—suggest a consciousness that floats free of its extreme bodily confinement. Bauby's description of his mental travel through space and time, the exploration of memory that is recorded in his book, confirms the reader's sense of Bauby's disembodied consciousness. Indeed, the initial stage of his composition process takes place only in his mind: "In my head I churn over every sentence ten times, delete a word, add an adjective, and learn my text by heart, paragraph by paragraph" (5–6). Yet to communicate these "bedridden travel notes" to a visitor or a reader, Bauby must link his composing consciousness to the body it inhabits. The radical changes in Bauby's body defamiliarize both speech and writing, revealing the multiple physical abilities that each communicative act requires. Speech has become a difficult and unreliable mode of communication for him; reflecting on his work with a speech therapist, Bauby writes: "You cannot imagine the acrobatics your tongue mechanically performs in order to produce all the sounds of a language. Just now I am struggling with the letter *l*, a pitiful admission for an editor in chief who cannot even pronounce the name of his own magazine!" (40).

In the fifth chapter of his book, "Alphabet," Bauby describes the system by which he communicates with visitors, and it gradually dawns on us, his readers, that the book has been produced in the same way. Using an alphabet arranged in order of each letter's frequency of use in the French language, he blinks to indicate the letter he desires. As Bauby explains:

> It is a simple enough system. You read off the alphabet (ESA version, not ABC) until, with a blink of my eye, I stop you at the letter to be noted. The maneuver is repeated for the letters that follow, so that fairly soon you have a whole word, and then fragments of more or less intelligible sentences. (20)

Conversing with Bauby involves both eye-to-eye and mouth-to-ear communication. In order to transmute his evanescent eyeblink into a written text, his interlocuter voices each letter, using the simple mediating technology of the alphabet board; Bauby's left ear hears the voiced letter (his right ear is deaf and the hearing in his left ear is impaired) and his eye blinks at the letter he wants; his visitor's eye interprets his blink and her hand transcribes the selected letter. While this process does not employ the parts of an author's body generally used in the act of writing, it produces a transparent text in which the means of production is not immediately apparent.

Bauby's writing practice is perforce a collaborative one, a practice in which his transcriber is directly, physically involved in creating the text. He makes clear that the active participation of another person, another body and mind, influences its production. Temperament, gender, and personal history shape the transcription of his words: "Because of nervousness, impatience, or obtuseness, performances vary in the handling of the code (which is what we call this method of transcribing my thought). Crossword fans and Scrabble players have a head start. Girls manage better than boys. . . . Meticulous people never go wrong" (20–22). The collaborative production of words can lead to what Bauby calls the "poetry" of mistranscription and of impulsive guessing. As an example of this poetry, he notes that once when he was asking for his glasses (*lunettes*, in French), his visitor asked what he wanted with the moon *(lune)*. Bauby's playful description of misreading underscores the indeterminacy of language and the uncertainty of communication, an uncertainty heightened by the process of collaboration. At the end of his narrative, Bauby tells the reader that he worked on the book daily with a single transcriber, minimizing—though surely not eliminating—the possibility of poetic errors, and he explains the role of Claude Mendibil, who transcribed these chapters letter by letter.[5]

Because of the unusual writing technology Bauby employs, his book is sometimes regarded as the literary equivalent of a freak show, an extraordinary textual body at which we can marvel from a distance. When I teach *The Diving Bell and the Butterfly* in a writing class, I try to redirect this voyeuristic gaze by suggesting to my students that the seeming strangeness of Bauby's composition process can help us to understand that every act of writing, even one that appears to be natural and effortless, comprises multiple physical and mental activities. Students often speculate that Bauby's very brief chapters, many of which are two or three pages long and read like prose poems, are a function of his labor-intensive composition process. By looking closely at a very specific mode of textual production—even or especially one as unusual as Bauby's—we become newly aware of how any text, not only one created in this particular way, depends on the body of the writer and the embodied reception and interpretation of its audience. The transparency and authority of Bauby's prose belies the painstaking collaborative effort it requires. However, Bauby chooses to highlight rather than to efface the material conditions of his book's composition, and in so doing he underscores the physicality of every act of writing.

In *Waist-High in the World: A Life among the Nondisabled,* and in numerous other collections of essays, Nancy Mairs contemplates the experience of disability. Referring to the angle of vision from her wheelchair, Mairs quips: "I 'Tell all the Truth—,' in accord with Emily Dickinson's instruction, 'but tell it Slant—' more literally than Emily ever envisioned" (*Waist-High,* 16). Literalizing the concept of point of view much as she literalizes the notion of voice in *Carnal Acts,* Mairs insists that the conceptual act of writing is shaped by the material circumstances of the writer's body. Like Robert Murphy, Mairs has adopted different writing tools as her disease, multiple sclerosis, has progressed and affected different parts of her body.[6] However, she mentions only in passing that she now writes using a computer with voice-activated software (*Waist-High,* 39). While she does not explore the effect of varied writing technologies on her work, Mairs frequently calls attention to the scene of writing, emphasizing the importance of her specific, embodied perspective. For example, she interrupts an essay on the nature of God to tell the reader that her Thirstbuster full of Diet Coke has spilled on the floor, and "since I can't reach down to mop it up, I'll have to continue working on this passage with my feet in a sticky brown puddle" (*Ordinary Time,* 184). Through narrative interruptions such as this one, Mairs suggests that the material conditions of writing, even when these conditions are comically mundane, influence her writing and thinking. As she contemplates God, sitting in her wheelchair with her feet in a puddle, she can only imagine a deity that has a sense of humor and a material presence in the world.

In an essay entitled "Body in Trouble," Mairs recounts her experience at a luncheon honoring the Dalai Lama, when 1,400 workshop participants suddenly streamed out of a meeting room and forced her and her wheelchair to cling to the wall so as not to be trampled. She writes: "Let me tell you, no matter how persuaded they were of the beauty and sacredness of all life, not one of them seemed to think that any life was going on below the level of her or his own gaze. 'Down here!' I kept whimpering at the hips and buttocks and bellies pressing my wheelchair on all sides. 'Down here! There's a person down here!'" (*Waist High*, 59). Mairs uses this anecdote to frame her literalized understanding of point of view and specifically of the notion of the marginal:

> 'Marginality' . . . means something altogether different to me from what it means to social theorists. It is no metaphor for the power relations between one group of human beings and another but a literal description of where I stand (figuratively speaking): over here, on the edge, out of bounds, beneath your notice. I embody the metaphors. . . . It may be this radical materiality of my circumstances . . . [that has] spurred me in the past, as [it] no doubt will go on doing, to put the body at the center of all my meditations, my "corpus," if you will. Not that I always write *about* the body, though I often do, but that I always write, consciously, *as* a body." (*Waist-High*, 60)

By claiming that her experience of the world, and thus her thinking and writing about that world, is crucially shaped by the particular body she inhabits, Mairs implicitly asks her readers to consider their own embodied experience and the location from which they write. After we read Mairs's essay, I ask my students what it means to "write . . . *as* a body." Many first-year students have not yet developed a self-conscious awareness of voice or a sophisticated theoretical apparatus, but they generally have a very well-developed sense of themselves as bodies. Whether they are athletes or library dwellers, whether they have bodies that conform to cultural norms of form and function or not, they often identify themselves with, and express themselves through, their bodies. Thus, Mairs's essay resonates with them and impels them to consider the relationship between embodiment and writing. Reflecting on their own embodied perspectives, students become aware that all of us, consciously or not, write *as* bodies.

———

In her collection of essays on blindness, *Sight Unseen*, Georgina Kleege makes clear that the act of writing is intimately bound up with the act of reading, not only because most writers are avid readers, but also because writers must read their own words as they write, and reread them as they revise and edit. Kleege describes in detail the different modalities of reading she employs—visual, aural, and tactile—and the ways in which these modalities shape both her writing process and her experience as a reader. Writing manually is difficult for Kleege because reading handwritten text is a laborious, painful, and uncertain process. Kleege's form of blindness, early-onset macular degeneration, creates a large blind spot in the center of her visual field but does not affect her peripheral vision. She explains that "as my pen travels across the page, everything to the left of it fades to blankness—my blind spot erases what I've just written" (195). The muscular strain of keeping her eyes focused and very close to the page gradually becomes painful: "If I continue writing as I am, my nose skimming the page, my eye peering through a heavy magnifying lens, the pain will deepen and spread, migrating to my forehead and my other eye" (192). Writing on a computer, she does not have to focus her eyes, and she can enlarge the words. Nonetheless, she must move her face very close to the screen to read her words and must use her magnifying lens to proofread. She also uses a closed-circuit TV reading device that enables her to magnify text up to a hundred times and to reverse an image from positive to negative, reducing glare. Describing her modes of writing, Kleege invites the reader to witness the process through which she writes the words we are reading—"At the moment I'm typing at 36 point. This *L* is about half an inch tall" (195)—and renders it impossible to disassociate her words from the body that produces them.

Whatever visual technology Kleege employs, words remain difficult to decipher. She explains, "As I stare at a word, it changes. I move my gaze around each letter, and it seems to reconfigure before my eyes. . . . 'Wood' could be 'weed' or perhaps 'ward,' or even 'word'" (200). This uncertainty and mutability, the ever-present possibility of misreading, requires that she attend closely to each letter. Linking her labor-intensive method of visual reading to the critical practice of the New Critics, Kleege recalls:

> When I first heard the expression 'close reading' as an English major in college, I felt a tremendous sense of affirmation. This was the Yale English department, where close reading was something like a religion, and hearing the phrase made me feel that I belonged. I always read close. I always read every word, every syllable, every letter. So the literary practice, to read every word, to dwell on them, to contemplate not only their meanings but connotations, resonances, and history, came very naturally to me. . . . I felt physically well-suited, if not predestined, to be a close reader. (197–98)

Kleege makes a rhetorical move here similar to the one by which Nancy Mairs reinterprets the notion of the marginal. She literalizes, tongue in cheek, the concept of close reading, revealing its origin in physical posture and pacing. Recounting that the first time she met her husband, he saw her hunched over a book in the library, her nose scraping the page, she suggests that perhaps he perceived her as the "physical embodiment of close reading" (198). Illustrating both the materiality of metaphor and the materiality of reading, Kleege insists that reading and interpretation are physical as well as conceptual acts.

In a chapter entitled "Voices in My Head," Kleege discusses her primary method of reading—listening to recorded books—and ponders why this reading technology, increasingly popular with sighted people, is often considered to be "not really reading" (169). She points out that reading aloud is not an unfamiliar experience; most of us were read to as children, and many of us learned to read by reading aloud, sounding out the letters and syllables. This association with childhood, she posits, may cause adults both to think of aural reading as regressive and to desire the "comforting cocoon of narrative" it creates (171). While Kleege puzzles over the disclaimers that accompany this mode of reading, she acknowledges that listening to a voice on tape is fundamentally different from reading privately and silently. Reading aloud, she suggests, introduces an element of performance, and the listening experience is layered and mediated: "I interpret the text, the voice reading the text, the experience of the person reading the text" (183). The qualities of the reading voice, its inflections and intonations, shape her listening experience. The polished tones of professional readers sometimes distract her from the content; the idiosyncrasies of volunteer readers engage or annoy her.

Kleege asserts that aural reading is essentially collaborative: "Readers are not reading to me; we are reading together. I have a sense of a continuous back-and-forth commentary in which I bounce my own ideas off the readers' ideas, or what I perceive of their ideas from their intonation, mistakes, involuntary grunts and sighs" (181). Like Jean-Dominique Bauby's collaborative writing practice, aural reading depends on the participation of another body, another voice. Kleege traces her pleasure in this mode of reading to the experience of being read to by her mother, both before and after she lost her sight. Later, listening to books read aloud by her college roommate and her husband, she finds that responses to the text become "mutual property," that "we share the process of reading, a real-time event in the intimate space where ideas first take shape" (182). Reading Kleege's book, we cannot help but become aware of our own method of reading, the particular modality we use to take in her words. Even as she describes methods of reading familiar to most of us, Kleege defamiliarizes these methods, making us conscious of the material and social circumstances that shape our reading.

In the final chapter of her book, Kleege describes the process of learning braille as an adult. From childhood on, she was actively discouraged from studying braille, which was cast as an archaic method of last resort, appropriate only for the totally blind. She suggests that schools for the blind initially resisted using braille because it enabled blind children to communicate directly, without the mediation of a sighted reader, making oversight and discipline more difficult. Persisting in her desire to master braille, Kleege reexperiences the process of achieving literacy, at first feeling "adrift in a chaos of random and capriciously disarranged dots" (202). As she gains fluency, the language she uses to describe this mode of reading emphasizes its tactility: "For the first time in decades I felt in absolute and stable contact with the text. . . . I touched the words. Meaning flowed into my brain" (203). Reading braille not only liberates her from slow and tedious reading practices, but also stabilizes meaning. She experiences this way of reading, which requires that she stay "in touch with the text," as "certain, unequivocal"; each letter is "still, steadfast, unwavering" (203–4).

Discussing the ways in which current and future computer technologies extend and enhance the usefulness of braille, Kleege notes that a braille printer would allow her to produce braille versions of her own work-in-progress, that a scanner and CD-ROM enables braille users to generate braille versions of a wide range of print materials, and that a "'refreshable braille display board'" creates a braille version of anything on a computer screen. Reflecting on these technologies, Kleege comments: "Annie Sullivan lives on as microcircuitry and hardware" (216). Invoking the companion who helped Helen Keller to communicate, and with whom Keller had a stormy relationship, Kleege emphasizes that blind people no longer require the mediation or collaboration of another person to read or write. In this sense, the use of braille and of assistive technology allows people with visual impairments greater autonomy and authority in their practices of writing and reading.

Kleege makes clear that learning braille has been liberatory for her, and she challenges the privileging of vision as a mode of reading and more generally as a way of apprehending the world. She also challenges the view of tactile reading as an alien, bizarre, experience, noting, "To read with the fingertips seems to the sighted like trying to hear through the nose" (216). By describing in detail a variety of reading technologies, she defamiliarizes acts of literacy that many nondisabled writers both take for granted and view as natural. Teaching Kleege's essays in a writing class, I have found that students develop a heightened awareness that any writer or reader's tools—whether pencil or braille display board—function prosthetically, extending and enhancing what we can do without such tools. They realize, too, that over time we tend to naturalize these technologies, incorporating them into our communicative acts so that they seem to be an extension of our bodies. This awareness helps them to understand reading as an embodied practice inflected by history and culture. Inviting us to become conscious of the materiality of reading, Kleege rhetorically ruptures the transparency of her seamless, beautifully crafted prose. She asks us, readers of her essays, to attend closely to the act of reading, to rethink what it means to read.

Disability studies and composition studies share the critical strategy of examining concepts and practices that are often considered to be transparent, self-evident, and natural. Disability scholars examine the construction of bodily norms and explore how disabled bodies reinforce or challenge assumptions about what kinds of bodies are normal.[7] Extending this investment in the notion of normalcy to the field of composition studies, we might ask: What constitutes a normal writing practice? How can literacy practices that diverge from the perceived norm provide insight into what it means to write? Our practices of writing and reading are often unconscious and unexamined unless we are struggling with a writing project, experimenting with a new technology, or adapting to physical changes. Disability can "productively disrupt" assumptions about composition (Brueggemann et al., 368) and make us aware of writing *as* a technology. Because disability narratives frequently foreground the scene of writing, teaching these narratives in a composition classroom can enable students to understand writing as a practice that is influenced by specific material and social conditions. By calling attention to its material as well as its rhetorical context, disability narratives challenge us to think about writing as an embodied practice and about the written text as shaped by the particular circumstances of the bodies that produce and interpret it. In other words, they ask us to embrace literacy as a "carnal act."

NOTES

1. Christina Haas, *Writing Technology: Studies on the Materiality of Literacy*. For other examples of critical work that considers writing as an embodied practice, see the essays in *Rhetorical Bodies*, edited by Jack Selzer and Sharon Crowley and in *Rhetoric and Composition as Intellectual Work*, edited by Gary A. Olson. In the latter book, see especially Sharon Crowley's "Body Studies in Rhetoric and Composition," and John Trimbur's "Delivering the Message: Typography and the Materiality of Writing."

2. Georges Canguilhem makes a similar argument in *The Normal and Pathological*.

3. While an extended discussion of American Sign Language is beyond the scope of this essay, I want to point to it here as an example of a mode of communication that complicates received ideas about language and literacy. Lennard Davis claims that ASL, in which conversation is "received through the eye and generated by the hand" (*Enforcing Normalcy*, 103), challenges ideas about which body parts are normative for communicative acts and directs our attention to the physical origins of language. Making a case for deafness as a critical modality, Davis suggests that "the deafened critic must reinscribe language on the body, in the materiality of the sign as it is embodied in the larynx or the hand" (179). The Deaf community, of course, conceives of deafness not as a disability but as a cultural and linguistic difference. For an extended discussion of deafness and Deafness, see especially Davis, *Enforcing Normalcy: Disability, Deafness and the Body*; Brenda Jo Brueggemann, *Lend Me Your Ear: Rhetorical Constructions of Deafness*; and chapter 6 of G. Thomas Couser, *Recovering Bodies: Illness, Disability, and Life Writing*.

4. Because this technology generates a written sign that originates in a voice, it invests the written word with some of the qualities of orality. Dictation to another person also combines characteristics of oral and written communication. See Charles Lowe, "Speech Recognition: Sci-Fi or Composition," for a discussion of how speech recognition technology can influence the composition process, especially at the stage of invention. He suggests, for example, that the strategy of "freespeaking" might be more effective than "freewriting." Lowe predicts that this technology, while originally available primarily to people with disabilities, will become widely used for writing. My thanks to Patricia Dunn for sending me Lowe's interesting article.

5. G. Thomas Couser comments on another instance of collaborative authorship of a disability narrative, *Raise My Eyes to Say Yes* by Ruth Sienkiewicz-Mercer and Steven Kaplan. Sienkiewicz-Mercer has cerebral palsy and is unable to speak or write; because she was institutionalized for many years, she never received an education. Kaplan, a lawyer and disability rights advocate, writes the text based on communications with Sienkiewicz-Mercer mediated by a word board. Noting the considerable discrepancy between Sienkiewicz-Mercer's basic level of literacy and the fluent, educated voice of the narrative, Couser asserts that "in his desire to speak *for* her, Kaplan speaks *as* her in a way that may misspeak her," and asks: "What issues does collaboration raise in terms of the authority of the narrative and the authenticity of its voice?" ("*Signifying*," 114–15). While similar questions must be asked of *The Diving Bell and the Butterfly*, Bauby's literary career and self-conscious humor about being misspoken lend his narrative an authoritative voice. Bauby dedicates the book to his transcriber, Claude Mendibil, but she is not listed as a coauthor. See Couser's "Making, Taking, and Faking Lives: Ethical Problems in Collaborative Life Writing" for an extended discussion of collaborative autobiography.

6. Personal conversation with Mairs, 2000. Because she is no longer able to write manually, Mairs creatively employs a variety of technologies; for example, she signs books after a reading of her work by using an inkpad and a rubber stamp with her signature.

7. See Lennard J. Davis, *Enforcing Normalcy: Disability, Deafness, and the Body*, for a historical analysis of concepts of the norm and the normal body that has greatly influenced work in disability studies.

SUGGESTIONS FOR STUDENT ACTIVITIES

Material and Bodily Aspects of the Writing Process

As is often done in composition classrooms, ask students to map their own writing process and also to note the various technologies involved in the process and product of their written texts. For example, do they use a pencil, a special pen, a yellow or white legal pad, a typewriter, or a computer keyboard to compose? Do they talk into a tape recorder? Do they use a cell phone to instant message themselves writing ideas? Do they revise by hand or use a computer? Do they put their writing on the Web for a public audience? Then ask students to go one step further by also asking them to consider and discuss ways they might imagine adapting—changing, deleting, or adding to their writing process—if they could not complete one part of the process because of a change in their physical or mental state or health.

Writing the Body

Ask students to consider, discuss, and then write about how their writing (in act, process, and product) is connected to their bodies. How does one write *as* a body, *in* the body, *from* the body, *with* the body? How does the body matter in writing? Ask students to compare their findings with their reading experience (in this course or in general) for written texts in which the author expresses, in some way, his or her embodied, physical presence in the writing of the text.

Collaborative Writing

To explore the nature of *collaborative* writing when someone cannot "write" his or her story in a conventional sense (as highlighted in Lindgren's discussion of the memoir by Jean-Dominique Bauby), ask paired students to collaboratively compose a brief life narrative. One student would only be able to "tell" the story while the other would be the author, committing it to written text. Students could then discuss their observations about the issues they encountered surrounding this kind of "collaborative" writing: How well was their "told" story actually represented in writing? How did they feel about their own autonomy and authority in producing this written expression of their story—as written by another? How were their words, experiences, ideas, and tones enhanced, well-represented, or misrepresented?

7

"The Taming of the Sun": Finding the Joke in the Cancer Narrative of a Pedagogue

REBECCA KREFTING

Rebecca Krefting, a comedian, originally composed "The Taming of the Sun" as a stand-up comedy act that was intended to both educate and entertain multiple audiences at a cancer benefit: academic audiences (as a teaching narrative), cancer patients and survivors, their families, and doctors. She addresses the "exposure" of disability or illness (often confined to private or institutional places) in a public, but also institutional, space such as the college classroom. Her essay invites us to consider questions about the classroom as both a public and private space and the objective, disembodied authority of the teacher: What does it mean for students to "bear witness" to the reality of disease or disability as it affects their own, their teacher's, or each other's bodies in a classroom space? What changes, and what is challenged in the teacher's authority when he or she experiences disease, illness, impairment, or disability?

> The goal is to live a full, productive life even with all that ambiguity. No matter what happens, whether the cancer flares up again or whether you die, the important thing is that the days that you have had you will have lived.
>
> —GILDA RADNER, 1989

Deep in the poststructural heartland of representation, Ann Fox, disability theorist and playwright, notes in "But, Mother-I'm-Crippled!" that disability is/has been utilized as a dramaturgical tool in theater. She questions the authenticity of representations of disability in theater and television but appreciates that there are representations of disability at all, lest disability be rendered completely invisible. Similarly, Carrie Sandahl, performance artist, scholar, and author of "Queering the Crip or Cripping the Queer? Intersections of Queer and Crip Identities in Solo Autobiographical Performance" examines performance artists according to queer and crip cultures as well as the way in which they construct and claim their identities in front of the audience, such as their performance of queer or crip or both. She would argue that the performances of individuals are perhaps the *most* authentic and powerful medium of disability representation. Disability theorists such as Fox and Rosemarie Garland-Thomson have argued for some time that use of disability as a dramaturgical device undermines the authenticity of that experience and cashes in on popular but misleading rhetorical tropes such as wonder-awe, über-sentimentality, and the exotic. The critiques of such leitmotifs have done little to abate the frequency with which these types of representations are employed; therefore, live disability performance is vital to challenging erroneous and patronizing representations of disabled persons—that is, fostering the expression of legitimate self-constructed identities, unmediated/untampered with by societal ideations.

I began this endeavor by imagining myself telling a series of jokes that would, in effect, retell *my* story of skin cancer, for every person's experience of this will differ vastly based on their gender, race, sexuality, class, ability, and geophysical location. The previous sentence also begs closer analysis of the term "retell," the act of carefully constructing what aspects of the experience I choose to bring to bear. My authorship, or my authority to narrate, affords me the right to claim and frame my experience, and therein lies a great deal of power, a power that feminists have long struggled to legitimate in the academic sphere.

Including comedy in the piece was pointed and necessary. It becomes a means for me to educate and enlighten vis-à-vis laughter, affording me the catharsis of laughing at myself and my insecurities, as well as allowing me a modality to criticize/satirize medical institutions. Historically, humor has been deployed and employed mostly by men, often targeting women, sexual and racial minorities, and the disabled. My use of humor to undermine what could (and should?) have been a very negative experience topples traditional uses of humor and challenges the very notion of *how* I was supposed to experience skin cancer both then and retrospectively. Thus, humor is used as a tool of resistance, resistance to social constructions of medical dependency and patient passivity. Being able to evoke/command laughter places me in a position of power, a position uncharacteristic of someone dependent on the medical system, and allows me to direct the audience how to feel and experience this lengthy soliloquy.

In many ways my monologue is framed like Greg Walloch's *I'm Looking for Someone to Fuck the Disabled:* mine relies on similar methods of humorous interpretation and storytelling and also arises from multiple and intersecting marginalized identities, that is, queer female cancer survivor. Disability theorists conduct intersectional analyses of identity, because unlike other forms of marginalization, disability *always* intersects with race, class, sexuality, and gender. Like Walloch, I claim my queer identity, but unlike Walloch, instead of focusing on presenting a sexualized bodily difference, I focus on an aesthetic bodily difference (Sandahl, 37). This calls attention to many important issues, such as the tensions between able-bodiedness and impaired/infirm bodies and the movement from one space into another, respectively, and the cultural value placed on the body/beauty aesthetic. Additionally, the performance seeks to illumine power dynamics inherent in the doctor-patient relationship (the doctor as "knowing" and the patient as a trusting/passive recipient of that knowledge) and to trouble the relationship of instructor and student, creating important yet difficult questions about pedagogy—namely, How much does one reveal to students and at what cost?

References to teaching, throughout my piece, were made purposefully, to elucidate my own beliefs about the feminist pedagogue and the difficulties surrounding disclosure and personal testimony. What are the pedagogic ends/benefits to inviting your students to bear witness to your disability/impairment/illness and in what ways can this practice backfire? For example, during my undergraduate years, in a literature course, I watched as the students in the class harangued our professor for less work because he had been unable to be there for three or four classes. His father had died near the middle of the semester, and two weeks later his brother died. Based on my experiences as an instructor, I would suggest that issues of "weakness" and "dependency" be framed very carefully; however, surely this and the degree to which a teacher feels comfortable sharing with the class is largely contingent upon the group of students a teacher is dealing with.

Diana Herndl, cancer survivor and scholar, argues that teachers need to allow themselves the possibility/opportunity of presenting themselves more authentically, by modeling the postmodern fragmented selves we all are, rather than the quintessential monolithic instructor whose droning voice and superior wisdom is enough to make anyone find religion and begin praying for another Orwell or Huxley. For her, this authenticity would include honest updates about her health, since she is simultaneously undergoing chemotherapy alongside teaching. For me it meant allowing myself to reference the ongoing process of healing instead of feigning the absence of corporeality in the classroom. While my recovery seldom interfered with my "duties" as instructor, similar to Herndl's experience of cancer it prompted my desire to interpellate my dis-ease in order to foster class dialogue about what it means to be both in a position of authority (teacher) and one of corporeal vulnerability (in the form of visible facial disfigurement) and the effects it had on the students. As Herndl shows in her own classroom (the caveat being that that classroom is composed of graduate students), choosing to represent oneself realistically can be highly rewarding and beneficial for the exact same reasons that live disability performance remains vital to the disability community: it creates space for actual social relations based on shared truths, versus polite academic dishonesty that serves the institution(s), rather than the individuals. In my experience, expressing a desire to teach far outweighs any physical or health-related barriers to teaching "normally." Students want to know that you are invested in them, and they become more responsive when you illustrate that you are also invested in yourself; this models a healthy self-efficacy that better serves academic reciprocity by showing that you have more to offer when you keep your own integrity and love yourself, something that bell hooks calls "engaged pedagogy" (15). Inspired by the teaching of Thich Nhat Hanh, she believes that "teachers must be actively committed to a process of self-actualization that promotes their own well-being if they are to teach in a manner that empowers students" (15). Though there are no guarantees, it is this self-actualization that poses the best argument for why teachers should practice testifying to their humanness. In this way, this performance serves dual functions: It is an exercise in pedagogical testimony and it seeks to be an authentic representation of illness, a written testament to my being-ness.

THE PERFORMANCE

Stage Setting: A stool and a microphone (if necessary). The performance should be spoken, as if you were telling this story to an old friend you have not seen in a long time. You should be familiar and funny in your discussion of the events, and the words should feel natural, not forced.

I had this spot on my face, we'll call it a beauty mark—I always did—so my doctor referred me to a plastic surgeon, which was exciting because I've always wanted to go to a plastic surgeon . . . to get my boobs reduced, though, not a mole excavated. I was half-expecting one of the guys from *Nip/Tuck*, but my surgeon looked like he might do plastic surgery but he doesn't *DO* plastic surgery . . . if you know what I mean. He diagnosed me with having a "blue nevus" on my face, which actually sounds more like a car (or a rare plant or a rock) and not a type of mole—e.g., "Oh my . . . is that blue nevus yours (she says enviously)?" *(You can improvise here, just do whatever feels comfortable).*

After I had the blue nevus removed under local anesthetic I went to receive my results a few weeks later and was met by a student doctor who informed me that the biopsy results were malignant melanoma, which is the leading cause of death for skin cancer, but the least likely form of skin cancer to contract. I've never been lucky . . . and how can I think I am when the odds are that 1 in 82 women will get malignant melanoma of the skin. I'm still waiting on thank you cards from 81 other women who did not have to get melanoma. *(Sarcastically)* They should be coming in any day now. The chances of getting skin cancer are high, though, as skin cancer is the number one form of human cancer. Research shows that 1 in 5 Americans will get skin cancer, whether of the squamous, basal, or melanoma variety. Squamous and basal cell carcinoma are the most common variety, but rarely result in death. I was referred to an oncologist immediately, and handed several pages of diagnoses. I walked back to my office feeling . . . well I think that's all it was, just a sudden rush of feeling, like I was acutely aware of my alive-ness and of my mortality, like I had been sleeping and just awoke from a long nap. I ran into a student of mine as I made the trek from the hospital to University Hall, and all I could do was expel a rapid firing of questions. "How's school?" "How's the volleyball team going?" "Are you still friends with so and so?" "Am I still your favorite teacher?" "How much wood could a woodchuck chuck if a woodchuck could chuck wood?" This wasn't my time to begin challenging the idea of the persona of the feminist pedagogue, where I process my own subjectivity and then display it for my students. But I would eventually do just that with the class I was teaching, I just couldn't muster it at that moment.

Nothing really hit home until I called my partner of six years and realized that I couldn't say the word *cancer.* I kept saying, I have malignant melanoma . . . the malignant melanoma has progressed this far . . . the doctors recommend this for malignant melanoma. Like saying it suddenly meant it was true. According to the Jewish faith, specifically the teachings of the Mothers of the Dead, as long as you can pen someone's name, they will not leave this world. Instead of speaking in order to invoke someone to stay, I was staying silent, desperately longing for something to go. When I finally said the word *cancer* I began sobbing.

It's so hard, really, for a person to walk in on someone who is crying. It can be surreal, because you're just enjoying the day. You've had a tasty breakfast, you're pleased that you've managed to get to school, having successfully climbed the mini Mt. Everest stretching from the stadium to the Oval—hell, you might have had some real good sex the night before—and all of a sudden you walk right onto the set of *One Life to Live,* and the resident comic is getting cancer, and you think, "Damn, those writers are good!" *(Pause)* No one wants or expects the funny lady to cry, just like students don't expect their teachers to be anything but whole; but this is how my colleague found me, a watery mess, in the basement office.

My first visit to the oncologist was strange, because you have no point of reference for what is going to happen next. During physicals you know that the doctor is going to ask you to bend over or grab your nuts and cough (not me, I don't have nuts . . . I'm just saying). I had no idea what was in store for me, but in retrospect I think it was better this way . . . because there really isn't any good literature on the market that prepares one for an anal exam. Perhaps after sharing this experience with enough people, this will in fact change. I have some beginning ideas for pamphlet titles. The pre-exam brochure could be called "Explorations of the Deep: Asking the Right Questions." There would also be literature for the post-anal-exam patient, called "Working toward a Rebuttal." My oncologist came in the examination room with a cadre of other people (nurses, student doctors, interns, radiologists, cafeteria workers, and some reporters from Fox, which didn't surprise me in the least . . . 'cuz they're notorious for not covering any real news and what they do cover is usually shit). You'd think I was the only person with malignant melanoma they had ever seen. I joked about charging admission, but golly those medical people don't laugh at anything!! When the doctor said he was on the lookout for unusual moles, I said, "Hey, I may be strange, but I am no double agent, my friend." That's when he reached for the KY Jelly and told me to relax. Here I was essentially starring in a low-budget porn flick, let's call it *Doctor Down in My Delta,* but not being paid and surrounded by strangers, and I'm *supposed to relax.* The least they could have done is provide a little foreplay; a little nipple tweak would have done the job.

The oncologist informed me that surgery was necessary, and since the malignant melanoma had unusually rapid cell growth he was concerned that the cancer had moved into my lymph system, so he needed to find the nearest lymph site and excise several sentinel lymph nodes in order to determine whether the cancer had moved that far. It was not lost on me that the nomenclature of the body was closely aligned with war terminology. I sure did hope that my lymph nodes standing sentry were getting paid enough to fight hard, because if the cancer was in my lymph system I would begin the arduous and debilitating process of radiation and chemotherapy, but the long-term prognosis wasn't good ... most patients with systemic malignant melanoma don't live more than five years. I scheduled the surgery for the middle of June, fitting it neatly between quarters, so that I could still teach and take classes that summer. I scheduled it like I would a dentist appointment and most of the time tried to think of it as little more than just that. The possibility of what *could* be nagged at me, as did the knowledge that my face would never be the same after this surgery. It made me angry because I don't think I would have cared half as much if that cancer were anywhere else on my body. But it was on my face. My face. My face ... that I look at every day, that everyone can see, that was my most beautiful feature, that I use to make people laugh, not to be laughed at. I remember thinking to myself, take my hip, take my arm, take my breast (lord knows my back would thank you) ... but don't take my profile ... don't take my face.

The day of the surgery came faster than I would have liked ... but isn't that how things work? You can't get an orgasm to last more than a minute, but a month can pass in the blink of an eye. I wasn't allowed to drink anything the whole day before the surgery. I was so thirsty that dirty puddles looked refreshing. My procedure began hours after the time they told me it would, and I was concerned because I really wanted to be done in time to watch *Last Comic Standing*. I closed my eyes, and when I opened them again I was in the recovery room and I had just vomited all over myself. I guess they don't want you to have water for a reason ... but that puddle was just so inviting. I couldn't speak, so in order to indicate that I was okay I periodically flipped off the hospital staff, which I think they understood was a sensitive gesture, considering the circumstances.

For all my whining and pleading to be able to watch *Last Comic Standing*, I couldn't keep my eyes open to watch the show. Instead I slipped into a dreamlike fugue where I was the last comic standing, but I didn't have a face, rather a paper bag over my head. I think someone's already done that bit, though. The first time I went to the bathroom, my partner deftly navigated me back to bed. The second time, I stopped and looked at myself in the mirror while she tried to steer me away from that glass that would tell me the truth about how I looked. I looked in the mirror but couldn't find myself, just a haggard, sliced-up version of my face. I began crying, tears wetting my fresh incision, and didn't resist when my mom and partner moved me back to the bed. I didn't look at myself in the mirror for days after the surgery. I brushed my teeth and conducted my daily hygiene with downcast eyes, averted away from the inevitable. When I did look at my incision it was with clinical eyes, separating the incision from the rest of my face, in order to dab ointment or clean between the 58 stitches that traveled from my right eye across my cheek, around my ear, and down my neck. I couldn't feel my right ear or the right side of my face. My doctor said it would be a year or two before I would experience full sensation in those areas.

Five days after surgery, I began getting ready to teach my first day of class for the summer session. Despite my mother's misgivings about me working during the summer, I was resolved to continue life as usual. I slipped into my standard black skirt that I wear every first day of class and donned an airy purple shirt. I moved to the mirror to put on my pearl necklace and matching earrings, and my hands shook as I tried to grasp my nonfeeling ear lobe, slippery from the Neosporin I put around my ear three times a day. I stepped back and looked at myself—really looked at myself—how I imagined my students would see me. My face swollen and stained with the blue surgical dye they use to prep for surgery, my eyes black and blue from the anesthetic, my cheek tessellated with stitches that looked like a trail of black spiders walking across my face, and my right ear now higher than the other . . . and I began to weep. I cried for the physical beauty I believed I no longer had; I cried for my dream of becoming a famous comic; I cried for the gawking and staring I knew was mine to experience; I cried for my partner who loves me no matter what but who I knew would have to learn to love a different face; and I cried with relief, because I had gotten a phone call two days before . . . and found out that I was going to live.

It's been ten months since then, and some things have changed. I began dieting and have lost thirty-seven pounds. I exercise regularly and am eating food and using products that are anticarcinogenic. It's hard to get excited about carrot juice and flaxseed oil . . . but I manage to. If you see me walking around campus you'll probably notice me wearing a hat, sunglasses, and long-sleeve shirts. If you come close enough to hug me or kiss my cheek, you'll smell the sweet medicinal smell of sunscreen that I wear as a uniform these days. I see myself in the mirror every day, even talk to myself in the mirror, but I never avert my eyes anymore, because I like what I see—the puckered pink skin healing and smoothing out—it's still *my* beauty mark. I've been told it's my badge of courage, but I don't feel courageous . . . just eternally grateful. Someone asked me if I was angry at the sun, because it caused my cancer. I thought about it, and although some days it seems to be my adversary, beating down, leaving no room for shade, no corner not brilliant with its light, in a way it is also my ally, my friend, my high noon lover, because the sun touched me, caressed me, sang sweet nothings into *my* crooked ear. The sun kissed my face and I'm still here.

REFLECTING ON YOUR TEACHING

Exploring the Personal and Public Space of the Classroom

In what ways is the classroom a "personal" space? In what ways is it public? In a whole-class exercise, students might be asked to list observations—behaviors, beliefs, examples, interactions—that document how the classroom is *private* or *personal* and also how it is *public* or *institutional*. (They might divide themselves in half to construct these lists.) Compare your students' findings with how you, the instructor, use the space. Are you and your students perceiving the same use of space or different uses of space? How do your students' perceptions affect how you see your use of space?

Exploring Authority and Disability

In another exercise with students, the *authority* of the teacher might also be considered. What behaviors are expected of the teacher "as an authority" or as the leader of the class experience? How might these behaviors change or shift when a student or the teacher experiences disability, illness, or disease? (In considering such a question, students should be encouraged to think not just about the negative, all that is lost or "deleted," but also about what might be gained, added, innovatively revised, and so forth.) Students could also expand this exercise to consider the authority and ability deemed inherent in anyone who holds a given job or career position: doctor, lawyer, CEO, athlete, cook, parent, car salesman, artist, and so forth. It might be interesting to create cards with a number of different "occupations" or "roles" on them and let students each pick one and then discuss these in small groups. How would being "disabled" change, enhance, detract from, revise, shift, or supplement these positions? Discuss possible adaptations and accommodations to jobs that could be made.

SUGGESTION FOR STUDENT ACTIVITY

Exploring Humor and Disability

As another form of "adaptation" that is common in human behavior, students might be invited to discuss and explore further the possibilities of humor in disability. Do they know of jokes, cartoons, sitcoms, and so forth where disability is used "comically"? Can they analyze the structure and function of such "comic" representations of disability? Do they know of any other humorous approaches to disability that are, in fact, offered by people with disabilities themselves? If so, they might compare these with the more mainstream media's "comic" representations of disability. How can humor function effectively in relation to disability? Who can author disability humor? Such questions could make for an excellent in-class "debate" as students discuss, develop, and illustrate the benefits and drawbacks, the pros and cons, of making disability "funny." Students might also go online and look at the disability humor of writer and teacher Sharon Wachsler at www.sharonwachsler.com or disability cartoonist John Callahan at www.callahanonline.com/index.php. Also see Callahan's book *Don't Worry, He Won't Get Far on Foot*. After conducting research, students could write an analytic and reflective paper on disability humor.

8

Reflections on Writing and Teaching Disability Autobiography

GEORGINA KLEEGE

Georgina Kleege, a writer with a disability, a college teacher, and an author, uses disability autobiography and the teaching of disability autobiography to address issues that are central to disability activism and the field of disability studies. In the following teaching narrative, Kleege explores the many attitudes, interactions, reactions, and discussions that developed around disability autobiography in a course she taught at the University of California, Berkeley. Disability was part of both the course content (its subject) and the course form (its daily processes), and during the course, two common disability-related themes emerged: access and identity. Kleege exposes and explores the nuanced and complicated nature of disability identity as it is connected to the complex nature of "access." Who is and isn't disabled? How should and shouldn't one behave as disabled (and, likewise, as able-bodied)? Who represents whom when disability is involved? All of these questions and more occur in the interactions among students in a class where disability and writing are at the center of the syllabus.

The standard charge activists and scholars make against disability autobiographies is that they reinforce cultural stereotypes and hinder social change. These texts, such critics argue, perpetuate the notion that disability is a personal tragedy that happens to an individual rather than a set of cultural structures and practices that affect many individuals. As a writer and reader of disability autobiography, I believe it is possible to use one's personal experiences to comment on the culture one inhabits. I do not intend here, however, to defend or condemn specific authors or works or to debate the value of these texts as a facet of a social-change movement. I offer instead an impressionistic account of a course on disability autobiography that I taught at Berkeley recently. What stands out in my memory of the course has to do less

From *Publication of the Modern Language Association* 120, no. 2 (March 2005): 606–10.

with students' responses to particular texts and more with interactions among the students or between the students and me that often seemed peripheral to the topic at hand. This is, then, an autobiographical essay, a series of vignettes and portraits, rendered in all the randomness of lived experience. But it will, I hope, raise issues that are central to disability activism and disability studies.

The class was an upper-division English course and was cross-listed for credit in the disability studies minor. The students were mostly juniors and seniors majoring in English except for two majoring in psychology, two in political science, and one in film studies. Two or three students were minoring in disability studies. The texts I assigned were *The Story of My Life*, by Helen Keller; *Moving Violations*, by John Hockenberry: *Waist-High in the World*, by Nancy Mairs; *Past Due: A Story of Disability, Pregnancy, and Birth*, by Anne Finger; *Reflections: The Life and Writings of a Young Blind Woman in Post-revolutionary France*, by Thérèse-Adèle Husson; *The Little Locksmith*, by Katherine Butler Hathaway; *Autobiography of a Face*, by Lucy Grealy; and *Thinking in Pictures*, by Temple Grandin. I chose these books because they represented a range of time periods and of impairment categories. But, in all honesty, I chose these titles because at the time I had to submit the reading list that was to appear in the course listings; these were all books that I knew were readily available in alternative formats, specifically as books on tape produced by Recordings for the Blind and Dyslexic and the National Library Service for the Blind and Physically Handicapped. I did this for the convenience of me and any students with print disabilities who might enroll. Berkeley, like other institutions, has a disabled-students program that produces alternative-format texts for students who need them. But since I was new at the university, I did not know how well the program worked. I wanted to be sure that students who needed alternative formats would be able to obtain them, on their own if they chose, even before the semester began.

I prepared for the course with an extra level of trepidation. This was my first class at the university. I had never taught any of the assigned texts or taught autobiography as a genre. In addition to these typical new-course jitters, I was having a hard time obtaining the access accommodations I had requested. Despite Berkeley's history as the birthplace—or one of the birthplaces, anyway—of the independent-living movement, I heard repeatedly that it had been a long time since the university had hired a faculty member with a disability. The system in place was equipped to handle faculty and staff members who had recently acquired disabilities but not those who had been disabled a long time and who were expert on what accommodations were necessary. After months of phone calls, e-mail messages, and visits to various offices, the access I had requested was only approved a couple of weeks before the semester started, leaving me feeling rattled and resentful.

And so the semester began. On the first day, a student used the phrase "people who suffer from disabilities." I opted not to correct or challenge him because I didn't want to begin the semester flashing the badge of the language police. I couldn't tell if any of the disabled students in the room responded to his use of *suffer*. And I sensed from his labored delivery that he was self-conscious because his professor and several of his classmates were visibly disabled. He was struggling, aware that whatever term he used might be the wrong one.

As it turned out, he was struggling with more than language. Later in the semester, he disclosed that he had been recently diagnosed with a learning disability. Also, he was a recovering alcoholic. He said he had heard that some people consider alcoholism a disability, though he was uncertain about this. Still later, during a class visit by Anne Finger, he admitted that he identified with her descriptions of hospital practices because he had once undergone reconstructive surgery after having his "face rearranged in a barroom brawl," as he put it.

Later in the first week, a student came to my office to tell me that she had a learning disability and to discuss accommodation issues. I was impressed with her poise as she delivered this information. I confess I became a bit misty-eyed with the recognition that the disability rights movement had made a measurable difference within even this student's memory. It was not so long ago that someone with her impairment would not have been admitted to an institution such as Berkeley or that someone with my impairment would not have been employed as her professor. In the rapid-fire delivery with which she brought up the subject, I heard an echo of my former student self, back in the dimly remembered past when I had similar conversations with my professors. In my day, however, these conversations had a different aim. I was there to persuade them that they should not dismiss me out of hand, that although I had a disability I could still perform up to par, and that I would not ask for or expect any sort of special treatment.

I made a comment along these lines to the student. She said that while she was an old hand at talking to her professors about her impairment, it was easier to talk to a professor with a disability who was teaching a disability-related class, implying that in other classes and with other professors, this conversation was not always so comfortable.

Perhaps things have not advanced as far as I'd like to think?

Other students with disabilities were not having as smooth an experience. A student told me that she wanted to take the class but was having trouble enrolling, for a reason she did not immediately disclose. One day when I asked her how the process was going, she burst into tears. Her enrollment problems stemmed from the fact that she had dropped out of school the previous semester, because of chronic depression. Apparently, the assistant dean she saw refused to grant her a medical leave, refused to discuss her situation as a disability issue, and even refused to look her in the eye. For all I know, there may have been extenuating circumstances that the student did not reveal to me. She petitioned another dean and was eventually able to enroll. Still, her unpleasant encounter with the bureaucracy resonated too closely with my own protracted effort to obtain access for me to dismiss it as a random glitch in the system.

In class, we were reading Helen Keller's *The Story of My Life* as reissued by Roger Shattuck. It is an important new edition that restores material out of print for decades, but Shattuck's introduction begins this way:

> Helen was born a swan—fair-haired and fair-faced, without blemish or impediment, giving back as much joy to the world as she found in it. Then, before she learned to talk, an illness changed her into an ugly duckling. Her appearance did not substantially change. She did not become ugly. She became totally deaf and blind. That was enough to turn the swan into an uncontrollable creature who lost her world, her home, and her family to inner silence and darkness. Several years later another creature, this one half-blind, turned the ugly duckling back into a swan by holding her hand and teaching her a secret finger language. (ix)

Some students were appalled. "He calls them creatures," one said. "Sign language is not a secret," another pointed out. A third student, who referred to herself as the consummate English major, complained that "first he says one thing, then another. If you wrote something like that in an English class, the professor would be all over you." I always enjoy the image of English professors as avenging harpies, ready to eviscerate users of imprecise prose. But I was also pleased that these students, even at the beginning of the course, were able to identify the ableist attitude behind Shattuck's description. It allowed us to talk about Keller's enduring status as an icon and to examine the extent to which she promoted this thinking in her life writing.

Colleagues elsewhere had warned me that students often find John Hockenberry's *Moving Violations* off-putting for his rather aggressive style. My students found him at first a relief from Helen Keller. But in the second class they were personally affronted by his reasons for not enrolling in Berkeley in the early 1980s. He said that the campus was so accommodating to students with disabilities—he described it as merely "a sunny California sanitarium" (114)—that the education there must be substandard. This prompted me to ask what they knew about the history of the independent-living movement on the Berkeley campus. The disability studies minors provided a detailed account, but most of the class admitted they had never heard this history. Most students at Berkeley today are probably unaware of the history of the free-speech movement as well. My difficulties with obtaining accommodations and my student's dealings with the dean she perceived as unreceptive made the discussion of the independent-living movement a bit hard to take. On the one hand, I was pleased to think that students might draw some college pride from this history. On the other hand, I was all too aware of the risk that pride can turn to complacency and inaction.

At the end of our second class discussing Nancy Mairs's collection of essays *Waist-High in the World*, a student announced that he found Mairs to be nothing but a whiner. He was a student with a disability who had sought special permission to take the class because he was enrolled in another institution. He had, however, only been to class twice. After he made his remark, the rest of the class was utterly silent. I suspect they looked shocked, but I could not tell. When he came to class, he tended to interrupt and challenge anyone who spoke, and he often patronized the other disabled students in ways that offended everyone. He was hostile toward every text we read, particularly Lucy Grealy's *Autobiography of a Face,* an account of childhood cancer and facial disfigurement that paralleled his life story. As I learned later, he was writing his own autobiography. The other students perceived him as an outsider and griped about him when he wasn't there, though, as one admitted, discussions were always rowdier when he was present.

In the next class, three students did a detailed and minute analysis of some of Mairs's arguments. In one case, they took her to task for what they thought was a dismissive attitude about people with learning disabilities. Another criticized her for disparaging the idea that many people with disabilities would not seek a cure, because they perceived their impairments as integral to their identities. I sensed that even in their criticism of Mairs they were defending her against the blanket charge that she was nothing but a whiner. They were asserting that she engaged them intellectually and emotionally, even though they could not agree with everything she wrote. They admired her, not for overcoming but for articulating complex issues that were important in their own lives.

In many ways, the most challenging text we read was Temple Grandin's *Thinking in Pictures.* She is a person with autism who earned a PhD in animal science and works as a college professor and a designer of humane slaughterhouses. One student admitted that she did not find the author very likable since Grandin was always talking about herself and boasting of her accomplishments. I pointed out that it was perhaps in the nature of autobiographers to talk about themselves and asked if Grandin was less likable than, say, John Hockenberry. This launched a lively discussion of social behavior and the extent to which it is innate or learned. A student who had never spoken in class before said that Grandin made her think about how many social practices are founded on a notion of so-called normal personality traits. Some weeks earlier, during a conference about her paper, this student had described herself as pathologically shy and tentatively suggested that being so put her at a disadvantage in a course such as mine, where class participation was evaluated for part of the grade. Her comment in class reminded me of this conversation and also of the student with the disruptive personality who had called Nancy Mairs a whiner.

Two themes recur in all these anecdotes. The first has to do with access. Throughout the semester, I was struck again and again by the constant ebb and flow of this social-change movement. On the one hand, here I was teaching a course in disability autobiography at a major research university. On the other hand, issues of access, my own and my students', kept cropping up. Access needs to be at the forefront of our consciousness and our conversation as disability scholars and advocates. It needs to be on our minds in the way we compose a reading list, the way we conduct our classes, the way we evaluate our students. Although being disability studies scholars does not make us access specialists, I believe we cannot cede responsibility for access to specialists or accept without question others' prescriptions about who needs access and what kinds of access are appropriate.

The other theme that emerges from these reflections has to do with disability identity. Anyone who teaches literature is accustomed to the ways students tend to identify with people they read about. This may be especially true when we teach autobiography, where the development of the author's identity is often central to the text. In this class, the texts we read and the interactions we had in the classroom seemed to prompt some students to contemplate or to embrace a disability identity for the first time. For these students, identification emerged from a new scrutiny of the world around them, including the built environment and academic and social practices. In the disability community and the culture at large, people hotly debate the definition of disability. Are such conditions as shyness, addiction, and depression legitimate disabilities? This debate can fuel a reactionary backlash in which it is argued that since everyone has a trait that can be perceived as a disability in certain contexts, we are all disabled, and therefore no measures to accommodate anyone need to be taken. Over their lifetimes, our students will witness an evolution in this debate that I can only begin to imagine. The ways that they identify these issues as relevant, even central, to their own lives or the lives of their peers will press the debate beyond the reductive binary of disabled versus nondisabled and continue to exert pressure on the barriers to inclusion. And some of them will, I hope, write their own autobiographies, to be read and discussed by the next generation.

SUGGESTIONS FOR STUDENT ACTIVITIES

Investigating Access

What is access in relation to disability/ies? Students can take up this important question—which is also central to Kleege's essay—in several ways. They might conduct research, either online or in person at their campus offices for disability services, to discover what some common accommodations and forms (as well as issues) of access are in college classrooms for various kinds of disabilities. Students might be broken into smaller groups, and each group could be in charge of a certain "kind" of disability for this research. More personally, they might draft out their typical daily or weekly schedule—classes, work, activities, social events, where they go, when they do this or that, who they do it with, and so forth. Then they could imagine themselves as a student with a disability (sensory, physical, cognitive, learning, psychological, etc.) and add on an "access" layer to this draft: What is "accessible" or not? Why or how is it accessible or not? How could it be made more accessible?

Exploring Disability Identity

Students might be invited to explore the intricacies of disability identity in a number of ways as well. Using two large columns (on the chalkboard, whiteboard, paper, or PowerPoint slide) they might jot down ways to answer the questions: What *is* (a) disability? What is not (a) disability? It might be useful in such an exercise to begin with the reporter's standard questioning rubric: who, what, where, when, why, how? As students begin to develop the complexities in such a seemingly straightforward question, they can also carry it another step further by adding the questions, Who gets to "name" disability? Who can "claim" disability? Students who are interested could develop this inquiry into a research paper by examining the official terms of the Americans with Disabilities Act and related Supreme Court cases since its passage in 1990 that focus on defining who qualifies as "disabled" under the act.

Seeing Disability Identity

Another angle of disability identity might be explored by asking each student individually to generate a list of ten famous people they know who had a disability. Then let the individuals work in small groups to create a larger "master" list and to discuss their criteria, their common points, and what they learned from each other. The entire class can then also create a class list, although they should also be encouraged to explore the limits of their lists. Because many will struggle to come up with a list of ten famous people, ask students to explore why they cannot generate the list. What about our society keeps us from "seeing" disability? Where do you see and not "see" people with disabilities? Does their disability help or hinder their "famous" designation?

9

Teaching by Ear

STEPHEN KUUSISTO

As Stephen Kuusisto describes how he blends his listening experiences "on the street" with those he enacts (and encourages his students to enact) in his writing classrooms, he uncovers just how much of his teaching is a hearing occupation. Connecting the act and art of listening to the acts of memory, imagination, and "leverage" (the art of influence), he offers scenes from his own creative writing classrooms and his "real life" to illustrate these points. Kuusisto's essay reminds us of how disability can actually enhance teaching and classroom experiences and how, as literary and cultural studies critic Lennard Davis has argued, it can serve as a critical and experiential insight.

Igor Stravinsky once said, "To listen is an effort, and just to hear is no merit. A duck hears also." I love Stravinsky's remark because I'm a blind teacher of writing, and I strive to be better than a duck where listening is concerned. Teaching is often an auditory occupation. We listen for the nuances in a student's question, we learn his or her personal vocabulary, we hope to answer with insight and imagination.

Blindness changes how I listen in the classroom. Listening in class is similar to walking in traffic. My ears are vital to my mobility. Walking in New York City I notice that the wind says I've arrived within a few meters of a cross street. This is important because the cross street may be Eighth Street— a dangerous sluice of traffic that I must cross as I head south on Fifth Avenue. The wind, which always blows from the west, gives me my first sign. I have arrived at the street, and as my dog guide "Miss Corky" stops at the curb I must listen again. It's not enough to know that I'm where I want to be—even a duck can do this. Now I must listen through the masking wind and hear what the traffic is doing. The corner of Fifth Avenue and Eighth Street is an anomaly: wind pours from west to east, and as it moves through gaps between the buildings it produces a form of white noise and the sound of traffic vanishes as if by magic.

The first time I noticed this I was in fact walking and listening like a duck. I was going south on Fifth and eavesdropping as I walked, a kind of pleasurable activity when you're blind. Two students from NYU, both women, were talking about jazz. They had gone to the Blue Note to hear the famed Oscar Peterson. They had grown up on Madonna, but now they were grooving and stretching and I was happy to be hearing about it. Walking with a dog guide, you can do this sort of thing. Corky watches the world and takes evasive action—the dog anticipates the kid on roller blades and pulls her blind partner a few steps to the right. She sees there isn't enough room between a trash can and the adjacent parking meter to allow both of us to move ahead. So she finds another route. And the blind traveler begins to listen to the crowd. One can think of this as the auditory equivalent of people watching. And then Corky stops short. We're at the curb. She's trained to stop for street crossings. We stand together in the white noise of the wind. I think about Oscar Peterson and how he used to accompany Ella Fitzgerald. I remember Ella singing "Angel Eyes," and I tell Corky to go forward. This is my job as one-half of the dog-man team. I'm supposed to listen at the curb. The dog watches the traffic. I follow the flow of cars, and when I think things are safe I give the command to go. I'm thinking of "Angel Eyes" and Ella's dulcet "almost" whisper at the end of the song and Oscar Peterson's understated piano coming in for just a few bars. I say "forward" because I hear no traffic whatsoever.

What happens next is clear-cut: Corky pulls me backward and I feel a rush of air across my face. Then I hear the roar of a crosstown bus. The dog has saved my life. The dog is trained in a form of observation known as "intelligent disobedience": she knows that my commands must be evaluated and on occasion even disobeyed. I am alive because of this.

The street corner hides its traffic sounds. Who knew? But what if I approach the same corner with active ears? Is the situation the same? After my adrenaline is sufficiently lowered, I walk around the block and reapproach the same street corner. The wind is astonishing in both its force and its absolute efficiency at blocking the sounds of cars and buses and delivery trucks. I stand for a few minutes on the east side of Fifth Avenue on the north side of Eighth Street and listen with what I can only call reverence. Perhaps this is what Stravinsky means by "effort"—one is listening beyond the narrow coil of easy expectations. One is listening because in a very real sense one's life or future life may depend on what one discovers. And what I discover is that the wind has three distinct auditory characteristics. Who knew?

The big wind kills traffic noise. The whole world sounds like flags in a hurricane. The wind rips through the openings between the brownstones, and it is surely a god, as the Greeks well knew.

Under the big wind is a funny effect—I call it the durational absentmindedness of wind—for whole moments the wind doesn't exactly stop, but it changes direction, and when it does you hear everything in the city with absolute clarity. In addition to the trucks you hear the bicycle delivery men—you hear the chains of their bikes and the gritty noise of gears. You hear the clatter of a loose manhole cover as a bus strikes it. You hear a woman laughing on the far side of Fifth Avenue—she is a mezzo-soprano, loud and high and laughing enough to beat the band. And then she's gone. The world of things in motion has once again been swallowed by the wind.

The last trick of the wind is the most ingenious of them all. The wind can transmit sounds or echoes if it wants to. Between the white noise and my own pulse I can hear electric lines and something metallic clattering and something that sounds like an oboe, and of course I'll never know what this is. Nevertheless, the wind carries fragments of noise from far places like an absentminded uncle who doesn't remember what's in his old suitcase.

So I've learned that the business of listening has acoustic subcategories that are easy to miss. And I know that I am alive despite the fact that I was duck walking and duck listening one morning in New York. Archimedes said, "Give me a place to stand and I will move the earth." He was of course referring to his own discovery of leverage. In my own case a place to stand allows me the chance to listen with better appreciation, and this, too, is a kind of leverage. *Leverage* means "influence." Listening can be the art of influence, and nowhere is this more true than in the classroom.

That I've learned how to teach by learning how to walk and listen isn't surprising. Poets walk. The meters of poetry derive from the sounds of walking or running feet. Myth, or "mythos," as the Greeks called it, is the breath of the runner. The Greek runners listened because they ran at night and carried the news from one city to another. When I teach writing I aim to teach students about imagination and the sounds of their own words. I hope they will sense the fragile and often unheard music in their use of language. I want them to hear this in the writing of others and to find it in their own poems and stories. I try to help them learn how to listen as I do—to listen as if it matters.

My classes are conducted in a workshop format. Fifteen college students sit around a table and learn something about listening by learning how to talk about each other's work. They want to write about their lives. So I say to them, "Do you know that every time you remember something from your past you are really just remembering the last time you remembered it?" Two young women who always sit together are suddenly confused. "Isn't the past just like a photograph?" one of them says. I want them to listen beneath the wind. I say, "Have you ever gone back to the house of your childhood or to a room that was significant to you when you were small?" Everybody has done this. "How does it look when you see it again? Is it the same size?" It's never the same size. The rooms of childhood are always impossibly small when we revisit them. "But it looked so big," says a woman three chairs to my left, "That house was huge, and when I went back to Wisconsin last year I saw it was like a toy house."

Someone wants to know which house is the "real" house? There's a growing sense of discomfort—it's as if we were arguing that the senses are incorrect when we say that we see the sun rising. It's as though I've told the class the sun is a product of the imagination. We merely believe in its existence. Memories are merely imaginative propositions. The past is what we believe right now. What can we do?

I tell my students that you can prove the existence of the sun without photographing it. I tell them that you can calculate mathematically when an eclipse will occur. They all nod. (Because I can't see them I have to ask if they're nodding. They are nodding. They laugh.) We know from mathematics that the sun exists. The life of memory can also be subjected to careful analysis. We are now talking about the human ability—one of the great tricks of imaginative life—to see ourselves as characters in a play. We can be in the audience watching how we've negotiated the past. We can see that the old self doesn't know as much about the world as the new self does. And writing autobiography introduces these two selves to each other. Both of them are right when they see the house in Wisconsin. It was for the child a genuine castle. It was a sad sight for the grown girl. What does this mean? I keep asking questions, bouncing them around the room. "It means the grown girl has more memories than the girl," says one young man. He is listening now.

What I'm after in the classroom is to help students see that the imagination is really not so different from listening in the dark. And that the more carefully we listen, the more we sense is there, or was always there. The photograph is never interesting enough to stand for the past. The past, at least at first, is as blank as that wind on the corner of Fifth and Eighth. But then you slow things down and find complications and matters have changed.

I ask students to think about their earliest memories and encourage them to go below their stored visual impressions to remember the sounds as well. There was a whistling top that spun across a table. There were grandparents who spoke a different language and who sang sometimes. There was the sound of tires on gravel when your father came home. There was a mockingbird who sometimes became your only friend. Listen to memory and it rewards you. The past becomes richer.

As the semester progresses I learn how to hear the personal habits of expression in each student. I'll ask them if they meant something else when a sentence appears opaque to the class. Suddenly the student is off, telling a quick story about how that impenetrable sentence fell onto the page. Someone did something to someone else and a funny thing happened and for some reason it got left out of the essay. The student was duck-listening when he was typing. He forgot that the past and the imagination are fuller than we are tempted to believe at first. "You can open that paragraph up and put a whole scene in there," I tell him. And I point out that sentences that defy sense are always the shorthand left behind by the mind that has stopped paying attention.

In my life, listening and then listening again have become a method. I try to bring this to the study of writing by having my students listen to what they're saying in the classroom and more notably, have them listen once more to what they think they've heard from their private lives. In the blind world we call this revisiting of attention "orientation and mobility."

REFLECTING ON YOUR TEACHING

Oral and Auditory Practices

Patricia Dunn has argued in *Talking, Sketching, Moving* that writing teachers may overprivilege written texts in ways that do not help all learners. Kuusisto suggests that writing teachers could profitably add an oral and auditory dimension to their usual practices. Consider asking students not only to read their drafts aloud but to memorize and recite moving passages from assigned reading and their own compositions. Teachers might consider incorporating options for oral journals (as Dunn recommends). Another activity is to have students orchestrate a choral performance of their writing: each student chooses a line from his or her own paper. Then, working in small groups, students arrange their lines into stanzas. As a class, they work out an arrangement of all the parts and make a choral presentation of their writing, as an oral "musical" collage.

Universally (Re)Designing for All Learners

The above activities, which are focused around the sense of hearing, can be exclusionary for a deaf student. Can you rethink each activity using alternative senses (for example, exercises using touch) that would include deaf or hard-of-hearing class members and still achieve the same goal—to encourage learning through different bodily pathways?

SUGGESTIONS FOR STUDENT ACTIVITIES

My Life by Ear

Students could be asked to write their own short, descriptive passages or essays that focus on and feature auditory "images:" my room by ear; my roommate by ear; my family by ear; my Sunday morning by ear; a workout at my gym by ear; swimming by ear; my coffee shop by ear, and so forth. They could also enter memory and imagination, as Kuusisto suggests in this essay, by writing a passage about some place or scene in the past that they remember and bringing it forward via auditory description.

Students could also be encouraged to listen to a common event—taping their classroom, or an event they attend, for example—and then asked to write an observation and analysis of the sound of that particular place, event, or moment. No doubt it will be interesting to the students to compare (and contrast) their auditory "memory" and description of the shared event. What do some hear that others do not? Why?

10 The Ways We Disclose: When Life-Writing Becomes Writing Your Life

WENDY CHRISMAN

Wendy Chrisman reflects on the mutual responsibilities and bonds between teacher and student when self-disclosure occurs in a writing class. Chrisman narrates an instance in which a student writes about cutting. "I am immediately alert," she writes. "One reason I know this is that my background is in disability studies and critical theory, with a focus on mental health disorders. But I also know this because of my own 'invisible' disabilities, or disorders, and my own lengthy interactions with the mental health field and its practitioners." Chrisman uses a conference to gently convey her understanding to the student and to let her decide how much she wishes to confide. One conference leads to a series of conferences, and Chrisman's disclosure to her student of her own disorders allows them to share information, such as how to find the right doctor, fill out forms, and ask questions. When the student has a full-blown panic attack at Chrisman's office near the end of term and says she cannot go to the emergency room alone, Chrisman offers to go with her. To help calm her while they wait, Chrisman suggests that she write in detail about the episode, the hospital, the doctors. While teachers are not therapists, Chrisman concludes that her self-disclosure not only helped her student through a traumatic experience, it also helped her write therapeutically about a "vital" personal experience.

Disclosure. Perhaps this is a misnomer for the experiences that transpire between my students and me when one of us breaks that fragile bond between educator and pupil, authority figure and someone looking to be authorized. Because something indeed breaks. Narratives of trauma or personal tragedy always rupture the seams of a heretofore "normal" class. And once the narrative begins, the listener must always wonder, "Will there ever be closure?" while the teller must always wonder, "Whatever did I open?" Or, is it the other way around?

From *Lore: An E-Journal for Teachers of Writing.* www.bedfordstmartins.com/lore-sp03/ stairwell/content.htm?dis11

I am "officially" (though invisibly) disabled and therefore carry my disability to class every time I teach, and sometimes my personal life spills out as I stand talking in front of the class or during a conference with a student. And like silent radar, many of my students find my class a place to disclose their own personal narratives: narratives of tragedy, disability, and trauma; stories they've kept inside, tales not told only for want of a listener.

I was teaching a section of English 367.01: The American Experience at The Ohio State University—the class also functions as a "social diversity" requirement for OSU undergrads—to a class of twenty-four students. I subtitled the course "From the Margins to the Center: A Multicultural Look at America," and used Sheena Gillespie and Robert Singleton's *Across Cultures: A Reader for Writers.* The first set of readings we covered engaged the students in thinking about how our choices about race, gender, sexuality, class, disability, and so on, affect our lives, our families and friends, and beyond. Once they have submitted their first drafts, I leaf through the expected essays about being a part of multilingual families, bridging economic hardships, and coming out to friends and families. Then I come to one entitled "You Think I Won't Cut You? Cuz I'll Cut Me!" and I am immediately alert. I know that this is not a violent threat, but rather the work of a cutter—literally, someone who cuts herself as a means to control pain externally when she cannot control internal functions.

Cutting is closely related to obsessive-compulsive disorder and eating disorders in that they all are ways of internalizing and externalizing both pain and control—something that people with these disorders feel they are at continual odds with, and oddly, something they both lack and need. One reason I know this is that my background is in disability studies and critical theory, with a focus on mental health disorders. But I also know this because of my own "invisible" disabilities, or disorders, and my own lengthy interactions with the mental health field and its practitioners. So I pore over her essay and find that, indeed, my student has disclosed a very private and painful truth to me: she is a cutter. In fact, she also uses lighters to burn her skin, or she burns metal to hold against her skin. Her essay contained a host of other truths to tell. Her parents do not know the extent of her experiences she describes in the essay, nor do her friends. She is using drugs as another form of release (as yet she has not—or will not or cannot—pinpoint what the drugs provide a release *from*), she feels she needs more aggressive treatment than she is getting from her general practitioner, and she is doing this all on her own and needs help. At this point I realize I have said something in or out of class that has gotten her attention and helped her to make this choice: she *chose* to *disclose* to me.

Because of who I am, because of the field I chose to be in, Amy's disclosure is (to me) an invitation not just to reciprocate, but also to offer assistance if she wants it. My own ethics of care necessitates it. It is logical, polite, helpful, politically correct, insightful, humane—it is all of those things and more if my colleagues or I *choose* to offer a genuine response to someone who is in a similar situation and give that person assistance if she or he wants it. As educators of the humanities and as scholars of identity politics, this is what we *do,* who we *are.*

I do, however, know that offering advice about mental health takes on slightly different consequences than does suggesting, say, where someone might have their guide dog trained or where to go for lessons in American Sign Language. During the first draft of our first essays I have mandatory conferences with my students and I take this as an opportunity to let Amy decide if she wants to engage in conversation beyond the writing process of her essay. And she does: "Do you think that's weird or anything?" she asks of her cutting. And I respond: "Weird? No. Do I think that cutting is the most effective, safe, and healthy way to respond to what seem to be some overwhelming and ongoing issues for you? No, I don't think that either. Am I glad you felt you could use this essay as a place to write about this and that you could share this with me, yes, I am." Certainly I am downplaying this conversation for the sake of privacy issues, but the more telling story is not even in her first draft or this student-teacher conference. When I say the story is "more telling," I mean to say that the story tells something to my student and me. Her disclosure, and mine, paid off.

After a series of conferences and drafts with Amy, I did disclose that I am in fact sitting comfortably in several places on the American Psychiatric Association's diagnostic axes of disorders. It reads something like this: bipolar I, OCD, panic disorder, and so on. While my experiences only provide me with secondhand psychiatric advice to give, they do allow me to tell Amy the choices I made when I decided to go for help with my mental health, and more important, what to expect as consequences for those choices. And there are, indeed, many consequences associated with finding the right doctor, making the phone calls, visiting the offices, filling out forms, asking and answering questions, knowing what to say and how to say it, who to say it to and who *not* to say it to, and knowing what medications cause the worst side effects and have the best and worst efficacy rate. And so goes our exchange of information throughout the quarter as Amy continues drafting her essay. At the end of the quarter, when I am sitting in my office on a Friday afternoon leafing through final essays, Amy walks in for an unscheduled visit. It becomes obvious, to me at least, that she is having an episode of epic proportions. She sits at my desk and confides that she is indeed feeling like she is having an attack of some sort and is not quite sure what to do about it. At this point, Amy has not come to trust any of the psychiatrists she has seen, nor have any of the medications had time to take effect. My advice to her is that she can call her doctors and explain the situation, wait the episode out, or go to the emergency room. All of these suggestions are the standard responses given to me a hundred times before whenever I have had what I suspect she is having: a full-blown panic attack. Amy takes my advice, in the order given, and Monday morning she comes back to my office and tells me she still feels out of control and should go to the ER. But she is afraid to and has no one to go with her. So I offer to.

Waiting in the literal rubber room offers the most engaging moments for all of our disclosures to align with the process of writing. During the three-hour wait my student fidgets, rocks, thumps her feet, flicks the wall, hums, and in general is nervous, agitated, and lacking control of any kind. Since I have been in these rubber seats before because of my own disorders, I am able to look at this picture from a very different angle. I also want to keep at bay my own memories of being here twitching and restless and praying for the episode to be over, so I tell Amy: "This is where your final draft comes from. You have everything you need right here. You have a descriptive essay: describe the texture, the color, the smell of the rubber, the graffiti of the previous patients on the rubber walls. Compare and contrast the ways the three different doctors who are treating you ask you questions. Who is more clinical? Who is more 'therapeutic,' or 'personal'? Who seems like they don't want to be in psychiatry at all and why?" I hand her a notebook and pen and she begins taking notes, which calms her down somewhat and ultimately is helping her keep up with her schoolwork, despite the traumatic nature of this event. As she jots ideas down, random thoughts come to her, such as how to incorporate research into this essay. This leads to a humorous tangent on APA and MLA documentation and how I believe they may have a tiny bit to do with how I lost my own mind. Unfortunately, but not surprisingly, the ER will not give Amy anything for the panic attack because of her admitted past substance abuse. Yet, the rubber room became a crash course in Writing during/about/in Reaction to Trauma, and Amy and I both feel like something has progressed here.

All told, by the final draft Amy had written an A essay. Her writing was already comfortably in the A range, but yes, the content, the effort, and the learning and writing process I actually witnessed in Amy that quarter deserved more than an A; it deserved a medal. My interaction with Amy and other students who disclose such personal information is questionable to say the least. But what I carry from an experience like this is why, when my students disclose to me, I cannot stop myself from trying to pry their narratives open more. David Bleich (in *Know and Tell: A Writing Pedagogy of Disclosure, Genre, and Membership*), Peter Elbow (an expressivist compositionist who would argue that voice is central and authentic, and therefore leads to empowerment), and many others would be fruitful sources for me to draw on here to explain why I feel Amy's writing about her deeply moving and painful experiences were not only important but vital. But I would like to point toward another, perhaps equally appropriate source. I did not (and still do not) profess to be Amy's therapist or health-care professional of any kind. Yet how many times do we catch ourselves as teachers of composition in any sort of capacity saying, "Writing is therapeutic"? Or, "We like to write out our feelings"? And in this case, the essay was about personal identity, and how the choices made by the writer affected it. In *The Gift of Therapy: An Open Letter to a New Generation of Therapists and Their Patients*, Irvin Yalom describes a strikingly similar scenario to that of English departments, particularly in the area of composition: psychiatrists and therapists go to great lengths *not* to disclose any of their personal lives with their patients in order to not interfere with the patient's treatment. Yet Yalom firmly believes this is a boundary that can and should be blurred when in the best interest of the patient. So then, disclosing to a patient that you, too, have a history of mental disorders and understand the accompanying trauma, the possibilities of wellness, the medical jargon doctors toss around, and so on may be not only appropriate, but also beneficial.

When I look back on this exchange of information, the conversations, the shared experiences, I think of what I have lost and gained, and I can only speculate about the same for my student. I know Amy earned an A in my class. I know she learned a lot about herself that quarter: she became incredibly aware about mental health in general, and she became a good deal more expressive about her needs with her own family and friends. Did she lose anything? I don't know. Some privacy maybe. Did she feel humbled? Possibly. She definitely had lost a lot of blood from all that prior cutting, though. And what did I gain? A sense of myself—as a teacher, as someone with mental disorders, as someone who can actually organize things in the midst of chaos (though that defies the logic of being mentally disordered). And my losses? I decided to cut my losses in favor of my gains.

REFLECTING ON YOUR TEACHING

Self-Disclosure

Mental illness remains among the most stigmatized of all kinds of disability. The label carries a stigma with real, material consequences too: many insurance policies do not cover the costs, or they provide very limited coverage, for mental illness/health treatment; patients who are committed for psychiatric care can lose fundamental rights that other citizens take for granted; a record of mental illness may disqualify a person from some employment; actions that are routinely accepted appear threatening to some people if the person doing them is known to be or have been mentally ill. Disclosure of a mental illness, then, may be the most risky kind of disclosure in a classroom, for both student and teacher, and requires a high degree of trust on both sides.

Debates about disclosure in composition have usually revolved around the role of the personal essay (Chrisman refers to Bleich and Elbow, for example). But disclosure can occur even without personal topics in the writing classroom, and often does occur in a disability-themed writing class. Students may ask the teacher: "What has drawn you to the subject of disability?" Not all teachers who incorporate disability issues into their classes are themselves persons with disabilities. Some might have close friends or relatives with a disability; others might have an invisible or visible disability; still others might be interested in the topic but have no personal connection whatsoever. Before you incorporate disability issues in your syllabus, spend some time thinking about how you might answer such a question. In a teacher-training workshop, write for five to ten minutes on possible answers and possible student reactions to them. Then, in pairs, share your reflective writing and discuss how you wish to respond to this question.

SUGGESTIONS FOR STUDENT ACTIVITIES

Critically Thinking about Disability Stigma

Consider approaching the topic of disclosure not in personal terms but as an exercise in critical thinking about the social construction of disabilities and their varying stigmas. Together as a class, make a chart on the social hierarchies of disability, the relative risks of disclosing each type of disability, the stigmas associated with each type, the material consequences in terms of employment, civil rights, and so forth. For example, at the top of the disability hierarchy might be the heroic war veteran with a missing limb. His disability (and such a figure is usually depicted as a "he") is visible, a sign of patriotism and valor. There will probably be a good deal of debate about the range of stigmas and material consequences of each type of disability, and that could be a starting point for a mini research project; for example, finding employment statistics of people with disabilities.

Exploring Attitudes toward Mental Illness

Another way that Chrisman's essay can be useful is to open up a dialogue about mental illness, mood, or behavior disorders. Though one of the most hidden and unacknowledged disabilities, mental illness is actually quite prevalent on college campuses. Ask students to write a five-to-ten-minute reflection on how their attitude toward their teacher, friend, or even a family member might change if they know he or she had been treated for a mental disorder. Remind students that members of the class or even the teacher may have some form of mood disorder, and that you are not asking for confessional writing, although an option might be to write about self-disclosure or passing, as well. Then have students, working in small groups, discuss their reflections and share with the class the cultural assumptions in the label "mental illness." This approach to mental illness may allow students to explore issues hypothetically, to try on perspectives and shift through positions. Students could be asked to identify stereotypes or "us"/"them" thinking in their own writing, or to identify descriptors as being positive or negative. You might follow up the sequence of writing and then discussion by having students write back to themselves or one another after they have filtered their original words through the classroom dialogue.

Resources for Teaching Disability Concepts in the Writing Classroom

Introduction to Part Three

The texts gathered here provide practical resources for developing a writing class infused with disability issues and activities. We have provided excerpts to give instructors a preview of the many resources available as they plan their courses. These excerpts, drawn from longer works by writing and disability studies scholars, hone in on key disability studies concepts that are especially useful in the teaching of writing. Publication information for each of the sources is provided if you wish to assign the reading in its entirety to your students. Following each excerpt, we have also included multiple suggestions for employing these readings in your own classroom. The ideas for activities and writing prompts can be used independently of the texts.

Part Three is arranged in four thematic clusters, beginning with "Redesigning the Writing Classroom." The six pieces in this cluster demonstrate how a disability perspective and disability experiences can fundamentally alter the teaching of writing. When we acknowledge disability's presence and use it as a critical lens, new practices of teaching and learning, and new teacher-student relationships, emerge.

The four selections that make up the second thematic cluster—"Analyzing Language, Representation, and Narrative from a Disability Perspective"— examine how language and representations shape attitudes toward the disabled and convey ideologies about disability. We encourage instructors to place these analyses within the contexts of rhetorical and critical thinking. As models, these selections provide analytic tools that students can apply to projects and purposes of their own choosing. Students may wish to "test" some of the claims made by these authors by conducting their own rhetorical analyses or research. These selections, and the teaching suggestions following them, are especially useful in a writing class because they teach students to pay close attention to the effects of textual and linguistic details as they read and compose their own writing.

The third cluster, "Using Disability Concepts: The Norm, Gaze, and Embodied Knowledge," presents descriptions of important conceptual terms and areas of inquiry in disability studies: normalcy and "the norm"; staring (a critical extension of "the gaze"); "talking back"; multiple identities; embodied knowledge; "voice"; sexuality; and life itself (its quality, limits, definitions). These core concepts concern and inform much of the contemporary interdisciplinary field of disability studies, especially as it has been infused and invigorated by scholarly approaches from the humanities.

The last cluster, "Entering Cultural Debates: A Politics and Poetics of Disability," offers a range of essays and poetry exploring the history, hopes, and intersections of the disability rights movement. Whether writing as public intellectual, academic, or poet, these authors argue for the centrality of disability to democracy, culture, and public life; relate the oppression of people with disabilities to that of other minority groups; and celebrate disability's potential to transform politics and art.

11 From *Becoming Visible: Lessons in Disability*

BRENDA JO BRUEGGEMANN,
LINDA FELDMEIER WHITE, PATRICIA A. DUNN,
BARBARA HEIFFERON, AND JOHNSON CHEU

This collaborative essay argues for stronger intersections between disability studies and composition studies in order to challenge and effectively change our ideas about such concepts as "writing," "composing," and "normal." The complete essay features six sections that examine the paradox of the "invisibility" of disability studies and awareness within composition studies; the social construction of learning disabilities; the rhetoric of backlash against disability, particularly learning disabilities; the challenge and rewards of teaching a single disability narrative in a composition classroom; ways to center an entire composition course around disability; and the new directions necessary to make composition studies meaningfully intersect with disability studies.

The excerpt offered here comes primarily from the fourth section, "Making Disability Visible to Students," written by Barbara Heifferon. In this section, Heifferon uses a provocative text by essayist Nancy Mairs to prompt a final writing assignment in her composition course. Heifferon argues that reading Mairs's essay and writing a response to it helped her students "move past the disabling and disenfranchising labels" assigned to disability, address "the invisibility of differently abled persons," and "debunk concepts of 'normalcy' and 'ideal bodies.'"

Why should these things—the attention to disability and the disappearance of such entirely unclear distinctions in the first place—matter? Issues of disability matter in composition studies and classrooms, first, because we have a long, proud history of making the invisible visible and of examining how language both reflects and supports notions of Other. We should be receptive to disability studies' powerful exposure of the dehumanizing societal constructions of disability and difference. Second, we also rightly pride

From CCC 52, no. 3 (2001): 368–98.

ourselves on our attention to practice—and on our refusal to separate it from the theoretical assumptions that explicitly or implicitly inform it. Disability and the presence of disabled students in our writing classrooms return us squarely to issues of practice that both interrogate and enrich our theories about literacy and empowerment. Third, connected to the first two reasons, because we already challenge the binaries of theory/practice, writing/thinking, and self/other, we should be well equipped—even eager—to embrace the critique of the (false) abled/disabled binary that is articulated by disability scholars such as Simi Linton, Lennard Davis, Rosemarie Garland-Thomson, David Mitchell, and Sharon Snyder. . . .

MAKING DISABILITY VISIBLE TO STUDENTS

As composition professionals we are in a unique position to challenge pervasive and misguided assumptions about disability. Introducing disability texts into the classroom not only makes disability visible, but also empowers students to see that "writing is intimately connected with issues of authority, identity, power, and confidence," as Patricia Dunn . . . state[s] that "if students are to become more sophisticated thinkers and writers, they should be both challenged and taken seriously." . . . Introducing a text written by a differently abled writer challenge[s] students in exactly the way Dunn advocates. . . .

One way to move past the disabling and disenfranchising labels . . . as well as the invisibility of differently abled persons is to debunk concepts of "normalcy" and "ideal bodies" in the classroom. Traditional students are most prone to such constructions of people and bodies, given their developmental stage of late adolescence. . . . [A] preliminary observation [of the following case study] could suggest future questions for researchers, such as . . . (1) Does introducing disability texts into the classroom raise awareness and increase visibility of differently abled people? (2) Do disability texts in particular challenge students' conceptions of "authority, identity, power, and confidence"? as Dunn stated and (3) Are there gender differences in reactions to disability texts?

. . . To situate this classroom description, we can point to the increasing acceptance of teacher research within our discipline. Teacher research "is not designed to investigate cause and effect; instead it aims to describe, as fully as possible, what happened in one teaching situation" (MacNealy, 243). . . . To summarize the situation, in the fall semester of 1996 the University of Arizona composition program gave a common final for all 130 sections of its first-semester, first-year composition classes. All . . . teaching sections of 101 were to give . . . students a copy of Nancy Mairs's essay "Carnal Acts" to read and discuss before the final.

In "Carnal Acts," Tucson writer Nancy Mairs responds to a request from a student at a small liberal arts college at which she has a speaking engagement to discuss how she lived with her disability of MS and how she found her writing voice. Mairs reviews the intimate details of how multiple sclerosis has affected her body and her sense of self, and she concludes that she cannot remain politely silent on such details if she is to write as a woman who has experienced birth, love, and disease. The intimate writing that she shares with her readers is what she ironically calls a "carnal act." Drawing on her own experiences, Mairs raises basic questions about living and writing; she uses research and her knowledge of feminist writers to develop her perceptions. As a woman who is physically challenged, Mairs confronts issues such as disability labels, stereotyping, and cultural biases toward the differently abled body.

In the essay, Mairs goes into explicit detail, especially after her failed suicide attempt from which her husband, George, rescues her. Her descriptions of her body and her honesty about being unable at times to cope with her disease are about as graphic as any text you can read. She doesn't make it pretty as she talks about a body that makes you fall, drop glasses in your hand, leak urine, and always feel tired no matter how much you sleep.

. . . I had expected emotional responses to Mairs's work, but was surprised at certain phenomena I observed. In the often heated and vehement student-led discussion about this work, I saw clear gender splits. The young women in the class were clearly moved by Mairs's words and were sympathetic and empathetic, and young male students were outraged, not just "grossed out" by descriptions of body functions and other things that go awry in MS, but angry, furious, livid in the classroom. One young male exclaimed in his final essay, "[This is] everything you don't want to hear." Other young men said that they were "uncomfortable" reading the text and wondered if she wrote it in order to "shock the reader."

. . . I followed my instincts to intervene when the voices in the classroom became overwhelming to the degree that students could no longer hear each other because everyone was talking at once. I suggested to my students that we rhetorically analyze the phenomenon we saw happening before us and make use of this teachable moment. What was it about disability issues in general, whether LD or physical disability, and Mairs's MS in particular that caused young women to react with such empathy and young men (for the most part) to react with such anger? Well, that question certainly shut down discussion for a few minutes. I then backed up and said I was not blaming men for reacting this way — I just wanted to understand why. I suggested that they take their anger into the finals, citing passages that repulsed them and arguing in a rhetorical analysis or writing personally in a reader response why Mairs did not reach her audience. Anger, any emotion in fact, is an excellent catalyst for writing well because students are engaged and motivated. As Dunn points out, Bruner and Oelschlaeger suggest that cogent arguments must also "evoke sentiment" in order to change minds (215). On the final exams, male students wrote about their initial reactions to Mairs's text with such terms and comments as: "lurid," "not easy to read," "offensive," "anger," "mad," and "reading those words infuriated me."

I tried to put myself into the shoes/often sandals in Arizona of the young men in my class. One of the issues I discovered by looking at their verbal and written reactions was that they were outraged at the schism between the idealized body image of women they see projected in the culture and the body image Mairs wrote about. Their reactions then generated another question for future research: Do male reactions hinge on the idealization of women's bodies? They were equally outraged by her admission of self-doubt, weakness, and disability. These young men are barely out of puberty at eighteen, still in it in many cases, just achieving sexual maturity or striving to. One male student writes: "At [this] point in my life, I [am] entering the transition state of moving from boyhood to manhood." Another male student writes, "This [separation between the mind and body] is largely due to social views of what the ideal person should be: able in both mind and body. . . . [P]eople in our society are expected to be both mentally and physically desirable." Their fantasies are based on women projected by our popular media, a media that offers no alternatives to the Barbie doll ideal, a totalizing gesture that wipes difference from our cultural map, rendering it invisible. As Susan Bordo documents in *Unbearable Weight: Feminism, Western Culture, and the Body*, "the vulnerability of men and boys to popular imagery, the contribution of their desires and anxieties, the pressures thus brought to bear on girls and women" are the fallout from the constructs our culture has created around youth and ideal bodies (46).

Mairs articulates the pressures on her as a female in this culture feeling, as most women do, unable to meet the ideals of female bodily perfection. When Mairs makes the invisible visible, she creates an emotional as well as intellectual dissonance for these young men. They see women as idealized sexual objects, while Mairs presents a real woman, one who bleeds, one who drops things and struggles to cope on a day-to-day basis. Many young male students form identities based on their own strong, healthy bodies, and because they are young and abled, their initial response to a disabled woman's body is an angry one.

The author challenged us to *see* ourselves beyond the packaged images that our culture sells us. As Bordo also articulates, "in our present culture of mystification—a culture which continually pulls us away from systemic understanding and inclines us toward constructions that emphasize individual freedom, choice, power, ability—simply becoming *more conscious* is a tremendous achievement" (30; emphasis in original). Mairs's essay succeeded in making such constructions more conscious and in increasing awareness.

In the finals, I thought I would get the same angry male responses as in class discussion. I told students in advance that I would not penalize them for writing against the grain as well as reading against the grain. Instead, their responses surprised me. I realized the young men had processed their dismay and gotten underneath and beyond it after the initial shock. The class discussion seemed to help them process the initial anger and move them from outrage to more awareness of and acceptance of difference. Not only did Mairs succeed in coming to voice herself in her essay, but she also succeeded in enabling young men who are still discouraged from expressing feelings to do so in response. Those feelings shifted dramatically, and that change was reflected in the final essays.

Texts on disability, honest, real, open texts such as Mairs's essay, have a valuable place in the writing classroom, particularly in a culture that continually blasts the able-bodied, idealized, and commodified body into our eyes and ears, and in a culture that often denies men the right to express their innermost feelings. I doubt a tamer text or a text that did not confront such stereotypes could have moved students so far from the previously unquestioned assumptions they carried with them, invisible and silent assumptions that render those with disabilities invisible and silent. Thus we moved from dismay to discussion past dissonance to the discovery of a place where disability texts in the classroom help students confront issues of authority and power. Students' ability to grapple with such texts that challenge the views they take for granted increases their confidence and enables identification with persons different from themselves.

REFLECTING ON YOUR TEACHING

Wild and Tame Texts

Heifferon suggests that it is the nature of the wild text that allowed her students to question assumptions they had about bodies and disability. Write a list of the texts you use in your classes. Using a scale of 1 to 5, where 1 is tame and 5 is wild, rank your texts. What is the purpose of using the tame text? What is the purpose of using the wild texts? Based on the answers your students provide in the preceding activities, how might you change your notion of wild or tame texts? How might you change which texts you use and what response you hope to elicit from your students?

SUGGESTIONS FOR STUDENT ACTIVITIES

Exploring Patterns of Reading Responses

In this excerpt, Heifferon suggests that she doubts "a tamer text or a text that did not confront such stereotypes could have moved students so far from the previously unquestioned assumptions they carried with them." She also muses over the gendered differences in reactions to Mairs's essay: "What was it about disability issues in general . . . and Mairs's MS in particular that caused young women to react with such empathy and young men (for the most part) to react with such anger?" Students in your composition classroom might explore either, or both, of these ideas.

For example, they could do comparative readings and brief reviews of several authors featured in this volume or in the bibliography at the end of this book (p. 271). First, they might determine which of the texts they compare are "tamer" or "wilder" than others. They will need to discuss and establish qualifications for these categories, of course; such a discussion asks them to consider carefully elements of writing such as tone and style. Once they have labeled their "tamer" and "wilder" texts and determined the features that make them "tame" or "wild," they could write a brief review of those pieces (or one of the pieces) that would include both summary and evaluative reaction. When all reviews have been drafted, students might exchange them in groups and then be asked to discuss among themselves how the "tameness" or "wildness" of the selected text or texts seems to affect their own reaction and evaluation of it or them. Do they notice patterns in their reactions to, interactions with, and evaluations of the texts and the degree of "tameness?"

Investigating Gendered Responses

Students could also be encouraged to continue this discussion by inserting "gender" as a factor in their reaction and discussion. Things will become considerably complicated here. Students might discuss or write further in response to questions such as these: Are there patterns in the way that women/men in the class respond to text A, B, or C? Does it seem to matter if the author is male or female in this reaction? What about a student's own gendered upbringing of values helps form her or his reaction to various disability texts? In what ways, in other words, do gender and disability seem interwoven? And how is being a "man with a disability" different from being a "woman with a disability" in our culture, based on their readings? How does gender matter in the way we seem to respond to men with disabilities and women with disabilities? Any of these questions might be addressed as well by looking for media representations of men and women with disabilities and applying the same questions.

12

From *Learning Differences: The Perspective of LD College Students*

PATRICIA A. DUNN

Dunn begins this excerpt by positioning herself in relation to learning disabilities—as an "outsider" who, like most of the other researchers studying learning disabilities, finds herself "researching a phenomenon that happened to others, not to them." This position encouraged her then to consult "the most expert people of all in this controversy," the "young people whose lives had been influenced, for good or for ill, by being labeled LD." Her interview, for example, with Nick, a college student who has been labeled "LD," provides her (and us, as readers of this text) "a unique perspective not available in the scholarly research." Nick reveals some of his self-taught learning and college survival strategies while also offering some remarkable insights through his advice for writing teachers regarding LD students (as prompted by Dunn in her interview with him). But what Dunn finds most "telling" in her interview with Nick, upon transcribing it later, is the obvious "self-deprecatory" stigma Nick seems to have internalized about himself because of his learning disability; the real disability for LD students, she concludes, "is a learned one: the inner belief that one is somehow inferior to one's peers."

After reading dozens of books and hundreds of articles by experts in the LD, reading, and writing fields, professionals who had themselves studied LD and conducted classroom and laboratory research, I still had almost as many questions as when I began my research several years ago. I also realized that these experts, for all their education and experience, were most likely not learning disabled. Like me, they were researching a phenomenon that happened to others, not to them. In a way, learning disabled college students are the most expert people of all in this controversy because they have lived amidst its chaos for a long time. No matter what the various PhD's were

From *Learning Re-Abled: The Learning Disability Controversy and Composition Studies* (Portsmouth, NH: Heinemann-Boynton/Cook, 2005), 96–153.

currently deciding about the existence and extent of learning disabilities, I wanted to hear from young people whose lives had been influenced, for good or for ill, by being labeled LD. . . .

NICK

The first person I talked with was Nick, who currently maintains a B average in college and participates in many social activities—dramatic productions, fund-raisers, and residence life workshops—all of which capitalize on his speaking skills, none of which involve a lot of reading and writing. He had been a physical therapy major, he told me, but the technical, complicated vocabulary of the major muscle groups had plagued him beyond his frustration level, so he switched to criminal justice, where he said he could learn more through listening. . . .

I learned much from my two -hour interview with Nick because his narrative provided a unique perspective not available in the scholarly research. Although Nick's elementary schoolteachers wanted him to be tested for LD, his mother did not want him to be stigmatized. In his early years of high school, another teacher wanted Nick to seek help, but he was too proud to risk going to the "resource room," a place he refers to in an autobiographical essay as the "reject room." He remained in a regular classroom, using what professionals might refer to as "compensatory strategies." He calls them "survival instincts." By listening carefully in class and craftily arranging group study sessions, Nick managed to get average grades through high school. Then he experienced several incidents, detailed below, that made him decide to get tested for LD, and ultimately labeled and provided with special services.

Because he was not officially labeled LD until his junior year in high school, he had limited, but insightful, experiences in that "resource room," a place where LD high school students are sent for extra help after they have been singled out from their classmates. (Christopher Lee, in *Faking It* [Lee and Jackson, 1992], calls his high school resource room "the stupid trailer.") In highlights of the interview, Nick talks about the students in this room, as well as about specific moments in his life that most shaped who he is today. He talks of ongoing problems and painful moments in his current college career that are related to his disability . . .

> **N:** I never missed a class, never missed school. In my whole high school career, I think I missed like maybe ten days. Class time was where I learned everything. I would just ask questions, and I just listened. Studying-wise, I always studied in groups, and everyone else would talk, and I would just pick it up auditorialy. . . .
>
> **P:** So how did you handle the reading comprehension on the Regents? Were you used to reading chunks like that?
>
> **N:** I—luckily I was able—I got labeled. I was able to take the Regents exam untimed. If I didn't take it untimed, I would have never passed. So that was a tremendous help because I never would have been able to finish the reading.

Like—a paragraph that takes most students, say, five minutes, would take me twenty minutes. My reading deficit is bad. That exam I was really nervous about because I didn't think I was going to pass. But I did. . . .

P: If you could speak to writing teachers, are there any specific dos and don'ts you would tell them regarding LD students?

N: I guess there's numerous dos and don'ts, but probably the number one don't would be to look at them differently—because a student usually is uncomfortable with their disability anyway, and any time a teacher almost looks down upon them and says, "You don't have to do this quality of work because you have a disability," that, in my mind, says that they don't think that we can do the work, so therefore they're not making us do the work. Therefore, they set a lower standard, and that perpetuates a continuously low quality of work. I see that happen continuously in high school as well as college. . . .

The supreme irony here is that serious, hardworking students like Nick are still being told, verbally or nonverbally, that they're lazy, when some are spending every waking moment doing schoolwork. They internalize what uninformed people say or imply about them. No matter how deeply buried, the low estimations teachers, parents, or peers have about these students' intelligence, even their morals, are revealed in sometimes offhand comments these students make about themselves.

Nick's story was fascinating as I spoke with him in person. Later, as I was transcribing the tape, I became more aware of quickly muttered comments he made, almost under his breath. Sometimes I had to play the tape on my stereo's highest volume to translate his remarks, but in many ways they are more revelatory than his more clearly articulated comments:

"she was allowing me to continue to be . . ."

"I didn't have the skills of the regular, normal students. . . ."

"not to better myself . . ."

". . . you learn to be ah—deceiving. . . ."

"If people want to say I'm stupid, I don't care because for most of the— sometimes I would agree with them. . . ."

"the wrong word . . . and that's due either to laziness or . . ."

In these words, Nick shows that he too, perhaps like some of the adults in his childhood, attributes his reading and writing difficulties to some kind of moral flaw. That young people are made to feel this way is outrageous. If we do nothing else in our various disciplines to alter educational philosophy and practice, if we agree on nothing else, we must change how society thinks of LD students, because students are absorbing these self-hating attitudes, in much the same way the self-deprecatory Brazilian peasants Freire describes began to think of themselves in the same negative way as did their oppressors (Freire [1970] 1988, 49).

And for LD students, *that* is the disability, and it is a learned one: the inner belief that one is somehow inferior to one's peers. Whatever initial difficulties someone like Nick might have with linguistic processing skills are compounded by the implication, or by the useless, potentially harmful advice, that if only he would try harder, concentrate more, spend more time—in short, if only he would be more normal—these problems would go away. When he follows this advice, spending far more time on schoolwork no doubt than are his self-righteous advisers, he sees only limited results and becomes even more alarmed with what he sees as his abnormality. Only the most determined, thick-skinned students continue to work so hard on written assignments. Many people feel it is not worth the aggravation and humiliation. They drop out. . . .

> **P:** Is there anything else you can think of? Absolute dos or absolute don'ts for college—
>
> **N:** Students? For college professors?
>
> **P:** For professors, or students, or anybody.
>
> **N:** The necessity, the skill, is *understanding*. The biggest thing is, don't be close minded about the issue—because who says you're right? I mean, society says you're right, but society's been wrong before, and so how do we know that your way of saying "This is the way it's going to be" is the right way? So I think open-mindedness—being open-minded about allowing the person to come to you and say, "This is what I have difficulties with," and not immediately saying, "Well, what makes you different than other students? What gives *you* special privileges?" You know, I had—I have a teacher this semester I *despise*. And he says to me, he says, "You know what? I think I was learning disability [sic] when I was young because I couldn't do this. . . ." And I'm like, thinking, "Well, maybe he was," but, he kind of like was looking down and saying, "If *I* didn't have it, why should you?" And like, in the middle of class, he'll like—like I walked in late the other day, and the professor said, "Nick, you want to take that test at seven o'clock, you know, your normal time outside of class?"—in front of the *whole* class! And you know, I can handle that because, like, I know what he's doing, and I'm just like, "Whatever," but most students would crumble. They would die. They would be like, "Ahhhh," and start crying and be like all emotional.
>
> **P:** Oh, yeah.
>
> **N:** And he's done that several times. So I think understanding is a big thing, understanding that you're not—just because you have your PhD, you don't—you aren't necessarily right.

SUGGESTIONS FOR STUDENT ACTIVITIES

Researching Stigma Historically

Invite students to explore the territory and tyranny of stigma, especially as it applies to disability. Such an exploration could take place in a number of ways. First, they might read about or consider other, more well-known scenes of stigmatization and groups stigmatized: Jews, gypsies, and people with disabilities in the Holocaust; treatment of African Americans before and leading to the civil rights movement; the attitude toward and treatment of women leading to women's suffrage or other key moments in the struggle for women's rights; or a more recent or local scene (perhaps even on their college campus or in their hometown). What do these events and elements of stigma have in common with the way that people with disabilities, especially students with learning disabilities in college, are perceived, treated, or interacted with?

Studying the Performance of Stigma

Finally, students might explore together the dynamics of stigma more deeply. This could be done in many ways. For example, they might all read together Dr. Suess's well-known story *The Sneetches* and conduct an analysis of how stigma and "othering" function in this story. Who gains from the process of stigmatization? What forces keep stigma in operation? Or, they might even imagine a "stigma scene." Some members of the class, for instance, could become the subject of stigma because they have non-brown eyes. How would this stigma be enacted? What would the non-brown eyes be allowed to do or not do? Where can they go or not? What are they allowed to say, or how are they allowed to speak or interact with each other and with brown-eyed people? How would their non-brown-eyed condition be "policed" so that their stigma is maintained? Once students enact such a "silly scene" around stigma they can often readily apply an analysis to the way that disability is stigmatized in our culture.

Visualizing Connections

Making use of the wealth of visual material and media representations that can be found online and in history books, invite students to look for images that link race- or gender-based civil rights movements globally or nationally with disability rights movements. Some good sources for such material, with regard specifically to disability and activist or civil rights protests, might be found at any of the following:

- *Ragged Edge Online* (disability activist newspaper), www.ragged-edge-mag.com
- The "Not Dead Yet" movement, http://notdeadyet.org
- ADAPT (movement for independent, noninstitutional living/homes for people with disabilities), www.adapt.org

Investigating Learning Disabilities

Students might place themselves in a journalist's position and investigate other narratives by people with learning disabilities or look for media accounts around "the learning disability controversy." How are narratives (interviews, autobiographies, documentaries) about or by people with learning disabilities organized? What themes and issues seem to arise across many of them? How do these themes compare with the larger media account of learning disabilities? As an extension of this investigation, students might be asked to plan an interview with a student on their campus who has a learning disability. What questions would they ask? How would they approach the various sensitive issues and themes they have learned about in their preliminary investigation with this "real person"? Another extension exercise might be to have students write a newspaper article about learning disabilities and the college student; this article could take the form of a letter to the editor (in response to perhaps another newspaper or news magazine piece they read in their investigation) or a feature story, for example.

13

From *Constructing a Third Space: Disability Studies, the Teaching of English, and Institutional Transformation*

JAMES C. WILSON AND
CYNTHIA LEWIECKI-WILSON

Wilson and Lewiecki-Wilson blend critical and rhetorical theory and their own pedagogical practices to create a "third-space" classroom that is modeled on the performative speech act that critic Judith Butler defines. In the first part of their essay, which is not reprinted here, the authors summarize how encounters with disability are typically and routinely understood in our culture through already well-established rhetorics of individual rights, the mythic norm, victimhood, bias, and injury. These scripts about disability are already with us, even in the classroom. The authors describe their attempts, then, to create a third-space classroom as a place where students and teacher work to "rewrite the scripts." That is, together teacher and students examine, think about, and work toward new ways of understanding disability. In this excerpt, Wilson and Lewiecki-Wilson enact an example of this third-space classroom through the use of written student responses made in reaction to a provocative disability documentary, Sharon Snyder and David Mitchell's Vital Signs: Crip Culture Talks Back.

Although we teach in different kinds of institutions and at different levels, we both teach writing, and we have found that many of the routine practices of writing pedagogy (student-teacher conferencing, small-group workshops, etc.) are effective or adaptable in accommodating the individual needs of disabled students. We talk to our classes at the beginning of each term or semester about learning differences, and we indicate that we are willing to accommodate different needs—for example, by providing large-print lecture notes, sending notes by e-mail, or allowing students to audiotape classes. We go further and convey that we are willing to adapt or codesign

From *Disability Studies: Enabling the Humanities,* ed. Sharon L. Snyder, Brenda Jo Brueggemann, and Rosemarie Garland-Thomson (New York: Modern Language Association, 2002), 296–307.

assignments with students to fit their particular learning strengths as well as to address particular learning needs. We let students know we are willing to codevelop with them strategies for success, and we stress that they have much to teach us and other students.

An important aspect of accommodation is access. By being flexible, teachers can compensate for less than ideal campus spaces and make learning more accessible. For example, if elevators are distant or unreliable, we offer to meet with students in alternate and more accessible (or just more comfortable) locations—the library, a computer lab, a student commons room, and so on. Access also means that a teacher be willing to conference by phone or e-mail.

Above all, we recommend openness in talking about disability. Because we have a disabled son, we often bring our experiences into the class as a way of representing the subject of disability without connecting it to any particular student present, thus introducing disability from the start. We mention that disabled students may, if they wish, identify themselves, and we offer opportunities for all students to conference privately with the professor, in person or by e-mail. We also incorporate the subject of disability into our curriculum in many of the composition, literature, and interdisciplinary classes we teach and encourage a variety of approaches, ranging from memoir writing and other forms of self-representation to critical and research projects connected to disabilities. However, we do not require personal topics or self-disclosure. Some students feel uncomfortable with the personal, while others welcome the opportunity to do serious work on a subject connected to their lives. Rather than approach disability as an identity, we integrate it into the curriculum as a social construction, a critical modality, and a community issue. We encourage nondisabled students as well to investigate disability issues and to reflect on the critical perspective gained from their investigations. . . .

Where should disability studies appear in the curriculum? We believe, as Rosemarie Garland-Thomson argues in "Integrating Disability Studies," that "it should be an integrated part of all the courses we design, just as many of us have begun to consider race, gender, and class issues as fundamental aspects of all disciplines and subjects of inquiry" (16).[1] In a number of the classes we teach (e.g., composition, women's studies, and graduate professional writing), we integrate readings from disability studies, memoirs by disabled writers, and videos made by disability activists. Assignments, depending on the particular course, might ask students to analyze cultural images of the disabled, explore new ways of representing the disabled in their writing, or reflect on the critical issues of difference in our culture. The students' reflective responses can be openings to discuss the ways that disability is familiarly encoded in language and social practices.

It has been our experience that when students encounter voices from disability culture, they tend to hear those voices in the common social scripts of individualism and individual rights based on a mythic norm: that is, they hear the rhetoric of victimhood, bias, and injury, and they place disability in the familiar mainstream-versus-minority construction. Consider these reflections written by seniors and graduate students in a medicine-and-science writing class after watching Sharon Snyder and David T. Mitchell's video *Vital Signs: Crip Culture Talks Back.*

After seeing the film I got the impression that persons with disabilities are offended by nondisabled persons who try to be pleasant, because they feel these pleasantries translate to pity. [. . .] To look at a person's disability and try to understand it through asking questions or entering into some sort of discourse with the disabled individual seems to me to be the only way to break the barriers, clarify the stereotypes, clear up the myths, and ease the discomfort of interactions between disabled and nondisabled individuals.

[This video] pointed out some of the underground currents of discrimination against people with disabilities. I use the terms 'underground' because I think many of the grievances discussed in the video are often swept under the carpet of mainstream culture, as a way for able-bodied people to ignore the pertinent issues and discriminatory acts encountered by our neighbors who happen to be on crutches, in wheelchairs, or disabled in some other way.

I liked the way the film was about the people, and got into their lives, childhoods, and feelings about being disabled and about how they are treated. Most films on the topic do objectify the [disabled], as many said, and turn them into something other than humans.

Until I watched the movie I did not picture disabled people as a different culture.

As probably intended, some of the interviews were harder to watch than others, but I got the distinct idea that [the producers] did not intend the audience to feel comfortable. [. . .] It also seemed appropriate that these people were speaking for themselves instead of having a celebrity (Jerry Lewis, for example) or a medical or political expert speaking for them or about them. [. . .] For me, it was very eye-opening [. . .] the fact that these people are so much more than their disabilities also jumps out. [. . .] The tendency for me especially is to not talk about the obvious, not to talk about the disability. [. . .] One thing I am wondering now that I'm thinking more about it is what exactly did the directors hope to achieve: awareness, attitude change, or some more concrete societal change? Who is the intended audience?

I'm always a bit skeptical when I watch a documentary about a politically charged issue. I have to say that [this one] wasn't much of an exception. I found it interesting that when presenting a culture in which 60 percent (I think it was said) are unemployed, the filmmakers chose to speak with individuals who were clearly educated and articulate. [. . .] So I wonder if the images presented aren't a little bit skewed and I wonder what the film would have been like if the makers had talked with some of the [unemployed majority].

We arranged these responses in an order that may suggest a movement from thinking about disability as a matter of individuals who suffer deficit or loss to seeing the disabled as a culture and disability as a social construction to be politically reclaimed, to use the disability studies theorist Simi Linton's term in *Claiming Disability*. Although such a movement would mirror the lines of argument of most disability studies theorists, our teaching goal is not to have students "reconstruct" their thinking about disability according to a "correct" theory. Rather, our goal is to encourage them to examine and conceptualize their encounters with disability. While we readily acknowledge that the work of engaging with and reseeing disability is indeed political, as the last student argues, we strive to keep class discussions reflective and reflexive — that is, in the form of thoughtful, open-ended conversations that include a critique of our enterprise. As students articulate the range of views inscribed in culture and reflect on these, their discourse can be vehicles for discussion and analysis and a starting point for the production of new thinking. As Kris Gutierrez, Betsy Rymes, and Joanne Larson argue in "Script, Counterscript, and Underlife in the Classroom: James Brown versus *Brown v. Board of Education*," the third-space classroom "requires more than simply 'adding-on' the student script; it requires jointly constructing a new sociocultural terrain in the classroom" (468).

As we are conceptualizing it, a third-space classroom is performative, to use Butler's term (*Excitable Speech*), calling into being new modes of address and inquiring into the uses and effects of language and cultural images. She writes:

> The performative is not a singular act used by an already established subject, but one of the powerful and insidious ways in which subjects are called into social being from diffuse social quarters, inaugurated into sociality by a variety of diffuse and powerful interpellations. In this sense the social performative is a crucial part not only of subject formation, but of the ongoing political contestation and reformulation of the subject as well. (160)

As Butler's word "insidious" makes clear, such remaking is not innocent. However, it is important to remember that all classrooms participate in subject formation and reproduce a social order that, as human agents, we may change. How we might (or might not) change it, why, and to what ends are all possibilities open to debate. . . .

In our teaching, we encourage students to examine the rhetorical constructions of difference and the dominant cultural narratives that both teachers and students employ. We do not offer answers but pose questions that turn a critical lens back on us and our projects, challenging students to think about the boundaries among academic disciplines, community, and discursive spaces.

The questions we put to students are ones we ask ourselves: How does disability studies change the boundaries of disciplinary knowledge? How should our society, our communities, and our universities take up diversity issues? In particular, how does disability help us think critically about the rhetoric and practices of pluralistic inclusion and consider new ways in which difference can really speak to, challenge, and transform institutions, communities, and people? How can disability studies address the material needs of the disabled, about 70 percent of whom are presently unemployed according to the 1998 National Organization on Disability–Harris Survey of Americans with Disabilities (Taylor)? Will access to the academy provide access to employment and economic space?

These questions cannot yet be answered definitively. However, we believe that by incorporating disability issues into the curriculum as widely as possible, by engaging with disability studies theory, and by rethinking disciplinary knowledge as a result of this encounter, teachers and students, the disabled and nondisabled can indeed participate in remaking the social and physical landscapes of the university. For this remaking to happen, teachers need to take the first steps in transforming their teaching in a way that allows them to engage with issues of disability and with the disabled. Then the question will become, Can the transformative process engendered by the third-space classroom extend beyond the university to other, larger, social spaces?

NOTE

1. See Linton, Mello, and O'Neill for a general discussion of incorporating disability into curricula; see Garland-Thomson ("Integrating Disability Studies") for ideas about incorporating disability specifically into literature classes.

SUGGESTIONS FOR STUDENT ACTIVITIES

Close Encounters of the Disability Kind

Ask students to examine and conceptualize their own encounters with disability. Allow them to write loosely and reflectively about any scene or scenes where they have encountered disability (in themselves, temporarily or permanently) or in others—for example, a random encounter with a stranger in some public space or a family member becoming disabled. On the chance that a student might imagine that they have *never* had a "close encounter of the disability kind" they might be encouraged to imagine, then, an encounter in their work or school lives that brought them "up close" with a person with a disability. They might recall such things as their own body positions, eye contact, or conversational comfort in this encounter. What did they expect might happen from or in the encounter and what really did happen? Were their expectations and reality the same?

Students could also extend this exercise from their own experience and brainstorm "close encounters" with disability that they have seen enacted in public and media spaces. What happens when a person with a disability appears on the silver screen or TV screen, in either scripted performances or in "real life" reporting of news events?

Social Scripting

Another direction students might go in with the ideas posited by Wilson and Lewiecki-Wilson would be to underscore the "common social scripts of individualism and individual rights" and "the rhetoric of victimhood." Can they name some of the plot lines and characterizations in these particular social scripts? Where can they point to for modern-day examples in operation? What are some of the common moves and motives in "the rhetoric of victimhood?" Again, where have they seen or heard such a rhetoric enacted lately? Creatively, students might be asked to collaboratively construct a short play that dramatizes, either straightforwardly or ironically, the "rhetoric of victimhood" or the "common social script of individualism." They could borrow easily from the plots and characters of many American novels or movies. What is lacking in familiar scripts of "disability as victimhood"? How might disability be understood not as "a script of individualism" but in terms of community?

14

From *Enforcing Diversity and Living with Disability: Learning from My First Teaching Year*

RAY PENCE

Taken from Pence's autobiographical, pedagogical, and critical essay, the following excerpt shows how Pence moves from being a teacher who struggled to appropriately use and address "diversity"—particularly through the use of African American texts in his syllabus—to a teacher who is diagnosed with a disability/chronic illness. Pence writes that he had been "preoccupied with the bodies of certain students" (the African American students who stopped coming to his class and did not turn in papers) when, later in the semester, he ironically faces the fact of his own body as disability "arrived to bring my body into my teaching." Pence's bodily experiences of limitation in movement and pain while teaching eventually led him toward disability studies. "I knew almost nothing about critical inquiries into whiteness and disability that were starting to attract widespread attention at around the same time I was getting ill," he writes. Pence's embodied experience led him to add disability to his syllabus and classroom discussions and toward a deeper inquiry into, rather than an enforcement of, "diversity."

I started learning about ability and disability during my second teaching semester, a time when I pressured myself not to colonize black bodies to serve my notion of diversity. Avoiding that abuse of power while being confident in my ability to teach the fiction and poetry that were part of my spring 1995 syllabus was the key to improvement. However, it soon became clear that I would handle situations involving black male students even less effectively than I had in the fall. This time, my emphasis on African American literature justified paternalistic interventions. Sterling Brown, Langston Hughes, Gwendolyn Brooks, and Toni Morrison were on my reading list for English 112: Composition and Literature. Why weren't my black students coming to

From *The Teacher's Body: Embodiment, Authority, and Identity in the Academy*, ed. Diane P. Freedman and Martha Stoddard Holmes (Albany: State U of NY P, 2003), 145–59.

class and turning in their work? I tried to answer the question by calling the students, seeking help from their academic advisors, dropping them from the course, and then asking the director of the composition program to "force add" them back into the class after I could no longer live with my decision. Once again, anxieties about the absence and presence of black bodies determined my decisions and priorities.

It took grave conflict with my own body to keep the second semester from turning into a repeat performance of the first. Psoriatic arthritis (PA), a condition I had never heard of until I had no choice but to listen, did not free me from dealing with real or imagined student problems. But the farther I went into territory from which there is no escape—chronic illness—the more I realized the need for new strategies to face difficulties that would, like students themselves, come and go. The first part of this chapter was about what went wrong with my teaching while I was preoccupied with the bodies of certain students; the rest addresses what happened when PA arrived to bring my body into my teaching. . . .

When people ask what my disability is (a common occurrence because it is obvious to others only during flare-ups), I usually tell them I have arthritis. This does not mean much because it can mean *too* much: There are more than one hundred kinds of rheumatic disease. (Theodosakis et al., 207). Saying that I have PA is more accurate and specific but still insufficient. PA takes five different forms: asymmetric polyarthritis, symmetric polyarthritis, arthritis mutilans, distal interphalangeal joints (DIP), and ankylosing spondyloarthropathy (Birks, 1–2). Because my symptoms correspond to four of these five variants, I still am unsure of the PA category I belong to. Though I have help from medical authorities and loved ones, learning the truth about PA is a solitary process because it is a rare condition that affects fewer than three million people in the United States (American College of Rheumatology, 1; Birks, 1). My health condition is marginalized even if I am not. There are no best-selling books offering cures or prevention of PA; I have never met a fellow "sufferer" (though I have found friendship with people who have other forms of arthritis, all of them women).

I would not begin learning all of this information until I received a definite PA diagnosis in the summer of 1998, more than three years after initial symptoms. To find out what the symptoms meant I made several disorienting visits to a local hospital whose specialists took over when the campus clinic could do no more. A gastrointestinal doctor looked for explanations of my stomach problems and anemia with upper and lower GIs and X rays. Many of the procedures took place during the midmorning hours, just after I had finished teaching.

In spite of the pain of my symptoms and the fear that went with the tests, I missed just one day of teaching and one seminar meeting and was proud that I had upheld the Protestant work ethic my father embodied.[1] The gastrointestinal specialist was also working hard but could find nothing wrong for all of his effort. Though my perception was clouded by sedatives that helped me through the lower GI, I can recall with clarity his frustrated tone when he told me I must go to a rheumatologist.

This was a turning point. My stomach pains had faded away, but my joints were worse than ever, and more of them were falling prey to the unknown assailant. While teaching sometime in April 1995, I tried to turn my head to face the students who sat to either side of me in our discussion circle but could not do so without agonizing effort. Other movements I had taken for granted brought unwelcome surprises. I learned to dread dropping things because I had to squat slowly and stiffly to retrieve them; bending from the waist became a faint memory. Plugging in an overhead projector or VCR triggered pain that shot from my elbow to my shoulder. Rising from a chair after just a few minutes created "locking" sensations in my lower back and ankles, which often did not feel as if they were there to support my decreasing weight.

Talking about these symptoms with my peers was an activity I usually avoided, in contrast to my compulsive discussions of problems with enforcing diversity (especially when the topic was "our" African American students). As for revealing to my students what I saw as physical and emotional weaknesses, this was out of the question. Our classroom environment, tense from the beginning because of the demeanor I adopted in reaction to the fall semester, had no camaraderie or trust. As the end of the semester neared, my symptoms intensified, and I struggled to be a minimally effective pedagogical presence. Students were less enthusiastic with each assignment and more willing to challenge me rudely. In bitter moments I told myself—and believed—that some of them would be happy to know I was ill. . . .

Now that I have lived and taught with PA for more than six years, I know from experience that emotional turmoil intensifies whatever symptoms I have, especially when that turmoil is associated with or generated inside the classroom.

But what interests me more than probable or certain connections between my reactions to teaching situations and my PA is the way my illness experiences are situated, culturally and socially. The postmodern theoretical context Arthur W. Frank uses in his study of the emerging genre of life writing about illness in *The Wounded Storyteller: Body, Illness, and Ethics* was also a setting for my initiation into the world of PA. Though I knew almost nothing about critical inquiries into whiteness and disability that were starting to attract widespread attention at around the same time I was getting ill, I was aware of the postmodern thought that influenced those inquiries. My first year of graduate school was an immersion in antifoundational philosophy that showed me the importance of Michel Foucault's analyses of institutional power and medical and clinical discourses. At the time I resisted much of what I read because it challenged my investment in humanism and Marxism. Later I realized that this difficult, disorienting thought had prepared me to interrogate the medical model of disability, which locates defects in individual bodies and their remedies in modern scientific practices. Chronic illness helped me find something useful in postmodern philosophy; postmodern philosophy made me want to assess my illness and myself as a life writer.

Acknowledging that PA has made me see things in postmodernism I did not notice before becoming ill is hard to do without turning this story into a variation on the theme of disability as a character builder. My main interest as a narrator is relationships between my body and mind, whose cohesion has been made clear to me by feminism, postmodernism, and PA. With its emphasis on postmodern critical theory, my first year of graduate school showed me sites for exercising agency and asserting identity I had not known. Becoming ill that same year was the beginning of moving toward such a site as a person with disability. Discovering disability studies was finding the site itself, a place where I can begin to make sense of how PA contributes to my social position, relationships, and responsibilities. Few concepts are more important to disability studies than the medical epistemology that the field challenges but cannot escape any more than people can be outside capitalism, heterosexism, patriarchy, and racism. Knowing about that model and its critique is one of the many empowering benefits of knowing about disability studies. In sum, disability studies manages my symptoms as much as Naproxen pills and Methotrexate shots do,[2] and this is a story of converging factors, not of causes and effects.

I have not always been as eager to share my story as I am now and wish I had kept a journal during the onset of PA. Comparing my initial reactions to PA with the perspective I have as a participant in two interdisciplinary fields, one dedicated to bringing disability to the attention of the humanities and the other committed to explaining change and conflict in the United States, would be useful. With its emphasis on life writing by people with disabilities who also theorize disability as scholars, disability studies is a community and context for stories like this. Fortunately, the flexibility that American studies and disability studies share should make the former field an additional space for disability narratives and help overcome past inattention to disability.

My own required coursework as a PhD student in American studies, which began in 1997, included no courses that addressed disability. What bothered me more than this exclusion at a time when disability studies was emerging was my failure to notice it sooner, especially considering my PA. That American studies would include class, ethnicity, gender, race, and sexuality seemed natural to me. When I thought of disability as a subject of scholarly interest I confined it to applied fields such as occupational therapy and special education. Bound by medical model thinking, I had trouble seeing that American studies was not as inclusive as I had assumed.[3] But American studies was also where I found peers and teachers who pointed me toward Simi Linton and Rosemarie Garland-Thomson, who urge dialogue between disability studies and American studies (Linton, 2–3; Garland-Thomson "Incorporating," 1).[4] Now I work on making the bulk of my reading and writing contribute to that conversation. . . .

An inclusive syllabus is a simple way to avoid returning to the narrow diversity definition of my past. Being attentive to the presence and absence of students with disabilities is more complicated and crucial. Over the past seven years my courses have been those that degree-seeking students take because they must and consequently are excellent sites for assessing campus diversity. As the reader knows, students of color are vastly outnumbered in the institutions where I have worked. Students with disabilities are usually not represented at all. Though a small handful of my students have had learning disabilities such as dyslexia, not one blind student or deaf student or wheelchair-using student has come through my door. People with disabilities and topics related to them were as invisible in the classes I taught as they were in seminars I took. In both cases I was too slow to recognize these disturbing realities, which showed me just how much I was a part of ableism.

There will always be one person with a disability in any classroom where I am teaching, but I anticipate retaining control over visibility of my PA, which seems to have stabilized, well into the future. On the few occasions when I have revealed my condition I have done so out of curiosity about how the news will be received and not because I have been all that comfortable doing so. One reason is the limits on how much of myself I will share with students who for the most part would rather be other places than my class. Perhaps things will change when I teach graduate students. Another reason is my reluctance to present myself to anyone as a person with a disability because I do not meet unofficial, informal, but nevertheless powerful public criteria. When I stand before my students I am passing as an able-bodied person, one who knows he should not reinforce social standards for competence and control. This says more about how I perceive my students than about the students themselves, but I feel I must avoid speaking of or showing my disability lest I lose authority. There have, of course, been exceptions to my silence. Sometimes I will give my perspective as a person with arthritis (not PA) when we encounter characters with a form of that condition. Just as it was crucial for me to overcome my ignorance about arthritis and whom it does and does not affect, it is important for students to see that many people who appear to be healthy do not always feel that way. In general, however, I have incorporated disability into my courses not by talking about myself but by making sure it is a category and a subject that deserves attention in its own right and in conjunction with other topics. . . .

NOTES

1. Since that time I have not missed a teaching session because of my illness, though there have been times when doing so would have been better for my students and for me.

2. Naproxen is a type of nonsteroidal anti-inflammatory medicine, a more potent form of over-the-counter products such as Aleve. Methotrexate is a toxic drug that was developed to treat cancer but has been effective against arthritis and psoriasis. I have taken Naproxen since May 1995 but began Methotrexate in 1998. The lack of dramatic results with Methotrexate in my treatment may validate what physicians suspect is true: The medicine is most effective when prescribed during the earliest stages of PA and other forms of arthritis.

3. George Lipsitz's address to the 1994 American Studies Association, titled "No Shining City on a Hill," is an example of this neglect. Lipsitz argues energetically that his field should align itself with various social movements but emphasizes ethnicity and race to the exclusion of people with disabilities and their cultures.

4. I am also intrigued by Linton's and Garland-Thomson's inclusive disability definitions. For Garland-Thomson disability is "the attribution of corporeal deviance—not so much a property of bodies as a product of cultural rules about what bodies should be or do" (*Extraordinary Bodies*, 6). Linton avoids Garland-Thomson's stress on physical disability with a broader definition. Disability is "a marker of identity [that] has been used to build a coalition of people with significant impairments" and a category open to those with "behavioral or anatomical characteristics marked as deviant, and people who have or are suspected of having conditions . . . that make them targets of discrimination" (Linton, 12).

REFLECTING ON YOUR TEACHING

Authority of Disability

In what ways would your authority as a teacher be threatened or changed by disability? First, make a list of the expected or common qualities of teachers and teaching, the typical dynamics of a college classroom, the stereotypes of "professor." Then compose a short reflective paper about the "authority" of disability on the teacher's body. In your reflection you might also consider the normalizing space of education (as evidenced in typical classroom behaviors and interactions) in general. What are "normal' classroom behaviors, interactions, processes? How is it that disability does or does not "fit" in that space?

SUGGESTIONS FOR STUDENT ACTIVITIES

Comparing Whiteness and Able-Bodiedness

Ask students to write an informal reflective paper considering the parallels between "whiteness" as an unexamined location and "able-bodiedness." In what ways do identifications of race/ethnicity and disability similarly depend upon a central norm? In what ways are race/ethnicity and disability different? After giving students a suitable amount of time to write, ask for volunteers to share their reflections, and as a class draw on the board a map or chart of the overlaps between the unmarked center of "normal" (white, nondisabled) against which race/ethnicity and disability are marked out. Also list the ways the categories differ.

Debate on Diversity

In another kind of related activity, ask students to stage a debate on the topic "disability as part of diversity." In what ways can they argue that disability is or should be part of the "diversity" umbrella (and requirements?) at their college? In what ways can they argue against its inclusion in college "diversity" requirements and foci? What assumptions do these arguments uncover about students' ideas about diversity and disability?

15

From *Visible Disability in the College Classroom*

MARK MOSSMAN

This excerpt starts at the point when Mossman begins to attend to the importance of disability autobiography laid alongside the growing body of theoretical and critical work in disability studies. Mossman links disability and autobiography as part of "the rhetoric of social change." Situating oneself within this rhetoric enables the person with a disability "to take some measure of control" over its meaning. To illustrate this theoretical claim, he uses a specific "dressing down" scene when he chooses, on the last day of a class he is teaching, to wear shorts. Such a clothing choice "meant dressing down into disfigurement and disability." Mossman's act invites more than just informality; it offers a constructive paradox to his students because they must confront "a disabled person performing a normalized activity— teaching."

Mossman ends with a moral to his story: We should strive to "authenticate disability" and to have disability be "understood as 'normal'" so that all students can "claim power, equality, and volition through performance, through the autobiographical demonstration of personhood."

As a person with a disability, I believe that telling stories, both in my scholarship and in the classroom, is doing something, making something happen, for telling stories, in the social context of disability, articulates the rhetoric of social change, enacts the autobiographical process that enables the disabled subjectivity in part to make itself, to take some measure of control and volition in its own construction. Further, when that subjectivity is in the socialized position of teacher and scholar, those stories become extremely powerful and pervasive, in that they become part of the fabric of the larger curriculum; disability narrative is a tool that can be used to open up areas of

From *College English* 64, no. 6 (July 2002): 645–59.

thought and experience, a weapon that strikes down the oppressive forces that work against equality, civil rights, and volition. In the postmodern cultures of the West, disability and autobiography are linked, inherently: in order for disabled persons to claim normality, we must often do so through discourse, through the perspective of autobiographical narrative and the performative construction of an "I," through, again, the story. Postmodernity allows such narratives to be articulated, for postmodernity is most often characterized by the deconstruction of the larger, more oppressive metanarratives, such as the construct of normality, that defined early modern and modern cultural practice. As a result, postmodernism creates a cultural dynamic of instability, a number of spaces where the body itself can become a potential utopian site: "Utopia in the postmodern era has, in effect, transferred its location to the solitary, private, individual body" (Morris, 137). Each individual, can, potentially, become empowered through storytelling; each person, no matter what his or her status or social context, can, potentially, resist the oppressive force of a master discourse by taking control of his or her narrative and constructing it as he or she chooses. In the cultural space of a postmodern undergraduate classroom, then, autobiographical disability narratives can and should become narratives of empowerment and agency, and our job in the classroom is to provide our students with the opportunities to articulate such volitional, empowered voices.

And so now I have yet another story to tell you. I wore shorts to class for the first time the other day. I did so with this project in mind. It was the end of the term, the last day of the spring semester. I had spent the weekend and early part of the week on an annual vacation to Florida, a very short trip that included four warm days of tennis, golf, and swimming. Needless to say, I was browned by the sun and nourished by a steady diet of seafood, exercise, and mental relaxation, and therefore I was still in a certain frame of mind: in the classroom I tend to be more formal in my dress, but on this day, the last day of class, I decided to dress down, to wear just shorts, a t-shirt, and sandals. In my case, of course, this meant dressing down into disfigurement and disability; and again, in my case, my choice of clothing also meant a choice in the way I would be understood: as a disabled person performing a normalized activity—teaching—the role or stigma of the super-crip would be available, certainly present in the rendering of my body.

The dynamics of that day in the classroom were in many ways a repetition of the scene initially narrated. I got to class early, and remained sitting down, my legs hidden underneath the large wooden desk at the front of the room. My students slowly came in and sat down; they talked to one another and to me, as was our typical procedure throughout the semester. It was comfortable, lots of talking and laughter. At 9:00 A.M. sharp, and after I had counted everyone present, I stood up and moved out from behind the desk to the front of the room. And, in that moment, my body—its exterior physical constitution—changed, became different, directly redetermined my interior self, a "new," "disabled" self; in a moment's time, then, my socialized role of instructor or professor was severely complicated by the disfigurement of my body. My body, as before, became an event, a hot site of cultural activity, the location of numerous "stories": inscribed upon my body in a single moment were narratives of disability as well as the standard narratives of the academy, simultaneous narratives, then, of both marginality and power.

I am used to the public reaction to my abnormal body, and I am used to these kinds of responses in the classroom. Again, I have a pronounced limp, and so there is always that moment when the class first sees me move, first sees the awkwardness of my gait, first recognizes and constructs physical difference. But this was *really* different; my disability was entirely visible, entirely open. As I stood before the class on that day my disfigurement was no longer hidden by the desk or with pants. The disfigurement of my natural body, the postmodernity of its acquired artificiality (with the prosthetic limb), were apparent to the mostly first- and second-year students—a sudden, explicit discovery. Their responses, indeed, were not surprising—eyes drifted unconsciously to the prosthetic limb, confused expressions clouded their faces, indicating uncertainty, a recognition of difference, a new construction of meaning being built for and applied to my body.

The clear visibility of my disfigurement and disability is what is significant here, for visible disability is what triggered the process of remaking my body in the first moments of class that day. Mitchell and Snyder have written that the "equation of physical disability with social identity creates a tautological link between biology and self (imagined or real) that cannot be unmoored—the physical world provides the material evidence of an inner life (corrupt or virtuous) that is secured by the mark of physical difference" ("Introduction," 3). This link between my biological construction and my inner self was firmly established that day, and as a result of my suddenly very open external disfigurement, my internal, invisible self was rewritten, remade by the students who were my audience, within an entirely new context. When I wore shorts to class, my disability and abnormality became authentic structures in the class for the first time. There could be no physical claim of normality on my part. Abnormality was physically present, and demanded some kind of recognition and absorption. The key evidence demonstrating this fact was my students' behavior. Those quick glances and unconscious stares denoted difference and created a unique environment: the instructor's body, normally the location of power in the classroom, was a deviant body, a body typically void of power in the practice of culture. Indeed, those stares, the recognition of difference itself, significantly reshaped the environment, changed the behavior of the class: no longer was the classroom a normalized space; now, with my visible presence, the only visibly disabled body in the room, the environment had changed, become different. The chit-chat mood of only a few minutes before had vanished. The class was cautious, quiet, tense. The free-floating discussion of the semester, the real comfort of this particular class, simply evaporated. In simple terms: it got weird; it got real weird.

My response, like that of my students, was a little uncertain. I felt their confusion and their embarrassment at feeling confused, their strong need to avoid "staring," to see sameness and allow inclusion, but also their equally strong need to observe, absorb, and understand my body and its newness, its suddenly different social status. Difference, abnormality: this was what was being constructed upon me, around me, through me, and of course I did not necessarily want that construction to take place; I did not want to be a super-crip, to be heroic or brave for simply being the professor at the front of the room, for doing my "normal" job with my "abnormal" body. I needed to take control of my body, to share in its story, in its social meaning. And so I told a story. I told the class, with what I am sure was an awkward start, how my body came to be as it is now, the complicated medical history of it. The story was short: numerous anomalies at birth; a large number of "corrective" surgeries through youth; then kidney failure in my late twenties, and now transplantation issues in my early thirties. The class listened; I remember saying that it was all "no big deal"; a few students nodded their heads, and then we moved on, and began our final discussion of the term, a talk that concerned Dylan Thomas's "Fern Hill."

The story, or explanation, worked, though: through it I was able to negotiate difference and abnormality, gain a measure of control over my own body and its making, claim and achieve inclusion and recognition as "normal." Indeed, I believe that the ultimate, larger result of that day in class was an undermining of stereotype, the construction of a new story of disability: my body, by telling its own story, as well as by simply being at the head of the class, directing discussion and conducting the class activity, resisted the many kinds of stereotypes or stigmas, including the poles of passivity and/or active heroism, often attached to bodies that are disabled. My body became a vehicle for social change, for my body, when it is placed in situations like that one, demonstrates that physical abnormality does not equal powerlessness and helplessness, or heroism and bravery, or anything else necessarily, but rather that disability equals normality and sameness.

My classroom experience here is not of course how visible disability usually works. Often when disability is visible, truly present in the physical moment, exclusion and a resulting discrimination are present in the interaction. If there is not a vehicle through which one may claim normality—such as the power allocated to the instructor in the classroom, or the agency of the particular individual—then exclusion, in some form, will almost always occur. Right now, for example, I am able to theoretically claim normality, in writing, with autobiography, by telling stories that everyone can understand and appreciate; I know that if I were speaking to you, my reader, along with all of the readers of this essay, most of whom are able-bodied and visibly normal, in a large forum or conference room, and if I were wearing shorts and a t-shirt to boot, the normality that I can claim here would not be possible, would not be nearly as close to being available in the interaction. In situations like the one narrated above the abnormality of the body typically overrides any claim of normality that the person may have. The body, when it is abnormal (or rendered as such), is in practice directly linked to the subjectivity the body performs, so that the subjectivity itself becomes abnormal, deviant. Visible disability, especially when it is the disenfranchised student in the college classroom who is disabled, often translates into such moments of exclusion and othering.

My ultimate point here, then, is obvious: we need to set up classroom environments that allow students to claim power, equality, and volition through performance, through the autobiographical demonstration of personhood. We need to use that same tautological link between the body and the self to build up normality and to wreck the negative constructs of abnormality. In other words, we need to authenticate disability, to make it a real, viable perspective on the world. Authentication happens when disability is understood as "normal," and in our classrooms this process of normalization happens only when we allow our students, all of them, to speak, to fully participate in the discussion, when we give them, all of them, a normalized status.

REFLECTING ON YOUR TEACHING

The Teaching Body

As the teacher, your body is extremely visible to your students. How you dress, act, and speak marks you in a particular way and sets particular standards or norms for your students. Write a self-reflection on how students perhaps "read" your bodily performance. Consider ways you might use your body to establish or challenge norms in the classroom.

SUGGESTIONS FOR STUDENT ACTIVITIES

Researching Different Kinds of Disabilities

Ask students to research and then discuss the differences between "visible" and "invisible" disabilities. They might begin by generating a list of questions that they have surrounding the distinctions between "visible" and "invisible" disabilities. They might also consider these questions: Why do we need these two categories anyway? How are these two dominant categories created and maintained in medical and social science research? How do they contribute to a hierarchy of disabilities? Likewise, how do "visible" or "invisible" disabilities appear in our literary and historical record? How do the media seem to respond to or deal with "visible" or "invisible" disabilities? What counts as "visible" or "invisible"? Do we behave differently when faced with "visible" disabilities? When and how can an "invisible" disability become "visible"? And likewise, when and how can a "visible" disability also be made "invisible"? What scenes, situations, interactions, and relationships construct a person with a disability as either "visible" or "invisible"?

Cloaking and Exposing Disability

In a more creative vein, students might pair up and have one member of the pair write a brief scene where a character operates with an invisible disability; then let the other member of the pair rewrite the scene with the disability made visible. When they are finished with these creative twinned scenes, they might also go on to engage in a critical discussion about their own work and the process involved in cloaking or exposing the character's disability in this scene: What shifts about the character and his/her relation to the plot or the other characters? How does the "visible" nature of the disability change that character? How (and why) can disability be "discovered" or "revealed" in literature (and, thus, in life)? How, too, can it be "cloaked," hidden, or downplayed? Is disability—whether visible or invisible—more than just a convenient metaphor or plot point in the scenes they have created? Why or why not?

16 Universal Design for Learning: A Brief Annotated Bibliography of Online Resources

COMPILED BY JAY DOLMAGE

This briefly annotated bibliography features eight online resources on Universal Design for Learning (UDL). As you may have read in Jay Dolmage's essay "Mapping Composition" (on p. 14 in this volume) UDL is a product of the disability movement. Adapted from the field of architecture (to design buildings and spaces that will meet the needs of all people throughout their lives), Universal Design for Learning sets out core principles of a flexible design for teaching that meet the needs of all (and different) learners. Some of the resources listed here connect UDL directly to the college writing classroom; others provide accessible overviews of UD in architecture and in innovative technologies for the disabled, which have improved the lives of all of us.

Bruch, Patrick L. "Universality in Basic Writing: Connecting Multicultural Justice, Universal Instructional Design and Classroom Practices." *Basic Writing E-Journal* 5, no. 1 (2004). www.asu.edu/clas/english/composition/cbw/journal_1.htm
This article connects the philosophy of UD with theories of multiculturalism in the classroom.
Dunn, Patricia A., and Kathleen Dunn DeMers. "Reversing Notions of Disability and Accommodation: Embracing Universal Design in Writing Pedagogy and Web Space." *Kairos* 7, no. 1 (2002). http://english.ttu.edu/kairos/7.1/
This Web-text offers suggestions for a Universally Designed composition pedagogy.
"Fast Facts for Faculty: Universal Design for Learning, Elements of Good Teaching." *The Ohio State University Partnership Grant Improving the Quality of Education for Students with Disabilities.* http://telr.osu.edu/dpg/fastfact/fastfactcolor/Universal.pdf
A great primer on UD, this pdf file lists some of the main concepts of UD as they might be practically implemented in the classroom.
Jacobs, Steve. "The Electronic Curb-Cut Effect." Developed in support of the World Bank Conference: *Disability and Development.* Copyright © 2000–2002 by NCR Corporation. www.icdri.org/technology/ecceff.htm

Tracing some of the history of usability and UD, Jacobs shows how innovations for people with disabilities have led to major shifts in our relationship with technology.

McAlexander, Patricia J. "Using Principles of Universal Design in College Composition Courses." *Basic Writing E-Journal* 5, no. 1 (2004). www.asu.edu/clas/english/composition/cbw/journal_1.htm

McAlexander offers suggestions for including UD principles in the writing classroom.

"Principles for Universal Design." Center for Universal Design, North Carolina State University. www.design.ncsu.edu:8120/cud/univ_design/princ_overview.htm

This list and the site from which it comes illustrate the origins of UD in architecture. Scholars at the NC State Center for Universal Design originated the concept, and the site now houses many useful materials related to both the history of UD and its future, including its uses in pedagogical design.

UD Education Online. www.udeducation.org/

A site designed for teachers and students, this resource includes discussion boards, links, and teaching suggestions. The site itself is highly accessible and customizable, linking form with content.

Welch, Polly, ed. *Strategies for Teaching Universal Design*. Adaptive Environments Center. www.adaptenv.org/universal/strategies.php

This book-length, edited collection of essays offers suggestions for teaching UD and on applying its concepts to pedagogy.

REFLECTING ON YOUR TEACHING

Evaluating and Redesigning for UDL

Ask students in your class at midterm or near the end of the semester to annotate and revise your syllabus to incorporate UDL principles and activities. Or, ask students to write an informal course evaluation (try to make this anonymous) in which they give you feedback about the variety and flexibility of teaching activities in your class. As a final step, collect and reflect on the evaluations and feedback from students and make notes toward redesigning your syllabus for the next time you teach.

SUGGESTIONS FOR STUDENT ACTIVITY

Research and Presentations on UDL

Ask students to work collaboratively with one or two of these online resources. Small groups or pairs of students could browse through the resource and then make a short, collaborative presentation to the rest of the class that outlines the key features of the site, anything interesting they learned from the resource; and ways they can now imagine that their own college classrooms could make (better) use of UDL principles.

For a follow-up project, the class could compile a descriptive list of UDL accommodations and characteristics. Then, using this list, students could evaluate a number of other classes they take: Which UDL principles did they find being used? Which were not used? Why or why not? This activity could be completed by individual reflective writing or by a class discussion.

Analyzing Language, Representation, and Narrative from a Disability Perspective

17 From *Reassigning Meaning*

SIMI LINTON

Simi Linton states that "a project of disability studies scholars and the disability rights movement has been to bring into sharp relief the processes by which disability has been imbued with the meaning(s) it has." Linton goes on to discuss language usage and its effects on attitudes and actions. She looks at words and labels ("nice" and "nasty" words, for example); commonplace phrases, such as "overcoming a disability," that contain embedded cultural norms and arguments about disability; and the structuring effect of language on people with disabilities, such as how familiar discourses of disability usually cast the disabled person in a passive role while the strong social stigma of "having a disability" typically makes people want to conceal their disability and "pass" as nondisabled. Linton's openly activist motive, to "reassign a meaning that is consistent with a sociopolitical analysis of disability," may not be one students or instructors necessarily share. But the attention she and the other authors give to language, representation, and narrative can be used to focus classroom work on close rhetorical and critical analysis of writing.

The term *disability*, as it has been used in general parlance, appears to signify something material and concrete, a physical or psychological condition considered to have predominantly medical significance. Yet it is an arbitrary designation, used erratically both by professionals who lay claim to naming such phenomena and by confused citizens. A project of disability studies scholars and the disability rights movement has been to bring into sharp relief the processes by which *disability* has been imbued with the meaning(s) it has and to reassign a meaning that is consistent with a sociopolitical analysis of disability. Divesting it of its current meaning is no small feat. As typically used, the term *disability* is a linchpin in a complex web of social ideals,

From Simi Linton, *Claiming Disability: Knowledge and Identity* (New York: New York UP, 1998), 8–33.

institutional structures, and government policies. As a result, many people have a vested interest in keeping a tenacious hold on the current meaning because it is consistent with the practices and policies that are central to their livelihood on their ideologies. People may not be driven as much by economic imperatives as by a personal investment in their own beliefs and practices, in metaphors they hold dear, or in their own professional roles. . . .

NICE WORDS

Terms such as *physically challenged,* and *able disabled, handicapable,* and *special people/children* surface at different times and places. They are rarely used by disabled activists and scholars (except with palpable irony). Although they may be considered well-meaning attempts to inflate the value of people with disabilities, they convey the boosterism and do-gooder mentality endemic to the paternalistic agencies that control many disabled people's lives.

Physically challenged is the only term that seems to have caught on. Nondisabled people use it in conversation around disabled people with no hint of anxiety, suggesting that they believe it is a positive term. This phrase does not make much sense to me. To say that I am physically challenged is to state that the obstacles to my participation are physical, not social, and that the barrier is my own disability. Further, it separates those of us with mobility impairments from other disabled people, not a valid or useful partition for those interested in coalition building and social change. Various derivatives of the term *challenged* have been adopted as a description used in jokes. For instance, "vertically challenged" is considered a humorous way to say *short,* and "calorically challenged" to say *fat.* A review of the Broadway musical *Big* in the *New Yorker* said that the score is "melodically challenged."

I observed a unique use of *challenged* in the local Barnes and Nobles superstore. The children's department has a section for books on "Children with Special Needs." There are shelves labeled "Epilepsy" and "Down Syndrome." A separate shelf at the bottom is labeled "Misc. Challenges," indicating that it is now used as an organizing category.

The term *able disabled* and *handicapable* have had a fairly short shelf life. They are used, it seems, to refute common stereotypes of incompetence. They are, though, defensive and reactive terms rather than terms that advance a new agenda.

An entire profession, in fact a number of professions, are built around the word *special.* A huge infrastructure rests on the idea that *special children* and *special education* are valid and useful structuring ideas. Although dictionaries insist that *special* be reserved for things that surpass what is common, are distinct among others of their kind, are peculiar to a specific person, have a limited or specific function, are arranged for a particular purpose, or are arranged for a particular occasion, experience teaches us that *special* when applied to education or to children means something different.

The naming of disabled children and the education that "is designed for students whose learning needs cannot be met by a standard school curriculum" (*American Heritage Dictionary*, 1992) as *special* can be understood only as a euphemistic formulation, obscuring the reality that neither the children nor the education are considered desirable and that they are not thought to "surpass what is common."

Labeling the education and its recipients special may have been a deliberate attempt to confer legitimacy on the educational practice and to prop up a discarded group. It is also important to consider the unconscious feelings such a strategy may mask. It is my feeling that the nation in general responds to disabled people with great ambivalence. Whatever antipathy and disdain is felt is in competition with feelings of empathy, guilt, and identification. The term *special* may be evidence not of a deliberate maneuver but of a collective "reaction formation," Freud's term for the unconscious defense mechanism in which an individual adopts attitudes and behaviors that are opposite to his or her own true feelings, in order to protect the ego from the anxiety felt from experiencing the real feelings.

The ironic character of the word *special* has been captured in the routine on *Saturday Night Live,* where the character called the "Church Lady" declares when she encounters something distasteful or morally repugnant, "Isn't that special!"

NASTY WORDS

Some of the less subtle or more idiomatic terms for disabled people such as *cripple, vegetable, dumb, deformed, retard,* and *gimp* have generally been expunged from public conversation but emerge in various types of discourse. Although they are understood to be offensive or hurtful, they are still used in jokes and in informal conversation.

Cripple as a descriptor of disabled people is considered impolite, but the word has retained its metaphoric vitality, as in "the exposé in the newspaper crippled the politician's campaign." The term is also used occasionally for its evocative power. A recent example appeared in *Lingua Franca* in a report on research on the behaviors of German academics. The article states that a professor had "documented the postwar careers of psychiatrists and geneticists involved in gassing thousands of cripples and schizophrenics" (Allen, 1996, 37). *Cripple* is used rather loosely here to describe people with a broad range of disabilities. The victims of Nazi slaughter were people with mental illness, epilepsy, chronic illness, and mental retardation, as well as people with physical disabilities. Yet *cripple* is defined as "one that is partially disabled or unable to use a limb or limbs" (*American Heritage Dictionary*, 1992) and is usually used only to refer to people with mobility impairments. Because *cripple* inadequately and inaccurately describes the group, the author of the report is likely to have chosen this term for its effect.

Cripple has also been revived by some in the disability community who refer to each other as "crips" or "cripples." A performance group with disabled actors call themselves the "Wry Crips." "In reclaiming 'cripple,' disabled people are taking the thing in their identity that scares the outside world the most and making it a cause to revel in with militant self-pride" (Shapiro, 1993, 34).

A recent personal ad in the *Village Voice* shows how "out" the term is:

> TWISTED CRIP: Very sexy, full-figured disabled BiWF artist sks fearless, fun, oral BiWF for hot, no-strings nights. Wheelchair, tattoo, dom. Shaved a+ N/S. No men/sleep-overs.

Cripple, gimp, and *freak* as used by the disability community have transgressive potential. They are personally and politically useful as a means to comment on oppression because they assert our right to name experience.

SPEAKING ABOUT OVERCOMING AND PASSING

The popular phrase *overcoming a disability* is used most often to describe someone with a disability who seems competent and successful in some way, in a sentence something like "She has overcome her disability and is a great success." One interpretation of the phrase might be that the individual's disability no longer limits her or him, that sheer strength or willpower has brought the person to the point where the disability is no longer a hindrance. Another implication of the phrase may be that the person has risen above society's expectation for someone with those characteristics. Because it is physically impossible to *overcome* a disability, it seems that what is *overcome* is the social stigma of having a disability. This idea is reinforced by the equally confounding statement "I never think of you as disabled." An implication of these statements is that the other members of the group from which the individual has supposedly moved beyond are not as brave, strong, or extraordinary as the person who has *overcome* that designation.

The expression is similar in tone to the phrase that was once more commonly used to describe an African American who was considered exceptional in some way: "He/she is a credit to his/her race." The implication of this phrase is that the "race" is somehow discredited and needs people with extraordinary talent to give the group the credibility that it otherwise lacks. In either case, talking about the person who is African American or talking about the person with a disability, these phrases are often said with the intention of complimenting someone. The compliment has a double edge. To accept it, one must accept the implication that the group is inferior and that the individual is unlike others in that group.

The ideas imbedded in the *overcoming* rhetoric are of personal triumph over a personal condition. The idea that someone can *overcome* a disability has not been generated within the community; it is a wish fulfillment generated from the outside. It is a demand that you be plucky and resolute, and not let the obstacles get in your way. If there are no curb cuts at the corner of the street so that people who use wheelchairs can get across, then you should learn to do wheelies and jump the curbs. If there are no sign language interpreters for deaf students at the high school, then you should study harder, read lips, and stay up late copying notes from a classmate. When disabled people internalize the demand to "overcome" rather than demand social change, they shoulder the same kind of exhausting and self-defeating "Super Mom" burden that feminists have analyzed.

The phrase *overcome a disability* may also be a shorthand version of saying "someone with a disability overcame many obstacles." Tremblay (1996) uses that phrase when describing behaviors of disabled World War II veterans upon returning to the community: "[T]heir main strategies were to develop individualized strategies to overcome the obstacles they found in the community" (165). She introduces this idea as a means to describe how the vets relied on their own ingenuity to manage an inaccessible environment rather than demand that the community change to include them.

In both uses of *overcome*, the individual's responsibility for her or his own success is paramount. If we, as a society, place the onus on individuals with disabilities to work harder to "compensate" for their disabilities or to "overcome" their condition or the barriers in the environment, we have no need for civil rights legislation or affirmative action.

Lest I be misunderstood, I don't see working hard, doing well, or striving for health, fitness, and well-being as contradictory to the aims of the disability rights movement. Indeed, the movement's goal is to provide greater opportunity to pursue these activities. However, we shouldn't be impelled to do these because we have a disability, to prove to some social overseer that we can perform, but we should pursue them because they deliver their own rewards and satisfactions.

A related concept, familiar in African American culture as well as in lesbian and gay culture, is that of *passing*. African Americans who pass for white and lesbians and gays who pass for straight do so for a variety of personal, social, and often economic reasons. Disabled people, if they are able to conceal their impairment or confine their activities to those that do not reveal their disability, have been known to pass. For a member of any of these groups, passing may be a deliberate effort to avoid discrimination or ostracism, or it may be an almost unconscious, Herculean effort to deny to oneself the reality of one's racial history, sexual feelings, or bodily state. The attempt may be a deliberate act to protect oneself from the loathing of society or may be an unchecked impulse spurred by an internalized self-loathing. It is likely that often the reasons entail an admixture of any of these various parts.

Henry Louis Gates, Jr. (1996) spoke of the various reasons for passing in an essay on the literary critic Anatole Broyard. Broyard was born in New Orleans to a family that identified as "Negro." His skin was so light that for his entire career as "one of literary America's foremost gatekeepers" (66) the majority of people who knew him did not know this. His children, by then adults, learned of his racial history shortly before he died. Sandy Broyard, Anatole's wife, remarked that she thought that "his own personal history continued to be painful to him. . . . In passing, you cause your family great anguish, but I also think conversely, do we look at the anguish it causes the person who is passing? Or the anguish that it was born out of?" (75).

When disabled people are able to pass for nondisabled, and do, the emotional toll it takes is enormous. I have heard people talk about hiding a hearing impairment to classmates or colleagues for years, or others who manage to conceal parts of their body, or to hide a prosthesis. These actions, though, may not result in a family's anguish; they may, in fact, be behaviors that the family insists upon, reinforces, or otherwise shames the individual into. Some disabled people describe how they were subjected to numerous painful surgeries and medical procedures when they were young not so much, they believe, to increase their comfort and ease of mobility as to fulfill their families' wish to make them appear "more normal." . . .

Both passing and overcoming take their toll. The loss of community, the anxiety, and the self-doubt that inevitably accompany this ambiguous social position and the ambivalent personal state are the enormous cost of declaring disability unacceptable. It is not surprising that disabled people also speak of "coming out" in the same way that members of the lesbian and gay community do. A woman I met at a disability studies conference not long ago said to me in the course of a conversation about personal experience: "I'm five years old." She went on to say that despite being significantly disabled for many years, she had really only recently discovered the disabled community and allied with it. For her, "coming out" was a process that began when she recognized how her effort to "be like everyone else" was not satisfying her own needs and wishes. She discovered other disabled people and began to identify clearly as disabled, and then purchased a motorized scooter, which meant she didn't have to expend enormous energy walking. She told this tale with gusto, obviously pleased with the psychic and physical energy she had gained. Stories such as hers provide evidence of the personal burdens many disabled people live with. Shame and fear are personal burdens, but if these tales are told, we can demonstrate how the personal is indeed the political. And further, that the unexamined connections between the personal and political are the curricular.

NORMAL/ABNORMAL

Normal and *abnormal* are convenient but problematic terms used to describe a person or group of people. These terms are often used to distinguish between people with and without disabilities. In various academic disciplines and in common usage, *normal* and *abnormal* assume different meanings. In psychometrics, *norm* or *normal* are terms describing individuals or characteristics that fall within the center of the normal distribution on whatever variable is being measured. However, as the notion of *normal* is applied in social science contexts and certainly in general parlance, it implies its obverse—*abnormal*—and they both become value laden. Often, those who are not deemed normal are devalued and considered a burden or problem, or are highly valued and regarded as a potential resource. Two examples are the variables of height and intelligence. Short stature and low measured intelligence are devalued and labeled abnormal, and people with those characteristics are considered disabled. Tall people (particularly males) and high scores on IQ tests are valued, and, although not normal in the statistical sense, are not labeled abnormal or considered disabled.

Davis (1995) describes the historical specificity of the use of *normal* and thereby calls attention to the social structures that are dependent on its use. "[T]he very term that permeates our contemporary life—the normal—is a configuration that arises in a particular historical moment. It is part of a notion of progress, of industrialization, and of ideological consolidation of the power of the bourgeoisie. The implications of the hegemony of normalcy are profound and extend into the very heart of cultural production" (*Enforcing Normalcy*, 49).

The use of the terms *abnormal* and *normal* also moves discourse to a high level of abstraction, thereby avoiding concrete discussion of specific characteristics and increasing ambiguity in communication. In interactions, there is an assumed agreement between speaker and audience of what is normal that sets up an aura of empathy and "us-ness." This process "enhances social unity among those who feel they are normal" (Freilich, Raybeck, and Savishinsky, 1991, 22), necessarily excluding the other or abnormal group.

These dynamics often emerge in discussions about disabled people when comparisons are made, for instance, between "the normal" and "the hearing impaired," or "the normal children" and "the handicapped children." The first example contrasts two groups of people; one defined by an abstract and evaluative term (the normal), the other by a more specific, concrete, and nonevaluative term (the hearing impaired). In the second comparison, the "handicapped children" are labeled abnormal by default. Setting up these dichotomies avoids concrete discussion of the ways the two groups of children actually differ, devalues the children with disabilities, and focuses on an "us and them" division of the population.

The absolute categories *normal* and *abnormal* depend on each other for their existence and depend on the maintenance of the opposition for their meaning. . . .

PASSIVITY VERSUS CONTROL

Language that conveys passivity and victimization reinforces certain stereotypes when applied to disabled people. Some of the stereotypes that are particularly entrenched are that people with disabilities are more dependent, childlike, passive, sensitive, and miserable and are less competent than people who do not have disabilities. Much of the language used to depict disabled people relates the lack of control to the perceived incapacities, and implies that sadness and misery are the product of the disabling condition.

These deterministic and essentialist perspectives flourish in the absence of contradictory information. Historically, disabled people have had few opportunities to be active in society, and various social and political forces often undermine the capacity for self-determination. In addition, disabled people are rarely depicted on television, in films, or in fiction as being in control of their own lives—in charge or actively seeking out and obtaining what they want and need. More often, disabled people are depicted as pained by their fate or, if happy, it is through personal triumph over their adversity. The adversity is not depicted as lack of opportunity, discrimination, institutionalization, and ostracism; it is the personal burden of their own body or means of functioning.

Phrases such as *the woman is a victim of cerebral palsy* implies an active agent (cerebral palsy) perpetrating an aggressive act on a vulnerable, helpless "victim." The use of the term *victim,* a word typically used in the context of criminal acts, evokes the relationship between perpetrator and victim. Using this language attributes life, power, and intention to the condition and disempowers the person with the disability, rendering him or her helpless and passive. Instead, if there is a particular need to note what an individual's disability is, saying *the woman has cerebral palsy* describes solely the characteristic of importance to the situation, without imposing extraneous meaning.

REFLECTING ON YOUR TEACHING

Thinking Critically about Language Choices

Linton lists euphemisms—*physically challenged, handicapable, special*—and teases out their narrative implications. She does not intend to join the "language police," nor would that be an advisable role for teachers. One reason she calls into question the language we use when we talk about disability or people with disabilities is that the term a group prefers to call itself changes over time (and this could be a topic of discussion and research). Taking up Linton's challenge to "reassign meaning" to such "crippling" language use, students should be encouraged to think critically about language, not to memorize a set of rules or enact an unquestioned etiquette. Revisit your course syllabus or a lesson-plan unit, and consider ways of extending Linton's challenge to think critically about language and its narrative implications to other areas of language use often subject to euphemizing, or charges of "political correctness."

SUGGESTIONS FOR STUDENT ACTIVITIES

The Language of Naming and Claiming

Rhetorically focused assignments might ask students themselves to investigate words and phrases associated with disability and persons with disabilities (and/or the terms used to name other groups) and their effects. Such an investigation would go beyond merely staging in-class debates, which tend to reaffirm established attitudes and common usages. For example, students might interview or survey people about terms and labels, then organize and reflect on their findings. They could research etymologies and reflect on the changes over time in the meanings of words. They could find current examples in newspapers, particularly in feature stories about people with disabilities or in reviews of films featuring a disabled character or a plot line involving disability, write about the contexts in which such words are used, and surmise the rhetorical purposes and intended or unintended effects.

Disability Etiquette

Students might research "disability etiquette" and examine the angles, lessons, and purposes of such polite behavior: What can be discerned about the authors or producers of such etiquette? What is learned about the "receiver" or "subject" of such etiquette? Why is this organization, site, or source concerned about "disability etiquette" to begin with? What terms and language use are and are not recommended by this source?

Writing on Language Choices

Students could also be asked to reflect specifically on the words they choose in their own writing: What words constrain their expression of new ideas? What "baggage" comes along with certain word choices? How do learning new ways of expression enable new ways of thinking? How easy or difficult is it to break with common usages? Students could write about the following questions: Who has the right to label and name? Which labels do students wish to "claim" (using Linton's term) and which do they not want to claim for themselves, and why? What is encompassed in the process of claiming a label or name?

Embedded Metaphors

Another fruitful assignment is to have students search newspapers for embedded disability metaphors (for example, "The USS *Cole* was crippled by a bomb," "The Yankees limped to victory") and share these with the class. This activity can lead to discussions about how metaphors work and about disability entailments. Such an assignment might be the first step of a sequence that moves toward getting students to locate and analyze how disability functions in literary texts.

18

From *Narrative Prosthesis and the Materiality of Metaphor*

DAVID MITCHELL

As David Mitchell writes in this excerpt, "disability pervades literary narrative, first, as a stock feature of characterization and, second, as an opportunistic metaphoric device." After students have discussed how embedded disability metaphors function in films (See "Suggestions for Student Activities: The Metaphorical Function of Disability in Films" on p. 188), they may be more able to "see" disability metaphors embedded in plots and used to develop characters and imply motive in literature. Mitchell argues that when disability appears, it "inaugurates the need to interpret human differences both biological and imagined" because it signals a variation from the norm. In literature, disability can signal inner moral corruption, as in the case of Shakespeare's Richard III, as well as innocent and pathetic victim, as in the case of Dickens's Tiny Tim. That is, disability has no fixed, stable meaning in itself, but operates to represent and show whatever social or psychological maladies the author wants to dramatize. In their coauthored book Narrative Prosthesis: Disability and the Dependencies of Discourse, *Mitchell and Sharon Snyder use the term* narrative prosthesis *to express this idea. (They employ a disability-related object— a prosthetic device—to name their concept!) Disability, Mitchell writes, is "a crutch on which literary narratives lean for their representational power, disruptive potentiality, and social critique." Ironically, Mitchell notes that disability has been "historically used to identify the working of dominant ideology in regard to nearly everything," except disability itself.*

LITERATURE AND THE UNDISCIPLINED BODY OF DISABILITY

This essay develops a narrative theory of shared characteristics in the literary representation of disability. It also seeks to demonstrate one of a variety of approaches in disability studies to the problem that disability and disabled populations pose to all cultures. Nearly every culture views disability as a problem in need of a solution, and this belief establishes one of the major

From *Disability Studies: Enabling the Humanities*, ed. Sharon L. Snyder, Brenda Jo Brueggemann, and Rosemarie Garland-Thomson (New York: Modern Language Association, 2002), 15–30.

modes of historical address directed toward people with disabilities. The necessity for developing various kinds of cultural accommodations to handle the problem of physical difference (i.e., through charitable organizations, modifications of physical architecture, welfare doles, quarantine, genocide, euthanasia programs, etc.) situates people with disabilities in a profoundly ambivalent relation to the cultures and stories they inhabit. The perception of a crisis or a special situation has made disabled people not only the subject of governmental policies and communal programs but also a primary object of literary representation.

My central thesis here centers not simply on the fact that people with disabilities have been the objects of representational treatments but also on the fact that their presence in literary narrative is primarily twofold: disability pervades literary narrative, first, as a stock feature of characterization and, second, as an opportunistic metaphoric device. Sharon Snyder and I have termed the perpetual discursive dependency on disability in the first instance *narrative prosthesis* (Mitchell and Snyder, *Narrative Prosthesis*). Disability lends a distinctive idiosyncrasy to any characters that differentiate themselves from the anonymous background of the norm. . . .

Physical and cognitive anomalies promise to lend a tangible body to textual abstractions; I term this metaphoric use of disability the materiality of metaphor. I contend that disability's centrality to these two principal representational strategies establishes a conundrum: while stories rely on the potency of disability as a symbolic figure, they rarely take up disability as an experience of social or political dimensions.

The narrative deployment of disability hinges on the identification of physical and cognitive differences as mutable categories of cultural investment. In literary narratives, disability serves as an interrupting force that confronts cultural truisms. John Limon has argued that, unlike science, literature functions as an "undisciplined discipline" that refuses to adhere to strict laws or established tests of proof (5). Instead, Limon characterizes literature as an upstart in the ranks of the truth-telling discourses of academic or research communities. Rather than legitimize its findings as a product of professional formulas, literature seeks to demonstrate that truth is a variable and contextual phenomenon produced by the convergence of institutional power, ideologies, and influence. Functioning without absolute standards or proof, literature can be said to behave like an unruly sister to the masculine domain of hard science. Limon demonstrates that as a result of this differentiation between literature and science, the literary surrenders its ability to produce truth while also gaining the advantage of flexibility or critique that its antidisciplinarity affords.

Like that of literature, disability's relation to the stable body is one of unruliness. As Sharon Snyder and I discuss in our introduction to *The Body and Physical Difference*, "disability might be characterized as that which exceeds a culture's predictive capacities or effective interventions. [. . . It] defies correction and tends to operate according to its own idiosyncratic rules" (3). Disabled bodies prove undisciplined because they refuse to conform to the controlling narratives of medical or rehabilitative science. In doing so, they are designated as pathological. The inherent vulnerability and variability of bodies serves literary narratives as a metonym for that which refuses to conform to the disci-plinary desire for order and rationality so apparent in empirical discourses. In this schema, disability acts as a metaphor and fleshly example of the body's un-ruly resistance to what Lennard Davis has theorized as the cultural desire to "enforce normalcy" *(Enforcing)*.[1] The body's weighty materiality functions as a textual and cultural other—an object with its own undisciplined language that exceeds the text's (and thus culture's) ability to control it.

Disability serves as a symbolic symptom to be interpreted by discourses on the body. Whether a culture approaches the body's dynamic materiality as a denigrated symbol of earthly contamination (as in early Christian cultures), or as a perfectible *techné* of the self (as in ancient Athenian culture), or as an object of social symbolism (as in the culture of the Renaissance), or as a classi-fiable object of bodily averages (as in the Enlightenment), or as specular com-modity in the age of electronic media (as in postmodernism), disability inaugurates the need to interpret human differences both biological and imagined. Whereas the able body has no definitional core (it poses as trans-parently average or normal), the disabled body surfaces as any body capable of being narrated as outside the norm.

In such a representational schema, literary narratives revisit disabled bodies as reminders of the real physical limits that weigh down transcendent ideals of the truth-seeking disciplines. In this sense, disability serves as the "hard kernel" or recalcitrant corporeal matter that cannot be deconstructed away by the textual operations of the most canny narratives or philosophical idealisms.[2] Representations of disability, then, allow an interrogation of static beliefs about the body while also erupting as the unseemly matter of narrative that cannot be textually contained. The coinage of the phrase "narrative pros-thesis" argues that disability has been used throughout history as a crutch on which literary narratives lean for their representational power, disruptive po-tentiality, and social critique. Yet, at the same time, literature avoids designat-ing disability itself as a source for derisive social myths that need to be interrogated. Instead, disability plays host to a panoply of other social mal-adies that writers seek to address. Disabled bodies show up in literary narra-tives as dynamic entities that resist or refuse the cultural scripts assigned to them. The out-of-control body of literature has been historically used to iden-tify the workings of dominant ideology in regard to nearly everything but the social construction of disability itself.

THE (IN) VISIBILITY OF PROSTHESES

The hypothesis of this discursive dependency on disability at first glance strikes most scholars and readers as relatively insubstantial. During a recent conference of the Herman Melville Society held in Völös, Greece, I met a scholar from Japan interested in representations of disability in American literature. When asked if Japanese literature made use of disabled characters to the same extent as American and European literatures, he honestly replied that he had never encountered any. On further reflection he listed several examples and laughingly added that of course the Nobel Prize winner

Kenzaburo Oe wrote almost exclusively about the subject. This surprise about the pervasive nature of disabled images in national literatures catches unaware even the most knowledgeable scholars. Readers tend to filter a multitude of disability figures absently out of their imaginations. For film scholarship on disability, Paul Longmore has perceptively formulated this paradox in his groundbreaking essay "Screening Stereotypes," by asking why we screen so many images of disability and simultaneously screen them out of our minds. This same phenomenon can be applied to literary discourses.

Our current models of minority representation in literature tend to formulate this problem of discursive neglect in the obverse manner. One might expect to find the argument in disability studies that disability is an ignored, overlooked, or marginal experience in literary narrative—that its absence marks an ominous silence in the literary repertoire of human experiences. In pursuing such an argument, one could rightly redress, castigate, or bemoan the neglect of this essential life experience in discourses that ought to have taken up the important task of exploring disability in serious artistic terms. In such an approach, disability would prove to be an unarticulated subject whose real-life counterparts could then charge that their social marginality was the result of a lack of representational interest outside medical discourses. Such a methodology would theorize that disability's absence proves evident a telling cultural repression to escape the reality of biological and cognitive variations. We might answer Longmore's query about screening out disability by pointing a finger at the absence of our images in mainstream and artistic discourses.

Yet disability occupies a rather unusual literary history, one that contrasts with the representation of many other minority identities. Even if we disregard the fact that entire fields of study have been devoted to the assessment, cataloging, pathologization, objectification, and rehabilitation of disability, one comes to be struck by disability's prevalence in discourses outside medicine and the other hard sciences. With regard to the relation between the social marginality of people with disabilities and their corresponding representational milieus, disability has suffered a different representational fate. While racial, sexual, and ethnic criticism have often founded their critiques on the pervasive absence of their experiences in the dominant culture's literature, images of disability abound in literary history. Once readers begin to actively seek out representations of disability in our literatures, it is difficult for them to avoid being struck by disability's tendency to proliferate in texts with which they believed themselves to be utterly familiar.[3] Consequently, as in the above mentioned anecdote about disability images in Japanese literature, the representation of people with disabilities is far from absent or tangential. Our critical models have failed to attend to questions of the utility of disability to numerous discursive modes, including literature. This failure to attend to disability's meanings in our critical models provides another, and more integral, explanation for why disability is so often screened out of our imaginations even as we consume them.

For the moment let us assume these proliferating images of disability to be fact. If such a characterization turned out to be more true than false, the historical marginality of disabled people would prove to occupy a much different cultural fate than that of other minority identities in literary narratives.[4] My working hypothesis is paradoxical: disabled peoples' social invisibility has occurred in the wake of their perpetual circulation throughout literary history. This question is not simply a matter of stereotypes or "bad objects," to borrow Naomi Schor's phrase.[5] Rather, the representation of disability strikes at the very core of cultural definitions and values.

What is the significance of the fact that the earliest known cuneiform tablets contain a catalog of 120 omens interpreted from the deformities of Sumarian fetuses and irregularly shaped sheep's and calves' livers? How does one explain the centrality of multiply disabled gods to Norse myths, such as the blind Hod, the one-eyed Odin, the one-armed Tyr, and the singular representation of Hephaestus, the crook-footed god, in Greek literature (see L. Bragg, "Mute God" and "Oedipus")? Why do our most memorable literary characters so often bear the blemish of a disability—Philoctetes, Richard III, Chillingworth, Captain Ahab, Holden Caulfield, Wallace Stegner's Lyman Ward, and so on? Why does the visual spectacle of so many disabilities become a predominating trope in the print medium of literary texts?

NARRATIVE PROSTHESIS

What calls stories into being, and what does disability have to do with this most basic preoccupation of narrative? Narrative prosthesis (or the dependency of literary narratives on disability) is the notion that all narratives operate out of a desire to compensate for a limitation or to rein in excessiveness. This narrative approach to difference identifies the literary object par excellence as that which has somehow become out of the ordinary—a deviation from a widely accepted cultural norm. Literary narratives seek to begin a process of explanatory compensation wherein perceived aberrancies can be rescued from ignorance, neglect, or misunderstanding for their readerships. As Michel de Certeau explains in his well-known essay "Montaigne's 'Of Cannibals': The Savage 'I,'" the development of the New World travel narrative is the movement of all narrative. A narrative is inaugurated "by the search for the strange, which is presumed different from the place assigned it in the beginning by the discourse of the culture" from which it originates (69). The very need for a story is called into being when something has gone amiss with the known world, and thus the language of a tale seeks to comprehend that which has stepped out of line. In this sense, stories compensate for an unknown or unnatural deviance that begs for an explanation.

The concept of narrative prosthesis evolves out of this specific recognition: a narrative issues to resolve or connect—to "prostheticize," in David Wills's sense of the term—a deviance marked as abnormal or improper in a social context. A simple schematic of narrative structure might run: first, a deviance or marked difference is exposed to a reader; second, a narrative consolidates the need for its own existence by calling for an explanation of the deviation's origins and formative consequences; third, the deviance is brought from the periphery of concerns to the center stage of the story to come; and fourth, the remainder of the story seeks to rehabilitate or fix the deviance in some manner, shape, or form. This fourth move toward the repair of deviance may involve an obliteration of the difference through a cure, the rescue of the despised object from social censure, the extermination of the deviant as a purification of the social body, or the revaluation of an alternative mode of experience. Since what we now call disability has been historically narrated as that which characterizes a body as deviant from shared norms of bodily appearance and ability, disability has functioned throughout history as one of the most marked and remarked on differences that propel the act of storytelling into existence. Narratives turn signs of cultural deviance into textually marked bodies. . . .

NOTES

1. There is an equivalent problem to the representation of disability in literary narratives in our own critical rubics of the body. The disabled body continues to fall outside critical categories that identify bodies as the product of cultural constructions. While challenging a generic notion of the white, male body as ideological proves desirable in our present moment in the realms of race, gender, sexuality, and class, there has been a more pernicious history of literary and critical approaches to the disabled body. In the introduction to *The Body and Physical Difference*, Sharon Snyder and I argue that minority discourses in the humanities all tend to deploy the evidence of "corporeal aberrancy" as a means of identifying the invention of an ideologically encoded body. Yet, "while physical aberrancy is often recognized as constructed and historically variable it is rarely remarked upon as its own legitimized or politically fraught identity" (5).

2. In the book *The Sublime Object of Ideology* (98), Slavoj Žižek extracts the notion of the hard kernel of ideology from the theories of Jacques Lacan. For Žižek, the notion of the hard kernel represents that underlying core of belief that refuses to be deconstructed away by even the most radical operations of political critique. More than merely a rational component of ideological identification, the Žižekian hard kernel represents the irrationality behind belief that secures the interpellated subject's illogical participation in a linguistically permeable system.

3. A brief catalog of disabled representations in literature includes some of the most influential figurations of suffering humanity across periods and cultures: the crippled Greek god Hephaestus; Montaigne's sexually potent limping women; Shakespeare's hunchbacked king, Richard III; Frankenstein's deformed monster; Charlotte Brontë's madwoman in the attic; Melville's one-legged, monomaniacal Captain Ahab; Nietzsche's philosophical grotesques; Hemingway's wounded war veterans; Morrison's truncated and scarred ex-slaves; Borges's blind librarian; Oe's autistic son.

4. The documentation of disability's proliferation in literary texts is evidenced in new works, including Davis's *Enforcing Normalcy*, Garland-Thomson's *Extraordinary Bodies*, and Mitchell and Snyder's *The Body and Physical Difference*.

5. For Naomi Schor a bad object is a discursive object that has been ruled out of bounds by the prevailing academic politics of the day or one that represents a "critical perversion" (xv). My use of the phrase implies both these definitions in relation to disability. The literary object of disability has been almost entirely neglected by literary criticism in general, until the development, in the mid-1990s, of disability studies in the humanities; and disability as a topic of investigation still strikes many as a perverse interest for academic contemplation. To these two definitions I would also add that the labeling of disability as a bad object nonetheless overlooks the fact that disabilities fill the pages of literary interest.

SUGGESTIONS FOR STUDENT ACTIVITIES

The Metaphorical Function of Disability in Films

This excerpt is perhaps the most challenging one reproduced here. After summarizing Mitchell's main ideas in a handout, an instructor could ask students to put Mitchell's ideas to the "test" by finding examples and then analyzing, writing, and reflecting on their narrative and metaphorical functions. Mitchell presents a number of paradoxes that could be easily summarized and then "tested" by students. For example, he notes the pervasiveness of disability in literature: it is everywhere, but also seemingly nowhere, overlooked both by a process of "screening out" and by the fact that it functions typically to signal something else. This paradoxical absence/presence lends itself to a prewriting, viewing, and then reflective writing sequence.

Disney movies and fairy tales are fertile ground. For example, students could be asked to recall a movie like *Finding Nemo* and to prewrite briefly on it, noting any disability in it that comes to mind. Prewriting provides a space to surface students' opinions about the presence/absence conundrum: Often, students are resistant to the idea that a popular movie is "about" disability, and this tension can be productive. Students could then be given some of Mitchell's concepts of how disability functions as metaphor for character development and plot. Mitchell argues that, indeed, disability actually "propel[s] the act of storytelling into existence," and he offers the following schema of a narrative structure based on the operating of disability:

- Some difference "is exposed to the reader."
- The narrative includes or implies some reason for the difference, some account of origins and development.
- The difference becomes the center of the story's movement.
- The plot moves toward fixing or compensating for the difference (or, we would add, its inverse, toward punishment for the difference).

After explaining this narrative schema, instructors could screen one or two scenes of the film, asking students to take notes on what propels the plot, on character development, and so forth. These notes could be used to inform a post-screening class discussion, and form the basis for a short reflective paper in which students might critically reflect on, or argue with, Mitchell's claims, analyzing whether and/or how the film employs disability metaphors and plot.

Expanding the Prosthetic Analysis

Students are often already experts at media analyses, finding and analyzing texts in highly innovative ways that may well connect with and expand the "prosthetic" analysis. Students can bring their own selected short clips from movies and TV shows to share and analyze with the entire class. Such an activity can lead to larger writing assignments, and also deeply engaging class discussions. Students have shown us how shows such as *South Park* and *Family Guy* surprisingly touch on a host of disability issues; they include plots and situations concerning disability, characters with disabilities, and issues of language related to disability.

19

From *Conflicting Paradigms: The Rhetorics of Disability Memoir*

G. THOMAS COUSER

Instructors can use this excerpt from G. Thomas Couser to provide students with several additional plot schemes to analyze cultural discourses about disability embedded in narratives. In addition to sketching their typical plots, Couser explains how the power and familiarity of schemes endow them with persuasive rhetorical effects. "People with disabilities may be granted access to the literary marketplace on the condition that their stories conform to preferred plots and rhetorical schemes." Couser describes several rhetorics that reinforce conventional attitudes: the rhetoric of triumph (a story of triumph over adversity, the overcoming of obstacles); the medical paradigm; horror, or "Gothic rhetoric"; and the rhetoric of spiritual compensation or conversion.

Couser also describes plots and rhetorics that can contest received attitudes about disability: by generating "outrage at ill-treatment," or narrating a disabled person's movement from institution to living in the community. He concludes that political rhetoric, moving from individual story to social issues of disability, can directly represent disability as a social construction.

To marginalized people, autobiography may be the most accessible of literary genres. It requires less in the way of literary expertise and experience than other, more exalted genres. It seems to require only that one have a life—or at least one considered worth narrating—and sufficient narrative skill to tell one's own story. Most literary scholars would agree that autobiography has served historically as a sort of threshold genre for other marginalized groups. Within the American literary tradition, witness the importance of autobiography to African Americans, Native Americans, and women, for example. Presumably, it might serve disabled people this way as well. It is not

From *Embodied Rhetorics: Disability in Language and Culture,* ed. James C. Wilson and Cynthia Lewiecki-Wilson (Carbondale: Southern Illinois UP, 2001), 78–91.

just the apparent accessibility of autobiography—a kind of negative qualification—that recommends it but also something more positive: the notion that autobiography by definition involves self-representation. If marginalization is in part a function of discourse that excludes and/or objectifies, autobiography has considerable potential to counter stigmatizing or patronizing portrayals of disability because it is a medium in which disabled people may have a high degree of control over their own images.

Yet there are serious obstacles in the way of realizing the counterhegemonic potential of the disability memoir. Obstacles can be found at three distinct junctures: having a life, writing a life, and publishing a life. Like minority racial or ethnic status, disability may disqualify people from living the sorts of lives that have traditionally been considered worthy of autobiography. Insofar as people with disabilities have been excluded from educational institutions and thus from economic opportunity, they will be less likely to produce the success story, perhaps the favorite American autobiographical subgenre from Benjamin Franklin on. That their disqualification lies not in individual incapacity but in social and cultural barriers does not change the fact that people with disabilities are less likely to live the sorts of lives considered narratable and less likely to be encouraged to display themselves in autobiography. One aspect of this discrimination, shared with other minorities, is the internalization of prejudices. Those who accept society's devaluation of them are less likely to consider their lives worthy of autobiography. Stigma serves to silence the stigmatized.

Writing a life is an aspect of accessibility that may seem secondary, but it is pertinent here because it is peculiar to disability. Despite important recent developments in assistive technology (such as voice-recognition software), the process of composition itself may be complicated by disability. People who are blind, deaf, paralyzed, or cognitively impaired are disadvantaged with regard to the conventional technologies of writing, which take for granted visual acuity, literacy in English, manual dexterity, and unimpaired memory. For people with many disabilities, the process of drafting and revising a long narrative may be too arduous. At this juncture, people with disabilities may be disadvantaged in ways that do not apply to racial and ethnic minorities and in ways that may not be immediately apparent to those who are not disabled. If a disability is such that it requires collaboration in the production of an autobiography, questions arise as to the agency, authority, voice, and authenticity of the self-representation.

Furthermore, it is not enough to produce a manuscript. Publishing—as distinct from printing—a life involves negotiating access to the marketplace through intermediaries who may have their own agendas. A third problem, then, may be located in the genre as defined by the literary marketplace, which may impose hegemonic scripts on a disempowered group. It is here that "rhetoric" and "disability" crucially intersect. In effect, people with disabilities may be granted access to the literary marketplace on the condition that their stories conform to preferred plots and rhetorical schemes. What characterizes these preferred rhetorics is that they rarely challenge stigma and marginalization directly or effectively. Indeed, their appeal to the reading public may vary inversely with the degree to which they threaten the status quo. This essay will distinguish a few of the most common rhetorical patterns of autobiographical disability narrative with reference to some recent examples, moving from rhetorics that reinforce conventional attitudes—the rhetorics of triumph, horror, spiritual compensation, and nostalgia—to a rhetoric that contests received attitudes about disability—the rhetoric of emancipation.[1]

The first of the common rhetorics is so obvious as to require little comment. Because disability is typically considered inherently "depressing," it is most acceptable as a subject of autobiography if the narrative takes the form of a story of triumph over adversity. In this formula, a successful individual takes pride in, and invites the reader's admiration for, a recounting of his or her overcoming of the obstacles posed by disability. Needless to say, the lives that fit this paradigm misrepresent the experience of most people with disabilities. This paradigm nominates as the representative disabled person the Supercrip, who is by definition atypical. These may be "true stories," but they are not truly representative lives. This rhetoric tends to remove the stigma of disability from the author, leaving it in place for other individuals with the condition in question. In any case, the scenario, like the other preferred scenarios, is entirely congruous with the medical paradigm, which locates disability entirely within a "defective" or "abnormal" body. Disability is presented primarily as a "problem" that individuals must overcome; overcoming it is a matter of individual will and determination rather than of social and cultural accommodation.

Another rhetoric frequently employed in the representation of disability is Gothic rhetoric, or the rhetoric of horror. Here, disability is characterized as a dreadful condition, to be shunned or avoided. At worst, Gothic rhetoric encourages revulsion from disability; at best, pity for the "afflicted." Such rhetoric might seem unlikely to be used in first-person discourse, such as disability memoir, because it would reflect negatively on the author-narrator. But this deterrent vanishes when impairment is corrected or "transcended." From the standpoint of those who are cured or rehabilitated—or who otherwise destigmatize themselves—it is common to look back upon a period of disability as a Gothic horror. In this rhetoric, narrators represent their former condition as grotesque. Readers are invited to share narrators' relief at escaping marginalization. . . .

Used this way, Gothic rhetoric tends, of course, to confirm the worst stereotypes about disability, to reinforce stigmatization. But such rhetoric is sometimes also used in accounts that do not culminate in the removal of the narrator from the condition in question. When the source of horror is not the condition itself but the treatment of the condition, Gothic rhetoric has some counterhegemonic potential. Julia Tavalaro's account of the six-year period following her two strokes, during which she was assumed by hospital staff to be completely unaware of her surroundings, is a good example of the latter form of Gothic rhetoric—a medical horror story of inattention, indifference, and abuse. . . .

The rhetoric of spiritual compensation has also frequently been used to narrate experiences of disability.[2] Ruth Cameron Webb's *Journey into Personhood*, a recent memoir by a woman with cerebral palsy, is a particularly interesting example of this, in part because the rhetoric of conversion was not the only, or even the most obvious, rhetoric available to her. Given the outlines of Webb's life, one might expect her narrative to employ the rhetoric of triumph. For despite delays in her education, Webb got a PhD in clinical psychology and had a successful career counseling people with disabilities. . . .

Webb does not, however, narrate a secular success story — much less question the medical paradigm — because of a deeply ingrained sense of inferiority associated with her disability. In therapy she traces these feelings to being examined, naked, by physicians at her first boarding school. Her sense of invalidity is so great that it challenges her religious faith: "Often I wonder why God allowed me to be injured at birth. Have I done anything to deserve cerebral palsy? Why can't I walk and talk like everybody else?" (70) Here we see a biblical view of disability, that it is a mark of sin or God's displeasure with an individual. . . .

Only through spiritual compensation can she find a comic plot in her life. Part of the implicit "purpose" of her disability, then, is to make her a better Christian. She finds solace finally in her sense of value to God, who has assigned her a special mission on earth. . . . Such rhetoric invites readers to assent to the conditions of Webb's validation as a person. In her view, disability is her problem — a challenge given her by God for his own inscrutable reasons — not a social or political issue. . . .

A third rhetorical schema, the rhetoric of nostalgia, is illustrated in pure form by a recent memoir that was greeted by extensive press coverage and positive reviews: Jean-Dominique Bauby's *The Diving Bell and the Butterfly*. Written by the editor-in-chief of *Elle* magazine after a massive stroke to the brain stem left him almost completely paralyzed, this memoir was translated and published in the United States in 1997. Bauby's paralysis was so extensive that it left him deaf in one ear and mute, able to move only his left eye. Nevertheless, he managed to compose a memoir by blinking to select letters, one by one, as an attentive collaborator, Claude Mendibil, recited the alphabet for him.

Partly as a result of this extremely labor-intensive method of composition, the book is very short; it consists of a series of brief vignettes. The chapters range over a number of topics, but typically recount isolated memories of his life before the stroke. . . . Aware that he would never recover, though he might improve in certain limited respects, Bauby ceased to orient himself toward the future.[3] Partly, then, because his condition did not allow for his reintegration into the world of the nondisabled, he minimizes the narrative of rehabilitation. . . .

Since the author did not live long with disability, there is no question of his using his position as a prominent editor to offer personal testimony on behalf of others with disabilities. Rather, he earns praise in part for having undertaken, in forbidding circumstances, to create a book and for having written a book that is not "depressing" but "uplifting" because, rather than raising disturbing questions about the status of people with disabilities, it offers poignant accounts of pleasures and pastimes no longer available to him.

The diving bell is Bauby's image for his confinement in a kind of hermetic zone removed from the world of "ability." The butterfly is an image of the compensatory liberation of his mind so that it may float freely over his past, as his eye surveys the souvenirs and snapshots surrounding him in his room (3). The emphasis throughout is much more on the freedom of the butterfly than on the confinement of the diving bell. Indeed, one might say that, despite its occasional Gothic passages, the text tends to idealize Bauby's condition as one freeing him from mundane constraints to reminisce, fantasize, and "travel" (103): "There is so much to do. You can wander off in space or in time. . . . You can visit the woman you love, . . . realize your childhood dreams and adult ambitions" (5). In effect, then, Bauby treats his disability not as an experience of the body but as an experience of being "out of the body." . . . The effect is not to challenge or erase but to mark a distinction between past and present, function and dysfunction, ability and disability, living and remembering. Although there is little that physicians can do for him other than to stabilize his condition and minimize his discomfort, his narrative in no way challenges the medical paradigm. Compared with the rhetoric of horror, the rhetoric of nostalgia seems benign, and yet it too tends to marginalize disability insofar as it is rooted in an equation between severe disability and the end of life.

In contrast to the preceding memoirs and their rhetorics, my final example realizes some of the counterhegemonic potential of disability narrative. *I Raise My Eyes to Say Yes*, by Ruth Sienkiewicz-Mercer and Steven B. Kaplan, is the story of a woman with cerebral palsy so severe that she has never been able to walk, feed herself, speak, or write. After spending some time as a child in rehabilitative facilities, she was sent to a state hospital in Belchertown, Massachusetts, because her father changed jobs and his new insurance did not cover private hospitals. Upon entering this new facility at the age of twelve, Sienkiewicz-Mercer was misdiagnosed as mentally retarded, and she was then "ware-housed" with people who were either cognitively impaired or mentally ill.[4] Eventually, her abilities were recognized and gradually recultivated. In her midtwenties she was able to move out of the hospital into an apartment and to marry a fellow former patient—both beneficiaries of the new approach to disability that favored deinstitutionalization.

In her new environment, she was presumed to be a body without (much of) a mind. Though toilet-trained early on, she was diapered, dressed in a hospital johnny—all for the convenience of the staff—and supervised, rather than educated or rehabilitated. It was thus not her own severe impairments but the disabilities of her physicians that threatened to limit her development.[5] What saved Sienkiewicz-Mercer from languishing in the institution was her ability, using very limited means, to connect with those around her. Virtually the only moving parts of her body under her control were her eyes and her vocal cords. By making eye contact with other inmates and staff members, she was able to establish vital connections with them; by gesturing with her eyes, and coordinating nonverbal vocalizations with those gestures, she was able to communicate ideas and emotions about life around her in a kind of private language to receptive others. The most receptive were the captive audience of other similarly misdiagnosed patients. It was only through eye contact and private language that she and a few peers could establish that there was intelligent—and intelligible—life within them. In this initial bonding with other inmates we can see the beginnings of political consciousness shared with others in the same predicament, an element that distinguishes her account from those of Bauby and Webb.

The role of her "gaze" in self-construction, then, is crucial. Whereas the disciplinary medical gaze had sized her up (or rather, down) as mentally deficient, through her own inquisitive and aggressive gaze she managed to challenge or defy her misdiagnosis—and, not incidentally, to have a social life. Once her consciousness and intelligence were recognized, she was able to expand on and refine this method of communication, but she could never abandon it. In order for her to communicate with the staff and move herself beyond the limits assigned to her, she needed to make them respond to her gaze as well.

The writing of her text is only a more deliberate and extensive application of this means of self-creation. The medium of autobiography is an elaboration of the process of self-possession and self-assertion through manipulation of her gaze. Collaborative self-inscription is the means for releasing herself from the institution. Personal narrative is thus crucial to her physical and psychological emancipation. Rather than accepting her dependency as disvaluing, she exploits interdependency as a means of self-assertion. While not achieving independence (or subscribing to the ideology of personal autonomy), Sienkiewicz-Mercer moves herself through reciprocity to a position of greater power and mobility. (The reciprocity of her self-construction is attested to by the way in which her narrative vividly individualizes others also consigned to near-oblivion in the hospital.)

Although, like most personal narratives of illness and/or disability, the narrative has an undeniably comic plot, it is not a story of overcoming disability—at least not in the usual sense. It is not what Arthur Frank calls a "narrative of restitution"—a narrative of complete healing in which a physician would play a transformative role (77). Nor is it primarily a narrative of rehabilitation. Although she does learn to use various assistive technologies to communicate, Sienkiewicz-Mercer never manages to walk or talk, nor does she achieve autonomy. Her rhetoric is thus not that of triumph. Rather, she manages, with a great deal of help, to work around her impairment. The comic resolution is not a function of removing or correcting her impairment but of getting the world to accommodate her irreparable impairments, of removing the physical, social, and cultural obstacles to her integration into "mainstream society." In that sense, her narrative demonstrates what we might call the rhetoric of emancipation.

Indeed, *I Raise My Eyes to Say Yes* has interesting affinities with slave narrative. This narrative is reminiscent of a slave narrative both in the sense that, on the level of plot, it traces a movement from virtual imprisonment to relative freedom, and in the sense that her emancipation is a function of a broader movement to deinstitutionalize disabled people. Like many, if not all, slave narratives, it defies the ascription of mental deficiency to the body of the Other and exposes the confinement of those bodies as a contingent social phenomenon rather than a "natural" one. It has particular affinities, then, with those slave narratives elicited by sympathetic abolitionists, for Sienkiewicz-Mercer's account is in effect promoted and sponsored by individuals seeking to liberate people with disabilities and even to abolish their "institutionalization." . . .

To associate this disability memoir with slave narrative alone, however, would be perhaps to limit its resonance. It might also be considered a form of autoethnography, as Mary Louise Pratt defines the term: "instances in which colonized subjects undertake to represent themselves in ways that *engage with* the colonizer's own terms. If the ethnographic texts are a means by which Europeans represent to themselves their (usually subjugated) others, autoethnographic texts are those the others construct in response to or in dialogue with those metropolitan representations" (7). This narrative does display a kind of postcolonial impulse — the impulse to define oneself in resistance to the dehumanizing categories of the medical and health-service institutions (see Frank, 7–11). It's autoethnography, too, in that it is a first-person account of what Erving Goffman calls the "underlife of a public institution," the inmates' view of the asylum — the gossip, the games, the inside dope. Both as individual and institutional history, it supplements, challenges, and indicts official discourse, which assumes that standardized testing can adequately indicate the inner life of the subject in question.

To characterize it as standing in for other unwritten, perhaps unwriteable, accounts is to suggest its affinity with a more current first-person genre: testimonio. In an incisive discussion of testimonio, John Beverley has distinguished it from autobiography as follows: "*Testimonio* represents an affirmation of the individual subject, even of individual growth and transformation, but in connection with a group or class situation marked by marginalization, oppression, and struggle. If it loses this connection, it ceases to be *testimonio* and becomes autobiography, that is, an account of, and also a means of access to, middle- or upper-class status, a sort of documentary *bildungsroman*" (103). In this text we have a disability memoir that moves toward, though it may not fully occupy, the position with regard to the disability rights movement that testimonio occupies with regard to the movement for the rights of indigenous peoples. *I Raise My Eyes to Say Yes* is testimonio to the (considerable) extent to which its narrator speaks not as a unique individual but for a class of marginalized individuals, in ways already suggested. My term "rhetoric of emancipation" should perhaps be qualified here, then, insofar as it overstates the position from which Sienkiewicz-Mercer composes her memoir.[6] To be sure, she is liberated from the confining state hospital, but she narrates her account from within the context of an ongoing personal and collective struggle for recognition of the value and rights of people with disabilities. While the political critique within the text is muted, her story decisively represents disability not as a flaw in her body but as the prejudicial construct of a normative culture. It thus suggests the way in which personal narrative of disability may articulate and advocate the political paradigm of disability and thus align itself with testimonio as deployed in other modern liberation movements. . . .

NOTES

1. These different rhetorics are often combined within single memoirs, but in most cases one pattern dominates. My examples are chosen to exemplify particular rhetorical appeals.

2. See *Recovering Bodies*, 192–98, for a discussion of the use of paradigms of spiritual autobiography in disability narratives by Reynolds Price and John Callahan.

3. It also lacks any confessional dimension. Bauby may have been deterred from a more confessional mode because his stroke occurred at a time of great instability in his life; he had just moved out of the house he shared with his wife and two children. Writing memoirs, rather than a more self-exploratory autobiography, he worked around rather than through this life crisis.

4. Given her treatment, or mistreatment — her leg was once broken by a careless and clumsy aide and not immediately attended to — Sienkiewicz's story, like Tavalaro's, has Gothic potential, but the Gothic remains a minor element in her account, as in Bauby's.

5. Reading Sienkiewicz-Mercer's and Tavalaro's accounts against Bauby's exposes the role of social class in the ascription of disability. For Bauby, though he never leaves the institution, the hospital is not a site of oppression in the way that it is for her. This is in part because of his socioeconomic status, with all the clout and connections it entails. For him, the major problem is his locked-in condition; for Sienkiewicz-Mercer and Tavalaro, it is the institution's (mis)treatment of their condition, which they have no powerful advocates to question.

6. Although I do not have the space to explore it fully here, I cannot entirely omit a discussion of the mediation of the collaborative narratives under discussion. For the collaboration of a disabled subject with a nondisabled agent to produce an "autobiographical" text raises the same political and ethical questions that pertain to testimonio. In any collaborative account, the "rhetoric" in question may not be entirely attributable to the subject; indeed, it is generally the case that the "writers" of collaborative accounts will be more conversant with conventional narrative rhetorics. This is, after all, one reason that they are used.

In the case of Bauby, who was highly educated and sophisticated about print media, it is probably safe to assume that his collaborator functioned mostly as a scribe — active in prompting him with recited letters, but probably largely passive in the composition of the memoir. With Tavalaro and Sienkiewicz-Mercer, who were far less highly educated, their collaborators probably played much more active roles in the solicitation and composition of the memoirs. In both cases, the narratives contain texts attributable solely to the women themselves; in both instances, the disparity between the style of those texts and that of the collaborative text suggests that the voice of the memoir is not really that of its subject and putative narrator — regardless of the *accuracy* of the accounts, which both women were apparently able to ensure.

SUGGESTIONS FOR STUDENT ACTIVITIES

Charting and Analyzing Plots

Instructors might make a chart using Couser's terms (his rhetorics) with abbreviated descriptions of each plot type and its embedded rhetorical message. Leaving one or two blank spaces at the end of the chart, invite students to think up other typical plots, give them names, and tease out their embedded rhetorical messages. This might be a good group activity to encourage conversation and questions about these schemes. Students could then use their charts as aids in analyzing a range of popular cultural narratives.

Using and Analyzing Bodily Performances

Couser's tropes also lend themselves to acting out. Each of these rhetorics can be "embodied." Gothic, emancipatory, and triumphal narratives imply bodily attitudes and actions, and actors do incorporate bodily cues in their performances, often overrepresenting the bodily entailments of such concepts. A class might revisit film clips already screened and discuss actors' uses of bodily tropes. Then, in groups, students could explore additional ways of walking or talking through these tropes and present them to the class. Group performances could be followed by class discussion or short reflective writing on bodily rhetorics.

20 From *Rhetoric and Healing: Revising Narratives about Disability*

JACQUELINE RINALDI

Jacqueline Rinaldi discusses the therapeutic properties of writing: "At the core of a therapeutic rhetoric is an assumption that any experience of failure is amenable to being reconstructed in a way that makes that failure tolerable, even beneficial according to a different set of values." Rinaldi argues for a powerful view of rhetoric, not merely as a tool of analysis, but writing as a healing action that can "revise our lives." Melding rhetorical tradition to psychotherapy, and drawing on the work of Kenneth Burke, Rinaldi describes the healing process as an outcome of dialogue held with the self and/or with others. She concludes that "it may well be time to explore the therapeutic potential of the reflective prose that we ask our students to write in more traditional classroom settings."

Then medicine, too, it seems, is concerned with words.

—SOCRATES, *GORGIAS*

How may one transform his failure into profit, not in the sense of those who leave failure behind them, since that change would involve a profound forgetting, but in the sense of those whose structure of existence is made of the materials of their frustration?

—KENNETH BURKE, *TOWARDS A BETTER LIFE*

Community-outreach writing programs have been seen recently as opportunities for healing. In "Kitchen Tables and Rented Rooms: The Extracurriculum of Composition," Ann Ruggles Gere (building on studies by Shirley Brice Heath, Glynda Hull, and Patricia Bizzell) argues that in groups ranging from farmers sharing ideas on tractors and cows, to women coping with poverty or addiction, the group members rapidly come to see "that writing can effect changes in their lives" (75–77). Gere stresses a need for community-based

From *College English* 58, no. 7 (November 1996): 820–34.

literacies that cut across race, gender, and class, serving different groups of people with similar life-problems; through the writing process, she sees the possibility of "transformations in personal relationships" (80).

In the same vein, panelists at a 1992 CCCC session ("Spiritual Sites of Composing") emphasized the healing properties of writing, assigning a strong therapeutic function to an activity that is often considered to be merely cognitive. Over the course of five summers, C. Jan Swearingen sponsored support workshops for women's groups, encouraging them "to draw on the power of spiritual conviction" in "the tasks of making meaning" (Swearingen, 252); JoAnn Campbell used meditation with adults "seeking help with writing blocks" (Campbell, 247); and Beth Daniell, working with Al-Anon groups, found them motivated by a "deeply-held belief in the power of language to heal and to bring about and deepen spiritual experience" (Daniell, 241). Given their success in using writing for therapeutic purposes, they all endorsed an effort, in Gere's words, "to uncouple composition and schooling . . . [and] to focus on the experiences of writers not always visible to us inside the walls of the academy" (80). . . .

In a like manner, Reynolds Price, in his recent memoir, *A Whole New Life*, indicates that writing about the body was, for him, a powerful therapeutic tool in helping him convert a "mid-life collision with cancer and paralysis" into "consoling gains" that have blessed him with a new life. His journey, as he wrote his way through his illness, was from "black frustration" and "powerlessness" to a transformed state in which he was able to move beyond a preoccupation with his own disability to a sensitive awareness of those around him: "I learned to sit and attend, to watch and taste whatever or whomever seemed likely or needy, far more closely than I had in five decades" (vii, 190).

Typically, with the onset of disability, the impaired feel an acute sense of displacement, living as they do in a culture that privileges strength, beauty, and health over frailty, deformity, and illness. They correctly perceive that cripples generate discomfort, that wounds disturb, that damaged bodies affront. In his classic work, *Stigma: Notes on the Management of Spoiled Identity*, Erving Goffman reminds us just how discrediting a "failure, a shortcoming or a handicap" can be, noting that when stigmatized in terms of "spoiled identities," the impaired are likely to internalize their deficiencies as personal failings (3). Since MS strikes most adults during their most productive years—between twenty and fifty—its impact can be as psychologically devastating as it is physically debilitating. Before becoming entirely crippled, MSers may limp, stumble, and drop things; often, they need help with the simplest tasks—tying a shoelace, unscrewing a jar lid, putting out the garbage. Mundane worries over whether they can negotiate a curb or make it to the bathroom on time create an undercurrent of tension that is always burdensome and often frightening. Oscillating between periods of exacerbation when symptoms worsen and periods of remission when disability lessens, MSers may appear sick at times and healthy at others.

In *A Leg to Stand On,* neurologist Oliver Sacks explains just how complex any experience of bodily impairment can be. Citing Freud's observation that "the Ego is first and foremost a body Ego," Sacks asserts that our notion of "self" is intrinsically linked with the biological integrity of our body: "One may be said to 'own' or 'possess' one's body—at least its limbs and movable parts—by virtue of a constant flow of information . . . from the muscles, joints and tendons. One is oneself, because the body knows itself, confirms itself at all times by this sixth sense" of "proprioception" (81, 71). As victims of neurological damage, MSers well know what it is to live without this "sixth sense." They know, too, what it is to live with a disease so mercurial, so little understood by others, that they are often charged with abetting the anxiety and depression that worsen their condition, an accusation that stirs a tangled network of family misunderstanding. Chronic illness is thus far more than an isolated instance of physical failing; it is, as Arthur Kleinman indicates in *The Illness Narratives,* "transactional, communicative, profoundly social" (186). Yet, despite the physical and emotional hardships faced daily by MSers, Ann Spector and I had a strong sense that as our group committed themselves to writing and revising narratives about their disability they would gradually discover the healing power of their own rhetoric.

At the core of a therapeutic rhetoric is an assumption that any experience of failure is amenable to being reconstructed in a way that makes that failure tolerable, even beneficial according to a different set of values. In *Coping with Failure: The Therapeutic Uses of Rhetoric,* David Payne explores this idea and proposes that as most forms of therapy aimed at ameliorating a person's sense of inadequacy are rhetorical in nature, "failure and rhetoric are necessarily and fundamentally related" (147). Therapeutic discourse, according to Payne, draws lines of argument from a set of basic *topoi* to manage "self-society tensions, integrate or explain past-future discrepancies, or reconcile spiritual-material trade-offs" in ways that permit us to reconceive failures as "opportunities for self-growth and change" (44, 154). In its healing function, rhetoric identifies and treats our perceived sense of personal and social shortcomings.

While the foundations for a therapeutic rhetoric are strongly rooted in antiquity, the attention given today to the tranformative nature of such discourse aligns it just as solidly with modern rhetorical theory. Building on claims that rhetoric is epistemic, a heuristic for the construction of knowledge through argument (Chaim Perelman), that meaning resides in interpretation (I. A. Richards), that it is hermeneutical (Ann Berthoff), and that language is both sermonic (Richard Weaver) and hortatory (Kenneth Burke), therapeutic rhetoric underscores the intrapersonal nature of discourse that uses all available means of self-persuasion to convert "failure into profit" in a Burkean sense of these terms (*Towards,* 40). "In a society of perfect men," contends Henry Johnstone, Jr., "rhetoric would not be needed" (83). But being human, "our nature thus rooted in failure" as William James contends (130), most of us rely on rhetoric to mitigate feelings of inadequacy and to revise the meaning of our lives accordingly. . . .

Although in some quarters the notion that rhetoric can be healing, rather than merely agonistic, may seem untraditional, it remains true that a therapeutic concept is woven throughout Western rhetoric and finds its earliest articulation in the work of classical authors, who believed rhetoric as apt an instrument for healing spirit as for persuading mind.

In *A History of the Cure of Souls,* John T. McNeill reminds us that Socrates "was, and wished to be, *iatros tes psuches,* a healer of souls" (27). Despite his attack on the Sophists for what he considered their misuse of rhetoric in pandering to audiences, he argued that the philosopher's duty as physician to the soul was to minister to others through a "just" and "right rhetoric" (*Gorgias,* 249). In the *Phaedrus,* he explains that the art of rhetoric follows methods similar to the art of medicine: "In both cases you must analyze a nature, in the one that of the body, in the other that of the soul" (137). As implied by Gorgias, in Plato's dialogue of the same name, rhetoric which aims to heal the soul may also bring about cures of the body. In his own work, the "Encomium of Helen," Gorgias speaks of rhetoric as a "powerful lord" and argues that "the effect of speech upon the condition of the soul is comparable to the power of drugs over the nature of bodies" (53). Even Cicero, in his advice to those seeking to comfort the souls of others, recommended the use of "healing words," what Aeschyllus had called "*iatroi logoi*" (McNeill, 29).

In these ancient roots, then, we find the origin of the word "iatrologic," a term used by recent scholars to wed the fields of rhetoric and psychotherapy in describing our modern, secular approach to the cure of souls (Baumlin and Baumlin, 245–61; Corder, 138–40; Szasz, 25–40). In their article, "Psyche/Logos: Mapping the Terrains of Mind and Rhetoric," James and Tita Baumlin make important connections between these two disciplines, insisting that as psychology has enabled rhetoricians to apply new insights to textual analysis, rhetoricians have in turn influenced psychotherapy, "teaching that the patient's discourse is a radically textual event yielding its meaning to figurative analysis" (246). They conclude that psychoanalysis "has become literally the study of a patient's discourse, an explication of one's defensive tropes and schemes" (246). Psychologist Aaron Beck, in *Cognitive Therapy and the Emotional Disorders,* also confirms the links between these two fields, observing that psychotherapists rely extensively on rhetoric when offering "alternative rules for the patient's consideration" (256). Suggestions for clarifying "the distortions, self-injunctions, and self-reproaches that lead to . . . distress and disability," Beck insists, channel patients away from potentially harmful accounts of past events toward restructured narratives that create a healthy present (258). In the process, rhetoric may be said to mirror psychology, "each mapping the effect of *logos* or language upon *psyche*" (Baumlin and Baumlin, 246).

As evidenced in the work of both ancient and contemporary rhetoricians, then, when conceived as an "interpersonal" exchange between at least two persons, be it rhetor and audience or psychotherapist and analysand, rhetoric may be said to include iatrology as one of its many aims. But are there grounds for positing a curative role for a self-persuasive or "intrapersonal" rhetoric such as that used in written discourse? May rhetoric be considered therapeutic for writers who deliberate through inner speech, becoming an audience for their own words? If so, just how does one, in the words of Kenneth Burke, "transform . . . failure into profit, not in the sense of those who leave failure behind them, since that change would involve a profound forgetting, but in the sense of those whose structure of existence is made of the materials of their frustration"? (*Towards*, 40).

In *A Rhetoric of Motives*, Burke moves beyond the Aristotelian notion of rhetoric as persuasion aimed primarily at an outside audience to a modern post-Christian rhetoric that considers the individual as both subject and object of his own discourse. This shift of emphasis results in a focus on "ideas or images privately addressed to the individual self for moralistic or incantatory purposes" (38). Defining rhetoric from the point of view of the person "addressed," Burke believes that "a man can be his own audience, insofar as he, even in his secret thoughts, cultivates certain ideas or images for the effect he hopes they may have upon him; he is . . . an 'I' addressing its 'me'" (38). He may even invent "psychologically stylistic subterfuges for presenting [his] own case to [himself] in sympathetic terms" (39). To this end, then, "he is being rhetorical quite as though he were using pleasant imagery to influence an outside audience rather than one within" (38). When aimed at promoting personal or cultural well-being, Burke suggests that "stylistic subterfuges" may be highly ethical, enabling us to restructure long-held "pieties" or beliefs that no longer foster the health of soul or psyche. As Clayton Lewis explains in "Burke's Act in *A Rhetoric of Motives*," when reconceiving worlds other than the ones to which we are daily confined, we "transform discordances, disharmonies, perceived chaos and disorder, conflicts or other signs of difference into newly created orders" which, in turn, may change our "audience" and our "view of self" and "possibly change reality itself" (376). Thus, a Burkean view of rhetoric as "performative," rooted in a belief that we can convert "failure into profit," strongly suggests a place for healing in intrapersonal as well as interpersonal discourse—a finding that has important implications for those of us professionally involved in assisting others to present their own cases to themselves in "sympathetic terms."

One uses rhetoric for many purposes, say the Baumlins: "to express, to create, to praise, to blame, to analyze, to explore, to doubt, to destroy, to curse[,] . . . to cure and heal" (259). As the last of these purposes—"to cure and heal"—has long been ignored within our profession, it may well be time to explore the therapeutic potential of the reflective prose that we ask students to write in more traditional classroom settings. But, whether the move to link rhetoric with healing happens within the walls of the academy or in less structured settings as part of composition's extracurriculum, the critical issue is that it happen.

REFLECTING ON YOUR TEACHING

Talking about Disability in the Classroom

Mitchell's and Couser's pieces direct our attention to analyzing discourses of disability "out there." But disability is not very far from every person in a classroom. There may be students with disabilities in your class, whether apparent or not. Some students may have family members with disabilities, or have experiences of neighbors, schoolmates, or church members with disabilities. As citizens of a community and a nation, we all are affected by and contribute to discourses about disability that have effects in the world. When incorporating disability into the curriculum, we have to be careful not to (consciously or unconsciously) set up an "us" and "them" binary—casting "us" in the classroom as "normal" and "nondisabled," and the object of study "out there" as "them." In a teaching journal, keep track of how students and you as an instructor talk about disability (or another identity category). Do/did you or students fall into the "us" and "them" binary? In what contexts? Briefly, write a note to yourself about ways to avoid this trap. Practice other kinds of sentences that acknowledge the presence and/or possibility of disability in all of us.

SUGGESTIONS FOR STUDENT ACTIVITIES

Revising "Typical" Disability Narratives

We do not recommend that instructors push students to identify as disabled or claim a disability identity, but all students should be invited to write about their own experiences, to write about their own passions and pain, and to reflect on their contributions to cultural constructions of disability. One way to incorporate a rhetoric of healing that is both reflective and revisionary is to ask students to locate disability in relation to their own lives, to write about their own experiences with it, but to do so while consciously trying to create a narrative that "revises" the typical stories and plots of disability (as those in the critiques of Linton, Mitchell, and Couser). To express one's relationship with disability while avoiding commonplace rhetoric is indeed difficult. But this difficulty can be embraced as a generative aspect of the writing process—an aspect, perhaps, of any writing process. A sequence of short writing assignments and group work might look like this: Students begin by freewriting to uncover some relationship to a person with a disability or some experiences with disability. In groups, students examine each other's freewrites, with the goal of finding embedded disability metaphors or familiar schema—for example, disability as spiritual lesson ("it made me a better person"); or the encounter with disability that somehow reaffirms one's own "normalcy" ("it made me realize how good my life is"). Each student then does another round of freewriting, with the conscious intent of complicating the familiar schema or metaphor. Next, as a homework assignment students might be asked to write a dramatic scene or two that "shows" a more complicated meaning of their encounter with disability. Bringing these short preliminary writings to class, students might work on developing both the "shows" and "tells" aspects of their papers. In a final writer's memo accompanying this reflective and revisionary paper, students could comment on the difficulties and satisfactions of consciously trying to revise narratives and discourses to achieve a sense of personal and cultural healing.

Using Disability Concepts: The Norm, Gaze, and Embodied Knowledge

21 From *The Rule of Normalcy*

LENNARD DAVIS

Lennard Davis begins this essay with a critical examination of "grammar" itself, interrogating the policing of language (and behavior) that allows one critic to call into question his use of the word "normalcy" rather than "normality." Working through cultural, literary, and social history, Davis connects the "coincidences" that "normalcy and linguistic standardization begin at roughly the same time." Davis argues that ableism—the assumption of a standardized, nondisabled body and the oppression, othering, and condemning or belittling attitude placed on disability and people with disabilities—is also an aspect of the changes brought on by the Enlightenment, modernization, standardization, and democracy. Normalcy—as represented through bodily, linguistic, and cognitive standardization—comes to rule in the era of modernity. In Davis's view, ableism is but one "aspect of modifications of political and social practice that have both positive and negative implications and that can be changed through a political process."

When we say that "normality" is preferred over "normalcy," what exactly do we mean? We mean that some or a preponderance of experts in the field have agreed that a certain word is more "normal" than another word. How is the norm determined? By usage, to an extent. By logic, to an extent. By reference to grammatical patterns worked out from other languages like Latin and Greek. In other words, by social convention. For example, since "normalcy" is credited by the *Oxford English Dictionary* as having an American origin, we can imagine that the neologism would be discounted by some British lexicographers as a colonial malapropism, only another example in the decline of the empire's standards.

From Lennard Davis, *Bending Over Backwards: Disability, Dismodernism, and Other Difficult Positions* (New York: New York UP, 2002), 102–18.

If we think of the distinction between prescriptive grammar, the body of didactic rules that tells us how to write and speak, versus descriptive grammar, which aims to describe how language is used in a variety of settings, we can understand how truly socially constructed are grammatical "norms." Prescriptive grammar arose in the seventeenth and eighteenth centuries in an attempt to regularize the English language, which had no grammar, to the level of the revered Latin and Greek, which being dead languages had to have grammars and rules so that they could be taught in schools. Scholars at the time had fretted over the fact that English had no grammar, so the grammatical conventions of Latin were applied in a procrustean way to English, whether they fit or not. During this time, the first English dictionaries were compiled, so that spelling and meaning could be normalized, and so that printers could standardize their productions. In other words, language was regularized, and the effort of speaking and writing came under the jurisdiction and control of a class of scholars, men and women of letters, and other professionals who tried to make spoken language, in its transformational complexity, fit into rather arbitrary, logical categories. As Georges Canguilhem wrote, when French grammarians of the Enlightenment "undertook to fix the usage of the French language, it was a question of norms, of determining the reference, and of defining mistakes in terms of divergence, difference."

Why I am mentioning grammar and language usage in the context of a discussion of disabled or abnormal bodies is worth considering. When we think about normality, people in disability studies have generally made the error, I would say, of confining our discussions more or less exclusively to impairment and disease. But I think there is really a larger picture that includes disability along with any nonstandard behaviors. Language usage, which is as much a physical function as any other somatic activity, has become subject to an enforcement of normalcy, as have sexuality, gender, racial identity, national identity, and so on. As Canguilhem writes, "There is no difference between the birth of grammar . . . and the establishment of the metric system. . . . It began with grammatical norms and ended with morphological norms of men and horses for national defense, passing through industrial and sanitary norms."

Let me backtrack here for a moment and rehearse the argument I made in *Enforcing Normalcy* so that I can make clear to readers of this essay the direction in which I am going. In that book, I claimed that before the early to mid-nineteenth century, Western society lacked a concept of normalcy. Indeed, the word "normal" only appeared in English about a hundred and fifty years ago, and in French fifty years earlier. Before the rise of the concept of normalcy, I argued, there appears not to have been a concept of the normal, but instead the regnant paradigm was one revolving around the word "ideal." If one has a concept of the "ideal," then all human beings fall below that standard and so exist in varying degrees of imperfection. The key point is that in a culture of the "ideal," physical imperfections are not seen as absolute but as part of a descending continuum from top to bottom. No one, for example, *can* have an ideal body, and therefore no one has to have an ideal body.

Around the beginning of the nineteenth century in Europe, we begin to see the development of statistics and of the concept of the bell curve, called early on the "normal" curve. With the development of statistics comes the idea of a norm. In this paradigm, most bodies fall under the main umbrella of the curve. And those that do not are at the extremes—and therefore are "abnormal." Thus, there is an imperative on people to conform, to fit in, under the rubric of normality. Rather than being resigned to a less-than-ideal body in the earlier paradigm, people in the past hundred and fifty years have been now encouraged to strive to be normal, to huddle under the main part of the curve.

Is it a coincidence, then, that normalcy and linguistic standardization begin at roughly the same time? If we look at that confluence in one area in particular, we see that language and normalcy come together under the rubric of nationalism. As Benedict Anderson has pointed out, the rise of the modern nation took place largely in the eighteenth and nineteenth centuries when the varieties of polyglotism that had made up a politically controlled area were standardized into a single "national" language. Without this linguistic homogeneity, a notion of the modern nation-state would have had great difficulty coming into being. In addition, national literatures, both in prose and poetry, were made possible through the standardization of languages, the prescriptive creation of "normal" language practices.

While few now object to Anderson's thesis that language practices had to be standardized, homogenized, and normalized to allow for the creation of the modern nation-state, I think that the next step, which I want to propose in this essay, might be more objectionable. I would claim that for the formation of the modern nation-state not simply language but bodies and bodily practices also had to be standardized, homogenized, and normalized. In this sense, a national physical type, a national ethical type, and an antinational physical type had to be constructed. Here we see much work done in the nineteenth century on racial studies, studies of pathology, deviance, and so on— all with the aim of creating the bourgeois subject in opposition to all these abnormal occurrences.

This is where I want to return to my putative linguistic solecism. In thinking about the difference, or lack of difference, between normalcy and normality, I began to think of the suffixes which make all the difference in those two words. "-cy" seems to indicate a state of being, as does "-ity," but there are resonating differences. Both "-ity" and "-cy" turn adjectives into nouns—as "sexuality," "ethnicity," "formality," as well as "malignancy," "pregnancy," "immediacy." However, I would suggest, without insisting absolutely, that the use of "-cy" seems more strongly to denote a permanent state, as it does in "idiocy," "complacency," "malignancy." But interestingly enough, many words that describe not simply a corporeal state but a political state use the suffix—"democracy," "autocracy," "plutocracy," or "aristocracy." My thought, then, was to salvage my own oversight by making a valid distinction, much in the way that Jacques Derrida talked about "difference" and "differance." I would call "normality" the alleged physical state of being normal, but "normalcy" the political-juridical-institutional state that relies on the control and normalization of bodies, or what Foucault calls "biopower." Thus, like democracy, normalcy is a descriptor of a certain form of government rule, the former by the people, the latter over bodies.

This distinction allows us to think through ableism in a somewhat different way than we have in the past. Rather than conceptualizing ableism as a trait or habit of thought on the part of certain somatically prejudiced people, we can consider ableism to be one aspect of a far-ranging change in European and perhaps global culture and ideology that is part of Enlightenment thought and part of modernization. Further, and I think this is important, we can begin to move away from the victim-victimizer scenario with which ableism, along with racism, sexism, and the other "isms" have been saddled and which leaves so little room for agency. Instead, one can see ableism as an aspect of modifications of political and social practice that have both positive and negative implications and that can be changed through a political process.

REFLECTING ON YOUR TEACHING

Student Assessment

Write a short reflection in your teaching journal about your own grading and/or assessment practices. What forms of measurement do you use to assess student learning? What are the strengths or drawbacks of these ways of measuring learning? Are they effective with every student writer? Why or why not? Have you ever considered other kinds of evaluation? With what results?

SUGGESTIONS FOR STUDENT ACTIVITIES

Norms and Standardization

Ask students to explore the rule of normalcy as it applies to other aspects of body/mind standardization in our culture and then work to make connections back to normalcy/ability. For example, they might be encouraged to conduct research on the development of any number of now fairly accepted "standard" measures: "proficiency" tests in K–12 education within their state or district; the height/weight/body fat percentage charts (available for almost every age group); the IQ or Stanford-Binet test; the SAT or ACT college entrance exams; professional/graduate school entrance exams such as the GRE, LSAT, MCAT, GMAT tests; the mental retardation chart; the standard audiological measurement charts; the vision charts; or even the Rorschach tests. What is the story behind the development of any of these measures? What controversies arose and remain, or have surfaced anew in relation to these standardized tests? Who was involved and not involved in the decisions to establish such standards and measures? What is measured and not measured? What is the "standard" that is measured in this test? What kinds of people do and don't take this test or are judged by this standard? And finally, perhaps most important of all, students should be encouraged to analyze how a test they are researching creates a "norm" and deviations in relation to it, and to reflect on this construction. Students might be directed to Stephen Jay Gould's *The Mismeasure of Man* as an excellent resource.

Literacy Narratives and Standardized Testing

Invite students to write their own personal literacy narratives in relation to standardized testing of any kind that they have undergone. How did their own awareness of a/the "norm" function in their experience of "taking" and "passing/failing" such tests? What did they understand "the norm" to be? Students might wish to place their own narratives within the context of their research on standardized testing.

22 From *Animals in Translation*

TEMPLE GRANDIN AND
CATHERINE JOHNSON

Temple Grandin is possibly the most well-known autistic person in the United States. She achieved fame for her autobiography as a person with autism, her knowledge of animal behavior, and her inventions that allow more humane treatment of cattle, described in her books Emergence: Labeled Autistic *and* Thinking in Pictures: And Other Reports from My Life with Autism. *In the following excerpt, she and cowriter Catherine Johnson try to explain how autistic people think, by comparing their abilities to generalize or discern particularities to those of "normal" people and animals. People with autism have a superior ability for some tasks, such as finding a hidden figure, and this ability leads people with autism to "outperform normal people" in a number of jobs—from inspecting silk screens for flaws, to maintaining "quality assurance on submarine parts. This excerpt concludes with the statement, "We're letting a huge amount of talent go to waste, both in people who aren't 'normal' and in animals who are."*

LUMPERS AND SPLITTERS: WHAT MAKES ANIMALS AND AUTISTIC PEOPLE DIFFERENT

Charles Darwin first used the terms *lumpers* and *splitters* to describe the two different kinds of taxonomists. Lumper taxonomists grouped lots of animals or plants into big, broad categories based on major characteristics; splitters divided them up into lots of smaller categories based on minor variations. Lumpers generalize; splitters "particularize."

This is a core difference between animals and autistic people on the one hand, and normal people on the other. Animals and autistic people are splitters. They see the differences between things more than the similarities. In practice this means animals don't generalize very well. (Normal

From Temple Grandin and Catherine Johnson, *Animals in Translation* (New York: Scribner, 2004), 294–98.

people often over-generalize, of course.) That's why you have to be so careful when you're socializing an animal to socialize him to many different animals and people.

You have to do the same thing with training. Service dogs who are being trained to lead a blind person across the street don't generalize from one intersection to another, so you can't just train them on a couple of intersections and expect them to apply what they've learned to a brand-new intersection. You have to train them on dozens of different kinds of intersections: corners where there's a light hanging in the middle of the intersection and crosswalk lines painted on the pavement, corners where there's a light hanging in the middle of the intersection and no crosswalk lines, corners where the traffic lights are on poles, and so on.

This is why dog trainers always make people train their own dogs. You can't send a puppy away to obedience school, because he'll only learn to obey the trainer, not you. Dogs also need some training from every member of the household, because if only one person trains the dog, that's the only person the dog is going to obey.

And you have to be careful not to fall into *pattern training*. Pattern training happens when you always train the dog in the same place at the same time using the same commands in the same order. If you pattern-train a dog, he'll learn the commands beautifully, but he won't be able to perform them anyplace other than the spot you trained him in, or in any sequence other than the one you used during training. He's learned the pattern, and he can't generalize the individual commands to other times, settings, or people.

People who teach autistic children deal with exactly the same challenge. A behaviorist told me a story about an autistic boy he'd been teaching how to butter toast. The behaviorist and the parents had been working really hard with the boy, and finally he got it. He could butter toast. Everyone was thrilled, but the joy didn't last too long, because when somebody gave the boy some peanut butter to spread on his toast, he didn't have a clue! His brand-new bread-buttering skill was specific to butter, and it didn't generalize to peanut butter. They had to start all over again and teach him how to spread *peanut* butter on toast. This happens all the time with autistic people, and with animals, too.

It happens so much, and it's so extreme, that it's not right just to call animals splitters; animals are *super-splitters*. That's what being hyper-specific is all about.

It's not that animals and autistic people don't generalize at all. Obviously they do. The black hat horse generalized his original traumatic experience to other people wearing other black hats, and the little boy who could butter toast had generalized that skill to other sticks of butter and other pieces of bread. With training, a service dog learns to generalize what he knows about other intersections to new intersections he's never seen before.

What's different is that the generalizations animals and autistic people make are almost always narrower and more specific than the generalizations nonautistic people make. *Human with black hat* or *spread butter on bread:* those are pretty narrow categories.

THE HIDDEN FIGURES TALENT

To any normal person, being hyper-specific sounds like a serious mental handicap, and in a lot of ways it is. Hyper-specificity is probably the main reason animals seem less smart than people. How intelligent could a horse be if he thinks the really scary thing in life isn't a nasty handler but the nasty handler's hat?

Probably not too intelligent when it comes to school smarts. But being smart in school isn't everything, and high general intelligence comes at the price of high *hyper-specific intelligence.* You can't have both.

That means normal human beings can't have extreme perception the way normal animals can, because hyper-specificity and extreme perception go together. I don't know whether one causes the other, or whether hyper-specificity and extreme perception are just different aspects of the same difference in the brain. What I do know is that Clever Hans couldn't do what people do, and people can't do what Hans did. Hans had a special talent humans don't have.

Until we know more about it, I'm calling this ability the *hidden figure talent,* based on some research findings in autism. In 1983 Amitta Shah and her colleague Uta Frith tested twenty autistic children, twenty normal children, and twenty children with learning disabilities—all of them the same mental age—on the Embedded Figure Task. In the test, first you show the child a shape, like a triangle, and then you ask him to find the same shape inside a picture of an object like a baby carriage.

The autistic children did much better at finding the hidden figure than any of the other children. They almost always saw the figure instantly, and they scored 21 out of 25 correct answers on average, compared to an average of only 15 correct answers for both the learning disabled and the normal kids. That's a huge difference. It's so huge you could probably say normal people are disabled compared to autistic people when it comes to finding hidden figures. The autistic children were so good they almost outscored the experimenters! These were developmentally disabled kids scoring the same as normal adults.

I believe it, because a few years back I happened to come across a hidden figure test in *Wired Magazine,* and the hidden figures jumped out at me. For me, they weren't really hidden.

To my knowledge no one's ever tested animals on hidden figure tests, but I bet they'd do well. Probably the easiest way to do a hidden figure test with an animal would be to run a simple recognition task. Teach the animal to touch or peck a certain shape, then show him a picture with the shape embedded inside and see whether the animal can still find it.

Most people don't realize how valuable the hidden figure talent is in the right situation. In Maryland there's an employment agency for autistic adults that places its clients in jobs like quality assurance. They have one group of autistic men working in a factory inspecting logo T-shirts coming off the line for flaws in the silk-screening. Nonautistic people have a hard time seeing tiny differences between one silk-screened logo and another, but those autistic employees can pick up practically microscopic flaws in a glance. It's the hidden figure test all over again. To them the flaws in the silk-screening aren't hidden.

The agency's clients also outperform normal people in bindery work. When you're assembling corporate reports you have to be able to tell the front cover from the back cover quickly and accurately. To regular people the fronts and backs look alike, but autistic employees can always tell the front from the back, and they do it in a flash. Extreme perception lets them see all the tiny differences normal people can't see. The agency even has one autistic woman working quality assurance on submarine parts.

I thought about those employees not too long after 9/11 when news reports started coming out about how hard it is for people who work as luggage inspectors to spot weapons on their video screens due to *clutter*. If you're a normal human being and your job is to sit in one place all day long staring at a video screen, pretty soon you'll have trouble separating out the form of a weapon from all the other junk that's packed in people's bags. The screen is too cluttered, and everything blurs together. But that might not be a problem for autistic people, and I think airports ought to try out some autistic people in that job.

I think we're letting a huge amount of talent go to waste, both in people who aren't "normal" and in animals who are. That's probably because we don't really understand what animals could do if we gave them a chance. We're just leaving it up to animals like the seizure alert dogs to invent their own jobs.

SUGGESTIONS FOR STUDENT ACTIVITIES

Writing Critical Reflections

After introducing students to the history of normalcy provided by Lennard Davis, the criticisms of language and labeling offered by Simi Linton, and the analysis of how disability functions in literary texts by David Mitchell, students should be ready to think critically about how Grandin and her coauthor use language and comparison to describe the minds of people with autism. What are the benefits and drawbacks of comparing autistic thinking with animals' thought? What is gained? What is lost? What entailments come with the comparison?

Writing Manifestos of Lumpers and Splitters

Ask the class to divide themselves into two groups, Lumpers or Splitters, depending on whether they feel they are good at generalizing or whether they prefer to learn through an understanding of details and patterns. Once everyone has joined one or the other group, ask each group to brainstorm a list of benefits and drawbacks of their preferred manner of learning. Next, have each group collaboratively write a manifesto of their thinking style. Rhetorical flourishes should be encouraged. Read these aloud, and discuss as a whole class. Invite students, following this activity, to lump themselves into new groupings, or split their identifications between groups. If the two teams can record the key points of their manifestos on a blackboard, whiteboard, large notecards, or computers, so that the whole class can easily see their work, then the class can also easily realign, exchange, and bridge points between groupings.

23 From *The Politics of Staring: Visual Rhetorics of Disability in Popular Photography*

ROSEMARIE GARLAND-THOMSON

According to Rosemarie Garland-Thomson, people with disabilities have historically been both something to look at and something not to be looked at. Garland-Thomson examines our "ocularcentric" view—the way we privilege looking at objects—and develops a taxonomy of four visual rhetorics for disability, especially as they are displayed in modern photography, to help us understand assumptions about and categorizations of the disabled body. These four rhetorics are "the wondrous, the sentimental, the exotic, and the realistic." She notes that none of these rhetorics occurs discretely and almost all of them appropriate the disabled body as spectacle for the spectator. Ending with the "realistic," Garland-Thomson argues that the "visual rhetoric of the ordinary" exhibits "a climate of integration and diversity created by the disability rights movement and resulting legislation such as the Americans with Disabilities Act of 1990 (ADA)."

The history of disabled people in the Western world is in part the history of being on display, of being visually conspicuous while politically and socially erased. The earliest record of disabled people is of their exhibition as prodigies, monsters, omens from the gods, and indexes of the natural or divine world. From the New Testament to the miracles at Lourdes, the lame, the halt, and the blind provide the spectacle for the story of bodily rehabilitation as spiritual redemption that is so essential to Christianity. From antiquity through modernity, the bodies of disabled people considered to be freaks and monsters have been displayed by the likes of medieval kings and P. T. Barnum for entertainment and profit in courts, street fairs, dime museums, and sideshows.[1] Moreover, medicine has from its beginnings exhibited the disabled body as what Michel Foucault calls the "case," in medical theaters and other clinical

From *Disability Studies: Enabling the Humanities,* ed. Sharon L. Snyder, Brenda Jo Brueggemann, and Rosemarie Garland-Thomson (New York: Modern Language Association, 2002), 56–75.

settings, in order to pathologize the exceptional and to normalize the ordinary (*Birth of the Clinic*, 29). Disabled people have variously been objects of awe, scorn, terror, delight, inspiration, pity, laughter, or fascination—but they have always been stared at.

Staring at disability choreographs a visual relation between a spectator and a spectacle. A more intense form of looking than glancing, glimpsing, scanning, surveying, gazing, and other forms of casual or uninterested looking, staring registers the perception of difference and gives meaning to impairment by making it as aberrant. By intensely telescoping looking toward the physical signifier for disability, staring creates an awkward partnership that estranges and discomforts both viewer and viewed. Starers gawk with abandon at the prosthetic hook, the empty sleeve, the scarred flesh, the unfocused eye, the twitching limb, but seldom does looking broaden to envelop the whole body of the person with a disability. Even supposedly invisible disabilities always threaten to disclose some stigma, however subtle, that disrupts the social order by its presence and attenuates the bond between equal members of the human community. Because staring at disability is considered illicit looking, the disabled body is at once the to-be-looked-at and not-to-be-looked-at, further dramatizing the staring encounter by making viewers furtive and the viewed defensive. Staring thus creates disability as a state of absolute difference rather than simply one more variation in human form. At the same time, staring constitutes disability identity by manifesting the power relations between the subject positions of disabled and able-bodied.

The rapid flourishing of photography after 1839 provided a new way to stare at disability. In our ocularcentric era, images mediate our desires and the ways we imagine ourselves.[2] Among the myriad, often conflicting, and never indifferent images modernity offers us, the picture of ourselves as disabled is an image fraught with a tangle of anxiety, distance, and identification. As a culture, we are at once obsessed with and intensely conflicted about the disabled body. We fear, deify, disavow, avoid, abstract, revere, conceal, and reconstruct disability—perhaps because it is one of the most universal, fundamental of human experiences. After all, we will all become disabled if we live long enough. Nonetheless, in representing disability in modernity, we have made the familiar seem strange, the human seem inhuman, the pervasive seem exceptional. By the beginning of the twentieth century, for example, public displays of disabled people became inappropriate in the same way that public executions and torture came to be considered offensive. Disabled people were sequestered from public view in institutions and the private sphere as middle-class decorum pronounced it impolite to stare. Photography, however, has enabled the social ritual of staring at disability to persist in an alternate form. . . .

To look at the way we look at disability, I elaborate a taxonomy of four primary visual rhetorics of disability. They are the wondrous, the sentimental, the exotic, and the realistic. This template of visual rhetorics complicates the often restrictive notion of images as being either positive or negative, as communicating either the truth of disability or perpetuating some oppressive stereotype. Thus, I analyze more than evaluate. These visualizations of disabled people act as powerful rhetorical figures that elicit responses or persuade viewers to think or act in certain ways. The wondrous, the sentimental, the exotic, and the realistic converge and inflect one another in individual pictures as well as across all genres of disability photography. These visual rhetorics seldom occur discretely; rather, the photographs blend together in individual photographs. They wax and wane, shift and combine over time as they respond to the purposes for which the photographs are produced. Moreover, these rhetorics constitute part of the context into which all representations of disabled people enter. Not only do these representational modes configure public perception of disability, but all images of disabled people either inadvertently or deliberately summon these visual rhetorics and their accompanying cultural narratives. None of these rhetorical modes operates in the service of actual disabled people, however. Indeed, almost all of them appropriate the disabled body for the purposes of constructing, instructing, or assuring some aspect of a putatively nondisabled viewer.

The first visual rhetoric is the wondrous. The oldest mode of representing disability, the wondrous continues to find a place in modernity's framing of disability. This genre capitalizes on physical differences in order to elicit amazement and admiration. The antecedents of the wondrous disabled figures are the monsters of antiquity, who inspired awe, foretold the future, or bore divine signs, and freaks, who were the celebrities in nineteenth-century dime museums and sideshows (Garland-Thomson, "From Wonder"). The rhetoric of the wondrous springs from a premodern interpretation of disability as either augury or marks of distinction, whether representing good or evil. Oedipus, Teiresias, monsters, giants—even Shakespeare's Richard III— were imposing if ominous disabled figures.

A nineteenth-century example is Charles Tripp, the famous Armless Wonder, pictured eating with his toes in a carte de visite, one of the exceedingly popular photographic portraits commonly sold to augment and promote live appearances. This carefully choreographed portrait includes samples of his calligraphic skills, paper figures he's cut out, as well as the pen and scissors he used to accomplish such remarkable tasks. The silver tea set in the picture refers to other photos of him drinking from a cup with his toes. The composition is a visual résumé documenting Tripp's supposedly amazing accomplishments. The spectacle tries to elicit awe from the viewers, whose sense of their own clumsy toes makes Tripp's feet feat seem wondrous. . . .

Modernity secularized wonder into the stereotype of the supercrip, who amazes and inspires the viewer by performing feats that the nondisabled viewer cannot imagine doing. Contemporary wonder rhetoric emphasizes admiration rather than amazement, in part because bourgeois respectability now deems it inappropriate to delight in staring at disabled people. One example is a recent ad for adventure tours that features a rock climber using a wheelchair. Here the photographic composition literally positions the viewer as looking up in awe at the climber dangling in her wheelchair. By making the disabled figure exceptional rather than ordinary, the wondrous can estrange viewer from viewed and attenuate the correspondence that equality requires.

Sentimentality has inflected the wonder model, producing the convention of the courageous overcomer, contemporary America's favorite figure of disability. Even though armless calligraphers are no longer an acceptable form of middle-class entertainment, photos of disabled people who have adapted tasks to fit their bodies still ask their viewers to feel a sense of wonder. An advertisement for Habitat for Humanity, for example, pictures a disabled volunteer worker building a house. Like Tripp, this man is portrayed as entirely ordinary except for the detail of the fingerless hands holding the hammer, which occupies the center of interest, at once inviting and authorizing the stare. As is typical in disability photography, the text instructs the viewer how to respond to the picture, with a headline that says, "Extraordinary Volunteer, Unstoppable Spirit." The picture thus combines the narrative of admiration for overcoming disability with the narrative of empowerment characteristic of a post–disability rights movement consciousness. By making disabled subjects masters of ordinary activities such as climbing rocks, drinking tea, or using hammers, these photos create a visual context that elicits adulation for their accomplishing what the normalized viewer takes to be a superhuman feat.

———

The second visual rhetoric is the sentimental. Whereas the wondrous elevates and enlarges, the sentimental diminishes. The sentimental produces the sympathetic victim or helpless sufferer needing protection or succor and invoking pity, inspiration, and frequent contributions. The sentimental disabled figure developed as a part of the larger nineteenth-century bourgeois culture of fine feelings.[3] The pathetic, the impotent, and the suffering confirmed the Victorian bourgeoisie by arousing their finest sentiments. As the increasingly empowered middle class imagined itself capable of capitalizing the world, it began to see itself as responsible for the world as well, a stewardship that launched humanitarian and reform movements to which today's telethons are heir. This discourse of middle-class noblesse oblige operates on a model of paternalism, often trafficking in children and alluding to the cute, the plucky, the long-suffering, and the courageous.

The rhetoric of sentiment found an effective home in the photographic conventions of the poster child of mid-twentieth-century charity campaigns. The 1946 March of Dimes poster child echoes the spunky cuteness of freak figures such as General Tom Thumb. But where Tom Thumb delighted with his miniature adulthood, this poster child breaks hearts as he is propped vulnerably up in a corner of his crib in the before-and-after format. In order to catalyze the adult, to whom the photo addresses itself, this March of Dimes poster presents disability to the middle-class spectator as a problem to solve, an obstacle to eliminate, a challenge to meet. In such appeals, impairment becomes the stigma of suffering, transforming disability into a project that morally enables a nondisabled rescuer. The viewer's dimes, the poster suggests, will literally catapult the unhappy little fellow trapped in braces in his crib into a smiling and spirited tyke, striding with determination and gratitude toward the viewer. Sentimentality makes of disabled people occasions for the viewers' own narratives of progress, improvement, or heroic deliverance and contains disability's threat in the sympathetic, helpless child for whom the viewer is empowered to act. Whereas earlier sentimental literature accentuates suffering to mobilize readers for humanitarian, reform, or religious ends, the poster boy's suffering is only the background to his restoration to normalcy that results from "your dimes." The optimism of cure thus replaces the intensity of sympathy, testifying to an increasing faith in clinical treatment and scientific progress as modernity increasingly medicalizes and rationalizes the body.

The rhetoric of sentiment has migrated from charity to retail in late capitalism's scramble to capture markets. For example, the cover of a 1998 Benetton public relations brochure distributed in stores employs a chic sentimentality in documenting a school for developmentally disabled children Benetton supports and outfits. . . .

The third visual rhetoric is the exotic. The rhetoric of sentiment domesticates the disability figure, making it familiar and comforting. In contrast, the visual rhetoric of the exotic presents disabled figures as alien, distant, often sensationalized, eroticized, or entertaining in their difference. The exotic reproduces an ethnographic model of viewing characterized by curiosity or uninvolved objectification and informed by the proliferation of popular ethnographic photography that accompanied the era of Western imperialism. For example, nineteenth-century freak photography often transformed disabled people into "wild men" or other exotic "savages," whose impairments were translated into marks of alien ethnicity (Garland-Thomson, "From Wonder," 5). The exotic demedicalizes, fascinates, and seduces with exaggeration, creating a sensationalized, embellished alien.

The introduction of disabled models has exploded the contemporary fashion world in the last several years, returning the rhetoric of the exotic into disability photography. . . .

The exotic serves this commercial aim by upsetting the earnest, asexual, vulnerable, courageous image of disability that charity rhetoric has so firmly implanted. One image advertising wheelchairs presents a tattooed biker figure brandishing a hockey stick. The image alludes at once to the strong men and tattoo kings of the sideshows and then inflects it with a hyperphallic sexuality, completely rewriting the cultural script of the emasculated invalid and the male who becomes feminized by disability. As is typical with much popular disability photography, the text instructs the viewer on how to read this photo. The exaggeration characteristic of exoticization here marshals ironic hyperbole to mount a brazen, sensational parody, provocatively challenging the viewer by lewdly commanding, "Lick this!" Such representations preclude even a trace of the sentimental or the wondrous, insisting instead on the empowerment of the transgressive, even at the expense of distancing the spectator from the spectacle. . . .

———

The fourth visual rhetoric is the realistic. Where the exotic mode cultivates estrangement, realism minimizes distance and difference by establishing a relation of contiguity between viewer and viewed. The wondrous, sentimental, and exotic modes of representation tend to exaggerate the difference of disability to confer exceptionality on the object in the picture. The rhetoric of the realistic, however, trades in verisimilitude, regularizing the disabled figure in order to avoid differentiation and arouse identification, often normalizing and sometimes minimizing the visual mark of disability. Realism domesticates disability. Realist disability photography is the rhetoric of equality, most often turned utilitarian. The use of realism can be commercial or journalistic, and it can also urge the viewer to political or social action.[4]

Realism emerged as a property of portraiture, documentary, and medical photography of the nineteenth century. Documentary photography such as that made famous by Lewis Hine and Jacob Riis aimed photographic realism at the progressive obsession with social reform.[5] Documentary and journalistic photographies differ from charity and commercial photographies in that they do not solicit the exchange of money so directly but rather aim to democratically disseminate information intended to shape the viewers' actions and opinions. Hine and Riis recorded the fabric of the American underclass, exposing the supposed truth of the conditions in which it struggled. Hine photographed wounded workers whose disabilities robbed them of the male privilege and duty of work, and he featured children whose disabilities he felt stole their childhood. The caption below an amputee worker reads, "When a man's hand is mutilated, he keeps it out of sight" (Stange, 60). The implied message is that the social mandate to hide disability precludes entry into the workplace. Hine enlists disability in documentary photos ultimately to tell a cautionary tale: disability is a scourge that can and should be avoided in a world that works right. In spite of the political support and social acceptance the picture confers, the photograph nevertheless marks this worker as a person the viewer does not want to be.

A more sensationalized use of realism recently provoked controversy and roused political protests over what constitutes unacceptable looking at women's breasts. The Breast Cancer Fund, a San Francisco–based nonprofit organization dedicated to education about and funding of breast cancer research, mounted a public awareness campaign in January 2000 called Obsessed with Breasts, featuring three posters showing women boldly displaying mastectomy scars. The posters parodied a Victoria's Secret catalog, a *Cosmopolitan* cover, and a Calvin Klein perfume ad, all of which typically parade women's breasts in soft-porn modes that have become an unremarkable staple of commercial magazine advertising. The posters disrupt the visual convention of the female breast as sexualized object for male appropriation and pleasure by replacing the now normative, eroticized breast with the proscribed image of the amputated breast. The powerful visual violation produced by exchanging the spectacle of the eroticized breast, which has been desensationalized by its endless circulation, with the medicalized image of the scarred breast, which has been concealed from public view, was so shocking to viewers that many demanded that the images be removed. Of course, the censuring and censoring of images that demand a recognition of the reality of breast cancer ignited a vibrant controversy. The images intensify this forbidden version of the disabled breast by ironically juxtaposing it with the commonplace but virulently sexist eroticisation of the breast. The posters thus advance a potent feminist challenge not only to sexism in medical research and the treatment for breast cancer but also to the oppressive representational practices that make erotic spectacles of women's breasts an everyday thing while erasing the fact of the amputation that one woman in eight will have. By mocking the tired sensationalism of pornography, these pictures protest against the refusal of contemporary America to literally and figuratively look at breast cancer.

The visual rhetoric of the ordinary has emerged in a climate of integration and diversity created by the disability rights movement and resulting legislation such as the Americans with Disabilities Act of 1990 (ADA). While the post-ADA era is not without resistance and backlash to the integration of people with disabilities, the social environment is filling with disability in the popular press. Disability not only appears in the sensationalist underbelly of the press, where it always has, but also is tucked with various degrees of conspicuousness into the fabric of common visual culture. Department store and catalog advertising, for instance, has adopted the rhetoric of the ordinary both to appeal to disabled people as a market and to suggest an ethic of inclusion. L. L. Bean promotes a wheelchair backpack in its catalog; Walmart and many other stores feature disabled models and mannequins in everything from frumpy jog suits to evening gowns. Toy lines like Barbie and the upscale American Girl have wheelchair-using dolls. Such routinization of disability imagery not only brings disability as a human experience out of the closet, it also enables people with disabilities—especially those who acquire impairments as adults—to imagine themselves as a part of the ordinary world rather than belonging to a special class of untouchables and unviewables. Images of disability as a familiar, even mundane, experience in the lives of seemingly successful, happy, well-adjusted people can reduce the identifying against oneself that is the overwhelming effect of oppressive and discriminatory attitudes toward people with disabilities. . . .

NOTES

1. For a historical account of the display of disabled people as monsters and freaks, see Altick; Bogdan; Dennett; Garland-Thomson, "From Wonder"; and D. Wilson.

2. For an account of the ocularcentric in Western culture, see Barthes; Crary; Debord; and Jay.

3. For a discussion of the development of middle-class feeling as a form of distinguishing respectability, see Halttunen; for a discussion of how sentimentality uses disabled figures, see Garland-Thomson, "Crippled Little Girls."

4. To use the term *realistic* does not suggest that this visual rhetoric is more truthful, accurate, or real than the other modes discussed here. Realism's function is to create the illusion of reality, not to reproduce or capture reality's elusive and complex substance. Although more subtle perhaps, the rhetoric of realism is just as constructed and convention-bound as the rhetorics of the wondrous, sentimental, or exotic.

5. For further discussion of Hine, see Rosenblum, Rosenblum, and Trachtenberg.

SUGGESTIONS FOR STUDENT ACTIVITIES

Media-Watch Project

Ask students to search/research contemporary media—magazines, newspapers, the Internet, TV, and film—in order to bring forward advertisements, stories, and scenes that also feature a picture of a person with a disability. This will not be hard—in fact, the volume of images available will be likely to quickly astound students once they set to this task. They should each bring one to four images to class, and class members could work in "first screen" small groups to place the images into any of the four visual rhetoric categories discussed by Garland-Thomson: "the wondrous, the sentimental, the exotic, and the realistic." Students can then work alone or in pairs to develop short critical papers about a single image within any one category that they will share with the class. What features of this image make it wondrous, sentimental, exotic, or realistic? What is the nature of the triangulated relationship between the subject or person in the photo and the photographer who creates the image and the audience likely to view the final image? What do considerations of tone, angle, composition, and frame contribute to a "reading" of this image within or against its particular visual rhetoric category?

Composing Visual Rhetoric

Students could also be asked to design or create a series of images, imagined or actual, that might illustrate any or all of Garland-Thomson's categories. What subjects and scenes would they set up to capture the rhetorical angles of the wondrous, the sentimental, the exotic, and the realistic in relation to their own, contemporary understanding of disability?

24   *Gawking, Gaping, Staring*

ELI CLARE

Because it is so short and so powerful, we have reprinted Eli Clare's essay "Gawking, Gaping, Staring" in its entirety. Clare's poetic essay is a provocative performative piece incorporating historical notes from "freak show" subjects, her own experience as one who is often "gawked" at, and a developing theory of staring back. Clare leans in this essay toward both finding a language to name herself and finding role models and a community. "I am looking for friends and allies," she concludes, "for communities where the gawking, gaping, staring finally turns to something else, something true to the bone."

Gawking, gaping, staring: I can't say when it first happened. When first a pair of eyes caught me, held me in their vise grip, tore skin from muscle, muscle from bone. Those eyes always shouted, "Freak, retard, cripple," demanding an answer for tremoring hands, a tomboy's bold and unsteady gait I never grew out of. It started young, anywhere I encountered humans. Gawking, gaping, staring seeped into my bones, became the marrow. I spent thirty years shutting it out, slamming the door.

The gawkers never get it right, but what I want to know is this: Will you? When my smile finds you across the room, will you notice the odd angle of my wrists cocked and decide I am a pane of glass to glance right through? Or will you smile back?

Thirty years, and now I am looking for lovers and teachers to hold all my complexities and contradictions gently, honestly, appreciatively. Looking for heroes and role models to accompany me through the world. Looking for friends and allies to counter the gawking, gaping, staring.

I come from peoples who have long histories of being onstage—freaks and drag queens, court jesters and scientific experiments. Sometimes we work

---

From *GLQ* 9, no. 1–2 (2003): 257–61.

for money and are proud. Other times we're just desperate. We've posed for anthropologists and cringed in front of doctors, jumped through hoops and answered the same questions over and over, performed the greatest spectacles and thumbed our noses at that shadow they call normal.

William Johnson—African American and cognitively disabled in the mid-1800s—worked the freak show stage. He donned an ape costume and shaved his head, save for a tuft of hair at the very top, and became the monkey man, the missing link, the bridge between "brute" and "man." P. T. Barnum, showman extraordinaire and shaper of the institution of the freak show, named William's exhibit "The What-Is-It?" People paid to gawk, and William died a well-off man. The folks who performed alongside William affectionately called him the "dean of freaks." Today that question—What-Is-It?—still lingers, still haunts us, only now the gawkers get in for free.

Billy Tipton worked the jazz stage with his piano, saxophone, and comedy routines. Billy lived for fifty years as a female-bodied man. He married five times and adopted three sons. He turned down major, high-profile music gigs. He died of a bleeding ulcer rather than seek medical care. He was much admired by the men he played music with. This we know about Billy, but there is also much we don't know: how he thought of himself, his gender; what prompted him to make the move from woman to man; what went through his head as he lay dying in his son's arms. But really the questions I want to ask aren't about his gender but about his life as a musician. *Billy, what did your body feel like as your fingers raced into a familiar song, playing in front of great throngs of people?* The gawking started after his death as the headlines roared, "Jazz Musician Spent Life Concealing Fantastic Secret."

I listen to the histories and everywhere hear the words *cripple, queer, gimp, freak*: those words hurled at me, those words used with pride. When I walk through the world, the bashers see a fag, the dykes see a butch, and I myself don't have many words. I often leave it at genderqueer or transgender butch. The gawkers never get it right. They think I'm deaf or "mentally retarded." They think I'm a twenty-year-old guy or a middle-aged dyke. They can't make up their minds, start with sir, end with ma'am, waver in the middle. They think I'm that pane of glass.

Cripples, queers, gimps, freaks: we are looking for teachers and lovers—teachers to stand with us against the gawking; lovers to reach beneath our clothing, beneath the words that attempt to name us, beneath our shame and armor, their eyes and hands helping return us to grace, beauty, passion. *He cradles my right hand against his body and says, "Your tremors feel so good." And says, "I can't get enough of your shaky touch." And says, "I love your cerebral palsy." This man who is my lover. Shame and disbelief flood my body, drowning his words. How do I begin to learn his lustful gaze?*

Believing him takes more than trust. I spent so many years shutting the staring out, slamming the door. Friends would ask, "Did you see that person gaping at you?" and I'd answer, "What person?" It's a great survival strategy but not very selective. In truth, the door slammed hard, and I lost it all, all the appreciation, flirtation, solidarity that can be wrapped into a gaze. These days

I practice gawking at the gawkers and flirting as hard as I know how. The first is an act of resistance; the second, an act of pride. I am looking for teachers.

If I had a time machine, I'd travel back to the freak show. Sneak in after hours, after all the folks who worked long days selling themselves as armless wonders and wild savages had stepped off their platforms, out of their geek pits, from behind their curtains. I'd walk among them—the fat women, the short-statured men commonly called dwarfs and midgets, the folks without legs, the supposed half men/half women, the conjoined twins, the bearded women, the snake charmers and sword swallowers—as they took off their costumes, washed their faces, sat down to dinner. I'd gather their words, their laughter, their scorn at the customers—the rubes—who bought their trinkets and believed half their lies. I'd breathe their fierceness into me.

I am looking for teachers and heroes to show me the way toward new pride, new understanding, new strength, a bigger sense of self. Often it is history I turn to, history I grasp and mold in my search. I am not alone in this endeavor. I think of a kid we've come to know as Brandon Teena: twenty-one years old, living as a guy in rural Nebraska, revealed as female-bodied, raped and murdered by so-called friends. In the trans community, we've chosen him. Claimed him as an FTM based on how his life makes sense to us, without listening to his confusion.[1] Named him Brandon Teena without paying attention to the dozen other names he used. We have made him hero, martyr, symbol of transphobic violence. I think again of Billy Tipton. In the lesbian community, many have taken Billy as an emblem of the sexism in the jazz world of the mid-1900s. They shape his life as a man into a simple survival strategy that allowed him to play music. I myself read the life of William Johnson and find someone who turned a set of oppressive material and social conditions to his benefit and gained a measure of success and community. That reading strengthens me. But in truth William might have been a lonely, frightened man, coerced, bullied, trapped by freak show owners and managers. We use and reshape history, and in the process it sometimes gets misshapen.

At the same time, we all need teachers and heroes: folks to say, "You're not alone. I too was here. This is what I did and what I learned. Maybe it'll help." My best heroes and teachers don't live on pedestals. They lead complex, messy lives, offering me reflections of myself and standing with me against the gawkers.

The gawkers who never get it right. They've turned away from me, laughed, thrown rocks, pointed their fingers, quoted Bible verses, called me immoral and depraved, tried to heal me, swamped me in pity. Their hatred snarls into me, and often I can't separate the homophobia from the ableism from the transphobia.

The gawkers never get it right, but what I want to know is this: Will you? If I touch you with tremoring hands, will you wince away, thinking cripple, *thinking* ugly? *Or will you unfold to my body, let my trembling shimmer beneath your skin?*

These days, I practice overt resistance and unabashed pride, gawking at the gawkers and flirting as hard as I know how. The two go together. On the Castro, I check out the bears, those big burly men with full beards and open shirts. One of them catches my eyes. I hold his gaze for a single moment too long, watch as it slips down my body. He asks, "Are you a boy or a girl?" not taunting but curious. I don't answer. What could I possibly say? I walk away smiling, my skin warm.

In another world at another time, I would have grown up neither boy nor girl but something entirely different. In English there are no good words, no easy words. All the language we have created—transgender, transsexual, drag queen, drag king, stone butch, high femme, Nellie, fairy, bulldyke, he-she, FTM, MTF—places us in relationship to masculine or feminine, between the two, combining the two, moving from one to the other. I'm hungry for an image to describe my gendered self, something more than the shadowland of neither man nor woman, more than a suspension bridge tethered between negatives. I want a solid ground with bedrock of its own, a language to take me to a brand-new place neither masculine nor feminine, day nor night, mortise nor tenon. What could I possibly say to the bears cruising me at 3 P.M. as sunlight streams over concrete?

Without language to name myself, I am in particular need of role models. I think many of us are. Whom do we shape our masculinities, our femininities, after? Who shows us how to be a drag queen, a butch, a trannyfag who used to be a straight married woman and now cruises the boys hot and heavy, a multigendered femme boy/girl who walks the dividing line? I keep looking for disabled men to nurture my queer masculinity, crip style. Looking for bodies a bit off center, a bit off balance. Looking for guys who walk with a tremble, speak with a slur, who use wheelchairs, crutches, ventilators, braces, whose disabilities shape but don't contradict their masculinities.

And in truth I am finding those role models. There is a freak show photo: Hiram and Barney Davis offstage—small, wiry men, white, cognitively disabled, raised in Ohio. They wear goatees, hair falling past their shoulders. They look mildly and directly into the camera. Onstage, Hiram and Barney played "Waino and Plutano, the Wild Men of Borneo." They snapped, snarled, growled, shook their chains at the audience. People flocked to the "Wild Men," handing over good money to gape. I hope just once Hiram and Barney stopped midperformance, up there on the sideshow platform, and stared back, turning their mild and direct gaze to the rubes, gawking at the gawkers.

It usually takes only one long glance at the gawkers—kids on their way home from school, old women with their grocery bags, young professionals dressed for work. Just once I want someone to tell me what they're staring at. My tremoring hands? My buzzed hair? My broad, off-center stance, shoulders well muscled and lopsided? My slurred speech? Just once. But typically one long steely glance, and they're gone. I'm taking Hiram and Barney as my teachers.

The gawkers never get it right, but what I want to know is this: Will you? When I walk through the world, will you simply scramble for the correct pronoun, failing whichever one you choose: he not all the way right, she not all the way wrong? Or will you imagine a river at dusk, its skin smooth and unbroken, sun no longer braided into sparkles? Cliff divers hurl their bodies from thirty, forty, fifty feet, bodies neither flying nor earth-bound, three somersaults and a half turn, entering the water free-fall *without a ripple. Will you get it right?*

I am looking for friends and allies, for communities where the gawking, gaping, staring finally turns to something else, something true to the bone. Places where strength gets to be softened and tempered, love honed and stretched. Where gender is known as more than a simple binary. Where we encourage each other to swish and swagger, limp and roll, and learn the language of pride. Places where our bodies begin to become home. Gawking, gaping, staring: I can't say when it first happened.

NOTE

1. The following are used in this essay: *FTM*, a female-to-male transgendered or transsexual person; *MTF*, a male-to-female transgendered or transsexual person; *trannyfag*, a gay FTM.

SUGGESTIONS FOR STUDENT ACTIVITIES

Memories and Reflections on Staring

Students should be invited to explore staring—a more abrasive form of "the gaze" made so famous by film critics from Laura Mulvey forward. Being stared at is often an experience people with (visible) disabilities share. (Also see Mossman p. 165, Garland-Thomson p. 216, Mairs p. 234, Hockenbery p. 257, and Siebers p. 262, for example). Invite students to recall a moment of being stared at and write about it. Or, encourage them to explore moments they have stared at someone or some scene themselves or moments they have seen others stare. How is a "stare" different from "a gaze" or a "glance" or even "a look"? What kind of emotions are in place with the stare under examination? What are the power relations between the one being stared at and the one doing the staring, and also, perhaps, the one capturing the scene of the staring on camera?

The Dynamics of "The Stare"

Students could also be encouraged to write small research and critical reflection papers on numerous dynamics of "the stare." They would first need to brainstorm some of these possible dynamics. How long does it take before a "look" becomes a stare? What are some of the gendered and relational possibilities for staring: women at men; women at women; men at women; men at men; parents at children; children at adults; children at other children; "rich" at "poor"; "poor" at "rich"; teachers at students; and students at teachers. How do other cultures regard staring? Who can practice it? When, if ever, is a stare acceptable? What are the dangers of staring? What are the various kinds of stares?

25   From *Disabilities, Bodies, Voices*

JIM SWAN

In the larger essay from which this is excerpted, Jim Swan asks how disability texts of poetry, autobiography, criticism, fiction, and drama are different from work by African American, Irish, Jewish, Chicana/o or Asian Americans' work—that is, how they are not simply a new identity field. He concludes that it is disability's "embodied perspective" as a "necessary ground" that "must be a fundamental part of any curriculum in disability studies." In the following section, Swan turns his attention to the classroom and discusses whether or not it is advisable to use "simulation activities" to help students understand embodiedness. Swan points out that simulations cannot give a nondisabled person an accurate experience of a disability, and they typically result in reinforcing an ableist point of view. For example, a student may conclude from such activities, "I learned how hard it is getting around in a wheelchair on this campus. I'm glad I'm able to walk." Instead of using simulations, then, Swan incorporates exercises that get students to ponder their own "embodied perception and experience."

The tie between disability studies and an embodied semantics will be tested most immediately in the classroom, where it may be useful sometimes to offer students an opportunity to experience what it is like to be physically or perceptually impaired. Ear stoppers for a day, or a blindfold, wheelchair, or crutches do convey something like the experience. But there are limits to what these simulations of disability can tell us.

In August and September 1998, several members of the Internet discussion list Disability Studies in the Humanities (DS-HUM) joined in a penetrating discussion of whether classroom simulations of disability serve as effective teaching tools or just confirm stereotypes and prejudices. A repeated

From *Disability Studies: Enabling the Humanities*, ed. Sharon L. Snyder, Brenda Jo Brueggemann, and Rosemarie Garland-Thomson (New York: Modern Language Association, 2002), 283–95.

criticism was that simply trying on a disability (e.g., spending a day in a wheelchair) cannot convey the continuous, no-time-out experience of being impaired. Worse, it focuses too much attention on the impairment and too little on the social construction that turns impairment into disability. The risk is that a simulation will simply confirm nondisabled persons in their belief that they are normal and therefore superior to anyone who is disabled — though, of course, with the added belief that they are now sensitized with feelings of guilt and pity for the plight of the disabled. A suggested alternative is to consider how the technological culture, the materially constructed environment, which is the result of specific design and policy decisions, acts to enable even those who think of themselves as already enabled on their own. In this view, culture and technology, the telephone and the paved highway, the public school and the home mortgage function as prostheses to overcome the limitations and extend the capabilities of — in principle — all members of society. However, the prosthetic function of these facilities and institutions tends to be invisible and unacknowledged, making it possible to exclude certain groups from being considered worthy of the same prosthetic consideration as that given to others — without the exclusion appearing to be an exclusion at all.

In my classroom I avoid doing simulations, but I do use exercises that quickly raise basic issues about embodied perception and experience. Drawing on Lakoff's analysis of prototypes and category structures, I ask students to jot down the first thing they can think of that is a member of a particular category. The choices are usually predictable: bird (sparrow, robin, pigeon, but rarely ostrich or penguin), flower (rose, carnation, tulip, but rarely asphodel or foxglove), and so on. Unlike the classical model, which imposes an all-or-nothing set of criteria for category membership, where all members belong equally and completely to the category, in this model some are "better" members than others and are perceived as prototypes, while others are marginal but still qualify as members. So, the category person with a disability, the most frequent response by far is "someone in a wheelchair," confirming the visual semiotic that structures the category. Linton in her wheelchair is a "better" member of the category than Rosenblum in chemotherapy.

For another exercise, when reading a blind or deaf-blind writer with a class, I have asked students to do something very simple. First, they are to stand up and find some clear space where they won't bump into one another. Next, I ask them to stand on one leg. That's easy enough. Then I ask them to close their eyes. Immediately, most of them find that they must open their eyes or they will fall over. This exercise provides a good opportunity to start thinking about eyesight as an orienting, balancing, sustaining phenomenon. If people think about sight at all, they tend to think of it as the experience of an independent ego actively directing its gaze to pick out features of interest. But the experience of standing on one leg and almost falling over when we shut our eyes tells a different story. It's not the same as becoming disoriented in a darkened room, because there we are presumably standing on both legs. But on one leg, we experience directly how exposure to the structure of the visual field, its up-and-down alignment with the pull of gravity and light, directly affects our trust in the groundedness of the body and its orientation in space. Its opposite is proprioception, the nonvisual sixth sense that, if Descartes had recognized it, we might have been spared a lot of trouble about the mind/body split—our ongoing, barely conscious awareness of the position, orientation, and movement of our bodies and limbs in space. Some people lose their proprioception to disease, and the effect can be devastating. For they lose much of the sense of their existential selves and must deliberately watch their arms and legs in order to move and act effectively.[1] In the exercise, ideally, students who lose their balance with their eyes closed discover how visual perception shapes and sustains their experience, even in so trivial a matter as standing in a room. Perhaps they also discover their proprioception, which usually functions unnoticed under the dominance of the visual. There are always a few students who do not lose their balance, and they often turn out to be dancers or similarly trained athletes, or people who do yoga, tai chi, and the like.

These exercises provide a glimpse of the role of visuality in how we categorize the world and orient ourselves within it. What they do not do is attempt to simulate a disability or impairment, and it is important to see why such an attempt will most likely fail. David Goode, an ethnomethodologist, did a field study of two young teenage girls who, as victims of rubella syndrome, were almost completely deaf and blind and had never developed language.[2] The perceptual lack, and the lack of language in particular, put into question their status as experiencing subjects. Could Goode, or anyone, have access to their subjectivity? With one of them, Christina (or Chris), Goode came to see that her subjectivity was constructed in ways that depended on who was observing her: medical professionals, primary-care staff, family, or Goode himself. It appeared that only those who worked closely with Chris reported that she showed rationality and purpose in her activities. The higher up the chain of professionalization, the more negative and pessimistic was the assessment. According to physicians and specialists, she was severely retarded, uncommunicative, autistic, and unlikely to respond to (re)habilitation. Goode doubted such reports. Seeking to bracket out his own physical and perceptual biases as much as possible, he spent time wearing a blindfold and ear stoppers. But, very quickly, he understood that his self-imposed deaf-blindness could not match even the most elementary features of Chris's experience:

> When I tried to eat my meal while "deaf-blind," I realized that what I was trying to do while eating was to produce that course of events that I already understood to be "mealtime" through my participation in the hearing, seeing, and speaking culture. The "meal" was already in my head, so to speak, and the deaf-blindness only posed technical problems to me in trying to produce it deaf-blindly.
>
> This was not at all the kind of deaf-blindness that the children experienced, since their "meal" was not in their heads at all. Thus, while they ate, they would finger and feel their food, sniff the food, examine it carefully with their residual vision—things that I did not do and for which I had no particular motivation while experiencing my temporary deaf-blind meal. (25)

Chris's congenital deaf-blindness was impossible for Goode to match — impossible even if, all of a sudden, he were to become really deaf-blind. To be deaf-blind as she was, he would have to have been born that way. Moreover, like her, he would have to lack language, to have never produced or comprehended a linguistic utterance of any kind.[3] Such a lack would mean that he would have no way to form the question. "What is it like to be deaf-blind and have no language?" Or even to know that there was such a question to be asked.

Still, Goode does learn something from his simulated deaf-blindness, "such as the relative danger of a world that is unpredictable or unanticipatable. Relying primarily on the kinesthetic sense and sense of smell makes the experiential world relatively 'thin,' immediate, unpredictable, and therefore dangerous. [. . .] In a sense, one's world is collapsed to one's immediate bodily space" (25). . . .

NOTES

    1. See "The Disembodied Lady" in Sacks, *"Man,"* 42–52.

    2. Depending on when a pregnant woman is exposed to the disease, rubella syndrome (or German measles) affects the fetus with varying severity. The two girls observed by Goode were profoundly disabled, with mental retardation, heart deformity, and other developmental impairments, in addition to being deaf-blind and alingual. Other outcomes might be just deafness or blindness. For instance, Stevie Wonder's blindness is the result of rubella syndrome.

    3. Two concepts that are often confused are language and communication. People communicate with one another all the time with gestures and grunts, laughs and sobs, hugs, caresses, and blows. But none of this is linguistic, none of it is language. We commonly use metaphors, like "body language" or "the language of music" or "the language of mathematics," but these are still only metaphors. They do not describe the unique kind of communication, whether spoken or signed, that has both a semantics and a grammar and that enables users to produce and comprehend propositions. All language use is propositional, a fact underscored by Dadaist and other deliberate efforts to produce nonsense — for example, Hugo Ball's 1916 sound poem "gadji beri bimba" (Stewart, "Letter," 31–32). And all language use is situated and contextualized between speakers, whose meanings are contingent, negotiable, and revisable on the fly. No other form of communication is both propositional and contingently situated the way language is. Goode records all sorts of communication with Chris, but the two never exchange a linguistic utterance. Consequently, a fundamental question for Goode is whether he or Chris can enter into the other's world, or, even more fundamental, whether she can be said to be aware of existing in a world at all. For to conceptualize a world means being capable of using both metaphor and irony, both the capacity to say what something is by saying what it is like, and the understanding that such a description is unlike its referent ("My mistress' eyes are nothing like the sun" [Shakespeare's sonnet 130]), that it is contingent and never more than an approximation. It is this dual capacity that gives language its power and flexibility, that makes it something one can use, and only language makes this capacity available.

SUGGESTIONS FOR STUDENT ACTIVITIES

Critical Discussion of Simulations

Discuss simulation exercises with your class, since a number of courses and programs do use such activities. Ask students whether they have experienced these and what they learned from them. Consider reading aloud the passage on the limitations of simulation to prompt a further critical discussion. Ask students to consider the important difference between pretending to have a disability for an hour or a day and observing how people treat someone who is disabled. Can the class think of a simulation exercise that avoids the shallowness Swan describes? One such exercise might be to accompany a friend who uses a wheelchair for a day or half day (with the friend's permission, of course). Observe the way others greet and talk to you as you accompany your classmate. Then, write a short reflection on the attitude of others toward you (not on your approximation of the disability experience). What did you learn from this exercise?

Making Embodiment Conscious

Swan gives students exercises with category construction, or asks them to stand on one leg with closed eyes to feel their bodies' orientation and grounding in a physical environment. In addition to the exercise of standing on one leg, you could have students focus on experiencing their own body's senses of hearing or seeing by consciously focusing on how those senses work, not on experiencing their deprivation. For example, ask students to put their heads on their desks and close their eyes and listen for a full seven to ten minutes. Keep the classroom door open and ask students to focus hard on listening to their surroundings and to use their memories to record what they hear. After the allotted time has elapsed, ask students to quickly list everything they heard, including background noise like humming or buzzing, chairs scraping, paper crumpling, and so on. Share lists and discuss the sense of hearing (not loss of sight). How does it orient you in the world and structure your embodied experience? Deaf or hard-of-hearing students in a class might use this time to record a list of all the visual information they see around them for a parallel discussion of sight.

26 From *Sex and Death and the Crippled Body: A Meditation*

NANCY MAIRS

Nancy Mairs, a celebrated writer who has multiple sclerosis, meditates on how others treat a person with a disability. From the perspective of the person with a disability, life goes on; as Mairs states, "disability simply is the norm." But, she notes, doctors pathologize disability and often enact a parent-child relationship with their disabled patients, just as many people treat the disabled as children and deny their sexuality. Mairs is not recommending that others ignore the disability and treat the disabled as if they do not have a disability. Instead, she offers that we must "define these differences frankly" so that we can "discern the ways in which they do — and do not — matter."

Medical professionals tend to pathologize disability, assuming that people whose bodies or minds function in abnormal ways have something wrong with them. People with disabilities certainly do have something — demyelination of the single nervous system, seizures, a severed spinal cord, inflamed joints, an extra chromosome; the possibilities seem endless and pretty unpleasant — but the wrongness of that something depends on one's point of view. From a doctor's perspective, a disability is wrong because it deviates from the ideal norm built up during years of training and practice. But for the patient, disability simply is the norm. There is nothing wrong with me. In fact, for a fifty-five-year-old woman with multiple sclerosis, I'm just about right. I am occasionally ill, of course, being a mere mortal, but my disability itself is not a sickness. It's part of who I am. And I'm far more likely to thrive if you don't regard me as sick at my very core.

In another misconception, society as a whole tends to infantilize those with physical or mental limitations, and none do so more readily than

From *Disability Studies: Enabling the Humanities,* ed. Sharon L. Snyder, Brenda Jo Brueggemann, and Rosemarie Garland-Thomson (New York: Modern Language Association, 2002), 156–70.

doctors and their adjuncts. To some extent, paternalism infects their relations with all their patients—*patient* is a word that doesn't share its root with *passive* by accident—because doctors' apparent (and often real) power over life and death reduces us all to a childlike dependency on their superior knowledge. We reinforce their dominance through our docility. My father-in-law swallowed blood-pressure medication for years, never knowing—indeed, refusing to ask—what his blood pressure actually was. If I were a doctor, I think that sort of quiescence would drive me nuts, but I can also see its allure. Not only does it endow the practitioner with an almost shamanistic force but also it makes treatment much more efficient. Patients who demand explanations for every detail of their care eat up time; and time, as HMOs know only too well, is money.

The tendency for doctor and patient to slip into a patient-child relationship is exacerbated in the case of people with disabilities by the fact that they are usually, in some way, genuinely helpless. I, for instance, can no longer walk or even crawl; I must be dressed and undressed; I manipulate eating utensils with an overhand grasp; when the sole of my foot is scratched, instead of curling under, my toes flare in the Babinski response characteristic of newborns. In short, my central nervous system is, quite literally, regressing toward its infantile state. Understandably, others may have trouble remembering that these neurological deficits are not accompanied by spiritual, emotional, or intellectual regression. But even if they were—as they appear to be in Alzheimer's, for example—the end product would be not an infant but an adult, damaged, to be sure, but fully mature.

In no area of human experience does it better suit the general population to think of the disabled as children than in the sexual. On the whole, we are a society fixated on sexual images and issues without ever feeling quite at ease with them. Shortly before a melanoma was discovered in his small bowel, my husband became impotent—a word I have never heard uttered in ordinary social discourse, even though the condition is shared by a good ten million men in this country. When George mentioned his state to his oncologist, Dr. Ralph waved it off as the least of our worries. Only after George raised the matter over a period of months did Dr. Ralph finally refer him to a urologist.

One day, I mentioned George's persistent impotence to my mother. "Good heavens," she said briskly, "you can live without *that!*"

"I know I can," I replied. "I just don't *want* to."

She shrugged. What else could she do? As her response and Dr. Ralph's suggest, plenty of people dismiss sexual enthusiasm in fifty-year-olds as at least a little silly. Perhaps the only person who can sympathize with me is my eighty-six-year-old mother-in-law. Her libido continues to flourish, and she has the boyfriend to prove it.

When it comes to sexuality in the disabled, dismissal is apt to turn into outright repression. Made uncomfortable, even to the point of excruciation, by the thought of maimed bodies (or, for that matter, minds) engaged in erotic fantasy or action, many deny the very possibility by ascribing to them the innocence of the very young. (In this, of course, they are as wildly mistaken about immature as about adult sexuality.) Perhaps this disgust and denial stem, as the sociobiologists would probably have it, from the fact that such bodies are clearly less than ideal vehicles for the propagation of the species. Whatever its origin, the repulsion lies buried so deeply in consciousness as to seem natural rather than constructed. As a result, even someone with the best intentions in the world may fail to see a disabled woman whole. The parents of a congenitally disabled daughter may rear her to believe that she will never enter a sexually intimate relationship like the one that they enjoy themselves, may withhold information about reproductive inevitabilities like menstruation, may perhaps punish her for the sexual acting out that adolescence brings. Those responsible for her health may forget that she requires reproductive care or provide it in a manner so cursory that she is left baffled and ashamed.

All the same, in most cases she will long for intimacy, since desire arises not "down there," in an area that may possibly be numb, but "up here," in the libidinous brain. If she is heterosexual, she will likely discover that, although she may make close male friends, most men will not think of her as a romantic object. I am fortunate in having found a partner before I became disabled who has elected to remain with me for thirty-five years. Nevertheless, I can speak with some authority here, because in order to prepare an article for *Glamour*, I read several hundred letters from readers with disabilities. I can't report as confidently about lesbian women with disabilities because they didn't write in, although several respondents naively contemplated trying lesbianism as a solution to their sexual frustration. Anyone who cannot accept as normal both a disabled woman's desire and the grief she feels when it is thwarted will never see her as fully human.

In condemning some of the social attitudes toward women with disabilities that may increase their difficulty in receiving optimal care, I don't propose that such a woman should instead be treated just like a nondisabled woman. To do so would be neither practical nor ethical. Disability does set one apart from the general population, impinging on every decision. Only when we define these differences frankly, instead of politely ignoring them, can we discern the ways in which they do—and do not—matter.

SUGGESTIONS FOR STUDENT ACTIVITIES

Attitudes toward the Disabled in Film and TV

Ask students to do field research into cultural attitudes toward the disabled in film and TV shows. Do scenes with doctors and their disabled patients typically portray the disabled patient as childlike or nonsexual or pathologically deviant? After collecting some examples, students can write detailed descriptions of such scenes and analyze the attitudes toward the disabled conveyed in them.

Researching Disability, Gender, and Sexuality

Are men and women with disabilities considered differently in regard to sexuality? To build on the research project above, ask students to analyze depictions of the disabled according to gender. The highly acclaimed documentary *Murderball* (2005) might make an interesting case to study. Consider rereading the excerpt from "Becoming Visible: Lessons in Disability," where Barbara Heifferon writes about using Mairs's essay in a writing class (see p. 141 in this volume). She noted that male and female students had different reactions to Mairs's statements about her own sexuality.

Reflective Writing

Why does Mairs *not* suggest treating someone as if they had no disability? This makes an excellent discussion question and reflective writing prompt for a class. What is the effect of ignoring disabilities? What is the effect of treating everyone "the same"? Why might people with disabilities not want to all be treated just the same? What can this mean in relation to multiculturalism?

27 From *Citizenship and Disability*

MICHAEL BÉRUBÉ

*Michael Bérubé's essay offers readers a chance to understand the
broad importance of the Americans with Disabilities Act (ADA) amid hostile political
pressures to construe the law narrowly. He recounts his experience raising his son
Jamie, who has Down syndrome, marveling at all Jamie has learned in school, made
possible by the Individuals with Disabilities Education Act (IDEA). He notes that before such opportunities for education, people with cognitive disabilities were considered less than human. The effect of disability rights law has been not only to improve
the lives of particular people like Jamie, he argues, but also to enlarge our understanding of and respect for a shared humanity.*

In the six years since I published a book about my son Jamie, *Life As We
Know It*, a great deal has changed in Jamie's life—starting with his realization
that there is a book about him. When I completed the book Jamie was only
four, and had not yet entered the public K–12 system. But I did not stop serving as Jamie's recorder and public representative when I finished that book: I
still represent him all the time, to school officials, camp counselors, babysit-
ters and friends, to academic audiences, and to Down Syndrome Associations. I take it as one of my tasks to watch for important things he's never
done before, as a way of charting and understanding the irreplaceable and ir-
reducible little person he is, especially as he gets less and less little, and more
and more capable of representing himself.

Jamie is now in his sixth year of school, having entered kindergarten in
1997–1998. In the intervening years he has not continued to perform at grade
level (he is repeating fourth grade, at age eleven), and he has occasionally presented his schoolmates with some eccentric behavior. On the other hand, he
has learned to read, to do two- and three-digit addition and subtraction, to

From *Dissent*, 2003. www.dissentmagazine.org/article/?article=506

multiply two-digit numbers, and most recently to do division by single numbers, with and without remainders. My wife, Janet, and I did not teach him these things, but the minute it became clear that he could do them in school, we picked up the ball and ran with it. We've tried to make every available use of his startlingly prodigious memory, and we've learned that when he tells us that such and such bird is not a parrot but is instead a scarlet macaw, he's usually right. He has some idiosyncrasies that do not serve him well in school or in testing situations: at one point he memorized the numbers on the wrong side of his flash cards, the serial numbers that indicate each card's place in the deck. He likes to pretend that he does not know left from right, referring instead (with perverse delight) to his "left foot" and his "other foot." He is a stubborn ignatz, as people find whenever they try to get him to do something he has no interest in, or whenever his teachers or aides try to make him move from one task to another. For a while he tried to put off unpleasant tasks by telling his teachers or therapists, "Let's do that tomorrow"; before long he realized that this didn't work, and began saying instead, "We did that yesterday"—a ruse with which he has had some success.

His conversational skills are steadily improving, but unless you're talking to him about one of the movies he's seen or one of the routines he's developed at school or at home, you'll find that his sense of the world is sometimes unintelligible, sometimes merely a bit awry. He recently received an invitation to a classmate's birthday party (his third such invitation since we moved to central Pennsylvania sixteen months ago: we count and cherish each one), and Janet asked him what the birthday boy looked like: "He's a small boy," said Jamie, holding his hand around his shoulder level.

"What color is his hair?" she asked.

"Black," Jamie replied.

"What color are his eyes?"

"Blue."

"Does he wear glasses?" (Jamie has worn glasses for about five years.)

"No," Jamie said, "just eyes."

But then, Janet and I did not expect him to be able to describe his classmates at all. Nor did we expect him to be so talented a mimic; he can imitate both of us, just as he can imitate break dancers and gymnasts and snakes and lemurs. We did not expect him to be able to do multiplication or division; we did not expect him to open books and ask us to "read and tell all the things"; we did not expect him to be able to ask us "why" questions, as when he asked me why I could not leave him alone in a hotel room while I went to park the car. We did not expect him to win a spelling award in second grade for maintaining an average above 90 on his spelling tests for the year. We did not expect him to be designated by his classmates in third grade as the kid with the best sense of humor.

Over eleven years, then, we've come to expect that Jamie will defeat or exceed our expectations when we least expect him to. And from this I draw two points. One, he's a child. Two, and this is a somewhat more elaborate conclusion, although it can be derived from point one: it might be a good idea for all of us to treat other humans as if we do not know their potential, as if they just might in fact surprise us, as if they might defeat or exceed our expectations. It might be a good idea for us to check the history of the past two centuries whenever we think we know what "normal" human standards of behavior and achievement might be. And it might be a very good idea for us to expand the possibilities of democracy precisely because democracy offers us unfinished and infinitely revisable forms of political organization that stand the best chance, in the long run, of responding adequately to the human rights of the unpredictable creatures we humans are. That might be one way of recognizing and respecting something you might want to call our human dignity.

Jamie is, of course, one reason why I am drawn to the question of disability rights and their relation to democracy: every morning I take him to school, I know how very fortunate he is to be living under a social dispensation that entitles him to a public education alongside his nondisabled peers. But beyond my immediate interest in forwarding Jamie's interests, I want to argue that disability issues are—or should be—central to theories of social justice in a much broader sense. . . .

Disability is not the only area of social life in which the politics of recognition are inseparable from the politics of redistribution; other matters central to citizenship, such as immigration, reproductive rights, and criminal justice, are every bit as complex. Nonetheless, our society's representations of disability are intricately tied to, and sometimes the very basis for, our public policies for "administering" disability. And when we contemplate, in these terms, the history of people with cognitive and developmental disabilities, we find a history in which "representation" takes on a double valence: first, in that people who were deemed incapable of representing themselves were therefore represented by a socio-medical apparatus that defined—or, in a social-constructionist sense, created—the category of "feeblemindedness"; and second, in the sense that the visual and rhetorical representations of "feeble-minded" persons then set the terms for public policy. One cannot plausibly narrate a comprehensive history of ideas and practices of national citizenship in the post–Civil War United States without examining public policy regarding disability, especially mental disability, all the more especially when mental disability was then mapped onto certain immigrant populations who scored poorly on intelligence tests and were thereby pseudo-scientifically linked to criminality. And what of reproductive rights? By 1927, the spurious but powerful linkages among disability, immigration, poverty, and criminality provided the Supreme Court with sufficient justification for declaring involuntary sterilization legal under the Constitution.

There is an obvious reason why disability rights are so rarely thought of in terms of civil rights: disability was not covered in the Civil Rights Act of 1964. And as Anita Silvers points out, over the next twenty-five years, groups covered by civil rights law sometimes saw disability rights as a dilution of civil rights, on the grounds that people with disabilities were constitutively incompetent, whereas women and minorities faced discrimination merely on the basis of social prejudice. Silvers writes, "To make disability a category that activates a heightened legal shield against exclusion, it was objected, would alter the purpose of legal protection for civil rights by transforming the goal from protecting opportunity for socially exploited people to providing assistance for naturally unfit people." The passage of the Americans with Disabilities Act (ADA) in 1990 did add disability to the list of stigmatized identities covered by antidiscrimination law, but thus far the ADA has been interpreted so narrowly, and by such a business-friendly judiciary, that employers have won over 95 percent of the suits brought under the act. . . .

Rights can be created, reinterpreted, extended, and revoked. The passage of the ADA should therefore be seen as an extension of the promise of democracy, but only as a promise: any realization of the potential of the law depends on its continual reinterpretation. For the meaning of the word, just as Wittgenstein wanted us to believe (in order that we might be undeceived about how our words work), lies in its use in the language. Similarly, the Individuals with Disabilities Education Act of 1975 (originally the Education for All Handicapped Children Act) was not some kind of breakthrough discovery whereby children with disabilities were found to be rights-bearing citizens of the United States after all, and who knew that we'd had it all wrong for 199 years? On the contrary, the IDEA invented a new right for children with disabilities, the right to a "free and appropriate public education in the least restrictive environment." And yet the IDEA did not wish that right into being overnight; the key terms "appropriate" and "least restrictive" had to be interpreted time and again, over the course of fifteen years, before they were understood to authorize "full inclusion" of children with disabilities in "regular" classrooms. Nothing about the law is set in stone. The only philosophical "foundation" underlying the IDEA and its various realizations is our own collective political will, a will that is tested and tested again every time the Act comes up for reauthorization. Jamie Bérubé currently has a right to an inclusive public education, but that right is neither intrinsic nor innate. Rather, Jamie's rights were invented, and implemented slowly and with great difficulty. The recognition of his human dignity, enshrined in those rights, was invented. And by the same token, those rights, and that recognition, can be taken away. While I live, I promise myself that I will not let that happen, but I live with the knowledge that it may: to live any other way, to live as if Jamie's rights were somehow intrinsic, would be irresponsible.

Of course, many of us would prefer to believe that our children have intrinsic human rights and human dignity no matter what; irrespective of any form of human social organization; regardless of whether they were born in twentieth-century Illinois or second-century Rome or seventh-century central Asia. But this is just a parent's—or a philosophical foundationalist's—wishful thinking. For what would it mean for Jamie to "possess" rights that no one on earth recognized? A fat lot of good it would do him. My argument may sound either monstrous or all too obvious: if, in fact, no one on earth recognized Jamie's human dignity, then there would in fact be no human perspective from which he would be understood to possess "intrinsic" human dignity. And then he wouldn't have it, and so much the worse for the human race.

In one respect, the promise of the IDEA, like the promise of the ADA, is clear: greater inclusion of people with disabilities in the social worlds of school and work. But in another sense the promise is unspecifiable; its content is something we actually cannot know in advance. For the IDEA does not merely guarantee all children with disabilities a free appropriate public education in the least restrictive environment. Even more than this, it grants the right to education in order that persons with disabilities might make the greatest possible use of their other rights—the ones having to do with voting, or employment discrimination, or with life, liberty, and the pursuit of happiness.

IDEA is thus designed to enhance the capabilities of all American children with disabilities regardless of their actual abilities—and this is why it is so profound a democratic idea.

SUGGESTIONS FOR STUDENT ACTIVITIES

Rhetorical Analysis of "Citizenship and Disability"

The full text of Michael Bérubé's essay is available online at www.dissent-magazine.org/menutest/articles/sp03/berube.htm, making it accessible for classroom use. The full text includes Bérubé's story of Jamie, his son, interwoven with a political analysis that criticizes and addresses leftist U.S. politics for not understanding disability (which, for brevity, we have edited out here). Instructors might ask students to conduct a rhetorical analysis of this essay. How, for example, does Bérubé use the rhetorical appeals of ethos, pathos, and logos? Which appeals are the most persuasive and why? Students could also research *Dissent* magazine. From a quick perusal of other articles it publishes, what can be inferred about Bérubé's audience? How might Bérubé revise the piece for a broader public audience, and why?

Researching Cognitive Disabilities

Encourage students to conduct further research, individually or in small groups, on current medical or social approaches to Down syndrome (or related medical and social interventions around various cognitive disabilities). Ask students to present their informational findings to the class as a whole and discuss points of disagreement and similarity in the information they discovered. More experientially oriented students might conduct research on and read other IDEA-based accounts by people with disabilities: What has been the impact of IDEA on the person's education and life? What benefits and challenges were presented during the person's "inclusive" education under IDEA? The class might spend some time comparing the various accounts about IDEA that students read and researched.

28

From *Composing Bodies; or, De-Composition: Queer Theory, Disability Studies, and Alternative Corporealities*

ROBERT McRUER

Writing primarily to an academic audience, Robert McRuer artic-ulates the connections between normative and nonnormative bodies, institutions, and practices in this excerpt, linking the corporate university to heteronormative struc-tures. These same structures pressure composition programs toward practices of effi-ciency and measurability while they also posit composing as orderly, not messy, and students as docile, heteroabled bodies. McRuer argues for critical writing practices that de-compose such normative structures: We should not insist on finished products in a writing class or fixed student identities; instead we should have students "recog-niz[e] and participat[e] in the multiple and intersecting critical movements" by ask-ing them to interrogate race, class, gender, sexuality, and disability. He concludes with the hope that "disability studies and queer theory will remain locations from which we might speak back to straight composition, with its demand for composed/ docile texts, skills, and bodies."

Most teachers and students of writing experience the cultural practice of composition as a difficult, messy, disorienting affair—the encounter be-tween a writer and the blank page or computer screen, like any encounter between two bodies, can leave one, as Tina Turner suggests, dazed and con-fused. Turner's claim to have "read someplace" about the disconcerting ef-fects of the more general encounter between self and other, moreover, is amply borne out of anti-identitarian theories of the past few decades that doc-ument the impossibility—given the ways all identities are continually shaped and reshaped in and through multiple communities and discourses—of com-posing, or writing into existence, a coherent and individual self.

As Kenneth Burke argued more than fifty years ago, composition is a cultural practice that would seem to be inescapably—even inevitably—con-nected to order.[1] *Webster's Dictionary* authoritatively defines "composition" as a

From *JAC* 24, no. 1 (2004): 47–78.

process that reduces difference, forms many ingredients into one substance, or even calms, settles, or frees from agitation. Ralph Cintron, in his study of the uses of language and strategies of resistance in an urban Chicano/a community, describes composition or writing as a "discourse of measurement" that is, especially in the exclusionary institutional forms it usually takes within the academy, "highly routinized" and controlled by an "ordering agent" (210, 229).

How, then, do we acknowledge and affirm the experiences we draw from multiple academic and nonacademic communities where composing (in all senses of the word) is clearly an unruly, disorderly, cultural practice? Can composition theory work against the simplistic formulation of that which is proper, orderly, and harmonious? If composing is, as the dictionary definition suggests, somehow connected to labor, is it possible to resist the impulse to focus on finished products (the highly routinized, "well-made" essay; the sonnet sequence; the supposedly secure masculine or heterosexual identity) and to keep that labor in mind as we inquire into what composition means and into what it might mean in the future? What would happen if, true to our experiences in and out of the classroom, we continually attempted to reconceive composing as that which produced agitation? In what ways might that agitation be productive?[2]

Although it is by no means universally acknowledged (to judge by how little or how slowly pedagogical or institutional practices have changed), there is nonetheless widespread critical recognition at this point that composition, as it is currently conceptualized and taught in most U.S. colleges and universities, serves a corporate model of flexibility and efficiency.[3] What we might call the current "corpo-reality" of composition guarantees that instruction is often streamlined across dozens of classes at a given institution, with standardized texts (handbooks, guides to the writing and research process, essay collections) required or strongly encouraged (either by campus or departmental administrators or by publishing houses). Inside and outside the university, corporate elites demand that composition courses focus on demonstrable professional-managerial skills rather than critical thought—or, more insidiously, "critical thought" is reconceptualized through a skills-based model ultimately grounded in measurement and marketability, or measurement for marketability. The most troubling feature of our current corpo-reality is that composition at most institutions is routinely taught by adjunct or graduate student employees who receive low pay and few (if any) benefits: the composition work force, at the corporate university, is highly contingent and replaceable, and instructors are thus often forced to piece together multiple appointments at various schools in a region.

I find these arguments that composition serves a corporate model of efficiency convincing, and it is vitally important for teachers and scholars of composition and composition theory to remain attentive to the ways we are positioned to serve professional-managerial interests. In many ways, however, despite the material base of these critiques, they remain strangely *incorporeal*—in other words, these critiques are not yet especially concerned with theorizing *embodiment* and/in the corporate university. Perhaps this is because corporate processes privilege and imagine only one kind of body on either side of the desk: on one side, the docile body of the contingent, replaceable instructor; on the other, the docile body of the student dutifully mastering marketable skills and producing clear, orderly, efficient prose. . . .

SPEAKING BACK TO STRAIGHT COMPOSITION

If the fetishized finished product in the composition classroom has affinities with the composed heterosexual or able-bodied self, I would argue that the composing body, in contrast, is in some ways inevitably queer/disabled. [Eve Kosofsky] Sedgwick, after considering the features that characterize the composed heterosexual self, particularly listing (for more than a page) "the number and *difference* of the dimensions that 'sexual identity' is supposed to organize into a seamless and univocal whole," contends that queerness refers to "the open mesh of possibilities, gaps, overlaps, dissonances and resonances, lapses and excesses of meaning when the constituent elements of anyone's gender, of anyone's sexuality aren't made (or *can't be* made) to signify monolithically" (8). Able-bodied identity, similarly, emerges from disparate features that are supposed to be organized into a seamless and univocal whole: a standard (and "working") number of limbs and digits that are used in appropriate ways (for example, feet are not used for eating or performing other tasks besides walking; hands are not used as the primary vehicle for language); eyes that see and ears that hear (both consistently and "accurately"); proper dimensions of height and weight (generally determined according to Euro-American standards of beauty); genitalia and other bodily features that are deemed gender-appropriate (that is, aligned with one of only two possible sexes, and in such a way that sex and gender correspond); an HIV negative serostatus; high energy and freedom from chronic conditions that might in fact impact energy, mobility, and the potential to be awake and "functional" for a standard number of hours each day; freedom from illness or infection (ideally, freedom from the *likelihood* of either illness or infection, particularly HIV infection or STDs); acceptable and measurable mental functioning; behaviors that are not disruptive, unfocused, or "addictive"; thoughts that are not unusual or disturbing. Optimally these features are not only aligned but are consistent over time—regeneration is privileged over degeneration (read: the effects of aging, which should be resisted, particularly for women). If the alignment of all these features guarantees the composed able-bodied self, then—following Sedgwick on queerness—we might say that disability refers to the open mesh of possibilities, gaps, overlaps, dissonances and resonances, lapses and excesses of meaning when the constituent elements of bodily, mental, or behavioral functioning aren't made (or *can't be* made) to signify monolithically.

One could easily conclude from these circumstances that we are all disabled/queer, since all of us (at some point and to some degree—or to some degree at *most* points) inhabit composing bodies that exist prior to the successful alignment of all of these features. I want to both resist and advance this conclusion. Obviously, definitional issues have been central to both queer and disability rights movements—who counts as queer, who counts as disabled? As Simi Linton points out, following Carol Gill, "The problem gets stickier when the distinction between disabled and nondisabled is challenged by people who say, 'Actually, we're all disabled in some way, aren't we?' " (12–13). Similar complacent assertions are made about queerness—"actually, we're all queer in some way, aren't we?"—and I believe it is important to resist such assertions, recognizing them as able-bodied/heterosexual *containments:* an able-bodied/heterosexual society doesn't have to take seriously disabled/queer claims to rights and recognition if it can diffuse or universalize what activists and scholars are saying as really nothing new, and as really about all of us. In other words, the question "aren't we all queer/disabled?" can be an indirect way of saying, "you don't need to be taken seriously, do you?"

In some very important ways, we are in fact *not* all queer/disabled. The fact that some of us get beaten and left for dead tied to deer fences or that others of us die virtually unnoticed in underfunded and unsanitary group homes should be enough to highlight that the heterosexual/queer and able-bodied/disabled binaries produce real and material distinctions. However, recognizing that the question "aren't we all queer/disabled?" can be an attempt at containment and affirming that I resist that containment, I nonetheless argue that there are *moments* when we are all queer/disabled, and that *those disabled/queer moments are desirable.* In particular, a queer/disabled theory of composition argues for the desirability of those moments when we are all queer/disabled, since it is those moments that provide us with a means of speaking back to straight composition in all its guises. Instead of a banal, humanistic universalization of queerness/disability, a queer/disabled theory of composition advocates for the temporary or contingent universalization of queerness/disability.[4]

The flip side of the fact that there are moments when all of us are queer/disabled is the fact that no one (unfortunately) is queer/disabled *all* of the time—that would be impossible to sustain in a cultural order that privileges heterosexuality/able-bodied identity and that compels all of us, no matter how distant we might be from the ideal, into repetitions that approximate those norms.[5] Critical de-composition, however, results from re-orienting ourselves away from those compulsory ideals and onto the composing process and the composing bodies—the alternative, and multiple, corporealities—that continually ensure that things can turn out otherwise. If we are all *virtually* queer and disabled, *critical* queerness/disability and critical de-composition result from actively and collectively desiring disability and queerness. Instead of solely and repeatedly asking the questions Cintron rightly cites as central to "school-appropriate" writing instruction—" 'Have you chosen the right word?' 'Can this be made clearer?' 'Your argument here is inconsistent.' 'Are you being contradictory?' " (231)—we might ask questions designed to dismantle our current corpo-reality: How can we queer this? How can we crip it? What ideologies or norms that are at work in this text need to be cripped? How can this system be de-composed?[6]

I recognize that the general point I am making here is one that has been central to a certain mode of composition theory for some time. Although I want to complicate the project, I in fact believe that one of the conditions of possibility for my own analysis here is precisely the collective and ongoing project within composition theory of arguing for the difficult but necessary work of continually resisting a pedagogy focused on finished products.[7] To cite just one example, William Covino writes,

> In even the most enlightened composition class, a class blown by the winds of change through a "paradigm shift" into a student-centered, process-oriented environment replete with heuristics, sentence combining, workshopping, conferencing, and recursive revising, speculation and exploration remain subordinate to finishing. . . . While writing is identified exclusively with a product and purpose that contain and abbreviate it, writers let the conclusion dictate their tasks and necessarily censor whatever imagined possibilities seem irrelevant or inappropriate; they develop a trained incapacity to speculate and raise questions, to try stylistic and formal alternatives. They become unwilling and unable to fully elaborate the process of composing. (316–17)

As I asserted at the beginning of this essay, however, such critiques remain decidedly incorporeal—composition theory has not yet recognized (or perhaps has censored the "imagined possibility") that the demand for certain kinds of finished projects in the writing classroom is congruent with the demand for certain kinds of bodies. Not recognizing this congruence, in turn, can bring us to a point where the imagined solution is the sort of *disembodied* postmodernism Covino calls for. I'm suggesting that queer theory and disability studies should figure centrally into the work that we do in composition and composition theory—that, in fact, they already do in some ways figure centrally into that work, since the critical project of resisting closure that we have been imaging is a queer/disabled project. In other words, a subtext of the decades-long project in composition theory focusing on the composing process and away from the finished product is that disability and queerness are desirable.

DE-COMPOSITION IN PRACTICE

Desiring queerness/disability means not assuming in advance that the finished state is the one worth striving for, especially the finished state demanded by the corporate university and the broader oppressive cultural and economic circumstances in which we are currently located. It means striving instead for what Donna Haraway has called "permanently partial identities" (154). Indeed, through Haraway, we might understand disability/queerness as "not the products of escape and transcendence of limits, i.e., the view from above, but the joining of partial views and halting voices into a collective subject position that promises a vision of the means of ongoing finite embodiment, of living within limits and contradictions, i.e., of views from somewhere" (196). I invoke Haraway here briefly to underscore (although my earlier invocation of theorists such as Butler and Sedgwick should of course also affirm this) that desiring disability/queerness is a feminist project (ultimately, I think disability studies and queer theory should be unimaginable without feminism), and I would add that it is an antiracist and postcolonial project as well.[8] Critical de-composition, in other words, entails recognizing and participating in the multiple and intersecting critical movements—what Haraway calls "an earth-wide network of connections" (187)—that would resist, or stare back at, the corporate "view from above." Haraway writes, "We need the power of modern critical theories of how meanings and bodies get made, not in order to deny meaning and bodies, but in order to live in meanings and bodies that have a chance for the future" (187). . . .

Certainly, in this article I intend to position queer theory and disability studies at the center of composition theory, and in the interests of such a project, my highlighting of the ways in which disabled/queer questions and issues, or de-composing processes, haunt the newly-composed program is intended to affirm, in the face of dangerous transitions, what Paulo Freire called "a pedagogy of hope." I do not, however, centralize disability studies and queer theory in order to offer them, somehow, as the "solution" for either a localized or more general crisis in composition; queer theory and disability studies in and of themselves will not magically revitalize a sometimes-tendentious and often-beleaguered field. I am nonetheless hopeful that disability studies and queer theory will remain locations from which we might speak back to straight composition, with its demand for composed/docile texts, skills, and bodies. Despite that hope, and with the transitions at my own institution in mind, I recognize that composition programs are currently heavily-policed locations and that the demand for order and efficiency remains pronounced—mainly because that demand and the practices that result from it serve very specific material interests. Disability studies and queer theory, however, do provide us with ways of comprehending how our very bodies are caught up in, or even produced by, straight composition. More importantly, however, with their connection to embodied movements both outside and inside the academy, they simultaneously continue to imagine or envision a future horizon *beyond* straight composition, in all its forms. And that horizon is populated by multiple and de-composing bodies.

NOTES

1. Burke develops the following thesis throughout the final section of his *A Rhetoric of Motives*: "Order, the Secret, and the Kill. To study the nature of rhetoric, the relation between rhetoric and dialectic, and the application of both to human relations in general, is to circulate about these three motives" (265). Despite Burke's emphasis on relations among the various elements, order remains the privileged term, and is in fact the title of the section.

2. Of course, a significant body of work in composition theory, focused in various and contestatory ways on "process," has taken up some of the questions I introduce here. . . . Although I have revised them slightly, I draw the preceding paragraphs and the epigraphs to this essay from my introduction to the second edition of *Composing a Writing Program: An Alternative Handbook for the Program in Rhetoric and Composition at The George Washington University*. The second edition of this document, which was printed in August 1999, was collectively authored by twenty members of GWU's Expository Writing Program and was edited by Angela Hewett and myself. *Composing a*

Writing Program included, among many other topics, discussion of the wide range of composition theories that were in circulation at the university. At the time, faculty in the program intended to revise this document continually, although there was debate about whether it should take a temporarily final form annually or whether it should appear online, allowing for the more obvious deferment of any "final" form. A great deal of agitation, however, attended the second edition: although the final copying bill was relatively small, there was concern that the university, via the English Department, had paid for the document, which included a section openly discussing efforts on the part of graduate students and part-time faculty around the country to unionize (in actuality, the document was collectively paid for by members of the Writing Program). In my conclusion, I return to localized agitation and consider very briefly some of the ways in which GWU has designed initiatives that in effect work to contain what I call in this essay decomposition.

3. One could certainly argue that this truth is far from universally acknowledged because, as the work of Paulo Freire has repeatedly suggested, knowledge requires praxis to be genuine: "The oppressed must confront reality critically, simultaneously objectifying and acting upon that reality. A mere perception of reality not followed by this critical intervention will not lead to a transformation of objective reality—precisely because it is not a true perception" (*Pedagogy of the Oppressed*, 34). For a thorough discussion of what they call "the corporate university," see Nelson and Watt 84–98. According to Nelson and Watt, corporate universities include "universities that adopt profit-oriented corporate values," "universities that adopt corporate-style management and accounting techniques," and "universities that instill corporate culture in their students and staff" (89–90). A March 21, 2003, *Chronicle of Higher Education* article succinctly details the ways in which composition programs are particularly invested in (or, conversely, are serving as investments for) the corporate university; in a paragraph nodding directly towards GWU, the writer of the piece suggests, "Scholarship in the humanities has always kept its distance from the business school. But in some recent work in composition studies, ideas about discourse mingle with concepts from the corporate world" (McLemee, A16). . . .

4. Abby L. Wilkerson and I further develop the notion of queerness and disability as desirable in our introduction to *Desiring Disability: Queer Theory Meets Disability Studies*.

5. In Roland Barthes's terms, the virtually orgasmic and identity-disintegrating "text of bliss" is impossible to sustain in the context of a culture that privileges the text of pleasure: "the text that contents, fills, grants euphoria; the text that comes from culture and does not break with it, is linked to a *comfortable* practice of reading" (14).

6. For related discussions of *virtual* and *critical* disability, see my "compulsory" and "Good." At this point, "crip theory" is still in its infancy, though I am tempted to predict that it may ultimately have the same kind of generative yet contestatory relationship with disability studies that queer theory has with lesbian and gay studies. Carrie Sandahl's "Queering the Crip or Cripping the Queer? Intersections of Queer and Crip Identities in Solo Autobiographical Performance" puts forward one of the first attempts to delineate how crip theory might function.

7. Given the commitment to cultural studies content in the composition classroom that I detail in the next section, there are ways in which I am aligned with what has been called the "postprocess" movement in composition theory rather than with expressivist attempts to "discover" the processes individual writers employ or some attempts, by cognitivists and others, to delineate the components of "the" writing process. For overviews of debates about process in composition, see Lad Tobin and Newkirk, as well as Tobin, which provides a snapshot of the emergence of the postprocess movement (13–16). For more on postprocess theory, see Kent.

8. For work that explicitly links queerness, bodily difference, and race, see Lorde and Fisher. For theoretical explorations of these particular intersections, see Muñoz; Harper; and McRuer, *Queer*, especially chapters 1–3.

SUGGESTIONS FOR STUDENT ACTIVITIES

Researching Campus Diversity Initiatives

Both Bérubé (see p. 238 in this volume) and McRuer imply that disability theory provides a critical lens through which to understand the intersectionality of identities and marginalization in the United States. Many universities today are working hard to remedy the past exclusion of minority groups through multicultural/diversity initiatives aimed at increasing diversity and understanding among different groups on campus. Ask students to research their school's multicultural/diversity initiatives to find out whether or not "disability" is considered to be an issue on their campus, and whether these initiatives encourage exploring connections among diverse groups. Have them look at official school diversity statements, and interview or survey students and student groups such as lesbian, gay, bisexual, and transgender or African American or disabled student organizations. Such research might culminate in a class presentation or paper. For example, students might form hypotheses as to why disability is, or is not, perceived as a diversity issue on campus, and how the push for diversity facilitates or delimits awareness of the intersections of experiences or tensions among diverse groups. Encourage students to write into the margins, across the divisions and around the omissions, of the push for diversity on campus. To what extent do diversity initiatives imply an unspoken center, a "norm" of able-bodied whiteness, against which "diversity" is measured?

Researching Campus Accessibility

Another campus research project is to have students evaluate the accessibility of buildings and campus events to people with disabilities. One day, students might negotiate their campus using only officially marked disability entrances—not as tourists of the disability experience, but as critical cultural geographers. Ask students to keep a detailed descriptive journal of their experiences and to interview a range of people on campus to ascertain awareness of accessibility and attitudes toward the disabled.

29   *Breast Cancer: Power vs. Prosthesis*

AUDRE LORDE

In this powerful narrative from her book The Cancer Journals, *Audre Lorde recounts the "stages of pain, despair, fury, sadness and growth" she experienced after her surgery and treatment for breast cancer. A self-identified "Black Lesbian Feminist," a poet, and an activist, Lorde wants to acknowledge and integrate her experience of mastectomy into her identity and find a way to continue with her work. She discovers, though, that there is strong medical-social pressure to encourage women to appear "the 'same'" after mastectomy, whether through prostheses or reconstructive surgery. Lorde criticizes "the Cancer Establishment," for this "physical pretense," which leads a woman to "dwell in the past rather than a future" and "focus her energies upon the mastectomy as a cosmetic occurrence." Lorde was an early questioner of prosthetics, and while she concedes, "There is nothing wrong, per se, with the use of prostheses," she analyzes how they function. Some restore the ability to perform tasks, but others are purely for looks, solely to benefit the nondisabled: to allay their fears of the scarred, nonnormative body that reveals human vulnerability.*

On Labor Day, 1978, during my regular monthly self-examination, I discovered a lump in my right breast which later proved to be malignant. During my following hospitalization, my mastectomy and its aftermath, I passed through many stages of pain, despair, fury, sadness and growth. I moved through these stages, sometimes feeling as if I had no choice, other times recognizing that I could choose oblivion—or a passivity that is very close to oblivion—but did not want to. As I slowly began to feel more equal to processing and examining the different parts of this experience, I also began to feel that in the process of losing a breast I had become a more whole person.

After a mastectomy, for many women including myself, there is a feeling of wanting to go back, of not wanting to persevere through this experience to whatever enlightenment might be at the core of it. And it is this feeling, this

From Audre Lorde, *The Cancer Journals* (San Francisco: Aunt Lute Books, 1980), 55–65.

nostalgia, which is encouraged by most of the post-surgical counseling for women with breast cancer. This regressive tie to the past is emphasized by the concentration upon breast cancer as a cosmetic problem, one which can be solved by a prosthetic pretense. The American Cancer Society's Reach For Recovery Program, while doing a valuable service in contacting women immediately after surgery and letting them know they are not alone, nonetheless encourages this false and dangerous nostalgia in the mistaken belief that women are too weak to deal directly and courageously with the realities of our lives.

The woman from Reach For Recovery who came to see me in the hospital, while quite admirable and even impressive in her own right, certainly did not speak to my experience nor my concerns. As a 44 year old Black Lesbian Feminist, I knew there were very few role models around for me in this situation, but my primary concerns two days after mastectomy were hardly about what man I could capture in the future, whether or not my old boyfriend would still find me attractive enough, and even less about whether my two children would be embarrassed by me around their friends.

My concerns were about my chances for survival, the effects of a possibly shortened life upon my work and my priorities. Could this cancer have been prevented, and what could I do in the future to prevent its recurrence? Would I be able to maintain the control over my life that I had always taken for granted? A lifetime of loving women had taught me that when women love each other, physical change does not alter that love. It did not occur to me that anyone who really loved me would love me any less because I had one breast instead of two, although it did occur to me to wonder if they would be able to love and deal with the new me. So my concerns were quite different from those spoken to by the Reach For Recovery volunteer, but not one bit less crucial nor less poignant.

Yet every attempt I made to examine or question the possibility of a real integration of this experience into the totality of my life and my loving and my work was ignored by this woman, or uneasily glossed over by her as not looking on "the bright side of things." I felt outraged and insulted, and weak as I was, this left me feeling even more isolated than before.

In the critical and vulnerable period following surgery, self-examination and self-evaluation are positive steps. To imply to a woman that yes, she can be the "same" as before surgery, with the skillful application of a little puff of lambswool, and/or silicone gel, is to place an emphasis upon prosthesis which encourages her not to deal with herself as physically and emotionally real, even though altered and traumatized. This emphasis upon the cosmetic after surgery reinforces this society's stereotype of women, that we are only what we look or appear, so this is the only aspect of our existence we need to address. Any woman who has had a breast removed because of cancer knows she does not feel the same. But we are allowed no psychic time or space to examine what our true feelings are, to make them our own. With quick cosmetic reassurance, we are told that our feelings are not important, our appearance is all, the sum total of self.

I did not have to look down at the bandages on my chest to know that I did not feel the same as before surgery. But I still felt like myself, like Audre, and that encompassed so much more than simply the way my chest appeared.

The emphasis upon physical pretense at this crucial point in a woman's reclaiming of her self and her body-image has two negative effects:

1. It encourages women to dwell in the past rather than a future. This prevents a woman from assessing herself in the present, and from coming to terms with the changed planes of her own body. Since these then remain alien to her, buried under prosthetic devices, she must mourn the loss of her breast in secret, as if it were the result of some crime of which she were guilty.

2. It encourages a woman to focus her energies upon the mastectomy as a cosmetic occurrence, to the exclusion of other factors in a constellation that could include her own death. It removes her from what that constellation means in terms of her living, and from developing priorities of usage for whatever time she has before her. It encourages her to ignore the necessity for nutritional vigilance and psychic armament that can help prevent recurrence.

I am talking here about the need for every woman to live a considered life. The necessity for that consideration grows and deepens as one faces directly one's own mortality and death. Self-scrutiny and an evaluation of our lives, while painful, can be rewarding and strengthening journeys toward a deeper self. For as we open ourselves more and more to the genuine conditions of our lives, women become less and less willing to tolerate those conditions unaltered, or to passively accept external and destructive controls over our lives and our identities. Any short-circuiting of this quest for self-definition and power, however well-meaning and under whatever guise, must be seen as damaging, for it keeps the post-mastectomy woman in a position of perpetual and secret insufficiency, infantilized and dependent for her identity upon an external definition by appearance. In this way women are kept from expressing the power of our knowledge and experience, and through that expression, developing strengths that challenge those structures within our lives that support the Cancer Establishment. . . .

There is nothing wrong, per se, with the use of prostheses, if they can be chosen freely, for whatever reason, after a woman has had a chance to accept her new body. But usually prostheses serve a real function, to approximate the performance of a missing physical part. In other amputations and with other prosthetic devices, function is the main point of their existence. Artificial limbs perform specific tasks, allowing us to manipulate or to walk. Dentures allow us to chew our food. Only false breasts are designed for appearance only, as if the only real function of women's breasts were to appear in a certain shape and size and symmetry to onlookers, or to yield to external pressure. For no woman wearing a prosthesis can even for one moment believe it is her own breast, any more than a woman wearing falsies can.

Yet breast prostheses are offered to women after surgery in much the same way that candy is offered to babies after an injection, never mind that the end effect may be destructive. Their comfort is illusory; a transitional period can be provided by any loose-fitting blouse. After surgery, I most certainly did not feel better with a lambswool puff stuck in the front of my bra. The real truth is that certain other people feel better with that lump stuck into my bra, because they do not have to deal with me nor themselves in terms of mortality nor in terms of difference.

Attitudes toward the necessity for prostheses after breast surgery are merely a reflection of those attitudes within our society towards women in general as objectified and depersonalized sexual conveniences. Women have been programmed to view our bodies only in terms of how they look and feel to others, rather than how they feel to ourselves, and how we wish to use them. We are surrounded by media images portraying women as essentially decorative machines of consumer function, constantly doing battle with rampant decay. (Take your vitamins every day and he *might* keep you, if you don't forget to whiten your teeth, cover up your smells, color your grey hair and iron out your wrinkles. . . .) As women, we fight this depersonalization every day, this pressure toward the conversion of one's own self-image into a media expectation of what might satisfy male demand. The insistence upon breast prostheses as "decent" rather than functional is an additional example of that wipe-out of self in which women are constantly encouraged to take part. I am personally affronted by the message that I am only acceptable if I look "right" or "normal," where those norms have nothing to do with my own perceptions of who I am. Where "normal" means the "right" color, shape, size, or number of breasts, a woman's perception of her own body and the strengths that come from that perception are discouraged, trivialized, and ignored. When I mourn my right breast, it is not the appearance of it I mourn, but the feeling and the fact. But where the superficial is supreme, the idea that a woman can be beautiful and one-breasted is considered depraved, or at best, bizarre, a threat to "morale."

In order to keep me available to myself, and able to concentrate my energies upon the challenges of those worlds through which I move, I must consider what my body means to me. I must also separate those external demands about how I look and feel to others, from what I really want for my own body, and how I feel to my selves. As women we have been taught to respond with a guilty twitch at any mention of the particulars of our own oppression, as if we are ultimately guilty of whatever has been done to us. The rape victim is accused of enticing the rapist. The battered wife is accused of having angered her husband. A mastectomy is not a guilty act that must be hidden in order for me to regain acceptance or protect the sensibilities of others. Pretense has never brought about lasting change or progress.

Every woman has a right to define her own desires, make her own choices. But prostheses are often chosen, not from desire, but in default. Some women complain it is too much effort to fight the concerted pressure exerted by the fashion industry. Being one-breasted does not mean being unfashionable; it means giving some time and energy to choosing or constructing the proper clothes. In some cases, it means making or remaking clothing or jewelry. The fact that the fashion needs of one-breasted women are not currently being met doesn't mean that the concerted pressure of our demands cannot change that.[1] . . .

NOTES

1. Particular thanks to Frances Clayton for the conversations that developed this insight.

SUGGESTIONS FOR STUDENT ACTIVITIES

Illness as Disability

In what ways can major illnesses and their effects qualify as a "disability"? Ask students to use the Internet to research the definition of *disability* in the Americans with Disabilities Act (ADA) of 1990, and in major court cases since then. Students can also compare the ADA definitions with those offered on the World Health Organization and United Nations Web sites, or in the *Diagnostic and Statistical Manual of Mental Disorders,* Fourth Edition (DSM-IV). Then have them bring in their notes and form small groups to discuss whether a major illness like breast cancer could be considered a disability under the precedents of ADA rulings. Ask each group to draw up two lists: one with illnesses they believe would qualify as disabilities and another with illnesses that are serious but that might not qualify.

Reflecting on the Label *Disability*

Following the research above, ask students to write a short reflection on the benefits and drawbacks of broadening the label *disability* to include a wider range of conditions and impairments. Ask students to use specific examples to illustrate their thinking. Also, ask students to comment on the question of *who* actually gets to define the parameters of disability, and how this power is used—this reflection should help students to reflect on the power they have wielded in sorting and classifying disabilities.

Multiple Identities and Their Intersections

Audre Lorde writes eloquently about her multiple identity locations, and her need to integrate each into her life. To get students to explore and reflect on their multiple identities, consider the following activity. List a number of different identity categories on 3 × 5 index cards, for example, gender identity, race/ethnic identity, sexual-orientation identity, class identity, ability/disability identity, and geographical/national identity. Make enough copies of each category for every student in class. Bring these cards to class and line them up in stacks on a table. Invite students to select cards from the table that are meaningful to them. Next, ask students to freewrite on the back of the index card about the significance of that identity category to their sense of themselves.

A number of follow-up discussions and activities could occur at this point:

1. Ask students to regroup according to their identity cards. They could then share and discuss their writing.

2. Discuss which identity categories were most claimed, which least claimed.

3. As a continuation in exploring intersections, ask students to lay out their identity cards on their desks, and on a large sheet of paper map ways that the identities overlap each other, or conflict with each other.

4. Complete this exploration by having students write an autoethnographic essay about his or her multiple identities.

30 From *Public Transit*

JOHN HOCKENBERRY

A journalist for National Public Radio, a paraplegic, and a wheel-chair user, John Hockenberry recounts his attempt to use the New York City subway system, literally mapping the intersecting paths of the disabled and other minority groups. He decided, as he explains, to "wire myself with a microphone and a minia-ture cassette machine to record everything that happened along the way." To negotiate the warren of stairs and platforms, Hockenberry must crawl down and up hundreds of steps, dragging along his chair tied to his wrist. "Down there" he discovers another America—not only rudeness, dirt, and inaccessibility, but also an alliance with other minorities in this world below the surface. African American and Puerto Rican pas-sengers acknowledge and help him, whereas whites refuse to meet his eye as they step around and on him in their hurry to their important destinations.

When I returned to New York City from the Middle East in 1990, I lived in Brooklyn, just two blocks from the Carroll Street subway stop on the F train. It was not accessible, and as there appeared to be no plans to make it so, I didn't think much about the station. When I wanted to go into Manhat-tan, I would take a taxi, or I would roll up Court Street to the walkway en-trance to the Brooklyn Bridge and fly into the city on a ribbon of oak planks suspended from the bridge's webs of cable that appeared from my wheelchair to be woven into the sky itself. Looking down, I could see the East River through my wheelchair's spokes. Looking up, I saw the clouds through the spokes of the bridge. It was always an uncommon moment of physical in-tegrity with the city, which ended when I came to rest at the traffic light on Chambers Street, next to city hall.

It was while rolling across the bridge one day that I remembered my promise to Donna, my physical therapist, about how I would one day ride the rapid transit trains in Chicago. Pumping my arms up the incline of the bridge

From John Hockenberry, *Moving Violations* (New York: Hyperion, 1995), 296–310.

toward Manhattan and then coasting down the other side in 1990, I imagined that I would be able physically to accomplish everything I had theorized about the subway in Chicago in those first days of being a paraplegic back in 1976. In the Middle East, I had climbed many stairways and hauled myself and the chair across many filthy floors on my way to interviews, apartments, and news conferences. I had also lost my fear of humiliation from living and working there. I was even intrigued with the idea of taking the train during the peak of rush hour when the greatest number of people of all kinds would be underground with me.

I would do it just the way I had told Donna back in the rehab hospital. But this time, I would wire myself with a microphone and a miniature cassette machine to record everything that happened along the way. Testing my own theory might make a good commentary for an upcoming National Public Radio program about inaccessibility. . . .

The Jay Street station was a warren of tunnels and passageways with steps in all of them. To get to the A train track for the ride into Manhattan, I had to descend a flight of stairs to the sub-platform; then, depending on which direction I was going, ascend another stairway to the tracks. Because it is a junction for three subway lines, there was a mix of people rushing through the station in all directions, rather than the clockwork march of white office-garbed commuters from Brooklyn Heights and Carroll Gardens on their way to midtown.

I rolled to the stairs and descended into a corridor crowded with people coming and going. "Are you all right?" A black woman stopped next to my chair. She was pushing a stroller with two seats, one occupied by a little girl, the other empty, presumably for the little boy with her, who was standing next to a larger boy. They all beamed at me, waiting for further orders from Mom.

"I'm going down to the A train," I said. "I think I'll be all right, if I don't get lost."

"You sure you want to go down there?" She sounded as if she was warning me about something. "I know all the elevators from having these kids," she said. "They ain't no elevator on the A train, young man." Her kids looked down at me as if to say, *What can you say to that?* I told her that I knew there was no elevator and that I was just seeing how many stairs there were between Carroll Street and city hall. "I can tell you, they's lots of stairs." As she said good-bye, her oldest boy looked down at me as if he understood exactly what I was doing, and why. "Elevators smell nasty," he said.

Once on the A train, I discovered at the next stop that I had chosen the wrong side of the platform and was going away from Manhattan. If my physical therapist, Donna, could look in on me at this point in my trip, she might be more doubtful about my theory than I was. By taking the wrong train, I had probably doubled the number of stairs I would have to climb.

I wondered if I could find a station not too far out where the platform was between the tracks, so that all I had to do was roll to the other side and catch the inbound train. The subway maps gave no indication of this, and the commuters I attempted to query on the subject simply ignored me or seemed not to understand what I was asking. Another black woman with a large shopping bag and a brown polka-dotted dress was sitting in a seat across the car and volunteered that Franklin Avenue was the station I wanted. "No stairs there," she said.

At this point, every white person I had encountered had ignored me or pretended that I didn't exist, while every black person who had come upon me had offered to help without being asked. I looked at the tape recorder in my jacket to see if it was running. It was awfully noisy in the subway, but if any voices at all were recorded, this radio program was going to be more about race than it was going to be about wheelchair accessibility. It was the first moment that I suspected the two were deeply related in ways I have had many occasions to think about since.

At Franklin Avenue I crossed the tracks and changed direction, feeling for the first time that I was a part of the vast wave of migration in and out of the Manhattan that produced the subway, all the famous bridges, and a major broadcast industry in traffic reporting complete with network rivals and local personalities, who have added words like *rubbernecking* to the language. I rolled across the platform like any other citizen and onto the train with ease. As we pulled away from the station, I thought how much it would truly change my life if there were a way around the stairs, if I could actually board the subway anywhere without having to be Sir Edmund Hillary.

The inbound trains were more crowded in the last minutes of the morning rush, and back at the Jay Street station there was a roar of people rushing to catch that lucky train that might make them not late after all. As I was sliding my folded chair toward the steps down to the platform, a young black man with a backward baseball cap walked right up to me out of the crowds. "I can carry the chair, man," he said. "Just tell me where you want me to set it back up." I looked at him. He was thin and energetic, and his suggestion was completely sensible. I didn't feel like giving him my speech about how I didn't need any help. "Take it to the Manhattan-bound A train," I said. "I'll be right behind you."

One train went by in the time it took to get up the flight of stairs, but going up was still much easier than I had imagined. My legs dragged along cooperatively just as my theory had predicted. At trackside, the young man with my chair had unfolded it and was sitting in it, trying to balance on two wheels. A friend of his, he explained, could do wheelies ever since he had been shot in the back during a gang shooting. "Your chair has those big-ass wheels," he said, commenting on the large-diameter bicycle wheels I used, as if to explain why he was having some trouble keeping his balance. "I never seen those kinda wheels," he said, as I hopped back into the chair.

As the train approached, he asked me for some cash. I thought that I must be some kind of idiot to go through all this and end up spending more to get into Manhattan than anyone else on the subway that day. The smallest bill I had was a five. I handed it over to him and boarded the train, laughing to myself at the absolute absurdity of it all. When I looked up, I could see commuters looking up from their newspapers. They cautiously regarded my laughing, as though I had just come from a rubber room at Bellevue Hospital. I let out a loud, demented shriek, opening my eyes as wide as I could. The heads bobbed quickly back behind the newsprint.

On the last flight of stairs leading onto City Hall Plaza at Centre Street and Chambers, the commuters in suits poured into the passageway from six trains. There was not a lot of space, and people began to trip over me. One gray-suited man in headphones carrying a gym bag nearly fell down, but he caught himself and swore as he scrambled up to street level, stepping on one of my hands in the process. A tall black man in a suit holding his own gym bag picked up my chair and started to carry it up the stairs. In a dignified voice, he said, "I know you're OK, right?" I nodded.

Behind him, a Puerto Rican mother with two daughters identically dressed in fluffy flowered skirts with full slips and holding corsages offered to take my backpack and cushion up to the top so that I could haul myself without worrying about keeping track of the loose things. At the top, as I unfolded the wheelchair, the mother told me that she was on her way to get married at the Manhattan municipal building. Her two daughters were bridesmaids. She said she was going to put on her wedding dress, which she had in her gym bag, in the ladies' room before the ceremony. I wished her good luck and hopped back up into the chair as the commuters streamed by. It was a familiar place, the same spot I always rolled to so effortlessly off the Brooklyn Bridge.

I turned to roll away and noticed that the two little girls had come back. In unison, they said, "We will pray for Jesus to bring back your legs, mister." "Thank you," I said. As though I had just given them each a shiny new quarter, they ran back to their mother, who was waiting for them with her hands outstretched to take them across busy Centre Street. It was not the sort of thing I ever cared to hear people say, but after the ordeal of the subway, and the icy silence of virtually every white person I had met, I didn't mind at all. For once, I looked forward to riding home in a cab.

Since 1976, I had imagined a trip on the subway. I knew it was possible, while my physical therapist had known it would be utterly impractical as a form of transportation. We were both right, but neither of us could have imagined the America I found down there. The New York subway required only a token to ride, but on each person's face was the ticket to where they were all really going, the places they thought they never had to leave, the people they thought they never had to notice, or stop and apologize to for stepping on them. Without knowing it, I had left that America behind long ago. I discovered it alive and well on the F train.

SUGGESTIONS FOR STUDENT ACTIVITIES

Documenting Accessibility

As Hockenberry did, students could use tape recorders or film, digital, or video cameras to create a documentary about accessibility. Teams of students could film attempts to access buildings and major college events using officially designated "handicapped" entrances. Students could also interview a range of people on campus about accessibility. If a class takes on such a project, they should first contact their Institutional Review Board for guidelines about interviewing subjects and get written permission from those interviewed to have them included in the documentary. (Gaining IRB approval would likely provide an additional informative exercise in access and ethics—particularly where people with disabilities are concerned.) The class could follow up with a campuswide discussion, a collaborative class publication, or a documentary video or radio program.

Public Information Project

Students might also create maps of public transit routes, including access signs, in and around their campuses and campus areas for social activities. What barriers exist or have already been addressed? How would a student with X disability attend and participate in Y event on campus? As an additional and extended exercise, students might also discuss ways to make their maps available in multiple formats.

31

From *What Can Disability Studies Learn from the Culture Wars?*

TOBIN SIEBERS

Activist disability politics contributed to the passage of the ADA in 1990. Yet post-ADA activists are still struggling to ensure and expand the accessibility of the public sphere in transportation, as well as in architecture and art. While it may seem odd to link politics and poetics, disability studies makes visible their connections. According to Tobin Siebers, aesthetic values and judgments have depended upon the "healthy and able body" as a "political unconscious [that] represses the role of disability in cultural and aesthetic representation." Siebers elucidates "the group psychology that lies beneath the rejection of disability and accessible architecture from the public sphere." He recalls the history of "ugly laws" meant to banish people with disabilities from view, as he relates how beauty in architecture has been equated with "beautiful," essentially normative bodies. Both the ugly laws and architecture's exclusions of disabled bodies "expose the fact that the public's idea of health is itself based on unconscious operations designed to defend against the pain of disability."

My concern in this essay is threefold. First, I will be arguing that disability is a significant register in the many and various disputes that have come to be known as the "culture wars." The culture wars are not only about what culture will mean in the future but also about who deserves to be included in our culture, and the determining factor in these political decisions often depends on being able to display a healthy body and mind. Statements that label cultural attitudes, minority groups, lifestyles, and works of art as "healthy" or "sick" are not metaphors but aesthetic judgments about the physical and mental condition of citizens. My general purpose is to rethink the culture wars from the point of view of disability studies, a revision that entails a critique of the reliance of cultural and aesthetic ideals on the healthy

From *Cultural Critique* 33 (2003): 182–216.

and able body as well as an appreciation of alternative forms of value and beauty based on disability.

Second, I want to suggest that a political unconscious represses the role of disability in cultural and aesthetic representation. This issue is by necessity related to my first concern. Fredric Jameson argues that the experience of human community functions as a "political unconscious" that represents the "absolute horizon" of all interpretation (1981, 17).[1] The political unconscious, he concludes, determines the symbolism by which the forms of aesthetic objects are given as representations of community, but what has not been considered is whether the political unconscious may also regulate aesthetic forms, excluding those suggestive of broken communities and approving those evocative of ideal ones. My specific test case here is the controversial *Sensation* exhibition shown at the Brooklyn Museum of Art in 1999, but my main point will be that the inclusion of disability changes the definition of the political unconscious in surprising ways.

Third, I claim that aesthetics is pertinent to the struggle to create a built environment accessible to people with disabilities. The debate in architecture has so far focused more on the fundamental problem of whether buildings and landscapes should be universally accessible than on the aesthetic symbolism by which the built environment mirrors its potential inhabitants. While universal access must remain the ambition of the disability community, a broad understanding of disability aesthetics reveals the hidden inhibitions and defense mechanisms that work against advances in universal design and undercut the political and social participation of people with disabilities. It also shows that aesthetic disgust with disability extends beyond individual disabled bodies to the symbolic presence of disability in the built environment. In short, we see again the influence of a political unconscious. My particular goal is to give some idea of the group psychology that lies beneath the rejection of disability and accessible architecture from the public sphere. . . .

Do certain kinds of bodies have greater civil rights than others? Which is more important, the baby's body or the mother's body? Who should bear the cost to make public buildings accessible to people with disabilities? Who gets to have sex with whom? Whose bloodlines will Americans claim as their birthright? These are political questions for the simple reason that they determine who gains membership, and who does not, in the body politic, but the apparent oddity of the culture wars consists in the fact that the debates over these questions have used aesthetic rather than political arguments. The flash points in the battle are not on the Senate floor or in the chambers of the powerful but in classrooms, museums, theaters, concert halls, and other places of culture. Opposing sides tend not to debate political problems directly, focusing instead on the value of reading certain books; the decency of photographs, paintings, and statues; the offensiveness of performances and gestures; the bounds of pornography; the limits of good taste. The culture wars are supposed to be more about who has culture than who gets into the culture, and yet it is difficult to raise one issue without raising the other.

Aesthetics tracks the emotions that some bodies feel in the presence of other bodies, but aesthetic feelings of pleasure and disgust are difficult to separate from political feelings of acceptance and rejection. The oppression of women, gays and lesbians, people with disabilities, blacks, and other ethnic groups often takes the form of an aesthetic judgment, though a warped one, about their bodies and the emotions elicited by them. Their actions are called sick, their appearance judged obscene or disgusting, their minds depraved, their influence likened to a cancer attacking the healthy body of society. Such metaphors not only bring the idea of the disabled body to mind but also represent the rejected political body as disabled in some way. The culture wars appear to be as much about the mental competence to render judgment, the capacity to taste, and the physical ability to experience sensations as about a variety of controversial judgments, tastes, and feelings. They are as much about the shapes of the individual bodies accepted or rejected by the body politic as about the imagination of a common culture.

The status of disability, then, is not just one problem among others in the culture wars. Disability is in one way or another the key concept by which the major controversies at the heart of the culture wars are presented to the public sphere and through which the voting public will eventually render its decisions on matters both political and aesthetic. For to listen to opposing sides, the culture wars are about nothing more or less than the collective health of our country. . . .

Human communities come into being and maintain their coherence by imagining their ideal forms on the basis of other bodies. It is no accident, then, that descriptions of communities in disarray summon images of the disabled body and that, conversely, the appearance of disabled bodies in public provokes fears that the community is itself under attack or coming apart. The political unconscious accounts for this mutual identification between instances of form and perfect images of the body politic. It also accounts for the existence of so-called ugly laws—municipal ordinances that bar people from public spaces on the grounds that their appearance is offensive and poses undue legal liabilities. "Ugly laws" were found routinely in American city statutes until the 1960s and still exist in Columbus, Ohio; Omaha, Nebraska; and other municipalities. This typical example, no longer on the books in Chicago, demonstrates that the compulsion to maintain instances of ideal form in public buildings and streets echoes a primordial obsession with perfect, public bodies:

> No person who is diseased, maimed, mutilated or in any way deformed so as to be an unsightly or disgusting object or improper person to be allowed in or on the public ways or other public places in this city, shall therein or thereon expose himself to public view.[2]

Culture is not merely a web of symbols. It is a web of body symbols. Disability activists have focused so far on negative representations of the human body, on how the desire to represent perfect, individual bodies denigrates or excludes the experience of disability. If culture is really composed of body symbols, however, it means that the struggle by disability activists against negative body images must extend far beyond physical images of the individual human body to its symbolic resonance in other bodies. Beauty, order, and cleanliness in the built environment occupy a special position among the requirements of society because they apply to artificial bodies our preoccupation with our own body, including its health, integrity, and hygiene. Only an analysis of this powerful symbolic connection will explain why prejudices against the disabled body persist in the built environment, and only then will disability activists be able to shift emphasis from the individual human body to the imaginary bodies undergirding architectural theory, employment law, and conceptions of citizenship.

A man extending a cane before himself and a three-bedroom colonial home stretching a wheelchair ramp into the street are equally disconcerting to the public eye. Both ignite a vigorous, defensive impulse to cure or fix the offending body. Conversely, beautiful, harmonious constructions automatically summon ideas of elegant, graceful people, as in this description of the John Hancock building in Boston, designed by I. M. Pei: "Pei and his principal designer, Henry Cobb, devised a sixty-two-story tower proportioned as slimly as a fashion model, sequined in reflective glass panels." Other examples of the imaginary connection between body and building may be found throughout architectural theory both because the political unconscious exerts a stranglehold on the kinds of bodies acceptable in the built environment, and because modern architectural theories define the form and function of buildings with explicit reference to a politics of the body. Lewis Mumford claimed that the state of building at any period represents a "legible script" detailing the complicated processes and changes taking place in the body politic itself, while Louis Sullivan insisted that pure design in architecture maximizes utility by reproducing the essence of the human being. Of course, this essence represents human beings in normative terms, both physically and mentally. These and other aesthetic dictates represent architecture itself as providing a transcendental expression of human perfection, situating in the crafting of concrete, wood, plastic, and steel the ability to overcome limitations of the human body and mind, but they also use the built environment to maintain a spatial caste system at the expense of people with disabilities. This caste system not only targets individual disabled bodies for exclusion but also rejects any form of appearance that symbolizes disability.

Perhaps the most revealing example of the relation between the political unconscious and architectural theory exists in the work of Le Corbusier. In 1925 he conceived of a diagram, the *Modular,* that utilizes the proportions of the body to help architects design buildings and other human habitats. It was to provide a standard scale by which buildings and human beings could be connected. The modular presents the image of an upright male—six feet tall, muscular, powerful, and showing no evidence of either physical or mental disability. It pictures the human body as a universal type, with no consideration of physical variation. Ironically, Le Corbusier wanted to tie buildings to the human beings living in them, but his theories privilege form over function and establish one basis for what Rob Imrie has called the "design apartheid" of modernist architectural practices.[3] In fact, design apartheid describes with accuracy the exclusionary system apparent in many episodes of the culture wars. Works of art called ugly ignite public furor. Unaesthetic designs or dilapidated buildings are viewed as eyesores. Deformed bodies appear as public nuisances. Not only do these phenomena confront the public with images of the disabled body, they expose the fact that the public's idea of health is itself based on unconscious operations designed to defend against the pain of disability. . . .

NOTES

1. See also Dowling, *Jameson, Althusser, Marx* (1984), who provides a concise reading of the "primitive communism" important to Jameson's theories.

2. See Burgdorf and Burgdorf 1976, 863, whose account of ugly laws I follow. See also Lifchez 1987, 2 n2; and Imrie 1996, 15, 62.

3. Designers and architects learn to design buildings, environments, and products for "average" people, and, of course, the "average" person is always able-bodied. The incarnation of the "average" in the built environment excludes bodies that do not fit the norm and embeds in the flesh of that environment the desire to preserve the able body over all other forms and shapes. But the average person does not really exist, for someone who is average at one point in life fails to be average earlier or later on. Children and the elderly, for example, do not have average bodies. Averageness is a ratio used to reject human variation, and of these variations the disabled body is the easiest to exclude. See Imrie 1996, 19, 81–87, whose discussion of Le Corbusier and architectural standards is invaluable.

SUGGESTIONS FOR STUDENT ACTIVITIES

Reflecting on Accessibility

Siebers's analysis suggests that the busy people in the New York City subway who did not meet Hockenberry's eye may have been driven by the unconscious desire to build a barrier against the pain of disability that they feared facing in an encounter with him. In a disability activist project on our own campus, when a class blocked a building's nonhandicapped doors to force everyone to use the "accessible" entrance, video recordings revealed that nondisabled people had openly voiced their irritation at being slowed down by having to use out-of-the-way "handicapped" entrances. The point, of course, was to make the community aware of the inaccessibility of these retrofitted entrances. Does the irritation at being slowed down stem from feelings of vulnerability? Is having to slow down, to be inefficient in movement, associated in our culture with lack of success, lack of ambition, failure? Such questions are good topics for in-class reflective writing and discussion.

Researching Eugenics

Students are often very surprised to learn about the "ugly laws" Siebers refers to, and these make good topics of research, as do early-twentieth-century laws about sterilization, institutionalization, and the eugenics movement. Good starting places for research online include:

www.eugenicsarchive.org/eugenics   Information and images about the eugenics movement in the United States

www.disabilitymuseum.org   Historical information and images about the experiences of people with disabilities

Aesthetic Observation and Description

Invite students to creatively explore and test Siebers's claim that our ideas about "beautiful" buildings come from our ideas of "beautiful" bodies. Have them observe and describe the aesthetics of a particular building in close detail and then write about that building using a metaphor of the human body. Pushing this analogy a bit further, does a fully accessible, ADA-compliant building suggest a new or different kind of body? How might that body be described?

32 Poems with Disabilities and *Poet of Cripples*

JIM FERRIS

Tobin Siebers (see "What Can Disability Studies Learn from the Culture Wars?," p. 262 in this volume) reminds us that removing barriers to full inclusion has material and psychological components. Art can expose, reshape, or express the buried logics and human emotions surrounding psychological attitudes toward disability. Disability activism, like the activism of other minority groups, has led to the discovery and recovery of writers, poets, and topics once excluded from artistic canons. Poet Jim Ferris touches humorously on the poetics of politics and the politics of poetics in "Poems with Disabilities," which begins, "I'm sorry—this space is reserved/for poems with disabilities. I know/it's one of the best spaces in the book,/but the Poems with Disabilities Act/requires us to make reasonable/accommodations for poems that aren't/normal. . . ." In the second selection, "Poet of Cripples," Ferris assumes a Whitmanesque voice: "Let me be a poet of cripples. . . ./I sing for cripples; I sing for you," suggesting, as do Hockenberry (see p. 257) and Bérubé (see p. 238), that including disability will lead to a broader enumeration and celebration of our democracy and its citizens.

Poems with Disabilities

I'm sorry—this space is reserved
for poems with disabilities. I know
it's one of the best spaces in the book,
but the Poems with Disabilities Act
requires us to make reasonable
accommodations for poems that aren't
normal. There is a nice space just
a few pages over—in fact (don't
tell anyone) I think it's better
than this one. I myself prefer it.
Actually I don't see any of those
poems right now myself, but you never know

From Jim Ferris, *The Hospital Poems* (Charlotte, NC: Main Street Rag Publishing, 2004).

when one might show up, so we have to keep
this space open. You can't always tell
just from looking at them, either. Sometimes
they'll look just like a regular poem
when they roll in—you're reading along
and suddenly everything
changes, the world tilts
a little, angle of vision
jumps, focus
shifts. You remember
your aunt died of cancer at just your age
and maybe yesterday's twinge means
something after all. Your sloppy,
fragile heart beats
a little faster
and then you know.
You just know.
And the poem is right
where it
belongs.

Poet of Cripples

Let me be a poet of cripples,
of hollow men and boys groping
to be whole, of girls limping toward
womanhood and women reaching back,
all slipping and falling toward the cavern
we carry within, our hidden void,
a place for each to become full, whole,
room of our own, space to grow in ways
unimaginable to the straight
and the narrow, the small and similar,
the poor, normal ones who do not know
their poverty. Look with care, look deep.
Know that you are a cripple too.
I sing for cripples; I sing for you.

SUGGESTIONS FOR STUDENT ACTIVITIES

Defining Traits of "Disability Poetry"

Jim Ferris's recent book of poems, *The Hospital Poems*, won the 2004 Main St.
Rag Poetry Book Award. This short volume would make a good class text.
Students might discuss whether there is such a thing as a "disability poet-
ics," and if so, begin to define its traits. Students interested in poetry might

investigate the work of other poets with disabilities: Homer, Alexander Pope, John Keats, Lord Byron, Emily Dickinson, or more contemporary poets such as Larry Eigner, Mark O'Brien, or Elizabeth Arnold. Born with cerebral palsy, Larry Eigner began writing at a young age and published many books of poetry before his death in 1996. See <epc.buffalo.edu/authors/eigner> for more information about Eigner. Mark O'Brien lived in an iron lung after contracting polio as a child and was the subject of Jessica Yu's 1997 Oscar-winning documentary, *Breathing Lessons*. See <www.pacificnews.org/marko> for more information about O'Brien. Elizabeth Arnold's first book, *The Reef*, chronicles her life with cancer. An excerpt can be found at <washingtonart.com/beltway/arnold.html>.

Finding a Poetic Voice

Encourage students to create their own poetry and then to reflect on how creative writing enables expression of ideas and communication to audiences in different ways than prose. One activity we have had success with is to ask the class to brainstorm lists of words and phrases associated with disability. Then, ask each student to create a "found poem" or a poetic dialogue using some or all of the words on the list. Follow the activity by inviting students to read their poems aloud.

BIBLIOGRAPHY OF COMPOSITION AND
RHETORIC AND DISABILITY STUDIES SOURCES

Ｗe have accumulated and included all the references from the essays included in this sourcebook as well as resources that have been suggested in student activities in this selected bibliography. Our hope is that this resource will enable you and your students to become more familiar with the wealth of information on disability studies and incorporate it into your own courses and pedagogy.

Ackley, Katherine Anne. *Essays from Contemporary Culture.* 5th ed. Boston: Heinle, 2003.

Adler-Kassner, Linda, and Susanmarie Harrington. *Basic Writing as a Political Act: Public Conversations about Writing and Literacies.* Cresskill, NJ: Hampton Press, 2002.

Alcorn, Marshall W. *Changing the Subject in English Class: Discourse and the Constructions of Desire.* Carbondale: Southern Illinois UP, 2002.

Allen, Barry. "Foucault's Nominalism." In Tremain, *Foucault and the Government of Disability,* 93–107.

Altick, Richard. *The Shows of London.* Cambridge: Belknap-Harvard UP, 1978.

American College of Rheumatology. "Psoriatic Arthritis Fact Sheet." www.rheumatology.org

American Disabled for Attendant Programs Today. www.adapt.org

American Eugenics Archive. http://eugenicsarchive.org/eugenics/

Americans with Disabilities Act home page. www.usdoj.gov/crt/ada

"Americans with Disabilities Act of 1990." U.S. Senate Subcommittee on Disability Policy. www.usdoj.gov/crt/ada/adahom1.htm

Anderson, Benedict. *Imagined Communities: Reflections on the Origin and Spread of Nationalism.* London: Verso, 1983.

Arkin, Marian, and Barbara Shollar. *The Tutor Book.* New York: Longman, 1982.

Bachmann, Susan, and Melinda Barth. *Between Worlds: A Reader, Rhetoric, and Handbook.* 3rd ed. New York: Addison Wesley, 2001.

Barber-Fendley, Kimber, and Chris Hamel. "A New Visibility: An Argument for Alternative Assistance Writing Programs for Students with Learning Disabilities." *College Composition and Communication* 55, no. 3 (Feb. 2004): 504–35.

Barthes, Roland. *Camera Lucida: Reflections on Photography.* Trans. Richard Howard. New York: Hill, 1981.

Baron, Dennis. "From Pencils to Pixels: The Stages of Literacy Technologies." In Hawisher and Selfe, *Passions, Pedagogies and 21st Century Technologies,* 35–53.

A Roland Barthes Reader. Edited by Susan Sontag. London: Vintage, 1982.

Bartholomae, David. "The Study of Error." In Weese, Fox, Greene, *Teaching Academic Literacy: The Uses of Teacher-Research in Developing a Writing Program,* 175–94. Originally published in *College Composition and Communication* 31, no. 3 (1980): 253–69.

———. "The Tidy House: Basic Writing in the American Curriculum." *Journal of Basic Writing* 12 (1993): 4–21.

Barton, Ellen L. "Negotiating Expertise in Discourses of Disability." *TEXT* 16 (1996): 299–322.

Bauby, Jean-Dominique. *The Diving Bell and the Butterfly*. Translated by Jeremy Leggatt. New York: Vintage International, 1997.

Baumlin, James, and Tita Baumlin. "Psyche/Logos: Mapping the Terrains of Mind and Rhetoric." *College English* 51 (1989): 245–61.

Baynton, Douglas C. "Disability and the Justification of Inequality in American History." In Longmore and Umansky, *The New Disability History: American Perspectives*, 33–57.

Beck, Aaron. *Cognitive Psychology*. New Haven: Yale UP, 1972.

———. *Cognitive Therapy and the Emotional Disorders*. New York: Penguin, 1976.

Bérubé, Michael. "Citizenship and Disability." *Dissent* 50, no. 2 (2003): 52–57.

———. *Life as We Know It: A Father, a Family, and an Exceptional Child*. New York: Vintage, 1998.

Birks, Kristen. "What Is Psoriatic Arthritis?" Missouri Arthritis Rehabilitation Research and Training Center. www.muhealth.org

Bizzell, Patricia. "Basic Writing and the Issue of Correctness; or, What to Do with 'Mixed' Forms of Academic Discourse." *Journal of Basic Writing* 19, no. 1 (Spring 2000): 4–12.

Bleich, David. *Know and Tell: A Writing Pedagogy of Disclosure, Genre, and Membership*. Portsmouth, NH: Heinemann-Boynton/Cook, 1998.

Bogdan, Robert. *Freak Show: Presenting Human Oddities for Amusement and Profit*. Chicago: U of Chicago P, 1988.

Bordo, Susan. *Unbearable Weight: Feminism, Western Culture, and the Body*. Berkeley and Los Angeles: U of California P, 1993.

Bowe, Frank G. *Universal Design in Education: Teaching Nontraditional Students*. Wesport, CT: Bergin & Garvey, 2000.

Bragg, Lois. "From the Mute God to the Lesser God: Disability in Medieval Celtic and Old Norse Mythology." *Disability and Society* 12, no. 2 (1997): 165–77.

———. "Oedipus Borealis: The Aberrant Body in Barbarian Europe." *Disability Studies Quarterly* 17, no. 4 (1997): 258–62.

Breathing Lessons. Videocassette directed by Jessica Yu. Fanlight, 1999.

Brueggemann, Brenda Jo. "The Coming Out of Deaf Culture and American Sign Language: An Exploration into Visual Rhetoric and Literacy." *Rhetoric Review* 13 (1995): 409–20.

———. "An Enabling Pedagogy: Meditations on Writing and Disability." *JAC* 21, no. 4 (Fall 2001): 791–820.

———. *Lend Me Your Ear: Rhetorical Constrictions of Deafness*. Washington, DC: Gallaudet UP, 1999.

———. "On Almost Passing." *College English* 59, no. 6 (1997): 647–60.

Brueggemann, Brenda Jo, Linda Feldmeier White, Patricia A. Dunn, Barbara A. Heifferon, and Johnson Cheu. "Becoming Visible: Lessons in Disability." *College Composition and Communication* 52, no. 3 (February 2001): 368–98.

Bruffee, Kenneth A. *Collaborative Learning, Higher Education, Interdependence, and the Authority of Knowledge*. Baltimore: Johns Hopkins UP, 1999.

Burgdorf, Marcia Pearce, and Robert Burgdorf Jr. "A History of Unequal Treatment: The Qualifications of Handicapped Persons as a 'Suspect Class' under the Equal Protection Clause." *Santa Clara Lawyer* 15 (1976): 855–910.

Burke, Kenneth. *Language as Symbolic Action*. Berkeley: U of California P, 1966.

———. *A Rhetoric of Motives*. New York: Prentice Hall, 1950.

———. *Towards a Better Life*. Berkeley and Los Angeles: U of California P, 1966.

Butler, Judith. *Bodies That Matter: On the Discursive Limits of "Sex."* New York: Routledge, 1993.

———. *Excitable Speech: A Politics of the Performative*. New York: Routledge, 1997.

———. *Gender Trouble: Feminism and the Subversion of Identity*. London: Routledge, 1990.

Callahan, John. *Don't Worry, He Won't Get Far on Foot*. New York: Vintage, 1990. www.callahanonline.com/index.php

Campbell, JoAnn. "Writing to Heal: Using Meditation in the Writing Process." *College Composition and Communication* 45 (1994): 246–51.

Canghuilhem, Georges. *The Normal and the Pathological*. Translated by C. Fawcett and R. Cohen. New York: Zone, 1991.

CCC Ad Hoc Committee on the Ethical Use of Students and Student Writing in Composition Studies. "Guidelines for the Ethical Treatment of Students and Student Writing in Composition Studies." *College Composition and Communication* 52 (2001): 485–90.

Center for Universal Design, North Carolina State University. "Principles for Universal Design." www.design.ncsu.edu:8120/cud/univ_design/princ_overview.htm

Certeau, Michael de. "Montaigne's 'Of Cannibals': The Savage 'I.'" Chap. in *Heterologies: Discourse on the Other*. Translated by Brian Massumi. Manchester, UK: Manchester UP, 1986. 67–79.

Chrisman, Wendy L. "The Ways We Disclose: When Life-Writing Becomes Writing Your Life." *Lore: An E-Journal for Teachers of Writing*. www.bedfordstmartins.com/lore/

Cintron, Ralph. *Angels' Town: Chero Ways, Gang Life, and Rhetorics of the Everday.* Boston: Beacon P, 1997.

Clare, Eli. *Exile and Pride: Disability, Queerness, and Liberation.* Cambridge, MA: South End, 1999. Reprinted in Curtis et al., *Original Text-Wrestling Book,* 71–80.

_____. "Gawking, Gaping, Staring." *GLQ* 9:1–2 (2003): 257–61.

Colombo, Gary, Robert Cullen, and Bonnie Lisle. *Rereading America: Cultural Contexts for Critical Thinking and Writing.* Boston: Bedford/St. Martin's, 2001.

Corder, Jim. "A New Introduction to Psychoanalysis, Taken as a Version of Modern Rhetoric." *Pre/Text* 5 (1984): 138–69.

Couser, G. Thomas. "Conflicting Paradigms: The Rhetorics of Disability Memoir." In Wilson and Lewiecki-Wilson, *Embodied Rhetorics,* 78–91.

_____. "Making, Taking, and Faking Lives: Ethical Problems in Collaborative Life Writing." In Davis and Womack, *Mapping the Ethical Turn,* 209–26.

_____. *Recovering Bodies: Illness, Disability, and Life Writing.* Madison: U of Wisconsin P, 1997.

_____. "Signifying Bodies: Life Writing and Disability Studies." In Snyder, Brueggemann, and Garland-Thomson, *Disability Studies,* 109–17.

Covino, William A. "Rhetoric Is Back: Derrida, Feyerabend, Geertz, and the Lessons of History." In *Rhetoric: Concepts, Definitions, Boundaries,* edited by William A. Covino and David A. Jolliffe. Boston: Allyn & Bacon, 1995. 311–18.

Crary, Jonathan. *Techniques of the Observer: On Vision and Modernity in the Nineteenth Century.* Cambridge: MITP, 1990.

Crockett, Jean B., and James M. Kauffman. *The Least Restrictive Environment: Its Origins and Interpretations in Special Education.* Mahwah, NJ: Lawrence Erlbaum, 1999.

Crowley, Sharon. "Body Studies in Rhetoric and Composition." In Olson, *Rhetoric and Composition as Intellectual Work,* 177–87.

Crowley, Sharon, and Debra Hawhee. *Ancient Rhetorics for Contemporary Students.* Boston: Allyn & Bacon, 1999.

Curtis, Marcia et al., eds. *The Original Text-Wrestling Book.* Dubuque, IA: Kendall/Hunt, 2001.

Cushman, Ellen. "The Rhetorician as an Agent of Social Change." *College Composition and Communication,* 47, no. 1 (1996): 7–28.

Daniell, Beth. "Composing (as) Power." *College Composition and Communication* 45 (1994): 238–46.

Daniels, Harry, and Philip Garner, eds. *Inclusive Education: Supporting Inclusion in Education Systems.* London: Koge, 1999.

Davis, Lennard J. *Bending Over Backwards: Disability, Dismodernism and Other Difficult Positions.* New York: New York UP, 2002.

_____. "Crips Strike Back: The Rise of Disability Studies." *American Literary History* 11, no. 3 (Fall 1993): 500–12.

_____, ed. *The Disability Studies Reader.* New York: Routledge, 1997.

_____. *Enforcing Normalcy: Disability, Deafness, and the Body.* London: Verso, 1995.

Davis, Todd F., and Kenneth Womack. *Mapping the Ethical Turn: A Reader in Ethics, Culture, and Literary Theory.* Charlottesville: UP of Virginia, 2001.

Debord, Guy. *The Society of the Spectacle.* Detroit: Black, 1983.

Denzin, Norman K., and Yvonna S. Lincoln, eds. *Handbook of Qualitative Research.* Thousand Oaks, CA: Sage, 1994.

Derrida, Jacques. *Of Grammatology.* Translated by Gayatri Chakravorty Spivak. Baltimore: Johns Hopkins UP, 1976.

Diagnostic and Statistical Manual of Mental Disorders (DSM-IVTR Fourth Edition). Washington, DC: American Psychiatric P, 2000.

Dickens, Charles. *A Christmas Carol in Prose: Being a Ghost Story of Christmas.* Oxford: Oxford UP, 1954.

Dickinson, Emily. *The Complete Poems of Emily Dickinson.* Edited by Thomas H. Johnson. Boston: Little, Brown, 1960.

Dilks, Stephen, Regina Hansen, and Matthew Parfitt. *Cultural Conversations: The Presence of the Past.* Boston: Bedford/St. Martin's, 2001.

Disability History Museum. www.disabilitymuseum.org/

The Disability Rag and Resource. www.raggededgemagazine.com/archiveindex.htm

Dowling, William C. *Jameson, Althusser, Marx: An Introduction to the Political Unconscious.* Ithaca, NY: Cornell UP, 1984.

Duncan, Nancy, ed. *Bodyspace: Destabilizing Geographies of Gender and Sexuality.* New York: Routledge, 1996.

Dunn, Patricia A. *Learning Re-Abled: The Learning Disability Controversy and Composition Studies.* Portsmouth, NH: Heinemann-Boynton/Cook, 1995.

———. *Talking, Sketching, Moving: Multiple Literacies in the Teaching of Writing.* Portsmouth, NH: Heinemann-Boynton/Cook, 2001.

Dunn, Patricia A., and Kathleen Dunn DeMers. "Reversing Notions of Disability and Accommodation: Embracing Universal Design in Writing Pedagogy and Web Space." *Kairos* 7, no. 1 (2002). http://english.ttu.edu/kairos/7.1

Larry Eigner home page. http://epc.buffalo.edu/authors/eigner

Faigley, Lester. "Competing Theories of Process: A Critique and a Proposal." *College English* 48 (Oct 1986): 527–42.

Family Guy. TV show created by Seth McFarlane. Beverly Hills, CA: Fox Network, 1999–2002. www.familyguy.com.

"Fast Facts for Faculty: Universal Design for Learning, Elements of Good Teaching." The Ohio State University Partnership Grant Improving the Quality of Education for Students with Disabilities. www.telr.osu.edu/dpg/fastfact/fastfactcolor/Universal.pdf

Feldman, Ann Merle, Nancy Downs, and Ellen McManus. *In Context: Participating in Cultural Conversations.* New York: Longman, 2002.

Ferris, James. *The Hospital Poems.* Charlotte, NC: Main Street Rag Publishing, 2004.

———. "Poems with Disabilities." *Ragged Edge* (March/April 2000). www.ragged-edge-mag.com

Finding Nemo. DVD directed by Andrew Stanton and Lee Unkrich. Emeryville, CA: Pixar, 2003.

Fine, Michelle. "Working the Hyphens: Reinventing Self and Other in Qualitative Research." In Denzin and Lincoln, *Handbook of Qualitative Research,* 70–82.

Fine, Michelle, and Adrienne Asch, eds. *Women with Disabilities: Essays in Psychology, Culture, and Politics.* Philadelphia: Temple UP, 1988.

Finger, Anne. *Past Due: A Story of Disability, Pregnancy, and Birth.* Seattle: Seal, 1990.

Fisher, Gary. *Gary in Your Pocket: Stories and Notebooks of Gary Fisher.* Edited by Eve Kosofsky Sedgwick. Durham: Duke UP, 1996.

Flynn, Thomas, and Mary King, eds. *Dynamics of the Writing Conference.* Urbana, IL: National Council of Teachers of English, 1993.

Foucault, Michel. *The Birth of the Clinic: An Archeology of Medical Perception.* Translated by Sheridan Smith. New York: Vintage, 1975.

Fox, Ann M. "'But, Mother—I'm—Crippled!': 'Tennessee Williams, Queering Disability, and Dis/Membered Bodies in Performance.'" In Smith and Hutchinson, *Gendering Disability,* 232–50.

Fox, Tom. *Defending Access: A Critique of Standards in Higher Education.* Portsmouth, NH: Heinemann-Boynton/Cook, 1999.

———. "Standards and Access." *The Journal of Basic Writing* 12.1 (Spring 1993): 37–45.

Frank, Arthur W. *The Wounded Storyteller: Body, Illness, and Ethics.* Chicago: U of Chicago P, 1995.

Freedman, Diane P., and Martha Stoddard Holmes, eds. *The Teacher's Body: Embodiment, Authority, and Identity in the Academy.* Albany: State U of New York P, 2003.

Freire, Paulo. *Pedagogy of Freedom: Ethics, Democracy, and Civic Courage.* Lanham, MD: Rowman & Littlefield, 1998.

———. *Pedagogy of the Oppressed.* New York: Continuum Books, 1993.

Frielich, Morris, Douglas Raybeck, and Joel Savishinsky, ed. *Deviance: Anthropological Perspectives.* New York: Bergin & Garvey, 1991.

Gale, Xin Liu, and Fredric G. Gale, eds. *(Re)Visioning Composition Textbooks.* Albany: State U of New York P, 1999

Garland-Thomson, Rosemarie. "Crippled Little Girls and Lame Old Women: Sentimental Spectacles of Sympathy with Rhetorics of Reform in Nineteenth-Century American Women's Writing," *Nineteenth Century American Women Writers: A Critical Collection.* Ed Karen Kilcup. New York: Blackwell, 1988. 128–45.

———. *Extraordinary Bodies: Figuring Disability in American Culture and Literature.* New York: Columbia UP, 1996.

———. "From Wonder to Error: A Genealogy of Freak Discourse in Modernity." In *Freakery: Cultural Spectacles of the Extraordinary Body.* New York UP, 1996. 1–22.

———. "Integrating Disability Studies into the Existing Curriculum: The Example of 'Women and Literature' at Howard University." In Davis, *The Disability Studies Reader,* 295–306. Originally published in *Radical Teacher* 47 (1997): 15–39.

———. "Integrating Disability: Transforming Feminist Theory." *NWSA Journal* 14, no. 3 Fall (2002): 1–33.

_____. "The Politics of Staring: Visual Rhetorics of Disability in Popular Photography." In Snyder, Brueggemann, and Garland-Thomson, *Disability Studies*, 56–76.

Gates, Henry Louis. "White Like Me." *New Yorker* 72, no. 16 (June 17, 1996): 66–81.

Gere, Ann Ruggles. "Kitchen Tables and Rented Rooms: The Extracurriculum of Composition." *College Composition and Communication* 45 (1994): 75–92.

Gillespie, Sheena, and Robert Singleton. *Across Cultures: A Reader for Writers*. Boston: Allyn & Bacon, 1999.

Giroux, Henry A. *Border Crossings: Cultural Workers and the Politics of Education*. New York: Routledge, 1992.

Gladwell, Malcolm. "The Sports Taboo: Why Blacks Are Like Boys and Whites Are Like Girls." In Curtis et al., *Original Text-Wrestling Book*, 135–44.

Gleeson, Brendan. *Geographies of Disability*. New York: Routledge, 1999.

Goffman, Erving. *Asylums: Essays on the Social Situation of Mental Patients and Other Inmates.* Chicago: Aldine, 1961.

_____. *Stigma: Notes on the Management of Spoiled Identity.* Englewood Cliffs, NJ: Prentice-Hall, 1963.

Goode, David. *A World without Words: The Social Construction of Children Born Deaf and Blind.* Philadelphia: Temple UP, 1994.

Gould, Stephen Jay. *The Mismeasure of Man.* New York: Norton, 1981.

Grandin, Temple. *Thinking in Pictures: And Other Reports from My Life with Autism.* Foreword by Oliver Sacks. New York: Vintage, 1996.

Grandin, Temple, and Catherine Johnson. *Animals in Translation: Using the Mysteries of Autism to Decode Animal Behavior.* New York: Scribner, 2005.

Grandin, Temple, and Margaret Scariano. *Emergence, Labeled Autistic.* Novato, CA: Arena P, 1991.

Grealy, Lucy. *Autobiography of a Face.* Afterword by Ann Patchett. New York: Perennial, 2003.

Gutierrez, Kris, Betsy Rymes, and Joanne Larson. "Script, Counterscript, and Underlife in the Classroom: James Brown versus *Brown v. Board of Education.*" *Harvard Educational Review* 65 (1995): 445–71.

Haas, Christina. *Writing Technology: Studies on the Materiality of Literacy.* Mahwah, NJ: Lawrence Erlbaum Associates, 1996.

Hahn, Harlan. "The Political Implications of Disability Definitions and Data." *Journal of Disability Policy Studies* 4, no. 2 (1993): 41–52.

Halttunen, Karen. "Humanitarianism and the Pornography of Pain in Anglo-American Culture." *American Historical Review* 100 (1995): 303–34.

Haraway, Donna. *Simians, Cyborgs, and Women: The Reinvention of Nature.* New York: Routledge, 1991.

Harper, Phillip Brian. *Are We Not Men? Masculine Anxiety and the Problem of African-American Identity.* New York: Oxford UP, 1996.

Hathaway, Katherine Butler. *The Little Locksmith: A Memoir.* Foreword by Alix Kates Shulman. Afterword by Nancy Mairs. New York: Feminist P, 2000.

Hawisher, Gail, and Cynthia Selfe, eds. *Passions, Pedagogies and 21st Century Technologies.* Utah State UP, 1999.

Herndl, Diane Price. "Johnny Mnemonic Meets the Bimbo: Feminist Pedagogy and Post-modern Performance." In Freedman and Stoddard Holmes, *The Teacher's Body*, 59–68.

Herrington, Anne J., and Marcia Curtis. *Persons in Process: Four Stories of Writing and Personal Development in College.* Urbana, IL: National Council of Teachers of English, 2000.

Heubert, Jay P. "Disability, Race, and High Stakes Testing." In Losen and Orfield, *Racial Inequity in Special Education*, 137–65.

Hockenberry, John. *Moving Violations: War Zones, Wheelchairs, and Declarations of Independence.* New York: Hyperion, 1995.

Hodge, Robert, and Gunther Kress. *Social Semiotics.* Ithaca, NY: Cornell UP, 1988.

hooks, bell. *Teaching to Transgress: Education as the Practice of Freedom.* New York: Routledge, 1994.

Horner, Bruce. "Birth of Basic Writing." In Horner and Lu, *Representing the "Other,"* 3–29.

Horner, Bruce, and Min-Zhan Lu. *Representing the "Other": Basic Writers and the Teaching of Basic Writing.* Urbana, IL: National Council of Teachers of English, 1999.

Husson, Thérèse-Adèle. *Reflections: The Life and Writings of a Young Blind Woman in Post-revolutionary France.* Translated by Catherine J. Kudlich and Zina Weygand. New York: New York UP, 2001.

"IDEA 2004 Resources." U.S. Department of Education. www.ed.gov/policy/speced/guid/idea/idea2004.html

Imrie, Rob. *Disability and the City: International Perspectives*. London: Paul Chapman, 1996.

Jacobs, Steve. "The Electronic Curb-Cut Effect." NCR Corporation. www.icdri.org/technology/ecceff.htm

Jameson, Fredric. *The Political Unconscious: Narrative as Socially Symbolic Act*. Ithaca: Cornell UP, 1981.

Jay, Martin. *Downcast Eyes: The Denigration of Vision in Twentieth-Century Thought*. Berkeley: U of California P, 1993.

Johnson, Tonya Stremlau. "Deaf Students in Mainstreamed College Composition Courses: Culture and Pedagogy." *Dissertation Abstracts International* 57, no. 9 (1996): 3857A. (UMI no. 9706338).

Johnston, JoAnn B. "Reevaluation of the Question as a Teaching Tool." In Flynn and King, *Dynamics of the Writing Conference*, 34–40.

Johnstone, Henry W., Jr. "Some Trends in Rhetorical Theory." In *The Prospect of Rhetoric: Report on the National Development Project*. Edited by Lloyd Bitzer and Edwin Black. Englewood Cliffs, NJ: Prentice Hall, 1971. 79–90.

Keeping it Real: The Adventures of Greg Walloch (formerly titled *I'm Looking for Someone to Fuck the Disabled*). DVD directed by Eli Kabillio. Los Angeles, CA: Picture This Entertainment, 2001.

Keller, Helen. *The Story of My Life*. Edited by Roger Shattuck, with Dorothy Herrmann. New York: Norton, 2003.

Kent, Thomas, ed. *Post-process Theory: Beyond the Writing Process Paradigm*. Carbondale: Southern Illinois UP, 1999.

Kirby, Kathleen. "Re: Mapping Subjectivity: Cartographic Vision and the Limits of Politics." In Duncan, *Bodyspace*. 45–55.

Kirsch, Gesa. *Ethical Dilemmas in Feminist Research: The Politics of Location, Interpretation, and Publication*. Albany: State U of New York P, 1999.

Kirszner, Laurie G., and Stephen R. Mandell. *Patterns for College Writing: A Rhetorical Reader and Guide*, 8th ed. Boston: Bedford/St. Martin's, 2001.

Kleege, Georgina. "Reflections on Writing and Teaching Disability Autobiography." *Publication of the Modern Language Association* 120, no. 2 (March 2005): 606–10.

———. *Sight Unseen*. New Haven: Yale UP, 1999.

Kleinman, Arthur A. *The Illness Narratives*. New York: Basic Books, 1988.

Knipfel, Jim. *Slackjaw: A Memoir*. New York: Berkley Trade, 2000.

Knox, Paul L. "The Social Production of the Built Environment: Architects, Architecture, and the Post-Modern City." *Progress in Human Geography* 11, no. 3 (1987): 354–78.

Kooser, Ted. *Flying at Night: Poems, 1965–1985*. Pittsburgh: U Pittsburgh P, 2005.

Kroll, Barry M. "Cognitive Egocentrism and the Problem of Audience Awareness in Written Discourse." *Research in the Teaching of English* 12 (1978): 269–81.

Lakoff, George. *Women, Fire, and Dangerous Things: What Categories Reveal about the Mind*. Chicago: U of Chicago P, 1987.

Lane, Harlan, Robert Hoffmeister, and Ben Bahan. *A Journey into the Deaf-World*. San Diego: Dawn-Sign Press, 1996.

Leder, Drew. *The Absent Body*. Chicago: U of Chicago P, 1990.

Lee, Amy. *Composing Critical Pedagogies: Teaching Writing as Revision*. Urbana, IL: National Council of Teachers of English, 2000.

Lee, Jerome. "A Good Investment (Hiring Individuals with Disabilities)." *Newsweek*, June 23, 1997.

Lewis, Clayton W. "Burke's Act in *A Rhetoric of Motives*." *College English* 50 (1988): 368–76.

Lifchez, Raymond. *Rethinking Architecture: Design Students and Physically Disabled People*. Berkeley and Los Angeles: U of California P, 1987.

Limon, John. *The Place of Fiction in the Time of Science: A Disciplinary History of American Writing*. New York: Cambridge UP, 1990.

Linton, Simi. *Claiming Disability: Knowledge and Identity*. New York: New York UP, 1998.

Linton, Simi, Susan Mello, and John O'Neill. "Disability Studies: Expanding the Parameters of Diversity." In Shor, *Education Is Politics*, 178–92.

Lipsitz, George. "No Shining City on a Hill." *American Studies* 40, no. 2 (1999): 53–70.

Longmore, Paul. "Screening Stereotypes: Images of Disabled People in Television and Motion Pictures." *Social Policy* 15 (1985): 31–38.

———. "The Second Phase: From Disability Rights to Disability Culture." In Longmore, *Why I Burned My Book and Other Essays about Disability*, 215–24.

———. *Why I Burned My Book and Other Essays about Disability*. Philadelphia: Temple UP, 2003.

Longmore , Paul, and Lauri Umansky, eds. *The New Disability History: American Perspectives*. New York: New York UP, 2001.

Lorde, Audre. *The Cancer Journals*. San Francisco: Aunt Lute Books, 1980.

Losen, Daniel J., and Gary Orfield, eds. *Racial Inequity in Special Education*. Cambridge, MA: Harvard Education P, 2002.

Lowe, Charles. "Speech Recognition: Sci-Fi or Composition?" *Currents in Electronic Literacy* 4 (Spring 2001). November 19, 2003. www.cwrl.utexas.edu/currents/spr01/lowe.html

Lunsford, Andrea. "Cognitive Development and the Basic Writer." In Villanueva, 1979. Reprinted in *Cross Talk in Comp Theory, A Reader*.

Lunsford, Andrea A. *The St. Martin's Handbook*. 5th ed. New York: Bedford/St. Martin's, 2003.

MacNealy, Mary Sue. *Strategies for Empirical Research in Writing*. Boston: Allyn & Bacon, 1998.

Maggio, Rosalie, ed. *The New Beacon Book of Quotations by Women*. Boston: Beacon P, 1996. 126.

Mairs, Nancy. *Carnal Acts*. Boston: Beacon P, 1996.

_____. *Ordinary Time: Cycles in Marriage, Faith, and Renewal*. Boston: Beacon P, 1993.

_____. "Sex and Death and the Crippled Body: A Meditation." In Snyder, Brueggemann, and Garland-Thomson, *Disability Studies*, 156–70.

_____. *Waist-High in the World: A Life among the Nondisabled*. Boston: Beacon P, 1996.

Marks, Deborah. "Able-Bodied Dilemmas in Teaching Disability Studies." *Feminism & Psychology* 6 (1996): 69–73.

Matsuda, Paul Kei. "Basic Writing and Second Language Writers: Toward an Inclusive Definition." *Journal of Basic Writing* 22, no. 2 (2003): 67–89.

McAlexander, Patricia J. "Using Principles of Universal Design in College Composition Courses." *Basic Writing E-Journal* 5, no. 1 (2004). www.asu.edu/clas/english/composition/cbw/journal_1.htm

McLemee, Scott. "Deconstructing Composition." *The Chronicle of Higher Education* (21 March 2003): A16.

McNeill, John T. *A History of the Cure of Souls*. New York: Harper and Row, 1951.

McNenny, Gerri, ed. *Mainstreaming Basic Writers: Politics and Pedagogies of Access*. Mahwah, NJ: Lawrence Erlbaum Associates, 2001.

McRuer, Robert. "Composing Bodies; or, De-Composition: Queer Theory, Disability Studies, and Alternative Corporealities." *JAC: Journal of Advanced Composition* 24, no. 1 (2004): 47–78.

_____. *The Queer Renaissance: Contemporary American Literature and the Reinvention of Lesbian and Gay Identities*. New York: New York UP, 1997.

McRuer, Robert, and Abby L. Wilkerson. *Desiring Disability: Queer Theory Meets Disability Studies*. Spec. issue of *GLQ: A Journal of Lesbians and Gay Studies* 9.1–2 (2003).

Merriam, Sharan B. *Qualitative Research and Case Study Applications in Education*. San Francisco: Jossey-Bass, 1998.

Metzel, Deborah S., and Pamela M. Walker. "The Illusion of Inclusion: Geographies of the Lives of People with Developmental Disabilities in the United States." *Disability Studies Quarterly* 21, no. 4 (2001): 114–28.

Mindess, Anna et al. *Reading between the Signs*. Yarmouth, ME: Intercultural P, 1999.

The Miracle Worker. DVD directed by Arthur Penn. Century City, CA: MGM, 1962.

Mitchell, David T. "Narrative Prosthesis and the Materiality of Metaphor." In Snyder, Brueggemann, and Garland-Thomson, *Disability Studies*, 15–30.

Mitchell, David T. and Sharon L. Snyder. "Introduction: Disability Studies and the Double Bind of Representation." In *The Body and Physical Difference: Discourses of Disability*, edited by David T. Mitchell and Sharon L. Snyder, 1–31. Ann Arbor: U of Michigan P, 1997.

_____, *Narrative Prosthesis: Disability and the Dependencies of Discourse*. Ann Arbor: U of Michigan P, 2000.

Morris, David. *Illness and Culture in the Postmodern Age*. Berkeley and Los Angeles: U of California P, 1998.

Mossman, Mark. "Visible Disability in the College Classroom." *College English* 64, no. 6 (2002): 645–59.

Mulvey, Laura. "Visual Pleasure and Narrative Cinema." *Screen* 16, no. 3 (1975): 6–18. Reprinted in Mulvey, Laura. *Visual and Other Pleasures*, 14–27. Bloomington: Indiana UP, 1989.

Mumford, Lewis. *The Culture of Cities*. New York: Harcourt, Brace, and World, 1983.

Muñoz, José Esteban. *Disidentifications: Queers of Color and the Performance of Politics*. Minneapolis: U of Minnesota P, 1999.

Murderball. DVD directed by Henry Alex Rubin and Dana Adam Shapiro. New York: Thinkfilm, 2005.

Murphy, Christina, and Steve Sherwood. *The St. Martin's Sourcebook for Writing Tutors*. 2nd ed. New York: St. Martin's P, 2003.

Murphy, Robert F. *The Body Silent*. New York: Norton, 1990.

Mutnick, Deborah. *Writing in an Alien World: Basic Writing and the Struggle for Equality in Higher Education*. Portsmouth, NH: Heinemann-Boynton/Cook, 1996.

Nagel, Thomas. *The View from Nowhere*. New York: Oxford UP, 1986.

National Center for Education Statistics. "Students with Disabilities in Postsecondary Education: A Profile of Preparation, Participation, and Outcomes." http://nces.ed.gov/programs/quarterly/vol_1/1_3/4-esq13-a.asp

Nelson, Cary, and Stephen Watt. *Academic Keywords: A Devil's Dictionary for Higher Education*. New York: Routledge, 1999.

Newman, Robert D., Jean Bohner, and Melissa Carol Johnson. *Uncommon Threads*. New York: Pearson Education, 2003.

Not Dead Yet. www.notdeadyet.org

O'Brien, Mark. *Breathing*. Berkeley, CA: The Lemonade Factory, 1990.

———. *The Man in the Iron Lung*. Berkeley, CA: The Lemonade Factory, 1997.

Olson, Gary A., ed. *Rhetoric and Composition as Intellectual Work*. Carbondale: Southern Illinois U P, 2002.

———. Foreward. In Gale and Gale, *(Re)Visioning Composition Textbooks*, 4.

Ong, Walter. *Orality and Literacy: The Technologizing of the Word*. New York: Methuen, 1982.

———. "Writing Is a Technology That Restructures Thought." In Tribble and Trubek, *Writing Material*, 315–37.

Padden, Carol, and Tom Humphries. *Deaf in America: Voices from a Culture*. Cambridge, MA: Harvard UP, 1988.

Payne, David. *Coping with Failure: The Therapeutic Uses of Rhetoric*. Columbia: U of South Carolina P, 1989.

Pence, Ray. "Enforcing Diversity and Living with Disability: Learning from My First Teaching Year." In Freedman and Stoddard Holmes, *The Teacher's Body*, 145–59.

Plato. *Complete Works of Plato*. Edited by John M. Cooper and D. S. Hutchinson. New York: Hackett, 1997.

Porter, James E., et al. "Institutional Critique: A Rhetorical Methodology for Change." *College Composition and Communication* 51, no. 4 (2000): 610–42.

Powers, Judith. "Rethinking Writing Center Conferencing Strategies for the ESL Writer." In *The Allyn and Bacon Guide to Writing Center Theory and Practice*, edited by Robert W. Barnett and Jacob S. Blumner. 368–75. Boston: Allyn & Bacon, 2001.

Pratt, Mary Louise. *Imperial Eyes: Travel Writing and Transculturation*. London: Routledge, 1992.

Price, Reynolds. *A Whole New Life*. New York: Atheneum, 1994.

The Ragged Edge. www.ragged-edge-mag.com

Ramage, John D., John C. Bean, and June Johnson. *The Allyn and Bacon Guide to Writing, Brief Edition*. 3rd ed. New York: Pearson Education, 2003.

Reynolds, Nedra. "Composition's Imagined Geographies: The Politics of Space in the Frontier, City, and Cyberspace." *College Composition and Communication* 50, no. 1 (1998): 12–35.

Reynolds, Thomas J., and Patrick L. Bruch. "Curriculum and Affect: A Participatory Developmental Writing Approach." *Journal of Developmental Education* 26, no. 2 (Winter 2002): 12–20.

Richards, Amy. "College Composition: Recognizing the Learning Disabled Writer." *Journal of Basic Writing* 4, no. 2 (1985): 68–79.

Rinaldi, Jacqueline. "Rhetoric and Healing: Revising Narratives about Disability." *College English* 58, no. 7 (November 1996): 820–34.

Rose, Mike. "The Language of Exclusion: Writing Instruction at the University." *College English* 47, no. 4 (1985): 341–59.

Rosenblum, Walter, Naomi Rosenblum, and Alan Trachtenbers. *America and Lewis Hine*. Millerton: Apertune, 1977.

Sacks, Oliver. *A Leg to Stand On*. New York: Summit, 1984.

———. *"The Man Who Mistook His Wife for a Hat" and Other Clinical Tales*. New York: Summit, 1985.

Sandahl, Carrie. "Queering the Crip or Cripping the Queer? Intersections of Queer and Crip Identities in Solo Autobiographical Performance." *GLQ* 9, no. 1–2 (2003): 25–56.

Sedgwick, Eve Kosofsky. *Tendencies*. Durham: Duke UP, 1993.

Selzer, Jack, and Sharon Crowley, eds. *Rhetorical Bodies*. Madison: U of Wisconsin P, 1999.

Seuss, Dr. *The Sneetches and Other Stories*. New York: Random House Books for Young Readers, 1961.

Shakespeare, William. *The Life and Death of King Richard III*. Oxford: Oxford UP, 2001.

Shapiro, Joseph. *No Pity: People with Disabilities Forging a New Civil Rights Movement*. New York: Times Books/Random House, 1993.

Shaughnessy, Mina P. *Errors and Expectations: A Guide for the Teacher of Basic Writing.* New York: Oxford UP, 1977.

Shor, Ira, ed. *Education Is Politics: Critical Teaching across Differences.* Portsmouth, NH: Heinemann-Boynton/Cook, 2000.

_____. "Our Apartheid: Writing Instruction and Inequality." *Journal of Basic Writing,* 16, no. 1 (Spring 1997): 91–104.

Sibley, David. *Geographies of Exclusion: Society and Difference in the West.* New York: Routledge, 1995.

Siebers, Tobin. "What Can Disability Studies Learn from the Culture Wars?" *Cultural Critique* 55 (Fall 2003): 182–216.

Sienkiewicz-Mercer, Ruth, and Steven B. Kaplan. *I Raise My Eyes to Say Yes.* New York: Houghton Mifflin, 1989.

Smith, Bonnie G., and Beth Hutchinson, eds. *Gendering Disability.* New Brunswick: Rutgers UP, 2004.

Smith-Yackel, Bonnie. "My Mother Never Worked." In Kirszner and Mandell, *Patterns for College Writing,* chap. 6.

Snyder, Sharon L., Brenda Jo Brueggemann, and Rosemarie Garland-Thomson, eds. *Disability Studies: Enabling the Humanities.* New York: Modern Language Association, 2002.

Snyder, Sharon L., and David T. Mitchell, dirs. *Vital Signs: Crip Culture Talks Back.* Videocassette. Brace Yourselves, 1997.

Soliday, Mary. *The Politics of Remediation: Institutional and Student Needs in Higher Education.* Pittsburgh: U of Pittsburgh P, 2002.

South Park. DVD created by Trey Parker and Matt Stone. New York: Comedy Central, 1995–2006.

"St. Martin's Handbook." Bedford/St. Martin's, 2003. July 27, 2005. www.bedfordstmartins.com

Steinau Lester, Joan. *The Future of White Men and Other Diversity Dilemmas.* Berkeley, CA: Conari Press, 1993.

Sternglass, Marilyn L. *Time to Know Them: A Longitudinal Study of Writing and Learning at the College Level.* Mahwah, NJ: Lawrence Erlbaum Associates, 1997.

Stewart, Susan. "Letter on Sound." *Close Listening: Poetry and the Performed Word.* Ed. Charles Bernstein. New York: Oxford UP, 1998. 29–52.

Stiker, Henri-Jacques. *A History of Disability.* Translated by William Sayers. Ann Arbor: U of Michigan P, 1999.

Strauss, Anselm, and Juliet Corbin. *Basics of Qualitative Research.* 2nd ed. Thousand Oaks, CA: Sage, 1998.

"Students with Disabilities in Postsecondary Education: A Profile of Preparation, Participation, and Outcomes." *NCES, 1999–187,* Laura Horn and Jennifer Berktold. Project Officer: Larry Bobbitt. Washington, DC: U.S. Department of Education National Center for Education Statistics, 1999.

Stygall, Gail. "Resisting Privilege: Basic Writing and Foucault's Author Function." *College Composition and Communication* 45, no. 3 (October 1994): 320–41.

Sullivan, Patricia. "Feminism and Methodology in Composition Studies." In Sullivan and Kirsch, *Methods and Methodology in Composition Research,* 37–61.

Sullivan, Patricia, and Gesa E. Kirsch, eds. *Methods and Methodology in Composition Research.* Carbondale: Southern Illinois U P, 1992.

Swan, Jim. "Disabilities, Bodies, Voices." In Snyder, Brueggemann, and Garland-Thomson, *Disability Studies,* 283–95.

Swearingen, C. Jan. "Woman's Ways of Writing, or Images, Self-Images and Graven Images." *College Composition and Communication* 45 (1994): 231–48.

Szasz, Thomas. *The Myth of Psychotherapy: Mental Healing as Religion, Rhetoric, and Repression.* Garden City, NJ: Anchor, 1978.

Tavalaro, Julia, and Richard Tayson. *Look Up for "Yes."* New York: Kodansha, 1997.

Taylor, Humphrey. "Americans with Disabilities Still Pervasively Disadvantaged on a Broad Range of Key Indicators." *Harris Poll Library.* Harris Interactive. Poll 56. 14 Oct. 1998. 28 Aug. 2001 http://www.harrisinteractive.com/harris_poll/index.asp?PID=152

Theodosakis, Jason, Brenda Adderly, and Barny Fox. *The Arthritis Cure.* New York: St. Martin's, 1997.

Tobin, Lad. "Process Pedagogy." In *A Guide to Composition Pedagogies,* edited by Gary Tate, Amy Rupiper, and Kurt Schick, 1–18. New York: Oxford UP, 2001.

Tobin, Lad, and Thomas Newkirk, eds. *Taking Stock: The Writing Process Movement in the 90s.* Portsmouth, NH: Boynton, 1994.

Tough Guise: Violence, Media, and the Crisis in Masculinity. DVD directed by Sut Jhally. Northampton, MA: Media Education Foundation, 1999.

Tremain, Shelley, ed. *Foucault and the Government of Disability.* Ann Arbor: U of Michigan P, 2005.
———. "Foucault, Governmentality, and Critical Disability Theory: An Introduction." In Tremain, *Foucault and the Government of Disability,* 1–24.
Tremblay, Mary. "Going Back to Civvy Street: A Historical Account of the Everest and Jennings Wheelchair for Canadian World War II Veterans with Spinal Cord Injury." *Disability and Society* 11, no. 2 (June 1996): 149–69.
Trent, James W. *Inventing the Feeble Mind.* Berkeley, CA: U of California P, 1994.
Tribble, Evelyn B., and Anne Trubek, eds. *Writing Material: Readings from Plato to the Digital Age.* New York: Addison-Wesley-Longman, 2003.
Trimbur, John. "Delivering the Message: Typography and the Materiality of Writing." In Olson, *Rhetoric and Composition as Intellectual Work,* 188–202.
Tropea, Joseph L. "Bureaucratic Order and Special Children: Urban Schools, 1890s-1940s." *History of Education Quarterly* 27, no. 1 (Spring 1987): 29–53.
UD Education Online. www.udeducation.org
U.S. Department of Labor. *Delivering on the Promise.* Washington, DC: U.S. Department of Labor, 2002.
Villanueva, Victor, ed. *Cross Talk in Comp Theory, A Reader.* Urbana, IL: National Council of Teachers of English Press, 1997.
Vital Signs: Crip Culture Talks Back. VHS directed by Sharon Snyder and David Mitchell. Marquette, MI: Brace Yourselves Productions, 1997.
Wachsler, Sharon. www.sharonwachsler.com
Ware, Linda. "Writing, Identity, and the Other: Dare We Do Disability Studies?" *Journal of Teacher Education* 52, no. 2 (March/April 2001): 107–23.
Weaver, Margaret E. "Transcending 'Conversing': A Deaf Student in the Writing Center." *Journal of Advanced Composition* 16 (1996): 241–51.
Webb, Ruth Cameron. *A Journey into Personhood.* Iowa City: U of Iowa P, 1994.
Webb, Suzanne Strobeck, and Lou Ann Thompson. *Rhetorical Context: Readings for Writers.* New York: Longman, 2003.
Weese, Katherine L., Stephen L. Fox, and Stuart Greene, eds. *Teaching Academic Literacy: The Uses of Teacher-Research in Developing a Writing Program.* Mahwah, NJ: Lawrence Erlbaum Associates, 1999.
Welch, Polly, ed. *Strategies for Teaching Universal Design.* Adaptive Environments Center. www.adaptiveenvironments.org/universal/strategies.php
White, Linda Feldmeier. "Learning Disability, Pedagogies, and Public Discourse." *College Composition and Communication* 53, no. 4 (June 2002): 705–38.
Wilcox, Sherman, Ed. *American Deaf Culture.* Bartonsville, MD: Linstock Press, 1989.
Williams, John M. "Marketing to People with Disabilities." National Organization on Disability. www.nod.org
Wills, David. *Prosthesis.* Stanford, CA: Stanford UP, 1995.
Wilson, Dudley. *Signs and Portents: Monstrous Births from the Middle Ages to the Enlightenment.* London: Routledge, 1993.
Wilson, James C., and Cynthia Lewiecki-Wilson. "Constructing a Third Space: Disability Studies, the Teaching of English, and Institutional Transformation." In Snyder, Brueggemann, and Garland-Thomson, *Disability Studies,* 296–307.
———, eds. *Embodied Rhetorics: Disability in Language and Culture.* Carbondale: Southern Illinois UP, 2001.
Wood, Gail F. "Making the Transition from ASL to English: Deaf Students, Computers, and the Writing Center." *Computers and Composition* 12 (1995): 219–26.
Wrigley, Owen. *The Politics of Deafness.* Washington, DC: Gallaudet UP, 1996.
Yalom, Irvin D. *The Gift of Therapy: An Open Letter to a New Generation of Therapists and Their Patients.* New York: HarperCollins, 2001.
Yancey, Kathleen Blake. "Two Comments on Recognizing the Learning Disabled College Writer." *College English* 52, no. 3 (1990): 338–42.
"Your Rights under Section 504 of the Rehabilitation Act." US Department of Health and Human Resources. www.hhs.gov/ocr/504.html
Žižek, Slavoj. *The Sublime Object of Ideology.* New York: Verso, 1989.

ABOUT THE EDITORS

Cynthia Lewiecki-Wilson is professor of English and director of composition at Miami University, where she teaches the theory and practice of composition, writing, rhetoric, and disability studies courses. She has published in the *Journal of Assessing Writing, Journal of Basic Writing, College Composition and Communication, JAC, Rhetoric Review,* and *TETYC,* and is the coeditor of *Embodied Rhetorics: Disability in Language and Culture* (Southern Illinois University Press, 2001). She has recently worked with an interdisciplinary group at Miami to establish a disability studies minor.

Brenda Jo Brueggemann is an associate professor in English and an associate faculty in women's studies and comparative studies at Ohio State University, where she also serves as coordinator for the American Sign Language program and coordinator for the interdisciplinary disability studies minor. She is the author of *Lend Me Your Ear: Rhetorical Constructions of Deafness* (Gallaudet UP, 1999) and essays and articles on pedagogy, qualitative research, literacy, rhetoric, deaf and disability studies. She is editor of and contributor to *Literacy and Deaf People: Cultural and Contextual Perspectives* (Gallaudet UP, 2004) and coeditor and contributor of *Disability Studies: Enabling the Humanities* (Modern Language Association, 2002) and *Women and Deafness: Multidisciplinary Approaches* (Gallaudet UP, 2006). She serves as editor for the Gallaudet University Press "Deaf Lives" (autobiography and biography).

Jay Dolmage is an assistant professor of English at West Virginia University, where he directs the first-year writing program. Jay grew up as part of the disability rights movement in Canada. In his scholarship, Jay focuses on critical disability studies, rhetoric, and composition. His essays and reviews are forthcoming with or have been published in *Rhetoric Review, College Composition and Communication, JAC, Rhetoric Society Quarterly, Prose Studies,* and *Disability Studies Quarterly.*

INDEX

INDEX OF ACTIVITIES